Justice After Stonewall

Justice After Stonewall is an interdisciplinary analysis of challenges and progress experienced by the LGBT community since the Stonewall Riots in 1969. The Riots (sparked by a police raid in New York City) are a milestone in LGBT history. Within a short time, a new feeling of confidence emerged, manifested in new LGBT organisations and the first Pride marches. Legal and social change followed: from the decriminalisation of homosexual activities to anti-discrimination laws and the legalisation of same-sex marriage. This makes it tempting to think of modern LGBT history as an unequivocal success story. But progress was not achieved everywhere: in 70 States, same-sex relations are still criminalised; violence against LGBT persons still occurs, and transgender people still struggle to have their rights recognised.

The question whether the path since Stonewall represents success or failure cannot be answered by one discipline alone. This book breaks new ground by bringing together experts from politics, sociology, law, education, language, medicine and religion to discuss fields as diverse as same-sex marriage, transgender students, the LGBT movement in Uganda and LGBT migrants in the Arabian Peninsula, conversion 'therapy', and approaches to LGBT matters in Judaism, Christianity and Islam. What emerges is a rich tapestry of LGBT life today and its consideration from numerous perspectives.

Based on thorough research, this book is an ideal text for students and scholars exploring LGBT matters. At the same time, its engaging style makes it a particularly valuable resource for anyone with an interest in LGBT matters and their reception in today's world.

Dr Paul Behrens is Reader (Associate Professor) in Law at the University of Edinburgh Law School, UK. He is Member of the Expert Advisory Group to the Scottish Parliament on Ending Conversion Practices and has published several books on international law.

Sean Becker previously taught as a docent at the University of Amsterdam's PPLE College. He is currently pursuing postgraduate studies at Columbia Law School, New York, and the University of Amsterdam.

Justice After Stonewall

LGBT Life Between Challenge and Change

Edited by Paul Behrens
and Sean Becker

Routledge
Taylor & Francis Group
a GlassHouse Book

First published 2023
by Routledge
4 Park Square, Milton Park, Abingdon, Oxon OX14 4RN

and by Routledge
605 Third Avenue, New York, NY 10158

a Glasshouse book

Routledge is an imprint of the Taylor & Francis Group, an informa business

© 2023 selection and editorial matter, Paul Behrens and Sean Becker; individual chapters, the contributors

The right of Paul Behrens and Sean Becker to be identified as the authors of the editorial material, and of the authors for their individual chapters, has been asserted in accordance with sections 77 and 78 of the Copyright, Designs and Patents Act 1988.

All rights reserved. No part of this book may be reprinted or reproduced or utilised in any form or by any electronic, mechanical, or other means, now known or hereafter invented, including photocopying and recording, or in any information storage or retrieval system, without permission in writing from the publishers.

Trademark notice: Product or corporate names may be trademarks or registered trademarks, and are used only for identification and explanation without intent to infringe.

British Library Cataloguing-in-Publication Data
A catalogue record for this book is available from the British Library

ISBN: 978-1-032-26052-5 (hbk)
ISBN: 978-1-032-26055-6 (pbk)
ISBN: 978-1-003-28629-5 (ebk)

DOI: 10.4324/9781003286295

Typeset in Bembo
by Apex CoVantage, LLC

Contents

Notes on Contributors   ix
Foreword   xvi

Introduction   1

1 From Stonewall to the World: The Difficult Path
 to Recognition   3
 PAUL BEHRENS AND SEAN BECKER

PART 1
Justice After Stonewall? Aspects of Political and Social Acceptance   13

2 Challenges Past and Present: Political and
 Social Perspectives   15
 SEAN BECKER AND PAUL BEHRENS

3 The Development of the LGBT+ Community in the
 UK in the Last 50 Years   17
 SIR STEPHEN WALL

4 LGBT+ Youth Homelessness as a Consequence
 of Progress   28
 CARIN TUNÅKER

5 The LGBTI Movement Organising in a Time of Peril:
 A Case Study of Uganda   47
 CLARE BYARUGABA

6 'That's Really Why I Got Married I Guess':
   Heteronormativity and Openness About Same-Sex
   Coupledom   65
   DORA JANDRIĆ

PART 2
LGBT Rights Facing New Challenges   81

7 A Landscape of Change: Legal Perspectives   83
   PAUL BEHRENS AND SEAN BECKER

8 The Evolution of LGBT Rights in the UK: Is the Tide
   Starting to Turn?   86
   CAROLYNN GRAY

9 In the Name of the People? Plebiscites, Referendums
   and Same-Sex Marriage   105
   PAUL BEHRENS

10 The Intrinsic Value of Registered Partnerships and
   Marriage for Same-Sex Couples, Their Recognition
   Domestically and at the Strasbourg Court   125
   HELEN FENWICK AND ANDY HAYWARD

11 Changing Perceptions of Homosexuality as Revealed
   by the Law of Defamation in Scotland   146
   KENNETH MCK. NORRIE

12 'Lewd, Disgusting and Offensive': A Critical
   Discourse Analysis of the Law Lords' Ideologies
   Toward Homosexuality Between 1967 and 2004   163
   SEAN BECKER

PART 3
**The Continued Struggle for Equality: LGBT
Students, Identity and Language**   187

13 Living Identity: Perspectives from the Fields of
   Education and Language   189
   SEAN BECKER AND PAUL BEHRENS

14 Embedding LGBT Equality in the Curriculum and the
    Classroom   191
    ELEANOR CAPALDI AND AMANDA SYKES

15 Investigating the Experiences of Transgender Students
    in Higher Education in the UK – Pilot Study   204
    LYNNE REGAN

16 Queerly Fluent/Fluently Queer: On (Re)Creating
    Shared Identities in Second and Third Languages
    Among Migrant LGBTQ Populations in the Arabian
    Peninsula   225
    GAAR ADAMS

PART 4
Between Disenfranchisement and Inclusion: The LGBT Community and the Medical Sector   237

17 Changing Science and the Science of Change: Medical
    Perspectives   239
    PAUL BEHRENS AND SEAN BECKER

18 Disenfranchisement in British Healthcare: Being a
    Lesbian Non-Biological Mother   242
    LUCILLE KELSALL-KNIGHT AND CERI SUDRON

19 False Therapy, Real Harm: Aspects of Conversion
    Practices and Their Evaluation   248
    PAUL BEHRENS

PART 5
Faith and Justice: Religion and the LGBT Community   265

20 Between Understanding and Inclusion: Religious
    Perspectives   267
    PAUL BEHRENS AND SEAN BECKER

21 Jewish Approaches to LGBT+ in Texts, Culture and Ritual   270
    RABBI MARK L. SOLOMON AND HANNAH HOLTSCHNEIDER

22 Tradition and Transition: Methodological Approaches to LGBT Issues in Roman Catholic Theology After Pope Francis 286
NICOLETE BURBACH

23 Is There a Space to Fight Back? Exclusionary Queer and Islamic Spaces and Resistance from Queer Muslims 307
DREW DALTON

Concluding Thoughts 329

24 Stonewall at Fifty: Between Hope and Challenge 331
SEAN BECKER AND PAUL BEHRENS

Index 336

Notes on Contributors

Gaar Adams is a writer, educator and journalist. His longform arts, culture and environmental reporting from the Middle East and South Asia has been published widely, including in *The Atlantic, Foreign Policy, Rolling Stone, Al Jazeera, NPR, Slate* and *VICE*. His essays, photography and poetry have been featured in numerous anthologies, including 'Uncommon Dubai' (Uncommon, 2018), 'The Edwin Morgan Centenary Collection' (Speculative Books, 2020) and 'Glasgow' (Dostoyevsky Wannabe, 2022). He is a 2020 London Library Emerging Writing Fellow and teaches creative writing at the University of Hull. His debut book on queerness, migration and belonging in the Middle East will be published by Harvill Secker in 2024. He is currently completing his doctorate at the University of Glasgow and lives in London, UK. Twitter: @gaaradams

Sean Becker's, LLM, LLM, BSc (Hons), principal research interests lie in the fields of comparative law, international law and criminal law. He has previously taught at the PPLE College of the Faculty of Law at the University of Amsterdam and has served as Academic Chair on the executive board of UNISCA, an Amsterdam-based MUN/summer school. Sean Becker is the co-founder and former Amsterdam chapter president of Alpha Iota Sigma, an interdisciplinary honours society of the Association for Interdisciplinary Studies (AIS). After graduating with a BSc in politics, psychology, law and economics with a specialization in law from the University of Amsterdam's PPLE College in 2018, he obtained an LLM in general law from the University of Edinburgh in 2019, and a second LLM in international criminal law from the University of Amsterdam and Columbia University in 2022. His research largely reflects his interdisciplinary and comparative law background. He is also a scholar of the Studienstiftung des Deutschen Volkes (German Academic Scholarship Foundation), Germany's oldest and most prestigious scholarship foundation.

Paul Behrens, PhD, LLM, is Reader in Law at the University of Edinburgh, where his academic interests include LGBT rights, international criminal law, diplomatic law and questions of self-determination. He is Member of the Expert Advisory Group to the Scottish government on Ending Conversion Practices and has provided written evidence on that topic to the Equalities, Human Rights and Civil Justice Committee of the Scottish Parliament. He has also been invited to address the European Union Committee of the German Bundestag, the German Foreign Office and the Group of Latin American and Caribbean Ambassadors in London on issues of international law. In 2022, he was invited to address the Appeals Chamber of the International Criminal Court as *amicus curiae* on matters arising in the Ongwen case. In addition to his teaching at Edinburgh, Dr Behrens has been Visiting Lecturer/Visiting Scholar at Uppsala (Sweden), Stockholm (Sweden), Kiel (Germany) and other universities. His publications include *Diplomatic Interference and the Law* (Hart Publishing 2016) and, as editor, *Diplomatic Law in a New Millennium* (OUP 2017) and (with Henham) *Elements of Genocide* (Routledge 2012). Apart from academic articles, he regularly contributes to newspapers (including *The Guardian, The Scotsman, The Herald, Süddeutsche Zeitung, Frankfurter Rundschau* and *The New European*) on issues of international and constitutional law and has given television and radio interviews on these topics.

Nicolete Burbach, PhD, is Social and Environmental Justice Lead at the London Jesuit Centre. Her interests lie in the interface between philosophical theology and Catholic social thought, particularly issues of conflict, plurality and uncertainty in the teachings of Pope Francis. Her research looks to resource Pope Francis to navigate some of the difficult discussions arising around trans issues in the Church. She previously taught modules in Catholic social thought and in postmodern theology at Durham University.

Clare Byarugaba, BINB, is Equality and Non-Discrimination program officer at Chapter Four Uganda. She founded the first-ever Parents and Families, Friends of LGBTI children support group in Uganda; co-founded the first-ever LGBT swim team in Uganda; and uses advocacy through the law to promote the rights of LGBTI Ugandans. Between 2012 and 2014, she coordinated a national Coalition of over 50 diverse organizations that used their collective power to fight against the 2009 draconian Anti Homosexuality Bill. Byarugaba and the Coalition received the 2011 US State Department's Human Rights Defender Award for their tireless work. Directly related to this work, she was awarded the 2014 Oak Human Rights fellowship and the 2018 Aspen Institute's New Voices Fellowship. Byarugaba's most recent publications include (with Ashanut Okille) *My Child Is Different. A Baseline Study of the Perceptions and Experiences of Parents, Families and Their Lesbian, Gay, Bisexual, Transgender and Intersex Children in Uganda* (Chapter Four Uganda Publications 2019) and 'On the Front Pages', *World Policy Institute, Program for African Thought* (12 June 2018), at http://worldpolicy-africa.org/2018/06/on-the-front-pages/.

Eleanor Capaldi, MLitt, BA (Hons), was Research Assistant on the University of Glasgow-funded project 'Embedding LGBT Equality in the Curriculum and the Classroom'. She is also Co-Chair of the University's LGBT+ Staff Network and sits on the board of the University's LGBT+ Committee. Eleanor has worked in heritage communications and as LGBTQ+ Project Assistant at the Hunterian Museum at the University of Glasgow. Eleanor is currently undertaking a PhD exploring the lives of digitised artworks at University of Glasgow and the National Galleries of Scotland.

Drew Dalton, PhD, MSc, MA, BSc, is Senior Lecturer in Sociology at the University of Sunderland. His research focuses on HIV, stigma and ageing, global homo/bi/transphobia and queer Muslims. Originally from a charity and human rights background, Drew was the Chair of Hidayah, a U.K. nationwide organisation for queer Muslims, and he is currently the founder and Chair of ReportOUT, a global human rights organisation for sexual and gender minorities. He is currently examining the role of climate change and the impact of COVID-19 on LGBTQI+ populations and communities. Previous publications have been 'Cutting the Ribbon? Austerity Measures and the Problems Faced by the HIV Third Sector' (in Rushton/Donovan [eds], *Austerity Policies: Bad Ideas in Practice*, Palgrave Macmillan 2018, 173–195) and '"Just Take a Tablet and You'll be Ok": Medicalisation, the Growth of Stigma and the Silencing of HIV' (17:2 [2017] *HIV Nursing* 63–68).

Helen Fenwick, LLB, BA, is Professor of Law at Durham University, Joint Director of the University of Durham Human Rights Centre (until 2012) and a Human Rights Consultant to Doughty Street Chambers. She specialises in human rights, especially in relation to freedom of expression, discrimination on grounds of sexual orientation and counter-terrorist law and policy. She is author of *Media Freedom Under the Human Rights Act* (OUP 2006, with G Phillipson) and *Civil Liberties and Human Rights* (Routledge, 5th edn, 2017). Recent journal articles include 'From Same-Sex Marriage to Equal Civil Partnerships: On a Path Towards 'Perfecting' Equality?' (with A Hayward), (2018) 30(2) CFLQ 97–120; 'Rejecting Asymmetry of Access to Formal Relationship Statuses for Same and Different-Sex Couples at Strasbourg and Domestically' (2017) EHRLR 545 (with A Hayward); 'Terrorism Threats and Temporary Exclusion Orders: Counter-Terror Rhetoric or Reality?' (2017) 3 *European Human Rights Law Review* 247–271; 'Same Sex Unions at the Strasbourg Court in a Divided Europe: Driving Forward Reform or Protecting the Court's Authority via Consensus Analysis?' (2016) 3 EHRLR 249–272; 'Redefining the Role of TPIMs in Combatting 'Home-Grown' Terrorism Within the Widening Counter-Terror Framework' (2015) 1 EHRLR 41–56; 'Protecting Free Speech and Academic Freedom in Universities' (with I Cram) (2018) 81(5) *Modern Law Review* 825–873; and 'Finding 'East'/'West' Divisions in Council of Europe States on Treatment of Sexual Minorities: The Response of the Strasbourg Court and the Role of Consensus Analysis' (2019) 3 EHRLR, 247–273 (with D Fenwick).

Carolynn Gray, PhD, LLM, FHEA, PGCTLHE, is Senior Lecturer in Law and Law Subject Lead at the University of the West of Scotland. She writes and researches in subjects where the law intersects with the body, and she has a particular interest in LGBTQI+ rights. Her PhD, awarded in 2015, called for reform of the Gender Recognition Act 2004. Dr Gray is a graduate of the Universities of Strathclyde and Glasgow. Her recent publications include 'The GenderQueer in UK Law: Why Current Laws Are Insufficient' in S Mustasaari (ed) *Subjectivity, Citizenship and Belonging in Law: Identities and Intersections* (Routledge/Taylor & Francis, 2016) and 'R & F v United Kingdom' in S Cowan, C Kennedy and V Monro (eds) *Scottish Feminist Judgments: (Re)Creating Law from the Outside In* (Hart, Oxford, 2019).

Andy Hayward, PhD, LLM, LLB, SFHEA, is Associate Professor at Durham Law School. His research explores from both domestic and comparative law perspectives the legal regulation of adult relationships and, in particular, marriage, civil partnership and cohabitation. His primary focus is reform of civil partnerships, and he has written extensively on their history, development and future following the introduction of same-sex marriage. He published, with Professor Jens M Scherpe from the University of Cambridge, an edited collection entitled, *The Future of Registered Partnerships: Family Recognition Beyond Marriage?* (Intersentia 2018). More recently, he has given evidence to the Equalities and Human Rights Committee of the Scottish Parliament in relation to the Civil Partnerships (Scotland) Bill 2019 and was appointed Specialist Adviser to the Women and Equalities Committee of the UK Parliament in relation to their *Rights of Cohabiting Partners* Inquiry.

Hannah Holtschneider, PhD, is Senior Lecturer in Jewish Studies at the University of Edinburgh. She is a cultural historian, and her research interests span early 20th century Jewish history in Britain, Jewish migration history, the impact of the Holocaust on individuals and communities, Holocaust memorialisation and the representation of history in museums. In 2019, she published her third monograph entitled, *Jewish Orthodoxy in Scotland: Rabbi Dr Salis Daiches and Religious Leadership* (Edinburgh University Press), and with Phil Alexander and Mia Spiro she edited a special issue of the *Shofar: An Interdisciplinary Journal of Jewish Studies* 37:3, on 'Narrative Spaces at the Margins of British-Jewish culture(s)', which also included her article 'Narrating the Archive? Family Collections, the Archive, and the Historian'. Hannah is an LGBT+ Ally and served as the School of Divinity's Equality and Diversity Director in 2019.

Dora Jandrić, PhD, MA, BA, is Research Fellow at the School of Social Policy (University of Birmingham), currently doing research on LGBTQ+

adult social care assessment. She has published in the *International Journal of Ageing and Later Life*. She has also participated in three COST Action (IS1409 and IS1402) training schools and has presented her work at the 50th BSG conference in Lancaster (2021), UK; 13th ESA conference in Athens (2017), Greece; the AgingGraz (2017) conference in Graz, Austria; and others. At the School of Social and Political Science (University of Edinburgh), Jandrić obtained her doctoral degree on a project exploring the intersection of the past, present and future in the lives of older same-sex couples in Scotland. She is interested in ageing, temporality and LGBTQ+ studies.

Lucille Kelsall-Knight, DProfHW, MSc, BNurs, is Associate Professor in Children's Nursing at the School of Nursing and Midwifery, University of Birmingham. Her research interests focus on her clinical background, which includes acute nursing care, clinical skills and diverse families within healthcare. Her doctoral thesis explored the experience of lesbian parents in accessing healthcare for their adopted children. She has published several book chapters and peer reviewed articles in nursing journals, including (with Ceri Sudron) 'Non-Biological Lesbian Mothers' Experiences of Accessing Healthcare for Their Children' in *Nursing Children and Young People* (2020) (doi: 10.7748/ncyp.2020.e1237) and 'Qualitative Exploration of Lesbian Parents' Experiences of Accessing Healthcare for Their Adopted Children in England' in *British Medical Journal Open* (2021) (doi: 10.1136/bmjopen-2021-053710).

Kenneth McK. Norrie, PhD, LLB, DLP, FRSE, is Professor of Law at the University of Strathclyde and started his academic career as a medical lawyer, and his early publications are all in that field. Since moving to Strathclyde in 1990, his interest in Family Law has predominated, and his major specialisms within that field are child protection and same-sex relationships. He remains involved in teaching and research projects in most Private Law areas, including property, delict and International Private Law. He has written widely in these fields and in legal history.

Lynne Regan, EdD, MA, MEd, BSc, BA, works in Student Support & Wellbeing at the University of Kent and is Co-Chair of the university's LGBTQ+ Staff Network. Lynne completed BA Humanities, BSc Psychology and Master of Education at The Open University and MA Higher Education at the University of Kent. Her Doctorate in Education at The Open University looked at the experiences of transgender students in higher education in the UK. Twitter: @lynneregan31.

Rabbi Mark L. Solomon, MA, BA (Hons), is Minister of the Edinburgh and Leicester Liberal Jewish communities, Senior Lecturer in Rabbinic Literature at Leo Baeck College and Interfaith Consultant and Chair of the Beit Din (rabbinic court) of Liberal Judaism. He was born in Sydney, where he studied English honours at Sydney University. He studied at Chabad

Yeshivot in Melbourne and Israel, and he was ordained at Jews' College, London, in 1991. After coming out – the only serving orthodox rabbi to do so in Britain – he joined Liberal Judaism and worked at West Central Liberal Synagogue and The Liberal Jewish Synagogue in London. He has taught at Leo Baeck College since 1991, where he completed an MA in Jewish studies with a thesis on the medieval philosopher Hasdai Crescas. He is author of several articles on Judaism and homosexuality and editor of *Covenant of Love: Service of Commitment for Same-Sex Couples* (Liberal Judaism 2005), whose publication coincided with the introduction of civil partnerships in British law. It was the first such liturgy published by any Jewish movement. He is an honorary rabbi for the Jewish LGBT+ Group, was on the organising committee of the international conference of LGBT Jews in London in 1993 and has spoken at other international Jewish LGBT conferences as well as at the interfaith conference at Jerusalem World Pride 2006. He has been a trustee of the London Ecumenical AIDS Trust and consultant for the Jewish AIDS Trust (now JAT), and he has just stepped down after many years as trustee of the London HIV Chaplaincy. He is also a cantor and is deeply involved in dialogue with Christians and Muslims. He lives with his partner, the actor Lobo Chan, in North London.

Ceri Sudron, MSc, SFHEA, MCPara, is Head of Department Midwifery & Allied Health – Practice at Staffordshire University, having finished tenure as Course Lead for Paramedic Science at the University of Wolverhampton. Her research interests include CPR-induced consciousness, professionalism, organisational culture and LGBT+ health inequality. She is an Editorial Board member and an active reviewer for the *Journal of Paramedic Practice*. Her recent publications include (with Mays, Gregory and Kilner) 'Awareness of CPR-Induced Consciousness by UK Paramedics' (2019) 4:1 *British Paramedic Journal* 1–5 and 'A Concise History of the Paramedic Profession', in G. Eaton (ed), *Law and Ethics for Paramedics: An Essential Guide* (Bridgewater: Class Publishing 2019) 13–28. Sudron commenced her career as a paramedic with West Midlands Ambulance Service progressing to paramedic clinical mentor with South Central Ambulance Service and later as a Clinical Education Development Specialist with East Midlands Ambulance Service. Sudron completed her MSc in Practice Education in 2014 and focused on the leadership of professional practice culminating in a dissertation exploring the professional identity of the paramedic and the identification of professional attitudes and behaviour.

Amanda Sykes, PhD, is Academic Lead for the University of Glasgow's Transformation Team. She was principal investigator for the project 'Embedding LGBT Equality in the Curriculum and the Classroom', which reflects her commitment to reducing the emotional labour required by students in HE to hide who they are, so that they can use that energy for learning and being. Amanda is staff representative on the University of Glasgow's Gender and

Sexual Diversity Committee. In 2016, she attended the Stonewall Leadership course.

Carin Tunåker, PhD, is a Lecturer at the Kent Law School. She is a Social Anthropologist specialising in LGBT+ homelessness and intersectional disadvantages. She has worked frontline in the homelessness sector in South East England for over ten years. Dr Tunåker's recent work includes 'No Place Like Home: Locating Homeless LGBT Youth', (2015) *Home Cultures*, and she acts as consultant for LGBT+ homelessness projects across the UK. Her research interests are in housing, homelessness, social justice, gender, sexuality and social inequalities.

Sir Stephen Wall, GCMG, LVO, is a former British Ambassador to Portugal and former British Permanent Representative (Ambassador) to the European Union. He worked on global foreign policy for three Prime Ministers in 10 Downing Street. He was for six years Chair of the Council of University College London (UCL) and was the university's first equalities champion for LGBT issues. He was for four years Chair of Kaleidoscope International Trust, which supports LGBT+ activists around the world. He is the author of four books on the UK's membership of the European Union.

Foreword

What happened at the Stonewall Inn, Manhattan, in the summer of 1969 not only marked a watershed in the cause of LGBTI equality – it has continued to have a profound and lasting impact on the world.

The Stonewall Riots highlighted the shocking persecution and prejudice faced by members of LGBTI communities. In doing so, they inspired and emboldened LGBTI people across the world to come together and have pride in who they are.

Perhaps the most vivid symbol of that is the global phenomenon of Pride parades, which mark the anniversary of the Riots. They continue to be wonderful celebrations of LGBTI rights, freedom and acceptance. In particular, amidst the challenges of Covid-19, it has been hugely inspiring to see the LGBTI communities around the world celebrate Pride in new and creative ways.

However, the legacy of the Stonewall Riots runs much deeper. The 50th anniversary of the Riots in 2019 provided an opportunity to reflect on that legacy – and the progress that has been made in the years since. And that's why I am delighted to provide a foreword for this book, in which the authors discuss the journey the world has made towards LGBTI equally in the last 50 years.

It is important to remember that when the Stonewall Riots took place, sexual activity between men was still a crime in Scotland – and remained so for more than a decade afterwards. Even then, LGBTI people continued to face prejudice, discrimination and the denial of basic rights and freedoms. The introduction, in 1988, of Section 28, which prevented local authorities from the 'promotion of homosexuality' was one particularly egregious example of that.

Since then, and particularly in the last decades, things have changed slowly – but surely – for the better.

In 2000, the Scottish Parliament repealed Section 28, and since 2007, same-sex couples have been able to adopt. One of the proudest moments of my career came in 2014, when members of the Scottish Parliament, from all parties, came together to support equal marriage. In 2017, I delivered an official apology to all of those who had been hurt and victimised by the homophobic laws of the past, and that same day the Scottish government introduced legislation to automatically pardon men convicted under those laws – for activity, which is now, and should always have been, legal.

There is, of course, a great deal still to do to achieve true LGBTI equality in Scotland.

In particular, we know that, here at home, we must do more to protect and promote the rights of trans people, who still face significant prejudice and inequality – more than 50 years after the trans community played a vital role in the Stonewall Riots.

And worldwide, there are still many places where it simply isn't safe to be LGBTI. Discrimination, harassment, anti-LGBTI laws, violence and inequality are all too common, so we must continue to support steps towards equality wherever, and whenever, we can.

As we take those steps, it is vital that we continue to understand the lessons of the Stonewall Riots. They remain a powerful symbol of the enormous struggles that LGBTI people have faced in seeking to achieve equal rights. They remind all of us of the need to stand in solidarity with the LGBTI community – not just in the good times but at those times when the cause of equality faces its fiercest opposition. And as this volume shows, the spirit of Stonewall can and should continue to inspire us all – as we seek to build a fairer, more equal country, and a better, more tolerant world.

Rt Hon Nicola Sturgeon MSP
First Minister of Scotland

Introduction

Chapter 1

From Stonewall to the World
The Difficult Path to Recognition

Paul Behrens and Sean Becker

---

1. The Stonewall Story

In the early hours of 28 June 1969, police raided the Stonewall Inn, a bar on Christopher Street, New York that was popular with LGBT patrons of the city's Greenwich Village.[1] The reason given was that the police had a warrant to investigate the illegal sale of alcohol,[2] but it was certainly not the first time that gay bars had been the target of police activities, and that their patrons had been harassed by them.[3] 'They were easy arrests', said the Inspector leading the raid decades later, '[t]hey never gave you any trouble'.[4]

That, however, was about to change. Outside the bar, a crowd of about 400 people formed, shouting 'Gay Power', rushing the officers who had to retreat into the Inn and hurling bricks, bottles and garbage at them.[5] The next night, the people were gathering again, some throwing bottles, some lighting small fires.[6] The Riots would last several nights.[7]

Police harassment was not the only factor that made life difficult for LGBT persons then. In 1969, same-sex activities were still outlawed in all US States except Illinois.[8] In the medical field, pathologisation of homosexuality and

---

1 Jerrold K Footlick and Susan Agrest, 'Gays and the Law' *Newsweek*, 25 October 1976.
2 *New York Times*, 'Police Again Rout "Village" Youths', 30 June 1969.
3 Merle Miller, 'What It Means to Be a Homosexual' *New York Times*, 17 January 1971.
4 Dennis Hevsi, 'Seymour Pine Dies at 91; Led Raid on Stonewall Inn' *New York Times*, 7 September 2010.
5 *New York Times*, '4 Policemen Hurt in "Village" Raid', 29 June 1969. See also Footlick and Agrest (n 1); Hevsi (n 4). For a detailed account of the riots, David Carter, *Stonewall. The Riots that Sparked the Gay Revolution* (St Martin's Press 2004) 129–181. See also Morty Manford, 'Fearless Youth' in Eric Marcus (ed), *Making History. The Struggle for Gay and Lesbian Equal Rights 1945–1990* (Harper Collins 1992) 199–202.
6 *New York Times* (n 2).
7 Hevsi (n 4).
8 David Carter, 'What Made Stonewall Different' (August 2009) 16:4 *Gay and Lesbian Review Worldwide* 11–13.

DOI: 10.4324/9781003286295-2

transsexuality was still frequently done.[9] The relevant medical 'diagnosis' could have severe consequences, including institutionalisation and efforts to 'cure' the subjects – practices that included electroshock treatment, castration and prefrontal lobotomy.[10] Discrimination was prevalent and extended to the job and housing markets, but also to the public sector.[11]

It comes as little surprise that the combined force of the obstacles put in the way of LGBT persons left traces on their self-perception. Yet, in spite of all these difficulties, an LGBT culture did exist – there were, at least in the larger American cities, bars that welcomed LGBT patrons[12] and even some LGBT organisations had been created – the Mattachine Societies, the Janus Society, the Daughters of Bilitis[13] among others. There were early instances of organised lobbying efforts[14] and even examples of resistance to police harassment.[15]

And yet, the 1969 Riots were a watershed moment. That something unique had happened was clear even to contemporaries who, within days, put hope into 'gay power' as a newly minted movement.[16] On the first anniversary of the events, members of the LGBT community marched from Greenwich Village to Central Park – a development that gave the then president of the Mattachine Society New York the opportunity to reflect that gay people had 'discovered their potential strength and gained a new pride'.[17] And there have been far more ambitious attempts to categorise the events: it was the Boston Tea Party, it was Fort Sumpter;[18] it was the storm on the Bastille.[19]

It would indeed be difficult to deny that the events in Christopher Street were a driving force in the LGBT movement in the United States. In 1970, parades already took place in Chicago and Los Angeles as well[20] – forerunners of the modern Pride parades. Stonewall was remembered in the titles of publications and editions after the Riots (such as *Christopher Street* and the *Stonewall Inn*

---

9 International Classification of Disorders, 9th Revision, at 302.0 and 302.5.
10 Carter (n 8).
11 See Footlick and Agrest (n 1); Webster Schott, 'Civil Rights and the Homosexual. A 4-Million Minority Asks for Equal Rights' *New York Times*, 12 November 1967; Miller (n 3).
12 Webster Schott, 'Civil Rights and the Homosexual. A 4-Million Minority Asks for Equal Rights' *New York Times*, 12 November 1967. See also, on gay culture in the USA before 1969, Mab Segrest, 'Visibility and Backlash' in David Deitcher (ed), *Over the Rainbow* (Boxtree 1995) 84, 85.
13 Herbert Dick, 'They Stay in Background Here – Others Ask "Rights"' *The Atlanta Constitution*, 5 January 1966.
14 *Ibid.*
15 See Schott (n 12) and Carter (n 8).
16 See Lucian Truscott, 'View from Outside: Gay Power Comes to Sheridan Square' *Village Voice*, 3 July 1969, reprinted in Jason Baumann (ed), *The Stonewall Reader* (Penguin 2019) 117, 118.
17 Lacey Fosburgh, 'Thousands of Homosexuals Hold a Protest Rally in Central Park' *New York Times*, 29 June 1970.
18 Miller (n 3).
19 Hevsi (n 4) with reference to an interview with David Carter.
20 Miller (n 3).

Editions),[21] and they were joined by other publications that benefitted from the new feeling of empowerment, such as *Gay, Come Out!* and *Gay Power*.[22] The LGBT movement became more organised: after Stonewall, the Gay Liberation Front (GLF) began demonstrations in Greenwich Village;[23] the less radical Gay Activists Alliance constituted itself;[24] and in 1973, an umbrella organisation was formed – the National Gay Task Force.[25] In mainstream politics, LGBT issues became more visible too[26] – as did LGBT politicians themselves, with Kathy Kozachenko in 1974 becoming the first openly lesbian politician to win elected office in the USA.[27] Stonewall plays a role in more recent memorialisation, too: June, the month of the Riots, was, under President Barack Obama declared 'Lesbian, Gay, Bisexual and Transgender Pride Month'.[28] Under Obama, too, Christopher Park and the Stonewall Inn were designated the Stonewall National Monument.[29] David Carter, writing in 2009, was not far off the mark when he emphasised the importance of the Stonewall Riots as being 'of a different order'. He identified four reasons: the fact that this was a 'sustained uprising', the sheer number of people involved, the media coverage they attracted and the fact that they gave birth to new organisational structures as well as to a 'new political ideology known as "gay liberation"'.[30]

Nor were the ripples of Stonewall felt only in the United States. Pride parades, often around the anniversary of the Riots, began to take place in other countries as well,[31] and the name 'Christopher Street Day' under which Pride parades are hosted in some countries[32] still serves as a reminder of the events to which they owe their existence. And while in England and Wales decriminalisation had taken place two years prior to Stonewall,[33] the LGBT movement there is still indebted to the spirit of 1969. (A direct line can, in fact, be drawn

---

21 Carter (n 8).
22 Joe Sommerlad, 'Pride Month: What Happened at the Stonewall Riots and How Did They Inspire the LGBT+ Rights Movement?' *The Independent*, 4 June 2021.
23 Fosburgh (n 17). See also Bob Koehler, 'In their Own Words', in Deitcher (n 12) 66–67; Carter (n 5) 209–221.
24 Sommerlad (n 22).
25 Footlick and Agrest (n 1).
26 See on this Miller (n 3).
27 Steve Friess, 'The First Openly Gay Person to Win an Election in America Was Not Harvey Milk' *Bloomberg UK*, 11 December 2015.
28 Sommerlad (n 22).
29 *States News Service*, 'Secretary Jewell, Director Jarvis, Valerie Jarrett to Participate in Dedication Ceremony for Stonewall National Monument in New York City', 24 June 2016.
30 Carter (n 8).
31 Cf Benoît Zagdoun, 'En 1977, elles participaient à la première Marche des fiertés: "On était encore les anormaux"' *France Télévisions*, 24 June 2017. <www.francetvinfo.fr/societe/il-y-a-40-ans-elles-participaient-a-la-premiere-marche-des-fiertes-on-etait-encore-les-anormaux_2251103.html>.
32 Martyn Ziegler, 'Football Fans to Fly Flag for Gay Rights' *The Times*, 23 June 2021.
33 Sexual Offences Act 1967, c. 60.

between the first LGBT demonstrations in London and the GLF, and from there back to Stonewall.)[34] 'Stonewall', the prominent UK LGBT charity, took its name from the 1969 events, and when, in 2019, various LGBT personalities reflected on the impact of the Riots, the comment was made that the very word 'gay' had, before the uprising, not been commonly used to denote sexual orientation in Britain.[35] Chris Smith, the first openly gay Member of the Westminster Parliament, observed that Stonewall 'laid the foundation for all the campaigns for LGBT+ equality that followed', including in his examples the fights 'against Section 28, for an equal age of consent, for equal access to services' and for equal marriage.[36]

These reflections, however, also invite a more discerning evaluation of the summer of 1969. A long path still lay ahead – even in countries in which homosexual activities had been legalised. Decriminalisation did not end discrimination; homosexuals could face exclusion from the civil service[37] and from the military: in the United Kingdom, the ban on homosexuals in the armed forces was removed only after the European Court of Human Rights had ruled that the discharge of two servicemen on the grounds of their sexual orientation violated their rights under the European Convention on Human Rights.[38]

Section 28, which Chris Smith mentioned, was a 1988 provision that introduced into the law of England, Scotland and Wales a prohibition on local authorities on the promotion of homosexuality as well as the promotion of teaching 'in any maintained school of the acceptability of homosexuality as a pretended family relationship'.[39] The provision was problematic from the outset, not least because of the implied discrimination of LGBT students and those brought up by same-sex couples.[40] The law was repealed in 2003;[41] but when, ten years later, Russia passed a law that banned homosexual propaganda directed at persons below the age of 18, the parallels to Section 28 were not lost on observers.[42] The Russian law is still in force, as are laws in other Eastern

---

34 See Jason Okundaye, 'Ted Brown: The Man Who Held a Mass Kiss-in and Made History' *The Guardian*, 8 April 2021.
35 Louis Staples, 'Stonewall Riots Recalled: The Day We Cried "ENOUGH"' *The Independent*, 24 June 2019.
36 *Ibid.*
37 Miller (n 3) with regard to England and Wales.
38 ECtHR *Lustig-Prean and Beckett v The United Kingdom* (Applications nos. 31417/96 and 32377/96), Judgment, 27 September 1999, paras 104–105; Audrey Gillan, 'Gay Sailor Breaks Silence' *Guardian*, 28 January 2000.
39 Local Government Act 1988, c. 9, s. 28(1).
40 Cf *The Times*, 'Lord Rea Obituary', 22 June 2020.
41 S. 122 Local Government Act 2003, c. 26.
42 Ben Smith, 'Persecution of Sexual Minorities in Russia' *House of Commons Research Briefing*, 21 August 2013, 3.

European and Central Asian States that are likewise directed against LGBT 'propaganda'.[43]

The consideration of homosexuality and gender diversity as 'illnesses', which was so prevalent in the Stonewall years,[44] has not disappeared either – at least not from all segments of society and all regions of the world. Conversion practices – efforts to change the sexual orientation or gender identity of individuals – are still carried out, at times with severe consequences for their victims.[45] Within the European Union, only two Member States have, at the time of writing, banned these practices;[46] but initiatives for a prohibition are under way in several other jurisdictions.[47]

A particularly troubling situation is caused by the difficulties which transgender people face. In 2010, the Council of Europe called on Member States to take 'appropriate measures' for the legal recognition of a person's gender assignment, 'in particular by making possible the change of name and gender in official documents in a quick, transparent and accessible way'.[48] But when, in the United Kingdom, proposals were made to reform the Gender Recognition Act[49] to allow for the self-identification of trans persons, the debate on the very recognition of transgender persons returned with undiminished force.[50] It led to a split of the LGBT movement, with groups breaking away that purport to focus solely on lesbian, gay and bisexual rights,[51] as well as to a division of the feminist movement, with 'gender-critical feminists' causing a similar schism.[52] Some statements that were made in the debate[53] undoubtedly had the capacity to cause hurt and allow the conclusion that the journey to societal recognition has not been concluded. Trans women, it may be remembered, were

---

43 Human Rights First, 'Homophobia in the Baltic States: The Eurobarometer', 21 October 2015. <www.humanrightsfirst.org/blog/homophobia-baltic-states-eurobarometer>.
44 See above at (n 9).
45 Special Rapporteur on Torture and Other Cruel, Inhuman or Degrading Treatment or Punishment, *Relevance of the Prohibition of Torture and Other Cruel, Inhuman or Degrading Treatment or Punishment to the Context of Domestic Violence*, Report, General Assembly (12 July 2019), A/74/148, para 48.
46 European Parliament, *Declaration of the EU as an LGBTIQ Freedom Zone*, European Parliament resolution of 11 March 2021 on the declaration of the EU as an LGBTIQ Freedom Zone (2021/2557(RSP)), P9_TA(2021)0089, at K.
47 See Scottish Government, *Programme for Government 2021–22* (Edinburgh 2021) 50. <www.gov.scot/publications/fairer-greener-scotland-programme-government-2021-22/documents/>.
48 Council of Europe, *Recommendation CM/Rec(2010)5 of the Committee of Ministers to Member States on Measures to Combat Discrimination on Grounds of Sexual Orientation or Gender Identity* (31 March 2010), para IV.21.
49 Gender Recognition Act 2004, c. 7.
50 See *The Week*, 'The Trans Debate: A Fiercely-Fought Battleground in the Nation's Culture Wars', 12 November 2021.
51 Greg Hurst, 'Transgender Dispute Splits Stonewall' *The Times*, 23 October 2019.
52 *The Week* (n 50).
53 See, on the problem, Tara John, 'Anti-Trans Rhetoric Is Rife in the British Media. Little Is Being Done to Extinguish the Flames' *CNN Wire*, 9 October 2021.

among the first who threw bottles at the policemen in Christopher Street in June 1969.[54] It is sobering to consider that, without them, the Stonewall Riots may not have happened.

Outside the Western hemisphere, the challenges faced by LGBT persons can be considerably more difficult. The very manifestation of a non-heterosexual identity can lead to conflict with the law: in 70 States, same-sex relations are still criminalised.[55] Even where criminalisation does not exist, societal disapproval can be severe,[56] and such rejection has the potential of developing into other forms of discrimination and violence.[57] Government-sponsored and government-tolerated violence has not disappeared either: arguably one of the worst instances in that regard was the 'anti-gay purge' carried out by Chechnyan authorities in 2017, who abducted more than a hundred men suspected of being gay to detainment camps where they were 'humiliated, starved and tortured'.[58] If these difficulties to which the LGBT community is exposed are taken into account, an image emerges that allows for a different assessment of the summer of 1969. If Stonewall was indeed 'Bastille Day', it did not entirely manage to topple the *ancien régime*.

2. Investigating the Subject

What these developments demonstrate is that the question of how far the LGBT community has come in the 50 years since Stonewall escapes simple answers. The conclusions to such a query depend on numerous parameters. The group of beneficiaries of any progress varies depending on the part of the LGBT group under debate: the rights realised by lesbian, gay and bisexual persons are not necessarily mirrored by those held by transgender or intersexual persons. Geographical and cultural notions require consideration too: the situation of LGBT persons in Africa can differ considerably from that of their peers in Europe; within Europe, differences between West and East manifest themselves, and even within the same country, the situation in larger cities may differ considerably from that experienced in less populous and diverse communities.

---

54 Sommerlad (n 22).
55 BBC News, 'Brunei Stoning: Which Places Have the Death Penalty for Gay Sex?' 3 April 2019. <www.bbc.co.uk/news/world-45434583>.
56 See Boniface Dulani et al., 'Good Neighbours? Africans Express High Levels of Tolerance for Many, but Not for All' *Afrobarometer Dispatch No. 74* (1 March 2016) 3.
57 Eric Pichon with Gevorg Kourchoudian, 'LGBTI in Africa. Widespread Discrimination Against People with Non-Conforming Sexual Orientations and Gender Identities' (May 2019) *European Parliamentary Research Service* 5.
58 Greg Wilford, 'Chechyan LGBT Activists Urge Governments to Help Them Flee Persecution in Their Russian Homeland' *Independent* 20 May 2017; Tanya Lokshina et al., 'They Have Long Arms and They Can Find Me' *Human Rights Watch*, 26 May 2017. <www.hrw.org/report/2017/05/26/they-have-long-arms-and-they-can-find-me/anti-gay-purge-local-authorities-russias>.

Even the concept of progress invites more detailed contemplation: its requirements may be different for an LGBT person who comes out in a heteronormative but generally welcoming environment to one who has to coordinate various minority statuses – a person, for instance, who experiences their sexual identity as strongly as their belonging to a particular faith community. Engaging with these concepts is the main theme of this book; the research question underlying its parts is constituted by an attempt to understand the achievements that the LGBT community has realised since Stonewall and to assess the challenges that, more than 50 years after the summer of 1969, remain.

This is a task that reaches beyond the remit of one discipline and on which different subject areas can legitimately reach different conclusions. Even the notion of 'justice', which unites the parts of this volume, is not exhaustively evaluated through the toolset of one field alone: the impact of morality on justice, for instance, can be expected to receive an assessment in religious studies that differs from that which the law applies; both findings may vary from the concept of justice as measured against historical parameters.

The effort that informed this book is therefore deliberately multidisciplinary. The 20 contributors come from a wide range of areas and include academics, activists, writers and leaders of faith communities. But their combined engagement in an evaluation of LGBT matters between progress and challenge results in a unique perspective of a subject that has meaning far beyond the confines of a minority group and whose examination yields insights into the very structure of human society.

Part 1, dealing with political and social perspectives, traces the history of the LGBT community and the treatment it received in the wider society in the UK;[59] but it also engages with particular societal aspects that affect LGBT lives and which tend not to receive sufficient recognition in literature on LGBT matters – such as the question of youth homelessness among LGBT people[60] and the way in which their situation and internalised experiences shape the lives of older LGBT couples today.[61] Outside the situation in the UK, it explores the difficulties that the LGBT movement in Uganda faces, as well as the ways in which LGBT rights organisations managed to deal with these challenges and to achieve a measure of success.[62]

Legal perspectives form the main theme of Part 2. It explores the evolution of LGBT rights in the UK and the question whether the march towards progress is now witnessing a setback;[63] but it also engages with more specific aspects in the legal area, which have an impact on LGBT matters. That includes the

---

59 Sir Stephen Wall, Chapter 3 in this volume.
60 Carin Tunåker, Chapter 4.
61 Dora Jandrić, Chapter 6.
62 Clare Byarugaba, Chapter 5.
63 Carolynn Gray, Chapter 8.

question whether tools of direct democracy are suitable for the establishment of marriage equality or whether court judgments offer an alternative that may better accommodate the rights of minorities,[64] but also a critical evaluation of the recognition of same-sex partnerships and marriages, in particular in the case law of the European Court of Human Rights.[65] This part also reflects on the law of defamation in Scotland and examines insights which the treatment of defamatory statements offers about the way in which the perception of homosexuality has changed in the understanding of society as a whole.[66] It also offers a critical analysis of selected judgments by the House of Lords on homosexuality, with reflections on the underlying judicial attitudes and ideologies which the narrative emerging from these texts reveals.[67]

Part 3 investigates the degree to which LGBT identity and the struggle for equality have been reflected in the fields of education and language. It thus explores in how far the notion of equality can be said to have been realised in the classroom and engages with the challenges that LGBT students have to face in this regard.[68] But it also analyses the experience of transgender students in higher education, with insights on the way in which they perceive university environments, but also on the difficulties that still exist on the path towards inclusion.[69] Beyond the British perspective, it also investigates the role that language has played in community-building among the migrant LGBT population in the Arabian Peninsula, but also how linguistic obstacles have been overcome in an act of embracing or rejecting normative labels.[70]

Part 4 deals with the interrelationship between the LGBT community and the medical sector and focuses on particular aspects that arise in this context. It thus provides a critical examination of the way in which lesbian non-biological mothers may face experiences of disenfranchisement in the British healthcare sector,[71] but also a reflection on the impact that conversion practices have had both on the health and the human rights of their victims and of the evaluation that such practices have received.[72]

Part 5 is dedicated to questions that arise where religious viewpoints and aspects of LGBT life meet. It thus examines Jewish perspectives of LGBT matters and focuses in particular on the wedding ceremony – including the various approaches taken to it under different strands of Judaism and the interpretation

---

64 Paul Behrens, Chapter 9.
65 Helen Fenwick and Andrew Hayward, Chapter 10.
66 Kenneth McK. Norrie, Chapter 11.
67 Sean Becker, Chapter 12.
68 Eleanor Capaldi and Amanda Sykes, Chapter 14.
69 Lynne Regan, Chapter 15.
70 Gaar Adams, Chapter 16.
71 Lucille Kelsall-Knight and Ceri Sudron, Chapter 18.
72 Paul Behrens, Chapter 19.

that the relevant texts have experienced in that regard.[73] With regard to Roman Catholic theology, this part provides an engagement with the methodological approaches to LGBT issues that have materialised in this context, with particular room given to *Evangelium Gaudii*, the 2013 apostolic exhortation of Pope Francis.[74] With respect to Islam, it explores the situation of LGBT Muslims in the UK and investigates the challenges that persons in that group face today – both as members of their faith communities and as members of the LGBT community – and traces the search for a space in which they can realise their identity.[75]

Each of the five parts is introduced by a shorter chapter written by the editors, which provides an overview of the relationship that developed between LGBT matters and the relevant subject area especially since the days of Stonewall.[76] The Conclusion reflects on the findings of the main part of the book and provides a summary of the insights gained in the course of the individual chapters, in particular in light of the underlying questions which were raised at the outset.[77]

While the contributions to this book arise from different subject areas, they also offer the opportunity to reflect on themes that recur across these divides and which can be held to be of particular significance for a contemporary evaluation of LGBT matters. A principal theme is the dichotomy between social and legal influences on matters of LGBT relevance and on the LGBT community as a whole. The relationship between these influences gives rise to the question whether law or society had been motor (or hindrance) for the progress of LGBT rights. But societal norms also influence educational structure and thus shape directly the treatment of LGBT in the classroom, while language in turn is the filter through which society categorises its environment in all areas, including LGBT matters. Medicine occupies a particular place in the framework of legal and societal parameters: negative societal perceptions on LGBT persons leave their traces on the medical assessment of LGBT matters as well; yet at the same time, the medical profession has often shown itself as leading general societal attitudes on the path to progress, sometimes ahead of legal change.

In a similar way, the position of 'morality' and its interaction with LGBT matters has relevance to more than one subject area. Questions of morality certainly arise where the relationship between religion and LGBT matters is concerned; but the question of morals – or rather, their subjective societal perception – also plays a role where the criminalisation of conduct (such as

---

73 Rabbi Mark L. Solomon and Hannah Holtschneider, Chapter 21.
74 Nicolete Burbach, Chapter 22.
75 Drew Dalton, Chapter 23.
76 Chapters 2, 7, 13, 17, 20.
77 Sean Becker and Paul Behrens, Chapter 24.

consensual same-sex intimacy) is concerned. But even with regard to medicine – an area that, more than others, seems to be anchored in the mandates of scientific objectivity – questions of moral perception retain their place and can influence the assessment of LGBT matters and the LGBT community – a point which was revealed in some clarity in the early debates on the decriminalisation of homosexuality, including in submissions to the Wolfenden Report.

A third theme is formed by the fact that the LGBT community by itself does not form a monolithic bloc. Its members experience forms of belonging other than those to a group defined by sexual orientation or gender identity; and not all aspects of their belonging can easily be reconciled with each other. The question of intersectionality gains particular shape when members of a faith group seek to realise a non-heteronormative sexual orientation or a non-cisgender identity, and the challenges they face may derive from either community to which they belong. But intersectionality materialises in other fields as well – it arises also when a particular community defined by ethnic, societal or linguistic parameters challenges reconciliation with an individual's gender identity or sexual orientation but plays a role also where membership of a more traditionalist professional body causes conflicts with the realisation of the sexual life or the gender identity of one of its individuals.

The subject area and timing of the publication invite some observations on the technical side of this study. Various abbreviations are commonly used to refer to (non-heterosexual) forms of sexual orientation as well as to gender diversity. For the purposes of this book, and unless otherwise specified by the contributors, the acronym 'LGBT' (lesbian, gay, bisexual and transgender) is used to also embrace related concepts, such as intersex, questioning, asexual, etc.

Opinions expressed by the individual authors are their own; they are not necessarily indicative of the opinions of the institutions of which they may be members or of other contributors of this work.

The cut-off point for the consideration of factual and legal developments was 15 November 2021.

We owe a particular debt of gratitude to Phillipa Crichton-Stuart and George Revel, whose research assistance in the preparation of parts of this study has been truly invaluable and was greatly appreciated by the editors and the contributors of the relevant chapters.

Part 1

Justice After Stonewall? Aspects of Political and Social Acceptance

Chapter 2

Challenges Past and Present
Political and Social Perspectives

Sean Becker and Paul Behrens

Along with topics, such as abortion and the wearing of religious clothing and symbols, LGBT issues tend to polarise voters and feature in political campaign platforms. Historically, the dividing line can be drawn between the left and right sides of the political spectrum: the former traditionally more 'pro' and the latter more 'anti-LGBT'. In 1980, US President Jimmy Carter was the first president in US history to support an LGBT rights plank in the Democratic Party's platform.[1] By contrast, during the 1987 British elections, the Conservative Party targeted the Labour Party's active support for LGBT equality in their campaign advertisements.[2] One such poster shows a lineup of young men wearing badges reading 'Gay lib' and 'Gay sports day' accompanied by the slogan, 'Labour camp. Do you want to live in it?'[3]

The political spectrum's polarised stance on LGBT issues seemingly has begun to erode in recent years. During President Trump's acceptance speech at the 2016 Republican National Convention, he vowed to protect the LGBT community 'from the violence and oppression of a hateful foreign ideology'[4] – the first time the LGBT community had been mentioned in a Republican nomination address. However, a more complex picture emerges following closer scrutiny of his seemingly LGBT-friendly stance – most prominently, during his time in office he banned transgender service members from serving in the military.[5] Similarly, in the UK, Prime Minister Boris Johnson's wife assured

---
1 Trudy Ring, 'The 11 Most Significant Presidents for LGBT Americans' *The Advocate*, 1 October 2019; see also Office of Staff Secretary, 'National Gay Task Force Questionnaire', 20 December 1979.
2 Matthew Todd, 'Margaret Thatcher was No Poster Girl for Gay Rights' *The Guardian*, 10 April 2013.
3 Sophie Gadd, 'This Conservative Party Poster from the 1987 Election Is Pretty Shocking' *Mirror*, 6 April 2015; see also Todd (n 2).
4 *CNN*, 'Donald Trump's Speech at the Republican Convention, As Prepared for Delivery', 22 July 2016.
5 Hallie Jackson and Courtney Kube, 'Trump's Controversial Transgender Military Policy Goes into Effect' *NBC News*, 12 April 2019; President Biden reversed this ban five days after taking office (see 'Executive Order on Enabling All Qualified Americans to Serve Their Country in Uniform', 86 FR 7471, 25 January 2021).

DOI: 10.4324/9781003286295-4

the 2021 Conservative Party Conference that her husband was 'completely committed' to protecting and extending LGBT rights.[6] Johnson himself, however, had in the past referred to gay men as 'tank-topped bumboys,' compared same-sex marriage to bestiality and, while in office, was widely criticised for dragging his feet on banning conversion practices.[7]

Nonetheless, the world has seen positive developments in the realm of the LGBT community and politics as of late as well. In 2019, Mounir Baatour became Tunisia's first-ever openly gay presidential candidate.[8] Brazil's 2020 municipal elections saw four transgender persons[9] elected to city councils across the country.[10] In 2021, Luong The Huy became Vietnam's first openly gay candidate to run for a National Assembly seat.[11] And, also in 2021, conservative politician Nicholas Yatromanolakis became Greece's first openly gay minister.[12]

The LGBT community has faced both challenges and changes in the domain of politics over the past 50 years. The chapters in this part address these changes by highlighting both difficulties and developments.

Chapter 3 (Wall) outlines both the obstacles and positive changes in the UK's treatment of the LGBT community over the past 50 years. He identifies the driving forces behind these positive changes while also critically engaging with contemporary controversies.

Chapter 4 (Tunåker) examines the issue of homelessness among young LGBT people. Specifically, she explores the 'paradox of progress' relating to advances in LGBT rights and social outcomes of these, analysing the difficulties this group faces as well as outlining solutions on preventative and policy levels.

Chapter 5 (Byarugaba) analyses how the LGBT movement in Uganda was able to organise at a time of peril, disseminate a positive message against violence and discrimination and gather both international and domestic support.

Chapter 6 (Jandrić) discusses how heteronormativity impacts the lives of older same-sex couples. Her focus lies on the way social structures built around heteronormativity influenced the lives of non-heterosexual individuals in the past and how they impact their present relationships and imagination of possible futures.

---

6 Liam O'Dell, 'Carrie Johnson Says Husband Boris Is "Completely Committed" to Protecting and Extending LGBT Rights' *The Independent*, 5 October 2021.
7 Adam Bienkov, 'Boris Johnson Called Gay Men "Tank-Topped Bumboys" and Black People "Piccaninnies" with "Watermelon Smiles"' *Business Insider*, 9 June 2020; Paul Brand, 'Conversion Therapy: Human Rights Lawyers Demand Ban Amid Repeated Delays' *ITV News*, 1 October 2021.
8 Leah Asmelash and Brian Ries, 'This Tunisian Lawyer Is Hoping to be the Country's First Openly Gay President' *CNN*, 9 August 2019.
9 Erika Hilton and Thammy Miranda in Sao Paulo, Duda Salabert in Belo Horizonte, and Linda Brasil in Aracaju.
10 AFP, 'Historic Wins for Trans Candidates in Brazil Vote' *France 24*, 16 November 2020.
11 AFP, 'Vietnam's First Openly Gay Candidate Sets Sights on National Assembly Seat in Sunday's Vote' *Southern China Morning Post*, 21 May 2021.
12 Rachel Savage, 'Interview – Greece's First Gay Minister Hopes Appointment Helps Erode Homophobia' *Reuters*, 11 January 2021.

Chapter 3

The Development of the LGBT+ Community in the UK in the Last 50 Years

Sir Stephen Wall

You cannot write about the last 50 years by starting only 50 years ago. Stonewall is a massively important reference point for all of us. But there are, I believe, other, more *nationally* important events that determine how we got to where we are today. And the laws that were in force just over 60 years ago still weigh on modern LGBT communities, something to which I will return.

I am not going back on LGBT rights as far as the 16th century, except to make the point that the 60 or so men who were hanged for sodomy in the early decades of the 19th century lost their lives, thanks to a law passed in 1533.[1] And it was the late 19th century that gave us the Labouchere amendment[2] that created the offence of gross indecency, which made all forms of sexual intimacy between men a crime, punishable by one year's imprisonment with, or without, hard labour. That was the law under which Oscar Wilde and Alan Turing were convicted.[3] It was also the basis of about 95% of the blackmail cases, which came to the attention of the authorities.[4] It created a climate of fear and

---

1 Public Act, 25 Henry VIII, c. 6; This law was perpetuated in 1540 by 32 Hen. VIII c. 3 and by 2 & 3 Edw. VI, c. 29 but repealed by the Statute of Repeal 1 Mar. St. 1 c. 1 d. 3. The continuous history of sodomy as a capital offence dates from 1562 by 5 Eliz. c. 17, which revived the Henrician legislation. AD Harvey, 'Prosecutions for Sodomy at the Beginning of the Nineteenth Century' (1978) 21:4 *The Historical Journal* 941. It should also be noted that in his reservation, James Adair (see below at n 18) made reference to the history of criminalising homosexuality as grounds for rejecting the Committee's recommendations for decriminalisation, Reservations I, *Report of the Committee on Homosexual Offences and Prostitution* (Wolfenden 1957) Cmnd 247, para 3 (pp 118).
2 Criminal Law Amendment Act 1885 (48 & 49 Vict. c. 69), s. 11.; *See also* Introduction of the amendment, Hansard (HC Deb) 6 August 1885, vol 300 col 1397.
3 Parliamentary Archives, '1885 Labouchere Amendment'. <www.parliament.uk/about/living-heritage/transformingsociety/private-lives/relationships/collections1/sexual-offences-act-1967/1885-labouchere-amendment/> (accessed 21 July 2020).
4 Earl Jowitt, Hansard (HL Deb) 19 May 1954, vol 187, col 745. The overall debate took place under the title of '"Homosexual Crime"', Hansard (HL Deb) 19 May 1954 Vol 187 cc 737-67; Report, Wolfenden (n 1), paras 109–113 (pp 39–41); Wolfenden Committee, 'Memorandum submitted by one of the witnesses to be heard at 2.15 p.m. on Thursday 28th July' (PRO HO 345/8, CHP/69); *see also* Leslie Moran, *The Homosexual(ity) of Law* (Routledge 1996) 50–56.

DOI: 10.4324/9781003286295-5

danger affecting the lives of gay men (the law did not apply to women), which permeated much of the history of the 20th century.[5]

There was a brief respite, in London at least, in the blackout years of WWII, famously described by Quentin Crisp: 'Never in the history of sex was so much offered by so many to so few'.[6] Or sometimes quoted the other way round: 'by so few to so many'.[7]

That respite did not long outlast the war. By 1953, the Commissioner of the Met, Sir John Nott-Bower, was promising to 'rip the cover off all London's filth spots', and he 'enlisted the support of local police throughout England to step up the number of arrests for homosexual offences'.[8] In the first decade of the century, there were about 100 arrests of gay men a year.[9] By 1953, there were 5,680 recorded 'homosexual offences'.[10] The Home Secretary, David Maxwell-Fyfe, (later Lord Kilmuir) instituted what he called a 'new drive against male vice, which would rid England of this plague'.[11] He told the House of Commons in 1953 that 'homosexuals in general are exhibitionists and proselytisers and are a danger to others, especially the young'.[12]

The arrest of Lord Montague and Peter Wildeblood in 1953 saw their conviction in a trial, which was both a travesty and a Press sensation. The defence counsel, Peter Rawlinson, would go on to become a Conservative Attorney General. It was his experience of that trial, and others, that led Rawlinson to tell the House of Commons, when reform was finally being discussed in the 1960s: 'I have left the court at the conclusion of some trials sickened by injustice [. . .] To sit there and see a man, perhaps of talent and distinction, in the box, and to see the worthless wretched creatures being paraded there as witnesses for the Crown, pampered by the police as persons upon whom

---

5 Colin Spencer, *Homosexuality: A History* (Fourth Estate 1996) 275.
6 Quentin Crisp, *The Naked Civil Servant* (Jonathan Cape 1968) 157–160.
7 Jeffrey Weeks, *Coming Out, the Emergence of LGBT identities in Britain from the 19th Century to the Present* (Quartet 2016) 228.
8 Donald Horne, 'Big Names Involved in London Clean-Up of Male Vice' *The Daily Telegraph* (Syndey, NSW) 25 October 1953, 11 (paraphrasing by Horne). *See also* Keith Dockray and Alan Sutton, *Politics, Society and Homosexuality in Post-War Britain: The Sexual Offences Act of 1967 and Its Significance* (Fonthill Media 2017); Michael Peppiatt, *Francis Bacon: Anatomy of an Enigma* (Constable 2008).
9 Average of arrests under the charge of 'gross indecency between males' (the specific crime created by the Labouchere Amendment of 1885) between 1900 and 1910, Home Office, 'A Summary of Recorded Crime Data from 1898 to 2001/02'. <https://assets.publishing.service.gov.uk/government/uploads/system/uploads/attachment_data/file/116649/rec-crime-1898-2002.xls> (accessed 21 July 2020).
10 *Ibid*. Although arrests for 'gross indecency between males' in 1953 numbered 'only' 1,673, taken along with related charges of 'buggery' and 'indecent assault on a male', the total rises to 5,680 for 1953.
11 Mike Hutton, *Life in 1950s London* (Amberley Publishing, Reprint 2015).
12 Hansard (HC Deb), 3 December 1953, vol 521, col 1298 (Sir David Maxwell-Fyfe); *See also* Horne (n 8).

apparently there has been cast the mantle of perfection, to see it is to feel that it is a mockery by society [. . .]'.[13]

So, our modern story really begins with the Wolfenden Inquiry, set up by Maxwell-Fyfe in 1954 to inquire into both prostitution and homosexuality.[14] It was in no sense a liberal initiative: both vices were seen to be prevalent. What was to be done about them?

Wolfenden makes interesting reading. It provides what I think is the first coherent statement that homosexual men do not choose their sexuality. But in no sense is it a document about human rights as we conceive them. It is about whether private immorality should constitute a criminal offence. And, surprisingly, it is the Churches who were more inclined than others to accept that that distinction should be made: a grave sin (and they all thought it is as bad as you can get – which, by the way, is certainly what I was told when, at my Catholic prep school at the age of ten, I was caught kissing and fondling one of my peers) – was not the same as a crime in law.

Paradoxically, it was the Law Society and the BMA who took the view I would have expected the Churches to take. Here is the BMA's view: 'Not only are their actual practices repulsive, but the behaviour and appearance of homosexuals congregating blatantly in public houses, streets and restaurants are an outrage to public decency'.[15] The answer, according to the BMA, lay in religious conversion.[16] Good medical diagnosis there then.

The Law Society was equally clear: 'both buggery and gross indecency should remain criminal offences even when committed in private between consenting male persons of full age. The offences are productive of great evils [. . .] inasmuch as they (i) tend to reduce the inclination to marry; (ii) militate against the procreation of children; (iii) are calculated to result in damage to the State if they get too strong a hold; (iv) are likely (if legalised in private between genuine homosexuals) to contaminate others'.[17]

What is interesting in these testimonies is the constant refrain that same-sex activity is likely to be so enjoyable as to be irresistibly contagious.

Several courageous gay men did come forward to give testimony, and the Committee did hear a number of them. Not all Committee members treated

---

13 Hansard (HC Deb), 26 November 1958, vol 596, col 472 (Mr Peter Rawlinson (Epsom)).
14 Brian Lewis, *Wolfenden's Witnesses: Homosexuality in Postwar Britain* (Palgrave Macmillan 2016) 4–6.
15 *Ibid.*, 111.
16 There are multiple references to 'moral' education, in particular from religious persons, in the BMA's report on homosexuality. The last paragraph deals specifically with conversion by religious means, noting its 'success'. British Medical Journal, 'Homosexuality and Prostitution: B.M.A. Memorandum Of Evidence', Vol. 2, No. 4954 (17 December 1955) 165–170; *See also The Times (London)*, 'On this day December 16, 1955' <www.thetimes.co.uk/article/on-this-day-december-16-1955-tgbc386z3dz> (accessed 21 July 2020).
17 Council of the Law Society, *Memorandum*, June 1955, para 4; Lewis (n 14) 41, 42; Paul Rock, *The Official History of Criminal Justice in England and Wales, Vol 1* (Routledge 2019).

them kindly: James Adair's style of questioning was described as 'hostile',[18] and he added his own reservations to the report, in which he stated that '[e]xisting homosexual trends and tendencies are currently the cause of much public concern and disgust'[19] and that the 'presence, in a district, of [. . .] adult male lovers living openly and notoriously under the approval of the law' was 'bound to have a regrettable and pernicious effect on the young people of the community'.[20]

Nevertheless, a clear majority of the committee, led by Wolfenden himself (whose son was openly gay)[21] took the view, as Wolfenden put it: 'I think it can be argued that other forms of sexual misbehaviour (adultery, rape and many forms of heterosexual perversion) are more harmful both to the individual and society than are private homosexual acts between consenting adult males . . .'.[22]

The Conservative Government of the day (1957) (with Rab Butler as Home Secretary) fought shy of doing anything to implement the report's recommendations. The *News Chronicle*'s view ('To countless thousands of men and women homosexuality is regarded as something to be stamped out at all costs')[23] was just one of several similar reactions that led Butler to conclude that it would not be wise to go against strongly held public opinion on that matter.[24] Maxwell-Fyfe (now Lord Chancellor) refused to attend any Cabinet meetings where this 'filthy subject' would be discussed.[25] When the Report was eventually debated in Parliament, 14 months after its publication, Butler fell back on the same argument: a majority of public opinion would not wear it. Very few MPs, on either side of the House, supported the findings of the Report. Most condemned it. The Government Minister who wound up the debate concluded that 'the Government have to take note both of the risk of homosexuality spreading, and of possible corruption and degradation in society if it does, if the law is changed'.[26]

---

18 Lewis (n 14) 203.
19 Wolfenden (n 1), Reservations I, Mr Adair, 118, para 3.
20 *Ibid*, para 2.
21 J Weeks, 'Wolfenden, John Frederick [Jack], Baron Wolfenden (1906–1985)' *Oxford Dictionary of National Biography*. <https://doi.org/10.1093/ref:odnb/31852>. See also Robert Aldrich, Garry Wotherspoon, *Who's Who in Contemporary Gay and Lesbian History, Vol.2: From World War II to the Present Day* (Routledge 2005).
22 Rock (n 17).
23 *Ibid*.
24 Cf. Hansard (HC Deb) 26 November 1958, vol 596, cc 365, 370–371; Minutes of the Home Affairs Committee, 29 November 1957 CAB 134 (HA (57) 26); Simon James, *British Government: A Reader in Policy Making* (Routledge 2002) 67; Adrian Bingham, *Family Newspapers? Sex, Private Life and the British Popular Press 1918–1978* (Oxford University Press 2009) 190–191; *The Times*, 'Heavier Fines in New Laws on Prostitution: Commons Reactions to Wolfenden Report', 27 November 1958, 4–5, 10.
25 Leo Abse, *Private Member* (Macdonald 1973) 147; see also Robert Philpot, 'The Jewish MP Who Pried Open Britain's Closet Door' *The Times of Israel*, 28 July 2017.
26 Hansard (HC Deb), 26 November 1958, vol 596 col 502 (Mr David Renton) (Huntingdonshire) (Parliamentary Under-Secretary of State for the Home Office).

So, the persecution and prosecution of homosexual men continued. In response, in 1958, the Homosexual Law Reform Society was founded. It included the Archbishop of York among its members. It made the case for reform, but there was no question of speaking out, let alone coming out, or claiming a right to be gay. Tacitly, the Society bought into the idea that homosexuals were 'unfortunate people [who] deserve our compassion rather than our contempt'.[27] There was no question then of following the example of some of the much bolder homosexual organisations, which were already making their voices heard in the United States. A British opinion poll in the summer of 1963 found 16% of those questioned to be in favour of law reform and 67% opposed.[28]

Leo Absé, in the House of Commons, and Lord Arran, in the Lords, made their first attempts to get the law changed through Private Member's Bills in the 1960s.[29] It failed since the Government was not prepared to support it. Nor was there much support in Parliament. Roy Jenkins, the future Home Secretary, referred to a difficulty about the Labouchere amendment, as he perceived it: 'We wish that it was not there, but it is there and there is a difficulty about removing it lest it be thought that in doing so this House was proclaiming that homosexuality is a good thing. I do not believe that many people would take that view.'[30]

The Labour Government of 1964 was similarly reluctant. Various new objections were raised. Lord Dilhorne was worried about orgies. He had worked out that 'a homosexual act can be committed between more than two persons at the same time'.[31] If he had not enlightened us, we would never have worked that one out.

What would happen, it was asked, when English law was changed while the law in Scotland remained unchanged? What, for example, would the legal position be of English ships sailing from Scottish ports? Would the new laws apply to sailors on those ships?[32]

---

27 Hansard (HC Deb) 29 June 1960, vol 625 col 1455 (Mr Kenneth Robinson. Robinson was on the executive committee of the Homosexual Law Reform Society).
28 British Market Survey quoted in Chapter Seven of Rock (n 17), Chapter VII, footnote 164.
29 Leo Abse's Bill was tabled in 1961–1962: *Sexual Offences Bill 1962*, Parliamentary Archives HL/PO/PU/2/143. As for Lord Arran, see Hansard (HL Deb) 21 June 1965, vol 267 cc 287–317. See also Peter Dorey, *The Labour Governments 1964–1970* (Routledge 2006) 348–352.
30 Hansard (HC Deb) 29 June 1960, vol 625, c 1507 (Mr Roy Jenkins) (Birmingham Stechford).
31 Hansard (HL Deb) 21 June 1965, vol 267, col 361. The entire debate and vote on Amendment (No 7) to the Sexual Offences Bill runs through cc 361–375; see also Rock (n 17).
32 A number of contributions in the debates referred to the differences between Scots law and English/Welsh law. The predominant focus appears to be on the 'public interest test' in Scotland that was not present in England. See Hansard (HC Deb) 26 November 1958 vol 596 cc 475–6 (Peter Rawlinson); Hansard (HL Deb) 12 March 1965 vol 266 col 1467 (Lord Bolerno); Hansard (HL Deb) 21 June 1965 vol 267 col 426 (Lord Bishop of London); Hansard (HL Deb) 21 June 1965 vol 267 cc 439, 445 (Lord Boothby). See also Rock (n 17).

So, it was not until Labour was re-elected with a large majority in 1966 that the Government, under the influence of the reforming Lord Chancellor, Lord Gardiner, took a benevolent interest in the legislation and fostered its adoption.

One of the most ardent opponents of the Bill, the Conservative MP for Carshalton, Captain Elliot, was rather prescient in identifying while decrying one of the effects that, thankfully for us, passage of the law was to bring in its wake: 'I think it is worth considering the side effects of the Bill,' he said. 'We should, I presume, get a succession of plays on television and on the stage on the subject. We should get more books on it. We should get more clubs. I believe that the vice would be looked upon as a normal and natural part of our daily life, and all checks would be gone.'[33]

The law was passed in 1967.[34] It did not make an immediate difference to the lives of gay men. Sex in private was allowed, but 'private' effectively meant two men alone in a private house. It did not mean two men in a bedroom with the door locked and someone downstairs in the kitchen, let alone two men in a hotel room. Arrests for indecency and importuning increased. A friend of mine, a bit older than me, recalls that the private parties to which the police had turned a blind eye before 1967 were now the subject of police raids.

In the Civil Service, homosexuality remained a barrier to security clearance and therefore to employment. The Foreign Office, on the back of the Burgess and MacLean spy scandals of the early 1960s, had become almost paranoid on the subject. By the time I joined the Foreign Office at the age of 21 in 1968, I knew I was gay, although I was deep in self-denial and convinced that I could make myself be straight. In my security interview, I was asked if I had ever had any homosexual experiences: yes, I said, with another boy when I was ten. This, as I had hoped, was regarded as merely amusing. I was less prepared for the next question: 'Did I have any homosexual tendencies?' I was not a Catholic for nothing. I knew I was tempted, but was that a tendency? Well, yes it was. But I lied. No, I said. Fortunately, the lie detector was not then in general usage.

And this is where Stonewall becomes relevant to the British story. It is not just that the riots inspired a more militant activism by gay people. More generally, the climate of moral censure was in retreat. Authority was no longer receiving automatic respect. Religious observance was starting to decline. The contraceptive pill had liberated men and women from the constraints of the old sexual taboos. Inspired by Stonewall, the new Gay Liberation Front was out, loud, proud and assertive. *Gay News* began publishing in 1972. It was banned by WH Smith's.[35] But within four years, it had achieved a circulation of 20,000

---

33 Hansard (HC Deb), 19 December 1966, vol 738, col 1082 (Captain Elliot) (Carshalton).
34 Sexual Offences Act 1967, c. 60.
35 Bonnie G Smith, *Global Feminisms Since 1945* (Routledge 2000) 179.

and, business being business, Smith's had started to stock it.[36] I can remember, in the early 1970s, first encountering the erotic drawings of Tom of Finland. I couldn't believe my eyes. All my fantasies were suddenly in print, in public. Here was my guilty secret being proclaimed as something to shout from the rooftops. If there had been any doubt in my mind that I was gay, Tom of Finland removed the doubts. To a young, closeted Roman Catholic, it was wildly exciting and profoundly disturbing. I mention it only because quite a lot of young gay men of my generation went through similar revelations. But stayed firmly in the closet. For family reasons, religious reasons, societal reasons and employment reasons. I would have lost my job. My husband, Ted, who was a doctor at Great Ormond Street, would have lost his too if he had been known to be gay. Some of us married, in the hope that the love of a good woman would cure us. Our ex-wives paid a high price. They too were victims of the law and social attitudes.

This flowering of male gay rights also went hand in hand with a flowering of feminist activism, of which lesbian rights were a part. The first lesbian kiss on British television was in a BBC drama in 1974. But, or so I recall, the two movements moved in parallel rather than together. As far as male homosexuality was concerned, the new spring of hope was relatively short lived. Public disapproval of homosexuality increased from 62% in 1983 to 69% in 1985 to 74% in 1987.[37] The reaction to HIV and AIDS in the Press was one of vilification. 'Is there a homosexual conspiracy'? asked the *Sunday Telegraph* in 1985.[38] The belated, brutally candid public campaign to make people aware of the risks of HIV and AIDS probably did much to raise awareness (and was certainly much more responsible than the wilful neglect of the Reagan Government in the United States) but did nothing to diminish fears of a 'gay plague'. In 1988, when public awareness of AIDS was high, Gallup reported 60% of the population as thinking that homosexuality was not acceptable.[39] 155 gay men were murdered in the UK between 1986 and 1994.[40] A Gallup poll in 1991 found that 44% of lesbians had been physically abused and 72% verbally abused.[41]

Margaret Thatcher's infamous Party conference speech of 1987 ('Children who need to be taught to respect moral values are being taught that they have

---

36 Geoffrey Robertson, *The Justice Game* (Vintage 1999) 154.
37 Based on the number of respondents who considered 'sexual relations between two adults of the same sex' either 'always wrong' or 'mostly wrong', British Social Attitudes, 'Homosexuality', Table 1.7 <www.bsa.natcen.ac.uk/latest-report/british-social-attitudes-30/personal-relationships/homosexuality.aspx>.
38 G Turner, 'Is There a Homosexual Conspiracy?' *Sunday Telegraph*, 5 June 1988 (in Virginia Berridge, *AIDS in the UK: The Making of a Policy 1981–1994* (Oxford University Press 1996) 319).
39 *Sunday Telegraph*, 5 June 1988, quoted in Spencer (n 5) 383.
40 National survey by Stonewall, quoted in Spencer (n 5) 384.
41 Spencer (n 5) 384.

an inalienable right to be gay')[42] was the precursor of Section 28. But its very iniquity provoked a backlash, not least in Manchester where the Chief Constable James Anderton spoke of gays as 'swimming in a cesspit of their own making'.[43] He was lauded by *The Sun*: 'What Britain needs is more men like Anderton' whom it commended for taking the fight to 'gay terrorists holding the decent members of society to ransom'.[44]

Brave individuals were among the agents of change. As were campaigning organisations. As was popular culture. As early as 1960, the film *Victim* was a powerful, harrowing film about the blackmailing of gay men. The central character, a young, prominent, successful barrister ostensibly happily married, falls victim to blackmail for his help, and attraction, to a young man who later commits suicide. The barrister was played by Dirk Bogarde, at the time the number one cinema draw in the UK and the heartthrob of a million girls who did not know, as society at large did not know, that he was gay. Nor throughout a long life did Bogarde ever come out. It was nonetheless a courageous step for Bogarde, and the film had a big impact on public opinion. It was X-rated, i.e. not viewable by anyone under 18, and I was only 13 at the time. But my mother, who was a devout Roman Catholic, did see it. I doubt if she would have been understanding had she known that I was gay, but when I asked her about the film she said: 'People should not be treated like that'.

In the 1970s, 'gay' became more common on TV. We look back now at John Inman's portrayal of a shop assistant in *Are You Being Served?* and find it unpleasantly caricatural. The entire script of the show was outrageous. My late brother-in-law, an actor, played the part of Mr Rumbold, the luckless manager of Grace Brothers, in the show. He and other cast members would say to David Croft, the writer: 'We can't possibly say that'. To which Croft would reply, 'if you say it with an appearance of innocence you can get away with anything'.[45] I suspect the John Inman character was a stage society had to go through on the route to our acceptance. Comedy is often about taking the sting out of fear by mocking authority: the dentist, the hard-nosed policeman, the sergeant major.

---

42 Margaret Thatcher, 'Leader's Speech' Conservative Party Conference 9 October 1987; *See also* Joe Sommerlad, 'Section 28: What Was Margaret Thatcher's Controversial Law and How Did it Affect the Lives of LGBT+ People?' *The Independent*, 24 May 2018.

43 *Liverpool Echo*, 'Police Chief Raps Human Cess-Pit', 11 December 1986. *See also* James Cusick, 'Besieged Gays Win Some New Friends in the North' *The Independent*, 7 December 1996; Paul Flynn, *Good as You: From Prejudice to Pride* (Ebury Press 2017).

44 *The Sun*, 'A Plague in Our Midst' (Editorial) 11 December 1986. See also Susan Kingsley Kent, *Gender and Power in Britain 1640–1990* (Routledge 2002) 352; Andy McSmith, *No Such Thing as Society* (Constable 2010) 229; Matthew Todd, *Straight Jacket – How to be Gay and Happy* (Random House 2017); Flynn (n 39).

45 Author conversation with Nicholas Smith who played the part of Mr Rumbold in *Are You Being Served?*

Because the audience laughed at John Inman, it was OK to like the character he played. Thus, a gay man became popular.

Then came the portrayal of LGBT characters in soap opera, with the first lesbian kiss on *Brookside*, followed by the first male gay kiss on UK TV on *Eastenders*, 'EastBenders', as the condemnatory *Sun* immediately called it.[46] Michael Cashman had a brick through his window.[47] Gary Hailes (the other half of the gay kiss), suffered verbal abuse.[48] Hailes is straight and was taken by surprise. And then, as now, audiences did not always distinguish between the actor and the character they played.

Today, the television portrayal of LGBT people has become routine, and those who produce the Soaps, in particular, can take great credit for changing opinion. But there are still surprises. My niece, the daughter of the actor who played Mr Rumbold, is herself an actor. She plays a senior consultant, Serena Campbell, in the BBC soap, *Holby City*. The character she plays is lesbian and has had, in the show, a dramatic affair with another doctor, played by Gemma Redgrave. Catherine, my niece, has a huge following and mail from lesbian women who assert the importance of her character in changing opinion. One woman in her 50s wrote that the show had given her the courage finally to come out to her parents.

We have seen big progress in recent times. John Major removed the bar on the employment of LGBT civil servants in 1991.[49] New Labour lowered the age of consent and repealed Section 28.[50] Reluctantly, and because the UK was in breach of the European Human Rights Convention, the ban on gays serving in the military was lifted.[51] David Cameron persisted in pushing through the law on gay marriage despite massive opposition among members of his own party.[52]

We still face big issues. How many of us have been subject to homophobic abuse? In my and Ted's case, only once but it was threatening, frightening and disturbing. Most of us will have friends who, even in gay-friendly London, have suffered homophobic violence. The liberation we have enjoyed does not

---

46 Kevin O'Sullivan, 'It's Eastbenders' *The Sun*, 13 August 1986; Sebastian Buckle, *Homosexuality on the Small Screen: Television and Gay Identity in Britain* (Bloomsbury 2018).
47 Buckle (n 46).
48 John Marrs, 'GT Talks to the Original Gay Soap Couple' *Queer Archive*. <https://queerarchive.net/eastenders-kiss-shows-us-how-far-weve-come/> (accessed 21 July 2020).
49 Foreign and Commonwealth Office (UK), Circular 266/91 of 25 July 1991. *See also* Annika Savill, 'Inside File: Gay Diplomats Are Safer in the Closet' *The Independent*, 17 March 1994.
50 s. 122, Local Government Act 2003, c. 26. (This was the last vestige of s.28 Local Government Act 1988). Section 28 was repealed in Scotland by s. 34 Ethical Standards in Public Life etc. (Scotland) Act 2000, asp 7.
51 *Smith and Grady v UK* (1999) 29 EHRR 493. See Geoffrey Hoon (Secretary of State for Defence), Hansard (HC Deb) 12 January 2000, vol 342 cc 287–288; see also Richard Norton-Taylor, 'Forces Ban on Gays Lifted' *The Guardian*, 13 Jan 2000.
52 Marriage (Same Sex Couples) Act 2013, c. 30.

permeate all sections of our society. Not long after I came out, I met in London a young man in his 20s from Birmingham. He was British; his family of Pakistani origin. He was gay. He came to London because he did not dare meet other men in Birmingham. He had been married. He had a young daughter. His parents were pressuring him to re-marry his ex-wife. 'Could you not come out to your parents?', I asked. 'No', he said. 'It would bring shame on my family'. That man may spend most of his adult life doing what I and others of my generation did: hiding the people we truly are.

Most of us will have lesbian and gay friends with children. Maxwell-Fyfe's excoriation of homosexuals as a danger to the young finds just as sinister an echo in the campaign to stop the work of schools in getting it accepted that families come in many varieties. 'We are not homophobic', say the protesters at Anderton Park School.[53] But what they are saying to children and their parents is that there is something wrong with them, something unacceptable. That is an abuse. Scotland has been far clearer than the rest of the UK on this issue, although Damian Hinds, then Secretary of State for Education, has spoken up on the issue of LGBT inclusive education.[54] Are we less enlightened than were the Churches at the time of Wolfenden? Of course, people have the right to their religious beliefs. But we are a democracy, not a theocracy. We have to assert our human rights if we are not to be bullied into silent submission.

I cited some of the homophobic language of a bygone age. But that too finds its echo today in some of the debate about the rights of trans men and trans women. There are particular issues and concerns. They are not irrelevant. But I mentioned earlier the argument about English sailors on ships from Scottish ports. That particular problem was used to try to negate the entire case for homosexual law reform. The fundamental issue today is similar: do particular issues define what should be the basic question? And that question is: do we accept the rights of our fellow human beings to determine their own gender identity? My answer to that is an unequivocal 'yes'. That, in my view, should be the starting point. Then, we can address the concerns of which we all know. Germaine Greer was a defining influence for me as a young man. I admired her hugely. But I don't accept the view she propounds today on transgender persons.[55] Apart from the issues of rights that I have mentioned, whatever happened to tolerance and generosity?

My final example, from the past haunting the present, is this. 53 independent countries around the world were once British colonies, 35 of them still make it

---

53 Jane Haynes, ' "Disgusting and Shameful" – Anderton Park Primary School Head Speaks Out After LGBT Protest' *Birmingham Mail,* 25 May 2019.
54 Sally Weale, 'LGBT Classes "Decision for School", Not Parents, Says Damian Hinds' *The Guardian,* 9 April 2019.
55 Heather Saul, 'Germaine Greer Defends "Grossly Offensive" Comments About Transgender Women' *The Independent,* 26 October 2015.

a criminal offence for adults of the same sex to love one another as they wish. They do so because they still apply the old colonial laws that they inherited, just as we were getting rid of them. It is to the credit of Theresa May that she was the first British Prime Minister to apologise for the injustice of those laws and the harm done. The British Government is supporting those countries who want to modernise their constitutional laws and remove the injustice. I am not making a plug for the charity I am involved with that supports the courageous activists round the Commonwealth who risk their freedom, and even their lives, in the campaign for their rights. I am making a simpler point. In speaking about our LGBT+ community and of the progress we have made, our community in today's world has to include our brothers, sisters and those who are non-binary who still face the adversity from which we have largely been liberated.

Chapter 4

LGBT+ Youth Homelessness as a Consequence of Progress

Carin Tunåker

1. Introduction[1]

Although LGBT+[2] rights have progressed since the Stonewall Riots and LGBT+ people's lived realities in England have improved drastically since then, there is a dark side to this progress. Young people are now more confident to come out as LGBT+ at much earlier ages, and one of the consequences of this is a rise in LGBT+ youth homelessness. Due to a combination of political and legal advances in LGBT+ rights and an increased presence of charismatic LGBT+ role models in the media, youth are changing their outlook and engagement with sexuality and gender identity, but paradoxically this can lead to homelessness. For various reasons, young people encounter challenges that they may not have anticipated, and their experiences of coming out are far from what they had envisioned. There are contradictions between expectations and imaginaries based on media-fuelled visions of open arms, acceptance and perceived normality, contrasting with the lived realities of being out in contemporary England where discrimination, harassment and exclusion are still commonplace. I refer to this as 'the paradox of progress'.[3]

---

1 The author would like to acknowledge all of the young people who took part in this research project by sharing their personal experiences – without them none of this would have been possible. The research was made possible by funding and support by Porchlight and by the School of Anthropology and Conservation at the University of Kent, with special thanks to Dr Daniela Peluso, who supervised the PhD research, and to Claire Williams, Mike Barrett and the staff team at Porchlight's BeYou Project. Thank you also to examiners of the PhD, Dr Judith Bovensiepen and Professor Judith Okely, for invaluable advice, and to Keira Pratt-Boyden and peers/colleagues for edits and suggestions. For this publication, my gratitude also extends to Professor Sarah Vickerstaff, the School of Social Policy, Sociology and Social Research at University of Kent, and the Athena Swan team.
2 I use the acronym 'LGBT+', which stands for lesbian, gay, bisexual, transgender and any other sexual or gender identity. The choice of using the '+' sign with the acronym is a recognition that there is no limit to possibilities of how people can and do identify themselves. Many of the young people I spoke to were questioning their sexual and/or gender identities, identified as non-binary, genderqueer, as well as queer and pansexual.
3 Carin Tunåker, 'No Place Like Home' (2015) 12:2 *Home Cultures*; Carin Tunåker, *The Paradox of Progress: LGBTQ Youth Homelessness in South East England* [PhD Dissertation] (University of Kent 2017, unpublished).

DOI: 10.4324/9781003286295-6

In this chapter, I examine the experiences, circumstances and difficulties faced by young people (ages 16–25) who identify as LGBT+ who are residing in hostels, sofa surfing and rough sleeping in South East England. Following my ten years of experience working in homelessness services, as well as a year of in-depth ethnographic research with LGBT+ youth, I outline how this group is more prone to marginalisation, online risk-taking, sexual exploitation, mental health problems and homelessness than their heterosexual peers. According to the LGBT+ homelessness charity Albert Kennedy Trust (AKT), 24% of homeless young people in England identify as LGBT+.[4] This figure should act as an indication to policy makers and governments to take action to ensure that support is readily available for this group. Reports from the USA and Canada show that this too is a significant problem elsewhere, with numbers as high as 37% of homeless populations reported as identifying as queer.[5]

Through my own experience in the third sector, data collected by charities and local authorities showed unrealistic figures that obscured the severity of LGBT+ youth homelessness. This was due to the difficulty of monitoring taboo and sensitive topics, and likelihood is that this problem could be even more prominent than figures suggest. Subsequently, LGBT+ individuals who experience homelessness may not be recognised by funding bodies and the State as a significant population resulting in resources not being allocated to alleviate their challenges. The broader politico-legal advances in LGBT+ rights are not yet resonating fully in the everyday lived experiences of LGBT+ individuals, who experience multiple exclusions by living outside of the norm in terms of their sexuality/gender identities, as well as existing outside normative institutions, such as the educational system, the home and the family. In order to prevent homelessness as a consequence of progress, we need to navigate future policy-making and the allocation of funds with caution, and ensure the younger generations have appropriate advice, support and guidance to cope in a heteronormative world that often fails to meet their expectations and needs.

After a short introduction to the concept 'paradox of progress' and the political landscape in Britain and the South East or England, I discuss LBGT+ homelessness in depth with illustrated examples; reasons for LGBT+ youth homelessness; socio-political advances in LGBT+ rights in contrast to lived experiences; online/social media challenges; trans specific issues; and, lastly, action for change and recommendations for future interventions.

---

4 Albert Kennedy Trust, *LGBT Youth Homelessness: A UK National Scoping of Cause, Prevalence, Response, and Outcome* (The Albert Kenny Trust 2015).
5 John Ecker, 'Queer, Young, and Homeless: A Review of the Literature' (2016) *Child Youth Serv* 37.

1.1 The Paradox of Progress

The 'paradox of progress' is that although there are advances in society indicating that identifying as LGBT+ is no longer an issue, many individuals nonetheless continue to face issues in their communities and within their families, which in some cases may lead to homelessness. Therefore, perceived 'progress' correlates with high numbers, as mentioned previously, of young people who identify as LGBT+ in homelessness services. Also, the perception that society has 'progressed' hinders young people foreseeing the possible outcomes that might arise for them if they choose to reveal their non-normative identities and sexualities to others. 'Progress' is in itself a contentious concept; its meaning is highly variable and subjective. It carries with it a sense of evolutionary uni-directionalism, which postulates an understanding of time and history as linear, implying a movement forward.[6] There is therefore an implication that societies, beginning at one time and continuing from this point onwards, are geared towards optimal 'improvement' and towards becoming more 'civilised'. Engels, for example, believed that society moved from promiscuity and incest towards monogamy, which he contended was 'more civilised'; in other words, humanity made 'progress' as measured by sexual behaviours.[7]

The word 'progress' is often loosely used in common vernacular when speaking about the legislative and cultural 'improvements' made in regard to gay rights or general openness in relation to LGBT+ people. The changes seen in many post-industrial societies regarding the acceptance and normalisation of alternative sexualities and gender orientations, or the erasure of distinct gender categories, may indeed be considered by some as 'progress'.[8] However, for others, such as opponents of LGBT+ rights, these societal shifts do not concur with their idea of progression. The idea of 'queer' to those that hold firmly onto the binary two-sex system may be too challenging to accept. Indeed, my experience in my field site, and among most non-academics and non-queer people in South East England, has taught me that many are not even aware of the meaning of the word 'queer' or its reclamation as a positive affirming term. Nevertheless, 'progress' becomes part of the political narrative that crystalizes roles and expectations. Foucault famously argued that the history of sexuality

---

6 Maximilian C Forte, 'The Problem of Progressivism' (2020) *Open Anthropology* <http://openanthropology.org/progressivism.htm> (accessed 24 May 2022).
7 J Collier, M Rosaldo, and S Yanagisako, 'Is There a Family? New Anthropological Views' in Lancaster and di Leonardo (eds), *The Gender and Sexuality Reader* (Routledge 1997).
8 See relevant debates by D Cooper, 'A Very Binary Drama: The Conceptual Struggle for Gender's Future' (2019) 9:1 *Feminists@Law* and PB Preciado, *Testo Junkie: Sex, Drugs, and Biopolitics in the Pharmacopornographic Era* (The Feminist Press 2017).

is precisely this: a State discourse that changes and emerges through time.[9] 'Progress' is then yet another aspect of the State's 'biopower'.[10] Just because parts of societies across the world are developing openness to sexual practices and identities other than cis and heterosexual ones, this does not need to mean 'progress' in evolutionary terms nor does it mean that progress is happening evenly or elsewhere. Rather, progress indicates *change*, and it is a part of multiple and continual processes of practices, beliefs and ideologies. Kath Weston already argued more than two decades ago that the political and media narratives regarding 'progress' in LGBT lives, at the time she was writing, were not as straightforward as one might think.[11] She explained that it was never as simple as 'progress' equating to coming out as gay or trans being easy, or not 'a big deal' anymore. Building on Weston's argument, I contend that for many, it is in fact still 'a big deal' to 'come out', and it can have serious repercussions, such as homelessness. 'Progress' is often depicted in political narratives as a simple outcome of an evolving society,[12] but 'progress' has many facets and is subjective. One outcome of perceived 'progress' in LGBT+ acceptance, for example, is that youth are 'coming out' at earlier ages, at a time when they are still reliant on their families for subsistence, care and accommodation. As such, they are then encased by narratives of 'progress' and subsequently not necessarily prepared for any reality other than a progressive society, which unfortunately is not always what they encounter.

1.2 Homelessness in Britain and the South East of England

Parts[13] of the South East of England have a reputation for being conservative, not only in their political framework but also in public views and in lack of diversity of demographic composition. Throughout fieldwork, I repeatedly heard comments, such as '[The region] is pretty much as conservative as it gets', and 'You don't want to be different in [this region]' and 'unless you're white British, straight and a Christian, you can be sure to feel like an outsider'.

The region has beautiful landscapes and is also known for attracting a lot of tourism and wealthy inhabitants from across the country to enjoy the countryside and coastline scenery – something that is reflected in soaring house

---

9 Michel Foucault, *An Introduction. Vol. 1 of The History of Sexuality* (Robert Hurley trans, Penguin Books 1978); Michel Foucault, *The History of Sexuality, Vol. 2: The Use of Pleasure* (Robert Hurley trans, Vintage Books 1985).
10 Michel Foucault, *Discipline and Punish: The Birth of the Prison* (Penguin Books 1977).
11 K Weston, 'The Virtual Anthropologist' in A Gupta and J Ferguson (eds), *Anthropological Locations: Boundaries and Grounds of a Field Science* (University of California Press 1997) 163–184.
12 M Forte, 'Progress, Progressivism, and Progressives' *Zero Anthropology*, 28 February 2018. <https://zeroanthropology.net/2018/02/28/progress-progressivism-and-progressives/>.
13 Due to matters of anonymity and confidentiality, I refer to the entire area of the South East of England. A lot of my fieldwork took place in one county. I refer to this area mostly as 'the region'.

prices and a relatively high cost of living. As with any location, the region has its flipside. There are areas of deprivation and pockets of poverty and high levels of homelessness. Although the South East as a whole, excluding London, does not have the highest levels of homelessness in the country, there are certain areas where official homelessness figures are particularly high.[14]

Britain faces serious problems in homelessness, with drastic rises in the last decade of both rough sleeping, 'core homelessness' (e.g. acute homelessness and unsuitable accommodation) and statutory homelessness acceptances (households accepted by the State as homeless).[15] At the same time, we have also seen especially large peaks in households living in unsuitable temporary accommodation (such as B&B's), which has seen a 260% increase.[16] Young people constitute the bulk of this significant increase. They are particularly affected by the government's recent benefit freezes and hostile housing environments, and a common solution to solve acute homelessness for young people is temporary accommodation.[17] In the beginning of 2013, the government introduced several cuts to benefits relating directly to housing, which has since had a vast impact on homelessness nationally.[18] Cuts and changes to housing benefits and allowances for young people have already impacted on the levels of youth homelessness, and there is a need for greater sociocultural awareness in State decision-making that affects youth homelessness, particularly youth from working-class backgrounds who are routinely demonised and, subsequently, subject to forms of structural violence that prevent them from accessing support.[19]

2. LGBT+ Youth Homelessness

2.1 Why Are LGBT+ Youth More Likely to Experience Homelessness?

LGBT+ homelessness is still an emerging theme in academic research.[20] I argue here that potentially a much larger proportion than what we already know of young people who experience homelessness identify as LGBT+ or

---

14 L Reynolds, 'Homelessness in Great Britain – The Numbers Behind the Story' *Shelter*, November 2018. <https://england.shelter.org.uk/__data/assets/pdf_file/0020/1620236/Homelessness_in_Great_Britain_-_the_numbers_behind_the_story_V2.pdf> (accessed 21 July 2020).
15 S Fitzpatrick et al., *The Homelessness Monitor: England 2019* (Crisis 2019).
16 G Bramley, *Homelessness Projections: Core Homelessness in Great Britain [Summary Report]* (Crisis 2017).
17 I Anderson and S Thompson, *More Priority Needed: The Impact of Legislative Change on Young Homeless People's Access to Housing and Support* (Shelter 2005).
18 See a brief review of these cuts: Crisis, 'Bleak April of Multiple Cuts Will Increase Homelessness' (2013) <www.crisis.org.uk/news.php?id=624> (accessed 22 September 2016).
19 See Tunåker (2017) (n 3).
20 E Jackson, *Young People and Urban Space: Fixed in Mobility* (Routledge 2015); Fraser et al., 'LGBTIQ+ Homelessness: A Review of the Literature' (2019) 16 *International Journal of Environmental Research and Public Health* 2677.

are questioning their sexual/gender identity. There are many reasons for how sexual and gender identities are connected to a person's homelessness, and these are intertwined with further layers of personal and societal complexities.

The reasons for people becoming homeless are often multifaceted and accumulative, resulting from many occurrences and issues that have happened over time. I found through my fieldwork with LGBT+ youth that they mostly did not connect their sexual/gender identity with why they first experienced homelessness, or alternatively they did not want to discuss it as they felt it was too personal. Dunne *et al* argued, 'A homeless crisis is usually a process that extends over time and it is not always easy to identify original triggers'.[21] This partly explains why there is a large proportion of LGBT+ youth in homelessness services, and why counting how many young LGBT+ individuals who experience homelessness there are overall becomes a challenging, if not an impossible, task.

There is not always one identifiable primary reason for homelessness, and although sexual or gender identity may have played a part in the process, the young people may not themselves have worked out or processed the connection.[22] Dunne *et al* also state that the extent to which sexuality is involved in a person's homelessness is often underestimated by agencies who monitor this, as it is not always considered to be the *initial* cause for homelessness. For this reason, it is likely that reporting of this issue is incorrect.[23] Nevertheless, through the little research there is available on LGBT+ youth homelessness, it is clear that these young people are overrepresented in the homeless population, making this overrepresentation a significant concern that needs to be researched further. LGBT+ individuals who reside in hostels and day centres are possible to locate and will in most likelihood have developed relationships and trust with staff, making them identifiable and available to talk to and register/monitor for official figures. However, they are likely to represent just the tip of the iceberg of a vast problem.[24] Many LGBT+ young people who experience homelessness are hidden and uncounted, especially in rural

---

21 GA Dunne, S Prendergast, and D Telford, 'Young, Gay, Homeless and Invisible: A Growing Population?' (2002) 4:1 *Culture, Health & Sexuality* 106.
22 W O'Connor, and D Molloy, *Hidden in Plain Sight: Homelessness Amongst Lesbian and Gay Youth* (NCSR Stonewall Housing Association 2002); S Prendergast, GA Dunne, and D Telford, 'A Story of "Difference", a Different Story: Young Homeless Lesbian, Gay and Bisexual People' (2001) 21:4/6 *International Journal of Sociology and Social Policy* 64–91; M Cull, H Platzer, and S Balloch, *Out On My Own: Understanding the Experiences and Needs of Lesbian, Gay, Bisexual, and Transgender Youth* (Health and Social Policy Research Centre Brighton: University of Brighton 2006).
23 See Dunne et al. (n 21) 109.
24 See Albert Kennedy Trust (n 4).

areas; are living in precarious homes; rough sleeping; squatting; or staying in unsafe exploitative environments.[25]

Prendergast *et al* found in their study that among the young LGB people they interviewed in hostels, there were four ways in which their sexuality was connected to their status as homeless:

1. Homeless young people who happened to be gay
2. Those for whom homelessness brought opportunities to challenge an assumed heterosexual identity
3. Those for whom gay issues had greatly influenced their homeless status
4. Those who were homeless because they were gay.[26]

Prendergast *et al* attempt to explain that sexual identity, in *varying degrees*, is intertwined in the reasons why homelessness occurs. Sexual identity also serves as an explanation for the different reasons accounting for why young LGB people make up a quarter of the young homeless population. I met young people throughout my fieldwork that fell into, or somewhere around, these four categories in different ways. It is important to note that this study did not consider trans homelessness, which is a newer area of study with increasing importance.[27]

2.2 Experiences of Homelessness

I spoke with a young man called Tom,[28] who told me that he became homeless as a direct result of coming out to his dad. He said that he had known for some time that he was gay. When he finally decided to come out, he was so excited about it that he decided to write 'I am GAY' in large glittery letters across the wall in his room, in a bold expression of an identity that he said he finally felt proud to share with friends and family. Unfortunately, his father did not share his excitement, and Tom said that his father scrubbed off the writing on the wall immediately. Tom believed that his father was probably worried that someone in the neighbourhood would see it and shame the family. Tom explained that his mother, whom he did not live with at the time, was not completely against his stated sexual orientation, but she had sighed and said: 'you're gay? But I wanted to be a grandmother!' effectively demonstrating that the heteronormative preconceptions of family formations and biological

---

25 For particular vulnerabilities, see K Browne, *Count Me In Too: LGBT Lives in Brighton and Hove* (University of Brighton and Spectrum 2007).
26 See S Prendergast, GA Dunne, and D Telford, 'A Story of "Difference", a Different Story: Young Homeless Lesbian, Gay and Bisexual People' (2001) 21:4/6 *International Journal of Sociology and Social Policy* 69.
27 E England, *Homelessness Among Trans People in Wales* (Shelter Cymru 2019).
28 All names and identifying details are pseudonyms.

continuity are still prevalent.[29] Tom was 16 years old when he came out to his father, and after arguing with him for a few days, his father disowned him. This led to a period where he felt confused and began to experience housing impermanence.

> The first night after I left my dad's I was sleeping on the streets (for one night), and then social services picked me up and put me in foster care for about one week. Then they put me in a motel where I was for about four to five months. Then I went to the council and basically they said like 'we want nothing to do with you'. The council considered me intentionally homeless because I'd had arguments with my dad after coming out. So, they recommended that I shouldn't have come out to my dad, because it was this that caused the arguments, which essentially made me homeless. That's when I applied for [a hostel], it's supported housing, and you have key-working. After speaking to the council I kind of figured that I had to get on with it myself and get my own housing. I had help from the student support at college, who helped me look for options online and that's how I found the [the hostel]. I lived there for about two years, and basically when I had two months left before I had to leave, they told me that to apply for a council flat takes about nine months, so then I moved in with my partner at the time instead. We lived together for about three months, and then I moved out about just over a month ago and now I'm sofa surfing with friends again.

This scenario illustrates the way in which age, class and gender intersect with sexuality, which suggests that the reasons for becoming homeless are multifaceted.

Although advances have been made since the time of Weston's book, *Families We Choose*,[30] in which she demonstrated how being gay was not yet socially acceptable, society is still not set up to deal with the kinship ties that LGBT+ individuals set out to make, nor is identifying as LGBT+ in any way easy or straightforward. There are still 'lived consequences of difference' for LGBT+ people, as Allison Rooke explains following her research with lesbians in Brighton and Hove.[31] Experiences of 'thinly veiled contempt'[32] are still commonplace, experienced through diffuse and subtle hostility, from name-calling, ridiculing and subtle harassment. A young person coming out in a homophobic family home is vulnerable in many ways and may not perceive of

---

29 K Weston, *Families We Choose: Lesbians, Gays, Kinship* (Columbia University Press 1991).
30 See *Ibid*.
31 Alison Rooke, 'Navigating Embodied Lesbian Cultural Space: Toward a Lesbian Habitus' (2007) 10 *Space and Culture* 249.
32 See *Ibid*.

the possible negative outcomes of telling their parents that they are LGBT or +. Being forced to leave home at an early age means living independently before having the skills or means to do so. With the limited or non-existent support for those experiencing homelessness and for young LGBT+ individuals, this vulnerability increases greatly.[33] Furthermore, these young people may face additional difficulties when re-negotiating their sexualities/gender identities in society at large.

According to Miceli, the two dominant structures that most importantly affect and/or shape young people are their educational system and family.[34] The home and school, college or university are the places where young people spend most of their time, *unless* they are outside of the educational system or homeless. 'The home', as a concept, is for many associated with the 'ideal' family, and it begets idealisations of family life as I mentioned earlier, and as such 'the home' becomes a principal site where these heteronormative dominant ideologies are reproduced and internalised.[35] Coming out involves a repositioning in society and among social networks and family, and at times also challenging the ideals shaped 'at home'. As mentioned, homelessness is rarely attributable to simply one discernible reason but rather a combination or interlinking factors. In my fieldwork with LGBT+ youth, dysfunctional family dynamics, relating to domestic abuse, financial instability, substance misuse or mental health issues, were often cause for fear and precariousness that prevented young people from coming out to parents/carers. The internal fear of moving against what they perceived as the 'ideal' also contributed to them escaping home.

3. The Consequence of Progress

3.1 Political Narratives and Real Outcomes

In 2012, during the debates leading up to the same-sex marriage bill in England and Wales, a journalist wrote in the *Evening Standard* that: 'Gays have gone from the prison cell to the altar in 55 years'.[36] Many people no longer believe that coming out as gay or trans is 'such a big deal', and that generally, people are now accepting of all sexualities and genders.[37] It is easy to forget that the legislative changes for LGBT+ individuals have only occurred

---

33 See Tunåker (2017) (n 3).
34 M Miceli, *Standing Out, Standing Together: The Social and Political Impact of Gay-Straight Alliances* (Taylor & Francis 2005).
35 R Short, 'Foreword' in Irene Cieraad (ed), *At Home: An Anthropology of Domestic Space* (Syracuse University Press 1999).
36 Matthew d'Ancona, *The Evening Standard*, 12 December 2012, 14.
37 Matthew Todd, *Straight Jacket: How to be Gay and Happy* (Bantam Press 2016); Matthew Todd, 'Think Coming Out Is Easy Nowadays?' *The Guardian*, 1 September 2017. <www.theguardian.

over the past 55 years, and the necessary cultural changes and ontological securities that need to follow for a truly 'accepting' society will never happen simultaneously in parallel with legal advances. Throughout fieldwork, I encountered the real difficulties that LGBT+ individuals are still facing and the less tolerant opinions held by some of the general public in regard to same-sex marriages, alternative sexualities and trans individuals' rights. Although a significant change has happened in the last decade or so, large parts of South East England rest on a history of social conservatisms and non-inclusion.

Fieldwork in the South East of England on LGBT+ issues gave me two conflicting views of the area. On the one hand, I heard the opinions of people who believed that there are little or no issues for people who are LGBT+ anymore 'these days', because society has changed, and one can now express non-normative identities and sexualities without fear. On the other hand, I was often asked what the acronym 'LGBT' stood for and was met with either indifference about LGBT+ rights, ignorance or outright homophobia. In general, as I discussed earlier, the general public perceives this area of the country as not very open to difference or alternative/non-heteronormative lifestyles. During my fieldwork, I had regular contact with local community officers (police) and local council housing support officers who informed me of the frequent (at least monthly) homophobic hate crimes, homophobic abuse and the neighbourhood discrimination that were reported to them by LGBT+ individuals. One of the community officers told me: 'Anyone that is the slightest bit different here will have a difficult time. It is too "samey" – most people are White British and straight, which makes it hard to be anything BUT precisely that'. An older self-identified bisexual man also spoke to me in detail about how unfriendly and unaccepting he found his local area. He pointed out the significance that this region hosts the core of the Anglican Church: '[This area] is a very conservative place, it's the seat of the church for God's sake! There's nothing here promoting that [gay] lifestyle'. Likewise, an older gay man who had lived in the area for 20 years spoke passionately about his negative experiences: 'There's not enough visibility for the gay community [here], for example, you don't see flags. [The region] itself is "closeted". The general public is fine with gay pride [parades] as long as it's not on their doorstep'.[38] These two opinions show the importance of how space can be experienced. Human geographers have long been concerned with 'mapping desire'[39] and

---

com/commentisfree/2017/sep/01/coming-out-kezia-dugdale-homophobic-fear-of-rejection-gay-shame-lgbt> (accessed 21 July 2020).

38 Since this research, areas of the South East of England have made significant efforts to improve inclusivity for the LGBT+ community, for example through extending the Pride march. Nevertheless, local residents still hold negative views of 'promoting' LGBT+ issues, for example through public debates about visible flags on online community forums.

39 D Bell and G Valentine (eds), *Mapping Desire: Geographies of Sexualities* (Routledge 1995).

have debated the significance of LGBT activity in different places. For example, Bell *et al* argue that gender and sexuality are 'spaced', and likewise that space is gendered and sexed, thereby highlighting that spaces are socially constructed.[40] As the above interlocutor stated, the region was perceived as 'closeted' because public spaces were heteronormative, and there were no 'gay' indicators, such as the gay flag. Bell *et al* refer to this as 'the presumed *authentic* heterosexual nature of everyday space' (italics in original).[41]

In 2013, before the same-sex marriage bill was approved in England and Wales,[42] the local BBC Radio hosted a phone-in programme, where members of the public were encouraged to give their opinions in regard to the bill. One woman attempted to disguise her contempt by stating that she was of course happy for gay couples to exist, as long as they kept their private lives 'private'. She also stated that the right to marry was one step too far, as according to her: 'The gays have enough rights as it is!' She continued to explain that the sanctity of marriage between a man and a woman was one of the only pillars of society, where proper values were being upheld.[43]

In 2003, following the government's abolishment of Section 28 nationally,[44] one region in the South East was the only one to introduce its own clause in legislation, insisting that schools continue to prohibit the intentional promotion of homosexuality in education. The County Council leader at the time stated that:

> We must protect our children as they grow up. We believe that Section 28 is right in prohibiting the intentional promotion of homosexuality in our schools. The Section 28 debate is one of those defining moments in politics when the vast majority of ordinary people have risen to say enough is enough. They are leaving politicians in no doubt that to take away this safeguard would be a move too far away from traditional, deep-rooted family values. I took legal advice in December [1999] and we are determined to continue in [the region] the spirit and commitment of Section 28, irrespective of the government's intentions.[45]

---

40 D Bell, J Binnie, J Cream, and G Valentine, 'All Hyped Up and No Place to Go' (1994) 1:1 *Gender, Place and Culture* 34–47.
41 See *Ibid.*, 34.
42 The same-sex marriage bill was passed in England and Wales on 17 July 2013.
43 *BBC Radio* [local area], 'The Big Phone-In', 4 February 2013.
44 Section 28 of the Local Government Act 1988 prohibited local authorities from 'intentionally promoting homosexuality' or promote teaching of homosexuality as a 'pretended family relationship'. See <www.legislation.gov.uk/ukpga/1988/9/section/28/enacted>.
45 Audrey Gillian, 'Section 28 Gone . . . But Not Forgotten' *The Guardian*, 17 November 2003. <www.theguardian.com/politics/2003/nov/17/uk.gayrights> (accessed 21 April 2016).

Politicians today, two decades later, would most likely not openly air such homophobic statements, but the area nonetheless has strong influences from the political era that foregrounded such views.

3.2 LGBT+ Youth Use of Social Media

In the book, *Tales from Facebook*, Miller argued that Facebook is often dismissed as unreal or unimportant, but that it actually does indeed have profound impact on people's lives.[46] Facebook, and other social media, can enable people to feel embedded in different communities or in wider social lives.[47] Online lives are both real and imagined and serve as an extension of sociality. Furthermore, social media create the opportunity to exaggerate, manipulate and devise online personas in ways that would not be possible in face-to-face contexts. For example, Sam, a young person I interviewed, had found a male friend on Facebook that he started chatting with on a regular basis. He explained to me that at first, he was very excited to talk to someone who understood how he felt about being gay and happy to have found someone who actually lived in the local area. It took a while before he decided to meet the man in person, and when he did he realised that the man was older than what he had made himself out to be on his profile – by about ten years. Nonetheless, Sam told me that he did not know any better, and this man and all of his knowledge impressed him, so they entered into a secret relationship. It was not long before the relationship became volatile and the man became abusive. As Sam explained to me what had happened, he visibly shuddered and looked away as though he was ashamed. He said he felt as if it was to some extent his own fault, because he had let him carry on with the abusive behaviour. Sam revealed that the man had raped him on two occasions, and it was not until months later that Sam dared to admit this to anyone. Sam was victim-blaming himself by placing guilt on himself for the wrongful actions of his perpetrator.

The implications of constructing sexual identities through online platforms can be detrimental and potentially risky, as in Sam's case, but can also enable young people who do not have a social arena, where they are free to explore sexuality and gender, to do so in a broader social field. For LGBT+ youth, the Internet has created possibilities for socialisation that bring perils as well as opportunities. Importantly, it has opened up options that could prevent isolation and connect youths who are now coming out at an earlier age.[48] Feeling

---

46 D Miller, *Tales from Facebook* (Polity 2011).
47 I have been made aware through interaction with young people in local support groups that Facebook is now 'outdated', and most social media interaction takes place on Instagram and other platforms for their age groups.
48 FJ Floyd and R Bakeman, 'Coming-Out Across the Life Course: Implications of Age and Historical Context' (2006) 35:3 *Arch Sex Behavior*.

empowered by the surrounding global LGBT+ community and contemporary public attitudes towards LGBT+ rights through media and recent legislation encourages LGBT+ individuals to see sexuality and gender in a new light. The unanticipated implication, however, is that LGBT+ individuals may come out earlier than they otherwise would due to the support they receive from their online communities, and therefore may face potential difficulties[49] in family settings, which may result in rejection and homelessness.

4. Trans Youth

Since I completed fieldwork in 2012, there has been an increase in young people accessing support services in Kent who identify as trans, genderqueer, gender fluid or non-binary. Kent LGBT+ youth support groups now largely consist of gender-non-conforming young people, and support groups for parents also consist mostly of parents of trans children and young people.[50] Trans support and transition services in the UK have seen an exponential rise of young people requiring their service in recent years, with nearly an eightfold increase in referrals in five years.[51] Evidence also suggests that a quarter of trans individuals have experienced homelessness.[52] Trans youth face significant challenges as society struggles to keep up with terminology and ideology, and they face high levels of discrimination, abuse and harassment on a daily basis. Despite these indicators pointing to extreme vulnerability for this group and a high likelihood of homelessness, trans homelessness is still an under-researched topic and lacking in resources for prevention and specialist services.[53] Trans homelessness needs separate and additional consideration rather than being categorised as a subsection of the LGBT+ homelessness umbrella. Trans individuals have different issues to tackle than their LGB counterparts, and they are vulnerable to loss of housing for additional reasons, such as financial hardship due to difficulties in finding employment.[54]

Dan, who I supported throughout their[55] transition, found homelessness services to be their place of freedom and solace; however, this may not always

---

49 ST Russell and JN Fish, 'Mental Health in Lesbian, Gay, Bisexual, and Transgender (LGBT) Youth' (2016) *Annual Review of Clinical Psychology* 12.
50 Informal observations from support services provided by The BeYou Project.
51 University of Oxford, Identifying the health and care needs of young trans and gender diverse people, 2020. <www.phc.ox.ac.uk/research/health-experiences/research-projects/identifying-the-health-and-care-needs-of-young-trans-and-gender-diverse-people> (accessed 17 July 2020).
52 C Bachman and B Gooch, *LGBT in Britain: Trans Report* (Stonewall 2018).
53 See England (n 27).
54 See *Ibid*.
55 I use gender-neutral pronouns to describe Dan, because their choice of pronouns changed throughout their transition and may still be changing.

be the case for trans individuals.[56] Dan told me: 'My dad used to talk about "those gays" on telly, and tell me how much he hated them. How could I have stayed at home with him? I knew he would eventually find out what I was . . . a disappointment'. Dan left home and moved into their boyfriend's house at age 16. Their boyfriend, who they had met on Facebook, was 23 years old and from what I understood did not treat them very well. It was a controlling relationship, and Dan said that there was not any other option but to stay, because otherwise they would be homeless. The relationship finally ended when Dan's boyfriend assaulted them because of arriving late home one night. Dan moved to their grandmother's house outside of Kent but had severe mental health issues, self-harmed and, at a low moment, tried to end their life by taking an overdose of painkillers. Dan spent six months in institutional care for mental health issues and when discharged, moved straight into a supported accommodation hostel.

It was only a few weeks before I started seeing changes in Dan; they were thriving at the hostel. Their self-expression was contagious, and many others at the hostel started seeing them as a role model – some even told me they were questioning their own sexuality because they wanted to 'be like Dan'. According to rumours among hostel residents, a majority of the other boys in the hostel had either had a crush on Dan or had an affair with them. Dan coloured their hair blue and started wearing make-up. After two months in the hostel, Dan's independent living skills improved immensely, and they subsequently moved into a hostel with less support available. Dan started college and appeared to be doing very well, but throughout their journey there were many bumps in the road. Dan was at this point questioning their gender identity, something that they said they had hidden deep inside for many years, and each time it came to the surface, they drank heavily. When Dan first told me that they had questioned their gender previously, they described these times as 'phases' when they was just 'being weird', and hastened to add that: 'Luckily, I am over it now and I'm just normal again'. After a lot of encouragement from staff at the hostel, Dan slowly began to come to terms with these feelings and openly question their gender.

After Dan had lived at the hostel for some time, they started questioning their gender identity more seriously, and once gaining the trust of their key-worker dared to tell her about their inner private thoughts regarding gender. They slowly began their journey towards accepting a feeling that they said they had felt for a long time; that they was born into the wrong body – that they should be in the body of a girl. Slowly, with the help of transgender support groups, they began to transition, starting by first assenting feminine sides by getting hair extensions, learning how to do make-up and eventually changing their name from Dan to Danni. At the hostel, Danni said peers were curious

---

56 See England (n 27).

and asked questions, but Danni still felt a general acceptance about their new gender identity from them. Danni explained that it was difficult for everyone at first to use the correct pronoun, as they had always known 'her' as 'him', but nobody had been abusive or negative about the change, and Danni said they felt like they could be themselves there. Danni did, however, speak about difficulties in daily life outside of the hostel. When trying on clothes in a shop in the town centre, Danni was denied access to the female fitting rooms. On another occasion when seeking to make changes to their bank account, Danni was accused of trying to commit fraud, as the bank customer service attendant did not believe that they were a girl. This was based on their (male sounding) voice.

The daily difficulties of disclosing one's gender identity to others can result in a trigger to becoming homeless. Living as a trans individual requires a major life transition and a significant repositioning of one's self in the social world.[57] Following Foucauldian theory of discourse, Judith Butler argues that gender is an act of performance within the boundaries of discourse and power that is itself within the boundaries of legislation and social norms.[58] Thus, identity is performed through a series of repetitions (iterations), which are influenced by legislation. In order for laws to start constituting the norm, they must be repetitiously enforced in society to eventually have ontological effects.[59] Derrida also argued that in order to understand the process of iterability, we should also look for rupture or failure within each interstitial moment.[60] For example, Danni was forced to experience this rupture when they wanted to use the female fitting rooms and when the bank denied Danni's rights to their own account. As the literature from gay and lesbian studies shows,[61] having to relive such moments continuously is a tiring process and can lead towards distress and mental health issues. I argue that this tiring process of constant reiteration makes it difficult to live outside the norm.[62] The intersectional issues that accompany gender transitions, coming out and living a non-normative life, for example mental health issues, abuse, sexual exploitation, substance misuse or social isolation, also increase the risk of homelessness. As such, homelessness will always be a relatively high risk to those who live outside of the normative binaries of male and female, or outside of heteronormativity, as long as society adheres to these norms.

57 GA Dunne, *Lesbian Lifestyles: Women's Work and the Politics of Sexuality* (Macmillan 1997) 18–20.
58 J Butler, *Gender Trouble: Feminism and the Subversion of Identity* (Routledge 1990); J Butler, *Bodies that Matter: On the Discursive Limits of 'Sex'* (Routledge 1993).
59 J Butler, 'Performative Agency' (2010) 3:2 *Journal of Cultural Economy* 147.
60 J Derrida, *Signature, Event, Context [Limited Inc.]* (Northwestern University Press 1971).
61 M Hughes, 'Imagined Futures and Communities: Older Lesbians and Gay People's Narratives on Health and Aged Care' (2008) 20:1/2 *Journal of Gay & Lesbian Social Services*; S Pugh, 'Accessing the Cultural Needs of Older Lesbians and Gay Men: Implications for Practice' (2005) 17:3 *Practice*.
62 See Rooke (n 31).

5. Action for Prevention and Change

5.1 Practical Action

LGBT+ organisations and activists are already taking action in raising awareness and creating support for those in need. However, the support is often concentrated in urban areas and particularly LGBT+-friendly cities, and types of support vary vastly depending on location.[63] At the time of my research, support and information was available sporadically in the region where activists had taken time to run support groups in some geographical areas, but it was also reliant on hard-working volunteers and individual action, and therefore not consistent.[64] Importantly, the region also did not have any web-based and age-appropriate information available for young people identifying as LGBT+, which meant young people would be more likely to seek advice from unreliable or potentially dangerous sources on the Internet. Following several years of lobbying with local councils and local NHS commissioning groups, myself and senior management in Porchlight were able to seek funds to set up support for LGBT+ youth across one region of the South East and a dedicated website to signpost to available groups and services. The BeYou Project[65] went live in June 2018 and now provides consistent support in the region.

Although many (but not all) LGB young people I have spoken to have stated that they do not need or want support groups and that they feel comfortable in all spaces, many who identify as trans or are questioning sexuality and gender want and need peers and role models to talk to in safe spaces. Local councils, housing providers, youth centres and schools/colleges can make a difference by visibly showing their inclusiveness, with for example rainbow flags and organised events and also by ensuring that monitoring of sexual and gender identity is done correctly and respectfully at both the beginning and end of support in order to get more accurate figures. The following advice could be used by any local providers that work with young people:[66]

- **Un-taboo the subject:** make sure that the topic is talked about openly and regularly in public spaces without inhibitions. Making it a natural

---

63 Government Equalities Office, National LGBT Survey, 2018. <https://assets.publishing.service.gov.uk/government/uploads/system/uploads/attachment_data/file/722314/GEO-LGBT-Survey-Report.pdf> (accessed 20 July 2020).
64 Available support for LGBT+ individuals has fluctuated, with services commissioned for short time periods, and then decommissioned. National LGBT+ support helplines have been consistently available but not always local helplines.
65 BeYou Project, Online Events and Virtual Groups, 2018. <www.thebeyouproject.co.uk>.
66 Advice adapted from Carin Tunåker, *Flying the Flag: Making a Difference to Homeless LGBTQ Youth* (Porchlight 2014). <www.porchlight.org.uk/sites/default/files/porchlight-16pp-lgbtq-report_0.pdf>.

thing to talk about will encourage people who are not 'out' to feel at ease if they decide to take that step.
- **Challenge homo/bi/transphobia and common microaggressions:** discourage people from name-calling and saying things like 'that's so gay', and challenge any abusive behaviour on the spot so that everyone is aware of the stance of staff in the organisation.
- **Visible information:** have at least one poster about a support group, for example Stonewall posters and anything that mentions LGBT+. This indicates that it is an LGBT+-friendly space and tells people that they can be themselves without fear of stigmatisation.
- **Staff training:** ensure that staff are aware of current issues regarding sexual orientation and gender identity concerns, what the different terms mean and how to approach the subject. If no internal training is available, try if possible to seek out external training and/or ensure that the subject is brought up among staff in the organisation. Ensure all staff is aware of appropriate use of pronouns.
- **Monitoring:** how monitoring is carried out will have a vast impact on numbers and subsequently on funding, so it is highly important to ensure that staff feel comfortable in asking the necessary questions for accurate monitoring. Staff also need to continuously update records, as and when sexual or gender identity is disclosed (which may not be until a relationship has been established). A further suggestion is that organisations monitor 'questioning' of sexual and gender identities, as this will also flag the need for further support for those who are unsure of their identities.
- **Role models:** if possible, ensure that there are positive role models available for young people in the area. If there are no staff members to carry out mentoring, then look in the local area for LGBT+ groups that can provide this.
- **Support:** offer support for the emotional distress of having been excluded from home, and possibly friends, due to coming out. Indicate useful websites for specialist support, such as substance misuse, domestic abuse and trans specific services, and refer to mental health services if necessary.

5.2 Action on a Broader Political Level

As mentioned previously, legislative changes to LGBT+ rights are fundamental to political change but are only the beginning of a long journey towards social change. In order to come close to some form of equality, policies and laws also need to be accompanied by an education campaign that demonstrates that living alternatively is not negative, and this has to happen at primary school age if attitudes are to be normalised. Before social change happens, the negative cycles that can, and often do, result in homelessness will be difficult to prevent. A first step politicians can take is to not to be reliant on 'progress' or paint a utopian view of society as accepting and understanding when this is not yet the case. We may be working towards or approaching a post-gender era,[67] but we cannot assume that only law and policy changes are enough before such a time comes, if it ever does. Where we are now, LGBT+ individuals experience bullying, harassment, violence, abuse, mental health problems, self-harm, suicide ideation and homelessness at high rates,[68] and a combined effort from national and local governments, the media, civil society and the third sector is necessary. Resources are needed for young people to have (quicker) access to mental health support, to domestic abuse specialists, to substance misuse services, to homelessness services and to correct and age-appropriate advice online.

6. Summary

The reasons for why there are large numbers of LGBT+ youth among the homeless population are difficult to disentangle, since young people do not necessarily connect their homelessness to sexuality or gender. Furthermore, the monitoring of this issue within housing and homelessness organisations is questionable, as a result of which we may not have a realistic estimate to date of how many homeless LGBT+ youth exist. Since sexuality and gender are sensitive and personal topics, the disclosure of *different* sexual practices is unlikely at early monitoring stages. I argue, following Dunne *et al*, that sexuality and/or gender identity is a factor in young people's status as homeless but to varying degrees.[69] For example, there are those for whom being homeless is not at all linked to them coming out as LGBT+, those who experimented further with their identities because of the open environment at the hostels, as well as those that became homeless as a direct result of coming out to parents or carers.

The experiences of people who identify as LGBT+ in the South East of England demonstrate that living outside of the norm is still challenging, and that ideological and political changes have not yet resonated in people's everyday lives. The concern of high instances of LGBT+ youth homelessness raises questions in regard to whether legislative change has made an impact on the lived realities of young people that are disadvantaged and/or access homelessness services. Many areas in the South East are rural, and young people identifying as LGBT+ or who are questioning sexuality and gender are isolated and have less opportunities to meet other young LGBT+ people. Therefore, the

---

67 See *Preciado* (n 8).
68 Stonewall, *LGBT in Britain: Health Report* (Stonewall 2018).
69 GA Dunne, S Prendergast, and D Telford, *What Difference Does 'Difference' Make? Towards an Understanding of Homelessness for Young Lesbian and Gay People* (London School of Economics, Gender Institute 2001).

Internet and online communication (such as Instagram) become important arenas for LGBT+ identity construction and sociality. However, the negative consequence can be that the progressive attitudes shaped online do not always match up with the realities young people face in their local communities and parental homes.

Political shifts since the time of the Stonewall Riots 50 years ago towards equal rights, such as legalisation on same-sex marriage, as well as increased media presence of LGBT+ concerns, indicate positive and progressive change. Nevertheless, experiences of LGBT+ youth in this research show that Britain is still predominantly heteronormative in everyday attitudes towards LGBT+ individuals. Young people are encouraged by positive media portrayals to 'be who they are', but the consequence and paradox of this progress are that the realities they face in their families and local communities are often far from as positive or encouraging as they hoped and expected. Additionally, generational differences in attitudes towards 'alternative' sexualities and genders have in some families exacerbated the complex web of reasons for family conflict, which in turn serve as another catalyst in the LGBT+ youth homelessness crisis.

Government, local authorities, media and the third sector need to work together to create change and facilitate *prevention*. LGBT+ homelessness is a very real problem that is hidden from the public eye. It needs urgent attention and action.

Chapter 5

The LGBTI Movement Organising in a Time of Peril

A Case Study of Uganda

Clare Byarugaba

1. Introduction

At the June 1969 Stonewall uprising, a historic event that has been lauded for triggering a worldwide movement of LGBTI (lesbian, gay, bisexual, transgender, intersex) activism, activists in the USA decided enough was enough and fought back against oppression, institutional inequality and harassment.

The Ugandan LGBTI community had its own 'Stonewall moment' 40 years later, with the introduction of the infamous, draconian Anti-Homosexuality Bill 2009.

The purpose of the private member's bill was to establish complete consolidated legislation to protect the traditional family, prohibit any form of sexual relations between persons of the same sex and to prohibit the promotion or recognition of such relations in public institutions.

The proposed bill, which at inception proposed a death penalty clause for certain types of homosexual practices and life imprisonment for the 'offense of homosexuality', is considered to be one of the most repressive of its kind introduced in the 21st century.

The bill, which was signed into law in February 2014 and repealed by the Constitutional Court just seven months later, created a repressive environment for the Ugandan LGBTI community, a community that had until then been living outside the margins, enabled by a conservative society where sexuality and sex are taboo and rarely openly and honestly discussed.

In this chapter, I shall interrogate the activism that was galvanised by the fight against the Anti-Homosexuality Bill 2009. Particular focus shall be placed on the formulation of the Civil Society Coalition on Human Rights and Constitutional Law, also known as 'The Coalition'. From 2009 to 2014, the diverse Coalition successfully sustained the fight against the Anti-Homosexuality Bill, a piece of legislation that was widely favoured to pass in the first weeks of being tabled in the Ugandan Parliament.

This chapter shall examine the formulation of the Coalition, the strategies used by the convening factions to fight for LGBTI rights under decidedly unprecedented contexts, with particular attention to the role of the allies from the international community.

DOI: 10.4324/9781003286295-7

The world has a lot to learn from Uganda, and particularly from the Coalition, on how movements can effectively organise even while in peril.

2. The Context of Uganda: The Social, Economic, Political and Legal Framework for LGBTI Rights in Uganda

2.1 Legal Framework

Uganda's 1995 Constitution[1] provides for respect, promotion and protection of the rights of all persons. The Constitution, however, fails to list sexual orientation and gender identity as a protected ground against discrimination.

The Constitution must be considered in tandem with international human rights instruments, like the Universal Declaration on Human Rights, as well as supporting frameworks, like Chapter 1 of the African Charter on Human and People's Rights, at the sub-regional level that oblige the signatories to recognise, promote and protect human and peoples' rights.

Despite this progressive legal framework, the prevailing political and social climate in Uganda is unsympathetic to the recognition and protection of the human rights of LGBTI individuals. When it comes to equal representation, the LGBTI community is not given a voice or consulted on the formulation of public policy and institutional protection mechanisms. Consequently, these factors lead to the exclusion of LGBTI individuals in public interest processes and limit their freedom of expression about the challenges that negatively affect their lives and livelihoods. Further still, the absence of sufficient legal protections for LGBTI persons hinders their access to unbiased legal redress in case of violations relating to discrimination, harassment, blackmail, extortion, etc.

In both inherent and unambiguous ways, Uganda's legal framework is largely unfavourable towards LGBTI individuals.

Section 145 of the Penal Code criminalises same-sex sexual acts, referring to them as 'carnal knowledge against the order of nature'. One can be prosecuted under this law whether or not the sexual partner consented to the act(s), and it can carry a life sentence punishment. This law has been on the Ugandan books since the British colonial era.

The unfavourable legal environment and accompanying social castigations (such as shame and stigma) that are imposed upon LGBTI individuals may lead families and parents to subject their children to punitive methods of reprimand, such as conversion 'therapy', banishment from home, involvement of law enforcement to deal with the child, violence and withholding of financial support for school fees, to force the child to adopt 'heterosexual normalcy'.

---

1 Constitution of the Republic of Uganda, 2006. <https://ulii.org/ug/legislation/consolidated-act/0>.

Such adverse reactions to a child's diverse sexual orientation and gender identity often lead to broken or strained relationships, homelessness, depression, despondent children and broken families.

The Sexual Offences Bill (2015) seeks to expand criminalisation of same-sex consensual sex to include women who have sex with women, thereby broadening the scope of section 145 of the Penal Code to prohibit a female person from permitting anyone to have carnal knowledge of her against the 'order of nature'.[2]

The bill, which also contains fundamental and progressive new provisions, such as the criminalisation of marital rape, protection of children from sexual exploitation, making rape gender neutral and the criminalisation of sexual harassment and assault, is still being considered by the Ugandan parliament.

Prosecution of LGBTI suspects under section 145 of the Penal Code is often difficult due to the burden of proof, and inevitably detainees end up facing unrelated charges prescribed under the law, such as indecent practices, common nuisance, being idle and disorderly, being rogue and vagabond and personation – 'any person who falsely represents themselves'.[3]

2.2 Other Prohibitive or Anti-LGBTI Legislation and Policies

Chapter 303 of the Police Act gives police officers power to arrest suspicious individuals, which often include LGBTI identified persons. Suspects are often detained without charge for more than the legally prescribed 48 hours and are inevitably subjected to inhumane and degrading treatment, such as forced anal exams, blackmail and extortion and physical and verbal abuse while in custody.[4]

The Non-Governmental Organizations Act (NGO Act) was assented to by President Museveni in 2016. The act establishes an NGO regulatory body – the National Bureau for Non-Governmental Organizations. Among other tasks, the functions of the Bureau include establishing and maintaining a register of NGOs and issuing and renewing NGO permits. The Bureau also has the power to 'blacklist', 'suspend' or revoke the permits of an NGO (section 7(1)).[5]

---

2 HRAPF, Analysis of Sexual Offences Bill Uganda Children's Portal, The Sexual Offences Bill 2015, May 2016, 3. <https://hrapf.org/images/legalanalyses/160510hrapfanalysisofthesexualoffencesbill2015.pdf>.

3 HRAPF, Uganda LGBTI Violations Report 2016, September 2016, 22. <www.hirschfeld-eddy-stiftung.de/fileadmin/images/laenderberichte/Uganda/16_10_04_Uganda_Report_on_LGBTI_Violations_2016.pdf>.

4 Chapter Four Uganda, *Where Do We Go for Justice?* Report, February 2015, 10–22. <https://chapterfouruganda.org/sites/default/files/downloads/Where-Do-We-Go-For-Justice-.pdf>.

5 Non-Governmental Organisations Act, 2016 <https://ulii.org/akn/ug/act/2016/5/eng%402016-03-03>.

Under the NGO Act, any act deemed prejudicial to Uganda's security, interest or the dignity of its people is an offence, which, upon conviction, is punishable by a fine and/or a maximum of three years in prison (section 41(7)(c)). The law, however, remains silent on what would constitute this type of 'act'. This particular provision is seen to target organisations working on LGBTI rights issues.[6]

This has led to organisations failing to register due to the stringent requirements. Many LGBTI organisations therefore have to operate informally, putting them at risk of invasion from the same bureau that is meant to regulate them.

The overreaching powers of the NGO bureau, which is mandated to decide who should or should not be registered, affect NGOs working on the rights of LGBTI people. Organisations have had to hide the true nature of their work and alter names in order to be registered to become full legal entities.

Organisations that have refused to alter their names have been denied the rights to reserve a name by the Uganda Registration Services Bureau.[7]

The provision of the Act, which imposes special obligations on NGOs and seeks to prevent organisations from doing anything that would be prejudicial to the 'security of Uganda', the 'interests of Uganda' and the 'dignity of Ugandans' (section 44(f)), has been interpreted as the government's efforts to reintroduce in disguise the 'promotion of homosexuality' provision from the repealed Anti-Homosexuality Act[8] in order to restrict the work of LGBTI activists and LGBTI organisations.

The Public Management Order Act 2016 whose objective is to regulate meetings and to empower the police to permit meetings has essentially been used to close the spaces for Civic Engagement and to gag alternative or critical voices of dissent. While the Ugandan LGBTI community was able to organise at least four Gay Pride events between 2012 and 2016, at the height of violations facilitated by the Anti-Homosexuality Act, since the beginning of 2016, when the Public Order Management Act became law, the community has not been able to organise a Pride event successfully. The police has used the provisions of the Act to claim that organisers were holding illegal gatherings because they had no police permits. This is despite the fact that these Pride events were organised in private settings,

---

6 HRAPF, *Commentary on the Recently Passed NGO Bill 2015 and Its Implications on Organizations Working on the Rights of Marginalized Persons*, November 2015. <https://hrapf.org/index.php/resources/legal-policy-analyses/21-15-11-30-hrapf-analysis-of-ugandas-ngo-bill-2015-as-passed-and-its-impact-on-lgbti-and-other-organisations/file>.

7 *Deutsche Welle*, 'Gay Activists Take Ugandan Government to Court for Blocking Registration', 18 May 2017. <www.dw.com/en/gay-activists-take-ugandan-government-to-court-for-blocking-registration/a-38894514>.

8 Section 13, Anti Homosexuality Act 2014 <https://old.ulii.org/system/files/legislation/act/2013/2014/Anti-Homosexuality-Act-2014.pdf>.

like clubs – and not as a street parade that would normally warrant a permit. The police, which on one previous Pride event provided police protection, regressed back to pursuing a policy of raiding, disrupting and shutting down events organised by the LGBT community.[9] During one raid, police arrested over 15 activists and violently beat up revellers; one 23-year-old man was so scared of police that he jumped off the sixth floor and almost lost his life.[10]

While no official research has been conducted to find out how much of an effect the repressive legal, social and political environment has had on the economic livelihoods of the LGBTI community in Uganda, Professor MV Lee Badgett, a professor of economics at the University of Massachusetts, developed a model that estimates the economic cost of homophobia[11] and applied it to India as a case study.

In the findings, she said that homophobia in the form of violence, prison, job loss, discrimination, family rejection, harassment in school and the pressure to marry led LGBTI people to have less education, lower productivity, lower earning and more poverty, poorer health and shorter lives, as well as lower labour force participation.

On the health side, homophobia led to higher rates of depression, higher incidences of suicide or suicidal thoughts and higher HIV prevalence.

Consequently, she replicated the model for 39 other countries, where gay rights are limited and found a 'close connection between LGBTI rights and economic development on both an individual level and at a larger economy wide level'.[12]

While Uganda was not among the 39 other countries modelled, there are similarities in the political and legal situation for LGBTI individuals, and the findings cited in the report are a daily occurrence among the LGBTI community in Uganda.

2.3 The Social and Political Framework

2.3.1 The Right to Form a Family

The Children's Statute 1996 and adoption of Children's Rules of 1997, which has provisions relating to adoption, custody and maintenance, only consider heterosexual couples, while the definition of 'family' requires a wife and a

---

9 Human Rights Watch, *Uganda: Police Attack LGBTI Pride Event*, 5 August 2016. <www.hrw.org/news/2016/08/05/uganda-police-attack-lgbti-pride-event>.
10 *Ibid*.
11 MV Lee Badget, *Economic Cost of Exclusion of LGBT People*, December 2016. <https://events.development.asia/system/files/materials/2016/12/201612-economic-cost-exclusion-lgbt-people.pdf>.
12 *Ibid*.

husband. This provision blocks LGBTI couples from legally filing for adoption, hence violating their rights to form a family.

2.3.2 Violence, Harassment and Discrimination

Homophobia and transphobia are still very prevalent in Uganda, despite the annulment of the anti-homosexuality law in 2014, a law which essentially sought to legalise and normalise homophobia. The widespread lack of acceptance of LGBTI persons, even by their families, affects the livelihood and well-being of LGBTI individuals today.[13]

The findings of the Ugandan LGBTI violations report 2016[14] documented the high prevalence of homophobia and transphobia in Uganda orchestrated by state and non-state actors, even after the repeal of the anti-homosexuality law in August 2014.

Reported violations included forceful evictions, harassment from neighbours and families, blackmail and extortion from state and non-state actors, non-physical homophobia and transphobic threats, employment discrimination such as loss of jobs and lack of access to employment opportunities, loss of physical property, discrimination and harassment while accessing medical services, particularly for transgender identified individuals. In 2016, there were 52 documented cases of human rights violations, including physical attacks perpetuated by civilians from the general Ugandan community.[15]

The Ugandan LGBTI community has, since 2012, been able to organise at least four gay Pride events (not including gay Pride parades), of which three were still permitted to proceed. The police even went as far as to provide police protection to two of the Pride-related events that were organised at secluded beaches in the outskirts of the capital city. This all changed in 2016, however, when the Ethics and Integrity minister Simon Lokodo declared it his mission to shut down all the Pride themed events organised by the LGBTI community.[16]

The Minister who headed the only 'ethics' ministry of its kind in the world had so far ordered the raiding and shutting down of at least six events and

---

13 Ashanut Okille and Clare Byarugaba, 'My Child Is Different: A Baseline Study of Perceptions and Experiences of Parents, Families, and the LGBTI Children in Uganda' *Chapter Four Uganda*, February 2019. <https://chapterfouruganda.org/sites/default/files/downloads/My-Child-Is-Different.pdf>.
14 HRAPF, *Uganda Report of Violations Based on Sexual Orientation and Gender Identity* 2016, September 2016, 45. <www.hirschfeld-eddystiftung.de/fileadmin/user_upload/laenderberichte/Uganda/16_10_04_Uganda_Report_on_LGBTI_Violations_2016.pdf>.
15 Human Rights Awareness and Promotion Forum page 44, *Uganda Report of Violations Based on Sexual Orientation and Gender Identity 2017* <www.hrapf.org/index.php/resources/violation-reports/104-lgbt-violations-report-2017/file>.
16 Trudy Ring, 'U.S. Embassy Slams Cancellation of Pride in Uganda' *The Advocate*, 21 August 2017. <www.advocate.com/world/2017/8/21/us-embassy-slams-cancellation-pride-uganda>.

pledged to continue to do so as a priority of his ministry and for the sake of the protection of the values of Ugandans.[17]

These actions were endorsed by The Ugandan High Court in a ruling,[18] which found that the closure of a lesbian, gay, bisexual and transgender (LGBT) rights workshop in 2012 did not violate the rights of the applicants (the workshop organiser and three invited persons) because, in its words, it was 'reasonable and justified for the Minister to conclude that this workshop was engaging in direct and indirect promotion of same sex practices'.[19] It rejected the activist's argument that the purpose of the workshop to develop leadership skills and allowed the Minister's claim to stand that 'the training actually aimed at equipping participants to lead organizations which support homosexual acts and plan and implement projects which promote homosexual acts'.[20]

The ruling, which is currently under appeal, was a huge setback to the LGBTI community's rights to freedom of assembly and association, which are guaranteed for all Ugandan citizens under the Constitution. It further sets a bad precedent by putting all LGBTI public and private events at risk of police raids and disruption by order of the government.

The social, economic, political and legal framework conditions do not just affect LGBTI individuals personally but also affect the relationships with their families, parents and friends.

For example, if an LGBTI individual is poor due to failure to get a job, or has lower earnings due to homophobia and discrimination, they will not be able to financially provide for their nuclear and extended family, as is the norm within Ugandan society. This may lead to strained relationships with the family, who may correlate the individual's sexual orientation and gender identity with a perceived lack of responsibility and concern towards their family.

3. LGBTI Activism and Organisation in Uganda

LGBTI and queer activism in Uganda responded to the anti-gay law in numerous ways, first by choosing to galvanise and organise to fight against the Anti-Homosexuality Bill – even though the major aim of the law was to throttle any form of activism around LGBTI rights in Uganda.

The anti-homosexuality law was considered by many as a nail in the coffin for the LGBTI social movement, but they fought back. As a movement, they organised, despite the odds being against them.

---

17 *Chapter Four Uganda*, 'Uganda Police Disrupts, Shuts Down 2019 IDAHOT Event' *Chapter Four Uganda*, 17 May 2019. <https://chapterfouruganda.org/resources/reports-analysis/uganda-police-disrupts-shuts-down-2019-idahot-event>.
18 *Nabagesera & 3 others v Attorney General & Anor* (Misc. Cause No.O33 of 2012) [2014] UGHCCD 85 (24 June 2014) <https://ulii.org/ug/judgment/high-court-civil-division/2014/85>.
19 *Ibid*, Issue 1.
20 *Ibid*, Issue 2.

It was a fight for their lives, and just like the advent of the Stonewall Riots back in 1969, the community was fed up with being 'scapegoated' and persecuted simply for being different from the majority. The movement grew from only being represented by five organisations in 2003 to over 50 operating in Uganda in 2019, a clear indication of the resilience and ingenuity within a community that was dismissed as a minority and therefore easy to erase.

There are many factors that led to the growth of organising within the LGBTI movement, one of them being the successful formation of a Coalition that brought together a diverse group of organisations to fight the anti-homosexuality law in 2009.

3.1 The Anti-Homosexuality Bill and Its Effect on the LGBTI Community

In 2009, Uganda gained international and national notoriety when Parliament introduced the draconian Anti-Homosexuality Bill. The bill's intention was to extend the criminalisation of LGBTI individuals, with law makers in support of the law claiming that the existing laws against homosexuality were not strong enough.[21]

The bill, whose criminal sanctions ranged from seven years imprisonment to life imprisonment and the death penalty, was positioned to advance homosexuality to one of the most severe crimes in the country – on the same level of treason, murder and robbery.

Other provisions included a prison sentence and a fine that targeted people who failed to report suspected LGBTI individuals – this provision would have targeted teachers, doctors, lawyers who failed to report their LGBTI clients and could conceivably have been applied even to parents who were privy to their children's sexuality and gender identity but failed to report them to the authorities.[22]

The bill further proposed extended prison sentences for 'promotion of homosexuality',[23] which would have effectively meant the end of LGBTI rights advocacy in Uganda because any human rights work targeting the LGBTI community, whether directly or indirectly, could easily be construed as 'promotion'. Funding for LGBTI-related work would have also been discontinued.

Despite various advocacy efforts, including national and international pressure, a watered-down version of the bill that excluded the death penalty clause was passed by Parliament in December 2013 and assented into law in February 2014. On 1 August 2014, the Ugandan Constitutional Court declared the

---

21 Rodney Muhumuza, 'Uganda's Anti-Gay Bill Won't Contain Death Penalty' *Associated Press*, 30 November 2012.
22 Clause 14, in conjunction with clause 1 Anti-Homosexuality Bill 2009.
23 Clause 13 Anti-Homosexuality Bill 2009.

law null and void on the basis that Parliament did not have the constitutionally required quorum of one-third of Parliament members when the Act was passed on 20 December 2013.

Despite its annulment, the spirit of the law had wide-reaching consequences in the Ugandan society at large, including the creation of an environment of fear and complacency among sympathetic would-be supporters of LGBTI individuals and the community in general, including parents, families, NGOs, health service providers, legal practitioners and education providers who took up the task of implementing the law as guided by the provisions.[24]

By spreading negative misconceptions about the LGBTI community (such as involvement in the 'recruitment' of young people into homosexuality, claims that homosexuality is un-African and will lead to the destruction of the traditional family[25]) proponents of the Law fuelled and normalised homophobia, thereby leading to increased stigma towards LGBTI persons and inadvertently making them prone to violence and widespread institutional discrimination.

Although the anti-homosexuality law is no longer on the books, the negative effects of the legislation are still being felt by the LGBTI community.

3.2 The Civil Society Coalition on Human Rights and Constitutional Law

The Civil Society Coalition on Human Rights and Constitutional law was established in October 2009 in response to the tabling of a now infamous Anti-Homosexuality Bill.[26]

What is the Coalition, and how did it come about? The conditions for the Coalition's emergence included the seeds of resistance planted and grown by the Ugandan LGBTI community and the international influence pursued by the Anti-Homosexuality Bill's proponents and opponents.

Activists in the global south and others around world have a lot to learn from the Coalition, which is regarded as a model entity in LGBTI activism.

The Coalition, which was disbanded in 2015, had a membership of over 51 Ugandan civil society organisations, including human rights, academia, feminist, HIV and health, LGBTI rights, media rights and refugee rights organisations. The primary objective of the Coalition was to see the bill dropped from Parliament's agenda, to pro-actively contribute to elaborating a positive sexual

---

24 Human Rights Watch, *Uganda: Anti-Homosexuality Act's Heavy Toll*, 15 May 2015. <www.hrw.org/news/2014/05/14/uganda-anti-homosexuality-acts-heavy-toll>.
25 Sexual Minorities Uganda, 'Expanded Criminalisation of Homosexuality in Uganda: A Flawed Narrative' (2014) at <www.humandignitytrust.org/wp-content/uploads/resources/Expanded-Criminalisation-of-Homosexuality-in-Uganda-2014.pdf at 5>; *Deutsche Welle*, 'Uganda Introduces "Kill the Gays" Bill' 11 October 2019.
26 Anti Homosexuality Act 2014. <https://ulii.org/system/files/legislation/act/2013/2014/Anti-Homosexuality-Act-2014.pdf>.

rights agenda for Uganda and to strengthen the capacity of civil society organisations to engage in and contribute to these important human rights debates.

The Coalition provided one of the most fascinating and significant experiences of activism around sexuality in the modern-day moment. This is in the sense that it brought together a diversity of groups working on a diverse range of issues and representing varied experiences of engaging with the law, as well as with human rights concerns that were similar to what LGBTI individuals were suddenly faced with.

Second, the focus of the Coalition was not limited to a narrow notion of LGBTI rights but very basic questions about basic human rights and the clear targeted violations that the Anti-Homosexuality Bill would inflict on the Ugandan LGBTI community.

The third and perhaps most pioneering aspect was the type of strategies employed by LGBTI activists to form the Coalition – famed to be the first and most impactful of its kind in Africa.

The Coalition utilised various strategies to sustain the struggle against the rise of a peculiar and perhaps unprecedented form of state-sponsored 'homophobia' in Uganda, where the law was actively being pursued as an instrument for violence and discrimination against non-conforming sexualities and gender identities.[27]

The role of the international community in supporting the Coalition efforts to fight the anti-homosexuality law is the most complex and important part of the development of the Coalition and is analysed as follows.

It is a fact that without donor engagements and international pressure, the Anti-Homosexuality Bill would have easily passed in the first month of its introduction. Having high-level international allies helped activists to continue working in relative safety despite the unrelenting hostility that the anti-gay campaign stirred up in Uganda.

Even the public threats to cut aid to anti-gay countries, such as those that were made by the then British Prime Minister David Cameron,[28] were strategic for the following reasons: the bill finally caught the government's attention, particularly that of the Presidency and the Ministry of Finance. The government had since the introduction of the bill dismissed it as a private member's bill – thereby delegating the debate around the bill to Members of Parliament. When there was a threat posed by the conditioning of aid by foreign governments, the Head of Government Business to Parliament advised MPs not to

---

27 Civil Society Coalition on Human Rights and Constitutional Law et al., 'Uganda Report of Violations Based on Sex Determination, Gender Identity, and Sexual Orientation' (2014) <www.hrapf.org/index.php/resources/violation-reports/48-uganda-violations-report-october-2014/file>.
28 *BBC News*, 'David Cameron Has Threatened to Withhold UK Aid from Governments that Do Not Reform Legislation Banning Homosexuality', 30 October 2011. <www.bbc.com/news/uk-15511081>.

rush to pass the bill, citing the potential international backlash. This led to the occasional shelving throughout the bill's five-year raging debate.

International pressure also led to some members of Parliament expressing concern about voting for the bill openly and showing public support for the bill because they were afraid that the donor funds for their constituency projects would be compromised or withheld. This was a significant turnaround from a decidedly militant group of MPs that had vowed not to waste time with voting when the time came for the re-tabling of the bill.[29]

International pressure also showed that the Ugandan LGBTI community, which had been profiled by the Anti-Homosexuality Bill's damning provisions and ensuing debates, had important allies on their side, and that there would be economic and political consequences to the continued attack on their rights as Ugandan citizens.

Further to this is the fact that it brought attention to the issue of Ugandan LGBTI rights on both the national and international stage. The unfavourable PR that the Anti-Homosexuality Bill generated for Uganda facilitated more critical attention to other issues affecting Ugandans, such as rampant corruption, the unfavourable governance practices favoured by the ruling party and the deplorable state of public service facilities among others.[30]

While the Coalition had petitioned and advocated for international allyship against the anti-gay law, this engagement had both beneficial and detrimental consequences, as discussed as follows.

3.2.1 Benefits that the International Engagement Generated for the Coalition

International engagement and support provided much needed financial resources to fight the Anti-Homosexuality Bill in the absence of national support. The availability of funding to support human rights work also facilitated the advent of LGBTI organisations, from about five organisations in 2009 to over 50 to date.

In order to get allies to join the Coalition and the fight against this anti-gay law, the Coalition strategised with donors to leverage their support towards influencing their beneficiaries to join the Coalition. Human rights organisations were not given leeway to be complacent with the status quo by ignoring the plight of the Uganda LGBTI community.

We know that a number of the members of the Coalition joined to appease donors, while some joined because they saw this as an opportunity to add

---

29 Sulaiman Kakaire, 'Gay Bill: Why MPs Fear Open Vote' *The Observer*, 31 March 2013. <www.observer.ug/index.php?option=com_content&view=article&id=24518:gay-bill-why-mps-fear-open-vote>.
30 See on this Morris Latigo in Ariel Rubin, 'Anti Gay Law Diversionary – Latigo' *The Independent (Uganda)*, 16 December 2019. <www.independent.co.ug/anti-gay-bill-diversionary-latigo/>.

monetary value to their organisations by committing to the promotion of all forms of human rights, including LGBTI rights.

While it is considered and observed that most of the non-LGBTI organisations were part of the Coalition due to 'survival instincts' or as a way to appease their donors, the Coalition staff developed LGBTI rights inclusion training programmes in order to fully reign in their allyship support. The Coalition was able to train at least 30 organisations.

After the backlash against David Cameron's statement threatening to cut aid to countries with anti-gay laws (statements that were made outside the formal guidelines that had been issued to international partners, in view of the state of affairs on the ground), the Coalition was able to emphasise to well-intentioned foreign countries and influential public figures the need to formulate their responses against the anti-gay law based on the guidelines[31] from the Coalition, which was responsible for spearheading a coordinated national and international response against the Anti-Homosexuality Bill and in favour of LGBTI rights.

One of the most effective ways that international allies followed Coalition guidelines was by ensuring that all sanctions[32] issued against Uganda by the US government were in line with the Coalition guidelines after the Anti-Homosexuality Bill was signed into law by the President in February 2014.

These sanctions are anticipated to have accelerated the President's decision to order the Courts of Law to do away with the anti-homosexuality law, less than seven months after he had signed that law in the full glare of national and international media.

Despite the inevitable backlash and fallout that came on the heels of these sanctions, the anti-homosexuality law was annulled by the Constitutional Court on a technicality[33] in record time (a rare phenomenon within the Ugandan legal system where cases can take years to be adjudicated).

After the annulment of the law, Members of Parliament immediately embarked on efforts to retable the Anti-Homosexuality Bill, but these efforts were thwarted by President Museveni himself, who warned members of the ruling National Resistance Movement (NRM) party to go slow on their zeal to re-introduce a new law and advised MPs as follows: 'We over showed off after the enactment of the law which landed us into problems, because many countries passed similar laws quietly and got away with it'. He also reportedly

---

31 Civil Society Coalition on Human Rights and Constitutional Law, *Guidelines to National, Regional and International Partners on How to Offer Support Now that the Anti-Homosexuality Bill Has Become Law*, 1 August 2014 <www.pambazuka.org/gender-minorities/supporting-lgbti-struggle-uganda>.
32 White House, President Obama blog, *Further U.S. Efforts to Protect Human Rights in Uganda*, 19 June 2014. <https://obamawhitehouse.archives.gov/blog/2014/06/19/further-us-efforts-protect-human-rights-uganda>.
33 David Smith, 'Uganda's Anti-Gay Law Declared Null and Void by Constitutional Court' *The Guardian*, 1 August 2014. <www.theguardian.com/world/2014/aug/01/uganda-anti-gay-law-null-and-void>.

said that Uganda risked having its exports rejected on the US Market, which would have had adverse effects on the country's revenues.[34]

3.2.2 Counter-Productive Effects of Donor Engagement and International Support

The international support and donor engagement did take attention away from the grassroots LGBTI movement in Uganda – because the international response against the anti-gay law was understood as a Western imposition/agenda. For example, few in Uganda really recognised the efforts of the Coalition work and, in particular, the strategic masterpiece of the Constitutional Petition[35] that led to the annulment of the law.

Most national and international media attributed the Court's annulment of the law to Uganda having bowed to the overwhelming pressure and backlash that ensued after the law was passed.[36]

While all this was a contributing factor, it is also a fact that without the Coalition Petition, the law would have not been annulled.

Allies in the international community often spoke about the Ugandan LGBTI rights issue seemingly in isolation from other human rights abuses going on in the country, and their interventions in favour of LGBTI individuals often fell into the LGBTI 'Western agenda' trap, which frustrated efforts of spearheading the fight against the Anti-Homosexuality Bill as an urgent national matter.

Further to this point, it made Ugandans angry that a minority group that they were so ready to dismiss was able to enlist such international attention and outcry. The bill also proved to be a useful tool for politicians to divert attention from important socio-economic issues.[37]

The financial support that the Coalition and LGBTI organisations received from donors to support their work was often misconstrued to be purposed towards pushing an alleged gay agenda – accusations that involved bizarre, false claims of 'recruitment' of children into homosexuality and working to end traditional marriage in Uganda.[38]

---

34 Sulaiman Kakair, and Sadab Kitatta Kaaya, 'Museveni Okays "Private" Gays' *The Observer*, 13 August 2014. <https://observer.ug/component/content/article?id=33286:-museveni-okays-private-gays>.
35 *Oloka-Onyango & 9 Ors v Attorney General* (Constitutional Petition No. 08 of 2014.) [2014] UGCC 14, 1 August 2014. <https://ulii.org/ug/judgment/supreme-court-uganda/2014/14>.
36 Derrick Kiyonga and Siraje Lubwama, 'Museveni Behind Gay Law Victory?' *The Observer*, 3 August 2014. <https://observer.ug/news-headlines/33127 – museveni-behind-gay-law-victory>.
37 Daniel Kalinaki, 'While You Were Busy Frothing on the Mouth Over the Anti-Gays Law . . .' *The Monitor*, 27 February 2014. <www.monitor.co.ug/OpEd/columnists/DanielKalinaki/While--you-were-busy-frothing-over-the-anti-gays-law/878782-2223306-xrvnoc/index.html>.
38 David Smith, 'Uganda Bans 38 Organizations Accused of Promoting Homosexuality' *The Guardian*, 20 June 2012. <www.theguardian.com/world/2012/jun/20/uganda-bans-organisations-promoting-homosexuality>.

Public threats related to foreign aid conditionality, especially those that were poorly timed, just gave certain politicians an opportunity to counter the statements with the claim that they acted in defence of Uganda's sovereignty, and thus to gain more popularity back home. A good example of this is the exchange between the Speaker of Parliament Rebecca Kadaga and the Canadian Foreign Minister John Baird in 2012, which gave the Speaker an opportunity to resurrect the Anti-Homosexuality Bill while increasing her popularity in Uganda. She later promised to ensure passage of the anti-gay bill into law as a 'Christmas gift' to Ugandans, a promise that she saw to fruition in December 2013.[39]

The international community's public threats, sanctioned or otherwise, increased the government's propensity to scapegoat the LGBTI community in Uganda. Further still, the Ugandan media used their platforms to add fuel to this hatred by writing 'sensationalist' and dangerous stories,[40] which encouraged anti-gay vigilantism within the public.

It is also important to note that not all members of the international community were committed to fighting the anti-gay law. In fact, the main argument for the LGBTI community to enlist support from the international community, particularly in the USA, was that it gave them an opportunity to right the wrongs imposed on the community by American far-right wing Christians who had lost the cultural battles at home,[41] thereby making Uganda ground zero for their anti-gay campaigns.

One of them was Scott Lively, who arrived in Uganda in 2009 and helped to organise a 'Seminar on Exposing the Homosexual Agenda'.[42] Lively warned an 'audience of parliamentarians, parents and police officers that "legalizing homosexuality" was akin to accepting the "molestation of children and having sex with animals," and that homosexuals only wish to abuse and recruit children, promote divorce and spread the AIDS virus'.[43] Lively's dangerous

---

39 Yasiin Mugerwa, 'Kadaga, Canadian Minister in Gay Row' *The Monitor*, 24 October 2012. <www.monitor.co.ug/News/National/Kadaga - Canadian-minister-in-gay-row/688334-1594430-t0reff/index.html>; Elias Biryabirama, 'Uganda Says Wants to Pass Anti-Gay Law as "Christmas Gift"' *Reuters*, 13 November 2012. <https://uk.reuters.com/article/uk-uganda-homosexuality/uganda-says-wants-to-pass-anti-gay-law-as-christmas-gift-idUKBRE8AC0VC20121113>.
40 Warren Throckmorton, 'Uganda's Rolling Stone Blames Terrorist Attacks on Gays', 13 November 2010. <www.wthrockmorton.com/2010/11/13/ugandas-rolling-stone-blames-terrorist-attacks-on-gays/>.
41 Tierney Sneed and Teresa Welsh, 'What's Driving Homophobia in Africa?' *US NewsI*, 16 October 2014. <www.usnews.com/news/articles/2014/10/16/how-anti-lgbt-legislation-in-uganda-nigeria-and-gambia-is-shaping-africa>.
42 Wibke Timmermann, *Incitement in International Law* (Routledge 2016) 1–2.
43 Ben Appel, 'Notorious Anti-Gay Preacher Scott Lively and the Language that Kills' *HuffPost*, 13 June 2017. <www.huffpost.com/entry/notorious-anti-gay-preacher-scott-lively-and-the-language_b_593ec487e4b014ae8c69e2ac?guccounter=1&guce_referrer=aHR0cHM6Ly93d3cuZ29vZ2xlLmNvbS88&guce_referrer_sig=AQAAALnCZkdz5zusgCQJIeAIP1Rfrr3t4uoCtsfmfv4SyTQly3b-OTZA367Bz_3ENFawvaO3dejJr9Tid7hRuIItFbQiU3q9f-DfmppKR3Erm1IZWeGH0u5J8o61tS5uapS0maii5kmYvcZdVS53uAusL4_lS5_kW_jfRUWiTFMKaDUE>.

language was reportedly influential for the Anti-Homosexuality Bill a month later.[44]

3.2.3 Other Strategies Used by the Coalition to Build Allies and Fight the Anti-Homosexuality Law

Apart from building alliances with the international community, the Coalition had to devise means to enlist the support of Members of Parliament and the media – two groups whose opinions on the anti-homosexuality law and the general sexual rights debate were vital for shaping attitudes towards LGBTI individuals within the Ugandan society.

3.2.3.1 THE MEDIA

It can be argued that the Ugandan media were responsible for the rise in homophobia and transphobia in Uganda, as well as the rampant spread of anti-gay sentiments and negative attitudes that surrounded the debate of the bill.[45] From forcefully outing suspected LGBTI individuals without their consent to publishing subjective and dangerous falsified stories under headlines, such as 'Hang them; they are after our kids!', with the provision of the names and addresses of alleged homosexuals,[46] as done by the local tabloid *Rolling Stone* (not related to the US publication), the role of the media cannot be underestimated.

The Coalition understood the need to rein in the media's dangerous trajectory and sought legal redress on behalf of those targeted as well as through advocating for economic sanctions.

In 2011, the High Court of Uganda ruled in favour of activists affected by the *Rolling Stone* article,[47] by declaring that the publication of lists and the accompanying incitement to violence contravened their 'fundamental rights and freedoms' (i.e. their rights to human dignity and their constitutional right to privacy).

---

44 The Gay and Lesbian Review, 'How US Clergy Brought Hate to Uganda' (undated). <https://glreview.org/article/how-us-clergy-brought-hate-to-uganda/>.
45 World Policy, 'On the Front Pages', 12 June 2018. <https://worldpolicy.org/2018/06/12/on-the-front-pages/>.
46 Jim Burroway, '"Hang Them": Another Wave of Anti-Gay Vigilantism Strikes Uganda' *Box Turtle Bulletin*, 4 October 2010. <www.boxturtlebulletin.com/2010/10/04/26981>; Narnia Bohler-Muller, 'Hoping for a New Dawn of Tolerance' *The Mercury* (South Africa), 3 June 2011; *Kasha Jacqueline, David Kato Kisuule and Onziema Patience v Rolling Stone Ltd and Giles Muhame*, High Court of Uganda at Kampala, Miscellaneous Cause no 163 of 2010, Judgment, 30 December 2010. <https://sexualminoritiesuganda.com/wp-content/uploads/2018/08/2010-Kasha-Jacqueline-v-Rolling-Stone.pdf> (hereinafter 'Jacqueline et al').
47 *Ibid*.

The Court further issued a permanent injunction restraining the respondent from publishing the identities and addresses of the petitioners and all other homosexuals.

In 2014, Orange Telecom withdrew advertising from a Ugandan tabloid newspaper – *Red Pepper*, which had been outing LGBTI people indiscriminately[48] – thereby promoting anti-gay sentiments and endangering the LGBTI community in Uganda. The sanction was in response to the Coalition's guidelines to partners to consider economic sanctions in response to the enactment of law by the President in February 2014.

These two strategies served to disrupt the media's trigger-happy practices of actively violating the human rights of LGBTI individuals through subjective and deadly stories as well as through public outings of suspected LGBTI individuals. *Rolling Stone* eventually went out of business, and *Red Pepper* reduced the number of damaging reports about the LGBTI community.

3.2.3.2 MEMBERS OF PARLIAMENT

The majority of Members of the 8th Parliament in Uganda were in favour of the swift passage of the Anti-Homosexuality Bill. However, during the Coalition's advocacy efforts with Members of Parliament, a few of the MPs that were opposed to the human rights violations entailed within the provisions in the bill intimated that they could not publicly stand against the bill due to fear of retaliation, both by their peers and by members of their constituencies.

In response to this, the Coalition, together with development partners, worked with four MPs to develop the 2012 Minority Report[49] (which is within the jurisdiction of Members of Parliament). The report was tabled in Parliament and signified that not all MPs endorsed the Anti-Homosexuality Bill. This minority report also shaped alternative thinking about the human rights issues in the bill of a cross section of the Ugandan society and also showed that the LGBTI community had allies in Parliament.

The Coalition also organised workshops with the human rights committee of Parliament to educate them about the human rights concerns of the Anti-Homosexuality Bill. These training sessions were organised together with other human rights organisations that had human rights concerns about other bills that were being debated in Parliament.

---

48 Jim Burroway, 'Ugandan Tabloids Continue Outing Campaigns' *Box Turtle Bulletin*, 1 March 2014. <www.boxturtlebulletin.com/2014/03/01/62964>.

49 Parliamentary Watch Uganda, *Minority Report by Members of the Sectoral Committee on Legal and Parliamentary Affairs on the Anti Homosexuality Bill 2009*, November 2012. <http://parliamentwatch.ug/wp-content/uploads/2015/02/MINORITY-REPORT-BY-MEMBERS-OF-THE-SECTORAL-COMMITTEE-ON-LEGAL-AND-PARLIAMENTARY-AFFAIRS-ON-THE-ANTI-HOMOSEXUALITY-BILL-2009.pdf>.

This strategy was used in order to show the universality of human rights and as a way to ease the minds of MPs who were concerned about perceived or actual retaliation resulting in their association with LGBTI rights activists/ work. It was also a fact that MPs would not have been willing to attend the workshops if the Coalition had organised them with exclusive focus on the Anti-Homosexuality Bill.

Through these strategic interventions with MPs, the Coalition was able to educate Members of Parliament about the human rights, social and legal concerns of the bill and make the case as to why the bill should not be passed into law.

Despite the fact that Parliamentarians eventually passed the bill in December 2013, there was a more notable enlightened opposition expressed about the bill than there had been at its inception in 2009. A clearer accomplishment resulting from this strategic engagement with Parliamentarians came in form of the Constitutional Petition filed in 2014, which included at least one Member of Parliament as a petitioner.[50]

4. Conclusion

While the situation for LGBTI people in Uganda remains dangerous and uncertain, as shown in the preceding analysis, a number of dynamic LGBTI rights organisations and activists in Uganda are continuing to fight for equality in court through strategic litigation cases, documentation of human rights violations against the community, provision of legal aid to victims of discrimination and abuse and bypassing an overwhelmingly local anti-gay mainstream media to claim spaces to speak for themselves in hopes of changing the attitude of Ugandans who have been taught to hate and fear LGBTI people; all this in spite of the security risks involved.

The LGBTI community and their allies under the umbrella of the Civil Society Coalition on Human Rights and Constitutional Law demonstrated the value of allyship; it showed Ugandans that the struggle for sexual rights and the right to exist peacefully as your most authentic self are not just a 'Western issue'. It also showed the Ugandan society that the fight for human rights cannot be entrusted to duty bearers. After all, they advocated for and passed a bill that was wholly unconstitutional and one that would never have passed any human rights litmus test at both a national and international level.

The Coalition work, which was sustained for six years, showed the value of having diverse voices speak out and fight for the rights of those that are most marginalised in society.

The allies of the LGBTI community that courted and experienced backlash from society because they chose to fight a battle for LGBTI rights that was

---

50 The Hon Ox Odoi-Oywelowo, see *Oloka-Onyango* (above n 35).

hugely unpopular and unfortunately cost some advocates, like David Kato, their lives[51] remain a vital piece of the LGBTI rights movement in Uganda.

The Ugandan LGBTI community still has a very long journey to freedom and full realisation of their rights ahead, but the resolve to fight against the Anti-Homosexuality Bill (which was in essence meant to erase their existence) just goes to show that this young movement has a future. It shows that the work LGBTI activists are doing in the face of incredible risks will create a better life for those that come after them.

The lessons learned from the Stonewall uprising and all the battles that activists fought to achieve the kind of freedom the Western countries enjoy right now are a signal for the LGBTI community in Uganda not to give up even when there are considerable odds against them.

---

51 Xan Rice, 'Uganda Gay Rights Activist David Kato Found Murdered' *The Guardian*, 27 January 2011. <www.theguardian.com/world/2011/jan/27/ugandan-gay-rights-activist-murdered>.

Chapter 6

'That's Really Why I Got Married I Guess'

Heteronormativity and Openness About Same-Sex Coupledom

Dora Jandrić

1. Introduction

This chapter explores the impact of heteronormativity on the lives of older same-sex couples, exploring the openness about their sexual identity and relationship. The chapter draws on the data from a doctoral project at the School of Social and Political Science, at the University of Edinburgh, which explored how older same-sex couples in Scotland imagined their future. The data for the project, and for this chapter, were collected through interviews and written accounts by seven same-sex couples and were then analysed using thematic and narrative analysis. The principal findings of this chapter contribute to a better understanding of the impact of past events and experiences on the present and the future, and further support the argument that in order to study older age and the ageing experience, social scientists should employ the life-course approach and take into consideration the entirety of the lived experience of the research participants.

This part of the chapter offers an overview of key social and historical events that happened during the participants' youth and that impacted their lives in the past and present. The chapter then introduces the main theoretical frameworks that work to support the data presented in Section 3. As the research was situated in Scotland, the chapter presents relevant social and political events that happened in the past 50 years throughout Scotland and the United Kingdom, and it includes events, such as the Stonewall Riots, as they have been key in the development of LGBT equality in most Western societies.

1.1 Historical Context of the Participants' Youth

The age of the research participants ranged from 36 to 77, meaning that most of them lived before and after 1967, when homosexuality was decriminalised in England and Wales, and 1980 when the same happened in Scotland. Following these legal changes, it can be argued that the situation for the LGBT population, and especially for gay men, improved. However, despite the introduction of new legislation, there were still areas where homosexuality was stigmatised and othered. For example, homosexuality was declassified as a mental illness

DOI: 10.4324/9781003286295-8

by the World Health Organization as late as 1992,[1] pointing to the slow rate of change that followed the decriminalisation. In 1988, the then Prime Minister of the United Kingdom, Margaret Thatcher, introduced Section 28 of the Local Government Act,[2] which prohibited promoting homosexuality in schools and presenting same-sex relationships as acceptable family relationships. During the years between 1988 and 2000, there were many attempts to change the law for the LGBT population, such as lowering the age of consent to 16 instead of 21, which was rejected in 1994, and lowered instead to 18.[3]

The year 2000 marked a series of positive changes for the LGBT population in Scotland, mostly due to the devolution of the Scottish Parliament and a new legislative freedom over health and social work, education, local government and housing, justice and policing and tourism, among other areas. The establishment of the Scottish Parliament, following the referendum in 1997, allowed Scotland to move in a different direction from the rest of the United Kingdom, at least in terms of LGBT rights. In 2000, Section 28 was abolished in Scotland but not in England and Wales, where it was repealed three years later,[4] and the ban on LGBT people serving in the armed forces was lifted at the same time. In 2001, the age of consent for gay and bisexual men was equalised with that of heterosexual people.[5] The year 2004 saw the passing of the Civil Partnership Act,[6] which gave same-sex couples the right to form civil partnerships, giving them the same rights as married opposite-sex couples in England, Scotland, Wales and Northern Ireland. In 2007, the Adoption and Children (Scotland) Act[7] allowed same-sex couples equal rights in adopting and fostering children. Following this, the Marriage (Same Sex Couples) Act was passed in 2013[8] and came to power in 2014 in England, Scotland and Wales. The most recent developments include the 2017 posthumous pardon to all gay men who were prosecuted because of their sexuality and the introduction of same-sex marriage in Northern Ireland in 2020.

1.2 Heteronormativity and Othering of Non-Heterosexual Identities

The events outlined earlier happened while the research participants were in their teens and early twenties. Any other sexual identity apart from the heterosexual one was at that time perceived as a mental illness until 1973 and the

---

1 Key Dates for Lesbian Stonewall, Bi Gay, and Trans Equality, 2016. <www.stonewall.org.uk/about-us/key-dates-lesbian-gay-bi-and-trans-equality#2000s> (accessed 29 August 2019).
2 Local Government Act 1988.
3 See Stonewall (n 1).
4 See Stonewall (n 1).
5 Stonewall, Love Wins! Age of Consent Equalised for Gay and Bi men, n.d. <www.stonewall.org.uk/our-work/campaigns/love-wins-age-consent-equalised-gay-and-bi-men> (accessed 11 May 2022).
6 Civil Partnership Act 2004.
7 Adoption and Children (Scotland) Act 2007 (asp 4).
8 Marriage (Same Sex Couples) Act 2013.

removal of 'homosexuality from the psychiatric nomenclature'.[9] The idea that homosexuality is a mental illness had its roots in heteronormative assumptions that were then translated into the legal, medical and social spheres. Heteronormativity is a socially constructed concept, which privileges heterosexuality and opposite-sex coupledom and enforces gendered power relations.[10] By positioning opposite-sex relationships as the norm, heteronormativity excludes same-sex coupling, enforcing homophobia and even legitimising violence against LGBT individuals.[11] Growing up in such an environment had an impact on people's lives, and, as will be illustrated by the data in Section 3, the desire to fit into the norm often meant individuals shaped their identities in a way that meant hiding from their sexuality. Consequently, this way of life, which often included hiding one's sexuality and passing as straight, influenced the participants' 'well-being in later life and concerns relating to accessing formal health and social care provision',[12] emphasising the need to take a life-course approach when studying older age and different parts of people's identity. The life-course approach does not only allow for an exploration of the research participants' sexuality but their experience of ageing as well, and it serves as a good tool for studying the intersection of sexuality and age. As Victor[13] argues, the lives people lead in their later years have been influenced by the cultural and historical contexts of their youth, and for same-sex couples these contexts were often hostile and unwelcoming.

One of the reasons why heteronormativity had such a strong hold over different parts of social life and why LGBT identities were considered outside the dominant norm was the emphasis on the reproductive aspect of sexuality, which, according to Foucault,[14] gained power in the 18th century. Foucault[15] argued that the idea of deviant sexual behaviour and giving names to such behaviour opened different avenues for the development of various sexual identities, instead of silencing them and prescribing what was 'normal'. His ideas further strengthen the argument that sexual identity is socially constructed, and as such it can be defined and moulded by the dominant group, in this case the heterosexual male. In this context, forms of sexuality that are not heterosexual or serve a procreative purpose can be defined as deviant, lesser than and 'other'. Historically then, heterosexuality has been the dominant form of sexuality, and

---

9 Anthony RD Augelli and Arnold H Grossman, 'Disclosure of Sexual Orientation, Victimization, and Mental Health Among Lesbian, Gay, and Bisexual Older Adults' (2001) 16 *Journal of Interpersonal Violence* 1008, 1009.
10 Heather Brook, 'Re-Orientation: Marriage, Heteronormativity and Heterodox Paths' (2018) 19 *Feminist Theory* 345.
11 See *Ibid*.
12 Sue Westwood, *Lesbian, Gay, Bisexual and Transgender Aging*, vol 13 (2nd edn, Elsevier 2015) 864.
13 Christina Victor, 'Social Gerontology: Older People and Everybody Else' in K Komp, M Aartsen (eds), *Old Age in Europe: A Textbook of Gerontology* (Springer 2013).
14 Michel Foucault, *The History of Sexuality* (Pantheon Books 1978).
15 See *Ibid*.

it has shaped the private and public lives of individuals, either by making them full members of the norm or by casting them out through various devices, such as legal regulations, discrimination and even the organisation of public spaces.[16] The way in which the research participants reflected the impact of such norms on their lives was through the implicit and explicit themes that emerged from the narratives they shared during the research process.

1.3 Time, Stories and Identity

One of the main theorists who argued that language and memories are the building blocks of our identities was George Herbert Mead.[17] Mead was also one of the founding fathers of symbolic interactionism, a theory that states that individuals construct their identities and the world around them through interaction with others, and through exchanging meaningful symbols, most often in the form of language. Furthermore, Mead argued that an individual's identity is not fixed, but rather that it changes through the life course, and it depends on the sociocultural and historical contexts of the individual's life. As a primary example of this identity construction, this chapter uses sexual identity to illustrate the fluidity and context dependency of identity formation, arguing that sexuality is not binary but rather a spectrum of identities, which an individual can occupy in their lifetime.

When people talk about themselves, they often bring up stories from their past, the memories they choose to share with the person they are talking to. While these memories are a part of the individual's life, they are often retold in a different way than the way in which they happened. This is because our own personal memories are impacted by a collective memory of the community we belong to.[18] One of the examples that illustrates this intersection of the personal and collective are the events that happened on 27 June 1969 in New York, when police raided the Stonewall Inn and encountered resistance from its patrons, starting a four-night riot.[19] Even though Stonewall was not the first time the LGBT community resisted authority, 'other events failed to achieve the mythic stature of Stonewall and indeed have been virtually forgotten'.[20] The power of Stonewall lies in the collective memory of people who participated in it and those whose lives have been changed by the events in 1969. In this way, even the younger generations, and people who have not participated

---

16 Phil Hubbard, 'Sex Zones: Intimacy, Citizenship and Public Space' (2001) 4 *Sexualities* 51.
17 George Herbert Mead, *Mind, Self, and Society* (University of Chicago Press 1934).
18 Yadin Dudai, and Micah G Edelson, 'Personal Memory: Is It Personal, Is It Memory?' (2016) 9 *Memory Studies* 275.
19 Elizabeth A Armstrong and Suzanna M Crage, 'Movements and Memory: The Making of the Stonewall Myth' (2006) 71 *American Sociological Review* 724.
20 See Armstrong and Crage (n 19) 725.

in these historical events, share the memory of them because of their impact on the present.

In order to further illustrate how past experiences shape the present and the future, this chapter uses both small- and large-scale events that happened in the lives of the research participants. By doing so, it further illustrates the intersection of the three temporalities, the past, present and future, and it argues that the life-course approach is needed when studying time, ageing and identity formation. The following section of this chapter outlines the rationale for the participant selection and the methods used in the data collection, and it explains the data analysis process.

2. Methodology

2.1 Participants

The participants for this project were same-sex couples living in Scotland at the time of the interviews. At least one of the partners needed to be over 55 for the couple to be eligible to participate. The age of 55 was chosen to get a broad range of experiences of the participants and to include those still working, as well as those who were retired. Depending on the discipline, the beginning of older age is defined at different ages. Literature on sexual health sometimes defines older age as over 40[21] and older workers are those over 50,[22] and the World Health Organization places older age at 60.[23] It is difficult to reach consensus on when older age 'begins', as it depends not only on different social groups but also on historical and cultural contexts.[24] According to Neugarten, the age group 55 to 75, or the young–old, are 'relatively healthy, relatively affluent, relatively free from traditional responsibilities of work and family'.[25] Taking 55 as the reference point, the ages of the research participants ranged from 36 to 77, providing a variety of experiences.

The participants were all white British citizens, living in different parts of Scotland at the time of the interviews. Half of the participants had children from previous heterosexual relationships, and 12 out of 14 were over the age of 55. The total number of couples interviewed was seven, with four female and

---

21 Laura M Carpenter, Constance A Nathanson, and Young J Kim, 'Sex After 40? Gender, Ageism, and Sexual Partnering in Midlife' (2006) 20 *Journal of Aging Studies* 93.
22 Wendy Loretto and Sarah Vickerstaff, 'Gender, Age and Flexible Working in Later Life' (2015) 29 *Work, Employment and Society* 233.
23 World Health Organisation, 'Ageing and Health' (2015). <www.who.int/ageing/events/world-report-2015-launch/healthy-ageing-infographic.jpg> (accessed 27 August 2019).
24 John A. Vincent, Chris Phillipson, and Murna Downs, 'Introduction' *The Futures of Old Age* (Sage 2006).
25 Bernice L Neugarten, 'Age Groups in American Society and the Rise of the Young-Old' (1974) 415 *The Annals of the American Academy of Political and Social Science* 187.

three male couples participating in the project. The participants were recruited through Facebook outreach to groups and non-governmental organisations that worked with older LGBT people, such as LGBT Health and Wellbeing and LGBT Age.

2.2 Data Collection and Analysis

The data were collected through semi-structured joint interviews[26] and written accounts. The couples were interviewed jointly to get an insight into their daily lives as a couple and to explore how their conversations framed the couples' discussions about the past, present and future. The interviews were based on an interview guide but provided freedom for different topics to emerge, allowing for a development of new ideas throughout the interviewing process. The purpose of the first interview was to build rapport with the participants, to get to know them and hear about their relationship. The second interview focused more on their future and the written accounts. Each couple was asked to produce a written account of their future in a notebook I left them between the two interviews, which were from four weeks to six months apart. The couples were asked to do this together as a way of stimulating discussion around the future. During our second interview, the couple guided me through their account, explaining why they had put in what they did, and I followed up with questions to further explore their imagination of the future. The interviews were recorded, transcribed and read for content and accuracy, and the written accounts were copied into Word documents for easier import into the data analysis software (NVivo 11).

The data were analysed in two rounds. The first round included a thematic analysis to outline the main themes that emerged during the data collection process. These themes were then organised in NVivo and used in subsequent interviews as prompts for conversation. The second round of data analysis used narrative analysis to look at the transcripts in more depth. During this round, the focus was on the way in which the couples discussed the topics we were talking about, rather than the topics themselves. Narrative analysis allowed me to explore the lives of the participants through the stories they told and, as Mead argued, to construct their identities through the narratives they chose to share with me.[27]

3. Findings

This section presents the research data and focuses on the coming out stories of the participants. Coming out is one of the most important events in the life of an LGBT individual, regardless of when and how it happens. It symbolises

---

26 Alan Bryman, *Quantity and Quality in Social Research* (Martin Bulmer ed, Routledge 2004).
27 Peter Robinson, 'Ageing Fears and Concerns of Gay Men Aged 60 and Over' (2016) 17 *Quality in Ageing and Older Adults* 6.

a break with heteronormative standards and a decision to create, or reclaim, one's own sexual identity. The stories presented here capture just a small part of the coming out experience of the participants, but they nevertheless present an important milestone in their lives. This section also focuses on the intersection of the past and the present, and the comparison between the two temporal frameworks. One of the dominant themes in these narratives was the impact of heteronormativity on the participants' past, which was visible in the way in which they discussed their present. Even though the sociocultural context of Scotland is different today than it was in their youth, the participants' lives are still impacted by past experiences of heteronormativity, homophobia and discrimination.

When discussing their lives today, the couples often contrasted them to how things were in the past while they were younger. Fred, for example, discussed the difference between his and Robert's, his partner's, youth as gay men and the lives younger gay men were leading today:

> One of the problems is that gay people of our age, as we were all brought up at a time when what we did was illegal, we could be sent to prison for, we could lose our jobs for, etc., so people of our age may be less likely to be open than younger people. You might see lots of younger gay couples holding hands in the street, it will be very, very rare that you'll see, well me and Robert don't, because we were brought up in an era where to do so would have, at best, led to talks, and at worst, at a certain time, would have led to prosecution.
>
> (Fred, 67, second interview)

Fred's story illustrated how the behaviour he experienced in the past impacted the way he and Robert performed their relationship in public. Not showing public displays of affection was a way to avoid prosecution at the time when engaging in same-sex relationships, especially as a gay man, was illegal, up to 1967 in England and Wales and 1980 in Scotland. Both Fred and Robert lived in England before 1967, and they were aware of what was at stake if they engaged in a same-sex relationship or disclosed their sexual identity. As argued earlier, even though Fred was aware that there was more acceptance and inclusivity of LGBT people in Scotland today, he and Robert still remembered the fear they felt in the past. Fred's comparison of the younger and older generations of gay men also illustrated the different sociocultural contexts, in which the two groups came of age and formed their sexual identities. In the following extract, Fred further illustrates the interplay of the past and the present:

> . . . and of course, you guarantee confidentiality, but people in the closet are still going to be, I mean I know when I was in the closet. Even with confidentiality, it would have meant admitting things to myself as well.
>
> (Fred, 67, second interview)

This was Fred's reply to our discussion on the difficulty of recruiting older same-sex couples for participation in the research. Fred argued that the reason behind the older LGBT population being invisible and closeted in the present was the need to hide their sexuality in the past. This extract illustrated the fluidity of the past and present through Fred's way of talking about both temporalities as being intricately linked one to the other and sharing the role in the construction of life narratives and identities.[28] Moving between the present and the past allowed Fred to rationalise the thoughts he might have had in his youth, as he reflected on them from the point of view of a gay man who might not have the same fears in the present. The difficulty he experienced in admitting his sexual orientation to himself in his youth further implied how deeply ingrained heteronormativity was in his, and others', lives. Heteronormativity did not only make it difficult to come out as LGBT to one's family and friends, but to themselves as well, for fear of deviating from the established norm shared by the individual's community.[29] Another example of past norms impacting the identity formation of the participants comes from Sharon, who, now married to a woman, is still not sure about using the term 'wife', for fear that someone would make an assumption that she was in a same-sex relationship:

SHARON: And for me, at my age, I still think it's quite difficult to say, 'my wife'. I still want to say, 'my partner', because that kind of almost makes it ok. And it's not . . .
INTERVIEWER: There's no reason [for it not to be ok].
SHARON: Yeah, that's an age thing.
ANNA: I was filling out forms and I was like, 'Shit, should I be putting wife?' It's like I can cope with the question of 'are you married or single', cause that's quite straightforward, 'yeah I'm married' –
SHARON: People still assume when you say married that you're married to a guy.
ANNA: So that automatic bit of, you're looking at a form, it's like 'oh, when somebody reads this, and they're actually gonna pick up that it's two women'.
(Sharon, 64, and Anna, 46, second interview)

Sharon argued that it was her age that impacted her behaviour towards Anna and the term wife, and that using the non-gendered term partner, in Sharon's opinion, made their relationship more legitimate. Her perception of the terms husband and wife as strictly belonging to a heterosexual marriage could have

---

28 Stevi Jackson, 'Self, Time and Narrative: Re-Thinking the Contribution of G. H. Mead' (2010) *Life Writing* 123.
29 Lena Rosenberg, Anders Kottorp, and Karin Johansson, 'LGBQ-Specific Elderly Housing as a "Sparkling Sanctuary": Boundary Work on LGBQ Identity and Community in Relationship to Potential LGBQ-Specific Elderly Housing in Sweden' (2018) 65 *Journal of Homosexuality* 1484.

meant that they could not be used in a same-sex marriage. As Sharon said, it might have been that her age (she was 38 when she started her relationship with Anna in 1992) and the events she experienced growing up made these terms strictly embedded into the heteronormative idea of marriage, and the only way to describe their relationship would have been to use the term partner. As Anna was 20 years old when they met, she might not have shared the same lived experience as Sharon but still found it difficult to write down wife on any of the forms she had to fill out. Anna's argument implied that she was wary of using the term wife in case people noticed that both partners were female, which might have caused discomfort.

Robert's coming out story illustrated how heteronormativity framed the way he thought about himself and his sexuality:

> Yes, I was trying, I mean, I think that I was on a sort of denial trip all in all, and that I didn't sort of really, I always knew I was gay, but I managed to sort of hide from it and pretend it wasn't there. That's really why I got married I guess, but then when the marriage came to an end, that's when I really had to face it, you know.
>
> (Robert, 76, first interview)

Robert told the story of his marriage from the perspective of the present and explained why he believed he was doing it in the first place. This extract illustrated Mead's[30] idea of the past being constructed by the present, as the story of Robert's marriage changed its meaning as time went by. In his youth, he used marriage to hide his sexual identity from others and himself, believing that following the heteronormative path would make him normal and ordinary[31] in the eyes of his immediate community. However, reflecting on the reasons for this marriage from the present perspective, Robert was aware that he used the marriage to pass as straight[32] and to postpone or completely avoid coming out. In the end, he 'really had to face' his sexuality, implying how difficult it was to continue hiding from it.

Engaging in opposite-sex relationships in their youth was an experience that was shared among most of the participants. Some, like Robert, did so to pass as straight, and others, like William, were experimenting with their own sexuality:

> I didn't know myself for many years, so I presumed myself heterosexual, and had several heterosexual relationships 'till the 1980s. About the same

---

30 See Mead (n 17).
31 Dian Richardson and Surya Monro, *Sexuality, Equality & Diversity* (Palgrave Macmillan 2012).
32 Craig B Fuller, Doris F Chang, and Lisa R Rubin, 'Sliding Under the Radar: Passing and Power Among Sexual Minorities' (2009) 3 *Journal of LGBT Issues in Counseling* 128.

time as becoming sexually active with women, I became sexually active with men in an entirely different way. I was never then dishonest about it. I actually said what my feelings were to my women partners, and as the AIDS thing started, it developed, the woman I was with then had some concerns, but I just sort of decided at that point if I met a woman, I would forgo men while being completely open about eyeing up guys on the street. If I met a man, then I'd go on that journey. And, in that particular time I met a woman, and then I realised having sex, or from the fork in that direction, that was the wrong direction.

(William, 65, first interview)

The 1980s were a turbulent time for the gay men population in the United States and the United Kingdom, as the HIV/AIDS epidemic was starting to spread, eventually reaching its peak in the late 1980s and early 1990s.[33] The year 1980 marked an important milestone for the LGBT population of Scotland, as it was the year when homosexuality was decriminalised with the Criminal Justice (Scotland) Act.[34] Despite this positive political move, the HIV/AIDS epidemic stigmatised gay men and, as William explained earlier, raised concerns related to the spread of the disease outside the LGBT domain. William was honest about 'eyeing up guys on the street' while he was in relationships with women, and this might have added to their perception of him as promiscuous or exhibiting risky behaviour. Deciding to 'forgo' men if he met a woman, and vice versa, might have been his way to decrease the perception of himself as a source of infection, and engaging in a monogamous relationship added to the image of a good sexual citizen, which was based on the model of 'heteronormative marriage and family values'.[35] William's coming out story also illustrated the societal opinions about gay men in the UK at the time and the difficulties the LGBT population might have faced when, and if, they decided to come out, as well as during the process of questioning and experimenting with one's sexuality. William's partner, Peter, was 36 years old at the time of our interview and had come out during the early 2000s when he was in his early 20s. He explained he never experienced the things that William had, and he was more open about his sexuality from an earlier age:

So, I've been very, very, very lucky with friends and family, and even when I came out to my friends I made in the first few weeks of uni, they weren't bothered, so it's like, this is quite a good decade to be me, and I thought,

---

33 Dana Rosenfeld, Bernadette Bartlam, and Ruth D Smith, 'Out of the Closet and into the Trenches: Gay Male Baby Boomers, Aging, and HIV/AIDS' (2012) 52:2 *Gerontologist* 255.
34 Criminal Justice (Scotland) Act 1980.
35 Diane Richardson, 'Locating Sexualities: From Here to Normality' (2004) 7 *Sexualities* 391, 406.

compared to living life on much harder difficulties, as I know some people have previously.

(Peter, 36, first interview)

Peter's account illustrates how belonging to a certain generation influences lives and experiences.[36] He is aware of the differences in the coming out experiences between him and William, who was 29 years older than him, and experienced different struggles in his youth. While Peter and William were not members of the same birth cohort and should have had considerable generational differences,[37] they shared a common understanding of the same event, which extended through both their lives. Based on Hockey and James's[38] ideas, what William and Peter experienced was a period effect (i.e. having their lives impacted by the same historical event, albeit in different ways and to a varying extent):

WILLIAM: So, way back in history, 'cause I had come out just about the time we were fighting that [Section 28], it's immediate history has this appalling language of pretend families. [. . .] I think in our minds we both felt very strongly about the clause, I campaigned against it and Peter grew up under its shadow.
PETER: Yes, I was in school when that was around, and the first time I came to [city], came to this house, I'd spotted, in a frame, in a hallway downstairs, the document that was basically the founder's declaration of [organisation], William was one of the founders of that campaign. That's why I thanked him over lunch the next day, and, in particular on behalf of me and all my generation, my gay friends for that. And it got me to where I am today.

(William, 65, and Peter, 36, first interview)

Even though Peter and William did not belong to the same birth cohort, they did experience the same period effect of the legal implications of Section 28. This suggests that age and birth year were not in themselves the most important factors here, but rather the culturally and historically specific experiences that William and Peter encountered during their formative years. In this particular example, William was campaigning against Section 28 in his youth, while Peter experienced its effect in school. Peter's last sentence probably referred to his relationship with William, but it might have also expressed his position as a non-heterosexual man. Because of William's campaigning in the past, it was possible for Peter to come out and live in a more inclusive society. By noticing

---

36 Jane Pilcher, *Age & Generation in Modern Britain* (Oxford University Press 1995).
37 Ken Plummer, 'Generational Sexualities, Subterranean Traditions, and the Hauntings of the Sexual World: Some Preliminary Remarks' (2010) 33 *Symbolic Interaction* 163.
38 Jenny Hockey and Allison James, *Social Identities Across the Life Course* (Palgrave Macmillan 2003).

the document on William's wall, Peter reframed his past to fit the present, imagining that his coming out and living an openly gay life were results of William's actions in the past, once again reflecting Mead's[39] ideas that the events in the present shape the past, rather than the other way around. Telling the story about the events he experienced in the past allows Peter to present them as actual lived experiences and identity narratives, both of which play a key role in his identity construction.

Some participants discussed a lack of support in their youth and how this played a role in their coming out process. Rachel discussed her past fears about being out, and she expressed a hope that history will not repeat itself:

> I was in my 30s before I came out, 'cause I lived in such fear of what would happen to me if I told people I was gay, I was doing a PhD, at [University], and at the back of my head, and I don't know how, I must have had blinkers on, I must have just been living in total fear, I thought 'if anybody finds out I have feelings for women, they'll throw me off my course, they'll throw me out of the university'. I mean [name] University had a gay society, and all that, but I couldn't see that, 'cause I was just living in fear, so it didn't matter that it wasn't criminal for women, I still had the same amount of fear as maybe the men had. [. . .] I mean I don't want to go back to that.
>
> (Rachel, 58, second interview)

Rachel came out in the late 1980s and was at that time living in England. Even though homosexuality was decriminalised by then, Rachel was aware that gay men still feared coming out and argued she experienced the same fear about her own sexuality. During our second interview, Rachel mentioned seeing *Maurice*, a film about a young man discovering his sexuality and falling in love with another man. Even though the film was set in the Edwardian era, Rachel argued she felt a similar amount of fear in the 1980s, and that this fear stopped her from seeking support. Unlike Rachel, who was aware there were support groups around her, Jane explained she had no role models in her youth, and that made her coming out process more complicated:

> For me, it was complicated because I was married to a man at the time, and I was, I had two young children, so it just, as the dawning happened to me, I thought, I knew I was unhappy, and then started to think why that might be, and as I began to realise what was happening, I then thought 'well I can't do anything about this because I've got two small children', and I had no role models, nobody else that I knew was in a position like I was, and I just thought I will have to just forget it, because I can't do this

---

39 See Mead (n 17).

and make my children unhappy. So, I didn't do anything about it for a little while, but then the kids kept seeing me unhappy, so I thought, you know, 'this is not good'. I can remember my little daughter putting her hands on my face and looking up at me and saying: 'Mummy, why are you always so sad?' So, I thought 'I can't do this', I went for some therapy, at that time it was actually a lesbian counselling service in [city], and for me that was a big thing, and I knew that going to the service was safe, and I knew that the counsellor would absolutely understand what my issues were, and for me that was very important. So, that was transformational for me because I realised that both I had the strength and that my children would survive. And in fact probably thrive because it's much more important that children are supported by adults that are well and happy.

(Jane, 56, first interview)

In this extract, Jane explained how, in the long run, her children's happiness was more important to her than her own. She also argued that it was complicated for her to come out because she was in an opposite-sex marriage, which further illustrated the impact of heteronormative gender roles on her life and relationship, suggesting that her coming out process would have meant deviating from the norms she probably followed her entire life. For Jane, following such established norms implied that if she came out, she would suffer ridicule and rejection,[40] and the lack of role models enforced that perception. In the end, as she realised her unhappiness was being reflected on her children, she came out for their sake as much as hers, shifting the narrative from fear and rejection to acceptance. Once she decided to come out, she actively sought help in the form of a counselling service in the city she lived in, taking control of her coming out process.

4. Discussion

The extracts presented earlier illustrate the impact of heteronormativity on the participants' lives. While it was not mentioned explicitly, it was clear that heteronormative ideals framed the way the participants thought about their sexual identity. Two thematic areas have emerged from the data presented earlier, illustrating the impact of heteronormativity on the participants' lives in different aspects.

4.1 Past Experiences and Present Behaviour

As was outlined in the introduction and illustrated with Fred's and Sharon's stories, the behaviour they exhibited in the past, in order to hide their sexual

---

[40] Rebecca Van Voorhis and Linda McClain, 'Accepting a Lesbian Mother' (1997) 78 *Families in Society: The Journal of Contemporary Social Services* 642.

identity, could still be seen in their attitudes today. There was no public display of affection, and there was a reluctance in using words that would imply a same-sex relationship. This kind of behaviour did not only illustrate the grasp that past experiences held over the participants' lives, but it also showed how relevant these narratives were for them. By choosing to share these specific stories about their past and present, both Fred, and Sharon and Anna presented a part of themselves they wanted me, as the researcher, to hear. In this way, they actively participated in the construction of their present and past identities.[41] What their narratives also portray is how stories told about the past often change their meaning in the present, because they are based in a specific cultural and historical context. What was important in their youth might not be as relevant in their later life because of the changing social context, but they nevertheless carried these events and experiences with them through their lives. While their memory of these events might change, the impact on their identity will not.

What was also visible from the stories presented earlier was the reflexive process present in the discussion of past events. Robert, for example, needed to step away from his heterosexual marriage, both literally and figuratively, to be able to see it as a mechanism that he used to enforce heterosexuality. For him and for the other participants, being part of the norm was at times more important than being true to themselves, but it took time, and in some cases space, for some of the participants to see this behaviour from a different perspective. Once they came out, the things they did and the lives they have led before became part of their past, but they still remembered them and carried them into the present.

4.2 Individual and Collective Memory

Jedlowski[42] explains that memories are constantly 'selected, filtered and restructured' to fit the needs of the present, and, as Jackson[43] argues, it is the present that shapes the past. Collective memories emerge from shared historical events, such as the Vietnam War, for example, or, as was mentioned earlier, campaigns against Section 28 and the Stonewall Riots. Such memories help construct the events people might have not participated in, or if they have, the knowledge of such events helps in forming individual memories about what happened. Our own personal memories are the products of our own recollection, the collective memory of the society we live in and the memories of the people we interact with.[44] As was illustrated in William's and Peter's account, the individual

---

41 See Jackson (n 28).
42 Paolo Jedlowski, 'Memory and Sociology: Themes and Issues' (2001) 10 *Time & Society* 29, 30.
43 See Jackson (n 28).
44 See Dudai and Edelson (n 18).

memory of an event holds different meanings for different people, even when the event might have had the same impact on their lives. Retelling memories also shows how time can be perceived as non-linear,[45] as people go back and forth in time when talking to others.

The data also illustrated how a group of people can have a collective idea about the future, not only the past. As Rachel explained, she did not want history to repeat itself in terms of negative experiences for the LGBT population, and all the participants shared this wish. The stories they told about the past implied that the experiences they had were relevant in the formation of their sexual identity, but that they did not necessarily want them to happen again. Passing as straight, being considered normal and following the expected gendered norms were just some examples of past experiences that, in the participants' opinion, had no place in the future. This kind of collective thinking about the present and the future is possible for this group of participants because of their shared historical struggles.[46] The ability to construct a joint future further strengthens the idea that time plays an important role in the way we develop our identities, and that collective memories of the past help create imagined communities[47] of the future.

5. Conclusion

This chapter presented part of the data of a larger doctoral project and offered some new ideas in thinking about time and identity. It argued that time plays a key role in identity formation, particularly in the case of the older LGBT population, who experienced social movements during their lifetime differently than their heterosexual peers. The impacts of the past on the present were visible in the stories about the participants' behaviour and ideals they held, and the chapter argued that these past events were reconstructed through retelling them in the present. Adding to that, the shared historical experiences opened a possibility of a shared imagination of the future, creating a kind of collective future memory for the group of people who participated in the research. Finally, the chapter illustrated the importance of studying the life course of an individual or a couple, as without understanding the past, there can be no knowledge of the present and the future.

---

45 Pitirim Sorokin and Robert Merton, 'Social-Time: A Methodological and Functional Analysis' in John Hassard (ed), *The Sociology of Time* (Palgrave Macmillan 1990).
46 Jose Esteban Muñoz, *Cruising Utopia* (New York University Press 2009).
47 Benedict Anderson, *Imagined Communities: Reflections on the Origin and Spread of Nationalism* (Verso 1991).

Part 2

LGBT Rights Facing New Challenges

Chapter 7

A Landscape of Change

Legal Perspectives

Paul Behrens and Sean Becker

At the time of Stonewall, the law, in general, was not an ally of the LGBT community.

Numerous States still outlawed homosexuality, although a movement towards legalisation had already begun.[1] Yet in the USA, at the time of the Stonewall Riots, only one State (Illinois) had decriminalised homosexuality.[2]

In light of that, it is tempting to consider the legal developments since then a success story. Twelve years after the riots, the European Court of Human Rights (ECtHR) found that a law prohibiting homosexual acts among consenting adults constituted unjustified interference with the right to respect for private life.[3] The end of the 1980s saw the introduction of the first same-sex registered partnerships;[4] the following decade the conclusion of same-sex unions in various countries; and in December 2000, the Netherlands became the first country in the world to give same-sex couples the right to marry.[5] Transgender rights, too, have seen significant development, with several States simplifying the procedure by which persons can change their gender in official documents.[6] Progress for the rights of non-binary and intersex people was slower, but Australia led the way when, in 2003, it reportedly issued a passport to an intersex person, which allowed 'an X in the sex field'.[7]

---

1 See, for England and Wales, Sexual Offences Act 1967, c. 60.
2 *CE Noticias Financieras*, 'From Stonewall to 2021: How Pride Blossomed After a Bar Fight' 26 June 2021.
3 *Dudgeon v United Kingdom* (Application no. 7525/76), Judgment, 22 October 1981, para 63.
4 In Denmark. See Sheila Rule, 'Rights for Gay Couples in Denmark' *The New York Times*, 2 October 1989.
5 See I Lund-Andersen, 'Registered Partnerships in Denmark' in JM Scherpe and A Hayward (eds), *The Future of Registered Partnerships – Family Recognition Beyond Marriage* (Intersentia 2017).
6 *Agence France Presse – English*, 'Countries that Allow Transgender People Easy Status Change', 29 June 2021.
7 Morgan Carpenter, 'Ten Years of "X" Passports, and No Protection from Discrimination' *Intersex Human Rights Australia*, 12 January 2013 (citing the *Western Australian* newspaper).

DOI: 10.4324/9781003286295-10

The path towards acceptance has also extended to the legal profession itself. The rise of LGBT groups, such as the National LGBTQ+ Bar Association in the United States,[8] the LGBT+ Lawyers Division of the Law Society[9] in the United Kingdom and, internationally, the LGBTI Law Committee of the International Bar Association, provides evidence to that effect.[10]

And yet, it would be premature to speak of these developments as truly universal in nature. The fact must be borne in mind that in more than a third of all States, homosexuality remains unlawful,[11] with several countries retaining the death penalty for consensual same-sex acts.[12]

At the same time, there is, in considering the situation outside the Western hemisphere, a danger of generalisation that ignores the development in individual jurisdictions – such as the fact that, in 2019, Taiwan became the first Asian country to legalise same-sex marriage,[13] and that several African States have in recent years decriminalised same-sex activities: Lesotho in 2012, Mozambique in 2015, Botswana and Angola in 2019.[14]

Yet the prevailing division among different jurisdictions provides at least a partial explanation for the long road that the recognition of LGBT rights had to follow internationally as well. The Yogyakarta Principles of 2006, stipulating fundamental rights of LGBT persons,[15] remain a private initiative.[16] A 2008 Declaration, sponsored by France and the Netherlands in the General Assembly of the United Nations, is arguably a more reliable indicator of attitudes of UN Member States. The statement urged States to take all 'necessary measures [. . .] to ensure that sexual orientation or gender identity' may not be the basis for criminal penalties; but it led to a division within the UN,[17] with 66 States supporting it and 60 States backing an opposing statement.[18] And yet, even this development allows for a more discerning view: among the supporters of the

---

8 LGBTQ+ Bar, 'The National LGBTQ+ Bar Association and Foundation' <https://lgbtqbar.org/about/about-us/>.
9 Law Society, 'About the LGBT+ Lawyers Division' <www.lawsociety.org.uk/en/topics/lgbt-lawyers/about-the-lgbt-lawyers-division>.
10 International Bar Association, 'Lesbian, Gay, Bisexual, Transgender and Intersex (LGBTI) Law Committee' <www.ibanet.org/unit/Section+on+Public+and+Professional+Interest/committee/Lesbian%2C+Gay%2C+Bisexual%2C+Transgender+and+Intersex+%28LGBTI%29+Law+Committee/3282>.
11 *BBC News*, 'Homosexuality: The Countries Where It is Illegal to Be Gay', 21 May 2021 <www.bbc.co.uk/news/world-43822234>.
12 Lucas Ramón Mendos et al., 'State-Sponsored Homophobia. Global Legislation Overview Update' *ILGA World* (2020) 38.
13 Beh Li Yi, '"Happily Ever After" Eludes Taiwan, a Year After Asia's First Gay Marriages' *Postmedia Breaking News*, 21 May 2020.
14 *This is Africa*, 'Botswana Decriminalises Homosexuality', 12 June 2019.
15 Yogyakarta Principles (2006) <http://yogyakartaprinciples.org/principles-en/official-versions-pdf/>.
16 *Ibid*.
17 Patrick Worsnip, 'U.N. Divided Over Gay Rights Declaration' *Reuters*, 19 December 2008.
18 *Ibid*.

Franco-Dutch declaration were States who may not have been readily associated with LGBT rights, including several African States and three members of the Organisation of Islamic Cooperation.[19] In 2011, 85 States supported a joint statement in the Human Rights Council seeking an end to human rights violations based on sexual orientation and gender identity;[20] and in 2016, the UN Security Council, for the first time, expressly acknowledged violence against LGBT persons.[21]

The chapters in this part explore various aspects of the law and their impact on LGBT matters.

Chapter 8 (Gray) raises the question whether the achievements since Stonewall have reached their peak and may now come under threat again. Particular focus is placed on transgender rights and the current debate in this field.

Chapter 9 (Behrens) investigates the role that direct democracy has played in the regulation of same-sex marriage and evaluates the legitimacy of referendums, in particular with regard to the determination of minority rights.

Chapter 10 (Fenwick and Hayward) explores the development towards same-sex marriage both from a domestic perspective and through the lens of the ECtHR. It analyses the Court's current reluctance, especially in light of its 'consensus' doctrine, but also parts of its rulings that indicate a willingness to adopt a more open approach in the future.

Chapter 11 (Norrie) examines the impact that the social evolution of attitudes to LGBT matters has had on the law of defamation. The relevant judgements allow conclusions on the changing nature of perceived community values, but contemporary rulings also highlight the tension inherent in the status of homophobic statements, which, at present, may still benefit from the protection of freedom of expression.

Chapter 12 (Becker) critically explores the belief system that selected House of Lords judgements on LGBT issues reveal and draws conclusions on the division between the law on homosexuality and ideologies in the highest UK court that prevailed even 30 years after the decriminalisation of homosexual acts.

---

19 *Human Rights Watch*, 'UN: General Assembly Statement Affirms Rights for All', 18 December 2008. <www.hrw.org/news/2008/12/18/un-general-assembly-statement-affirms-rights-all>.
20 *State Department Documents and Publications,* 'Joint Statement on the Rights of LGBT Persons at the Human Rights Council. Fact Sheet', 23 March 2011.
21 *Thai News Service*, 'United States: UN Acknowledges Human Rights Violation Against LGBT Community', 17 June 2016.

Chapter 8

The Evolution of LGBT Rights in the UK
Is the Tide Starting to Turn?

Carolynn Gray

1. Introduction

Fifty years after the Stonewall Riots, it would be easy to believe that the rights of LGBT people have been achieved in the United Kingdom. This process has not been an easy one, but on the whole, in 2021, UK law provides those of us within the LGBT community with recognition and protection in almost all areas of life. However, recent antagonistic debates around the reform of the Gender Recognition Act 2004 (GRA 2004), the calls for a 'straight pride' parade,[1] along with the reporting of the demonstrations outside Anderton Park Primary School in Birmingham,[2] where some parents and members of the local community were demonstrating against the teaching of LGBT issues to children of primary school age,[3] highlight that perhaps the LGBT rights movement reached a pinnacle in the middle of this decade and may, in fact, now be under threat.

This chapter will examine the evolution of trans rights in UK law,[4] focusing largely on key legal developments from the 1950s in light of the recent proposals to reform the GRA 2004[5] and the debate that this has generated. In particular, this chapter will show how the trans rights movement is fragile and is now particularly susceptible to being undermined by a rise in anti-LGBT populist politics across Europe and further afield.

---

1 Patrick Evans, 'Calls for a Straight Pride Parade Cause Stir' *BBC*, 5 June 2019. <www.bbc.co.uk/news/blogs-trending-48527248> (accessed 1 June 2020).
2 Tara John, 'Kids Are Being Taught About LGBTQ Rights in These British Schools. Some Parents Are Saying No' *CNN*, 2 July 2019. <https://edition.cnn.com/2019/07/02/uk/birmingham-lgbtq-school-protests-gbr-intl/index.html> (accessed 1 June 2020); 'Birmingham School LGBT Protests 'Probably Harassment'' *BBC*, 10 June 2019. <www.bbc.co.uk/news/uk-england-birmingham-48580310> (accessed 1 June 2020).
3 See also *Birmingham City Council v Afsar* [2020] EWHC 864 (QB).
4 By this, I mean the law of England and Wales, Scotland, and where applicable Northern Ireland.
5 The UK government held a consultation on reform of the GRA 2004 from 3 July 2018 until 22 October 2018 and the Scottish government held a consultation on reform of the GRA 2004 from 9 November 2017 to 1 March 2018 and again from 17 December 2019 until 17 March 2020.

DOI: 10.4324/9781003286295-11

2. Progress So Far

Stonewall has been acknowledged by some as the turning point in relation to LGBT rights.[6] Some go as far as to say that in relation to discussions of LGBT history and rights that '[i]t is common to divide gay history into two epochs "before Stonewall" and "after Stonewall"'.[7] However, 'historians of sexuality have challenged the novelty of the events at the Stonewall Inn'.[8] Certainly, in the UK, it is somewhat of an overstatement to attribute the acquisition of Sexual Orientation and Gender Identity (SOGI) rights to the Stonewall Riots in New York, as the LGBT rights movement began here prior to Stonewall.

The history of LGBT rights in the UK is long and has its roots in medical and social changes beginning in the 1950s. In relation to the quest for trans rights specifically, it is not really possible to separate out that history from the history relating to the criminalisation of homosexuality, as both were entwined until the 1950s when work on transsexualism,[9] first as a focus of sexology and then as a discrete medical condition, developed:[10] until around the 1950s, there was no real separation of sexual orientation and gender identity as understood in the latter part of the 20th century and often laws criminalising male homosexual activity criminalised trans people also.[11]

2.1 The 1950s–1970s

For trans people, very little movement was made towards acknowledging their gender identity until the 1950s when a variety of different medical and social developments enabled some degree of separation of homosexuality and trans identity;[12] it could then be argued that developments in the 1950s, completely separate from the Stonewall Riots, enabled the contemporary understanding of sexual orientation and gender identity as distinct characteristics of one's

---

6 Elizabeth A Armstrong and Suzanna M Crage, 'Movements and Memory: The Making of the Stonewall Myth' (2006) 71 *American Sociological Review* 724–751, 724; Phil CW Chan, 'Protection of Sexual Minorities Since Stonewall: Their Lives, Struggles, Sufferings, Love, and Hope' (2009) 13 (2–3) *The International Journal of Human Rights* 129–141, 130.
7 See *Ibid*.
8 See *Ibid*.
9 Please note that the terminology of the time was such that the use of transsexual and transsexualism is appropriate in this context. Contemporary terminology is more inclusive, and therefore, elsewhere in this chapter the term trans will be used to encompass all whose gender identity differs from the sex assigned at birth (e.g. those who identify as the opposite sex to that assigned at birth but also to those whose gender identity is more fluid or non-binary).
10 For more on this, see Carolynn Gray, 'A Critique of the Legal Recognition of Transsexuals in UK Law' PhD Thesis, Glasgow University, 2015.
11 See Jeffrey Weeks, *Coming Out: Heterosexual Politics in Britain, from the Nineteenth Century to the Present* (Quartet Books 1977).
12 See Gray (n 10).

identity and paved the way for the development of SOGI rights separate from the movement in the USA, which has been attributed to the Stonewall Riots.

In the UK, the first sex reassignment procedures began in the 1940s,[13] but it was the 1950s that saw the start of some legal challenges in relation to changing one's birth certificate and saw the emergence of transsexualism as a distinct medical condition with treatment protocols.[14] One of the earliest, of what could be considered trans rights, cases was the Scottish case of *X, Petitioner*,[15] which, although short, provides a particularly useful example from which to gather an understanding of the ability to alter one's legal sex as opposed to one's physical sex. The case itself was not about legal recognition *per se* but rather about amending entries in the Register under the Registration of Births, Deaths and Marriages (Scotland) Act 1854 (the 1854 Act), where the individual had undergone sex re-assignment procedures. The case said nothing in itself about how the law determines the legal sex of an individual, but it did provide that registered sex cannot be changed unless an error was made when initially registering the child's birth or if a mistake had been noticed subsequently.[16] The law on amending Register entries was at the time governed by the 1854 Act s.63, which provided that errors of registration could be corrected and recorded in a separate register called the Register of Corrected Entries. It was held that to amend the Register following sex reassignment surgery was not within the ambit of s.63.[17]

Stating what was to become the mantra in applications for amendments of birth certificates following sex re-assignment surgery, sheriff-substitute Prain stated that '[t]he Register is essentially a record of fact at a fixed time; it is not, and is not intended to be, a narrative of events'.[18]

Although the discussion of the medical evidence in this case was very weak,[19] Prain did highlight that it was medical opinion that the petitioner firmly believed that she was a woman and that this belief did not appear to be derived from any mental abnormality.[20] Prain, noting that this case involved

---

13 Michael Dillon, the UK's first trans man, reportedly began taking testosterone in the early 1940s and underwent a series of surgeries through the 1940s, which are considered to be the first sex reassignment surgeries carried out in the UK. See Aidan Collins, 'Laurence Michael Dillon of Lismullen: World's First Transsexual Man' (2017) 210:3 *The British Journal of Psychiatry* 179.
14 Harry Benjamin is widely considered to be the father of the concept of modern gender dysphoria. See Harry Benjamin, 'Transvestism and Transsexualism' (1953) 7 *International Journal of Sexology* 12–14, in which it is believed that he first used the term 'transsexualism'.
15 *X, Petitioner* 1957 SLT (Sh Ct) 61.
16 i.e. if the individual had a medical condition which fell under the term 'Disorder of Sexual Development', but this was not apparent when the birth was registered.
17 See *X, Petitioner* (n 15) 62.
18 See *Ibid*.
19 See *Ibid*.
20 See *Ibid*. This is an important distinction to make because the case predated the later medical belief of the importance of mental pathology in relation to gender identity as medicine had not fully

'a genuine case of the very rare condition of transsexualism'[21] and, although having some degree of sympathy towards X, was unwilling to accept that X was female because her 'skin and blood tests still show X's basic sex to be male and that the changes have not reached the deepest level of sex determination'.[22]

The consequence for X was that she was constrained by the law to live as female but remain legally male. The position established in *X, Petitioner* continues to be the default position in 2020; one's sex remains that registered at birth, unless it can be established that a mistake has been made on registering the child's sex or, currently, following the enactment of the GRA 2004 a full[23] Gender Recognition Certificate (GRC) has been issued.[24] *X, Petitioner* was heard at a time when sex re-assignment surgery was largely a new phenomenon, and this case began the long process of trans individuals seeking legal recognition of their gender identity. This legal approach had serious implications for trans individuals in relation to various aspects of their lives, as will be shown in the remainder of this chapter.

The next major UK legal development in the pursuit of trans rights, albeit a negative one, was the case of *Corbett v Corbett*[25] in 1971. *Corbett* was heard at a time when SOGI rights were starting to emerge[26] and when medical developments were such that physical interventions to change one's body had advanced considerably. In this context, *Corbett* was an unfortunate step backwards, a step that would damage the quest for trans rights until the 21st century and which was, arguably, the case that was most damaging to the trans rights movement in the UK.

Corbett is of its time; the issue is that when the case was decided, there was no agreement between medical professionals regarding the causes of and treatment in relation to transsexualism. In addition, the *Corbett* judgement concerned one specific legal issue: could someone assigned male at birth (AMAB) but who transitioned to female enter into a valid marriage with a cisgender man? Ormrod J's judgement in *Corbett*, although troublesome for trans people who later sought legal recognition in the UK courts, was a thorough examination of transsexualism, as a medical condition, as understood at the time and also of the law of marriage in England. Although *Corbett* was never intended to be

---

articulated this until the medical condition 'transsexualism' appeared for the first time in the American Psychiatric Association's *Diagnostic and Statistical Manual of Mental Disorders* (DSM) in 1980.

21 See *X, Petitioner* (n 15).
22 See *Ibid*.
23 If an interim GRC is issued, then there are no legal consequences flowing from the GRC, and the individual remains legally of the sex registered at birth. Interim GRCs are largely used as a means of ending a marriage.
24 Gender Recognition Act 2004 s.9.
25 [1971] P 83.
26 Sexual Offences Act 1967 s.1 decriminalised male homosexual acts in private providing that both men were aged 21 or over. This law only applied in England and Wales.

the test for determination of one's legal sex, the judgement became such and had a detrimental impact on individuals in a number of areas of personal life for decades. Some commentators note the anomaly of the *Corbett* judgement becoming such an important piece of law given the court in which it was heard and the lack of appeal, and therefore its lack of precedential strength. However, this did not prevent *Corbett* from providing the test for determining legal sex then and now.[27] The arguments put forward in this case were that sex is essentially fixed at birth and dependent upon one's primary sex characteristics, which are supported by the natural development of secondary sex characteristics on puberty versus the argument that sex is more complicated than biology and includes aspects of one's psychological identification, which ought to be recognised by the law.[28] Ormrod J was at pains to determine the respondent's 'true' sex because, according to him, the existence of a valid marriage was dependent upon this.[29] From the remainder of his judgement, it became clear that true sex meant the respondent's biological rather than her psychological sex. The Court heard the expert testimony of several medical professionals, and Ormrod J observed that according to the medical experts 'there are at least four criteria for assessing the sexual condition of an individual'.[30] These were identified as chromosomes, gonads, genitals and psychology,[31] and where the first three 'are congruent, determine sex [. . .] accordingly and ignore any operative interventions'.[32]

The *Corbett* judgement has had a massive impact on legal sex determination and consequently on the lives of trans individuals and their families who sought recognition, rights and protection in law. Cowan argues that one particularly important legal outcome of *Corbett* was that the law confirmed that 'sex is not a matter of choice in law; rather it is an essential biological characteristic'.[33] Bell argues that when courts adopt the approach taken in *Corbett* and begin their enquiry with the question of whether a man 'who has surgery to change his physical characteristics is still just a man'[34] rather than the more inquisitive enquiry of what is the applicant's 'sex after surgery, hormonal therapy, and psychiatric counselling'[35] then 'the court's formulation of

---

27 Stephen Gilmore, 'Bellinger v Bellinger – Not Quite Between the Ears and Between the Legs – Transsexualism and Marriage in the Lords' (2003) 15:3 *Child & Family Law Quarterly* 295–311; Anne Barlow, 'W v W (Nullity: Gender) and B v B (Validity of Marriage: Transsexual) – a New Approach to Transsexualism and a Missed Opportunity?' (2001) 13:2 *Child & Family Law Quarterly* 225–240.
28 Corbett (n 25) 85[C]-[G].
29 *Ibid.*, 89.
30 *Ibid.*, 100[D].
31 *Ibid.*, 100[D]-[E].
32 *Ibid.*, 106[D].
33 Sharon Cowan, '"Gender Is No Substitute for Sex": A Comparative Human Rights Analysis of the Legal Regulation of Sexual Identity' (2005) 13 *Feminist Legal Studies* 67–96, 74.
34 Megan Bell, 'Transsexuals and the Law' (2004) 98 *Northwestern University Law Review* 1709, 1730.
35 See *Ibid.*

the question determines the outcome'.[36] By adopting the more inquisitive approach and framing their narrative in the latter form, the courts would open up the possibility of finding that someone who has undergone surgery to modify their body to make it congruent with their gender identity has in fact changed sex. UK Courts, however, were unwilling to take this approach. *Corbett* highlights what Bell terms the court's 'adherence to essentialist modes of inquiry'[37] so that the courts rely upon 'a stark distinction between "natural" and "man-made" organs, thus treating sex/gender as truly existing in a single, universal form'.[38] *Corbett* was a judgement that allowed for predictability in determination of sex, but it was also 'the basis of the separation of sex from gender in transsexuality cases'.[39] As Cowan argues, 'UK courts have adhered to this division [of sex and gender], treating gender as a social/psychological factor that can always be trumped by biological sex (particularly chromosomes)'.[40] This is an important issue: although it may seem that sex and gender can be used interchangeably, and indeed the terms are often confused, each term has a specific meaning. 'Sex' is understood as a person's biological make-up, which ranges from chromosomal make-up, possession of a particular type of gonad to widely differing secondary sex characteristics, such as body hair. Whereas 'sex' refers to biology, 'gender' refers to psychology and is therefore not as easy to determine definitively as sex.[41] However, had the Court been more willing to consider the importance of gender identity and psychological identification, then it is arguable that the respondent in *Corbett* would have been recognised as female and the marriage would have been deemed valid;[42] as it was, the marriage was deemed null *ab initio*, and decree of nullity was granted.

Between *Corbett* and the next UK case that concerned the legal recognition of an individual's gender identity, the UK government, in response to developments in EU law, enacted the Sex Discrimination Act 1975 (SDA 1975),[43] which made it unlawful to discriminate on the ground of sex in employment,

---

36 See *Ibid*.
37 See *Ibid*., 1731.
38 See *Ibid*.
39 See Cowan (n 33) 74.
40 See *Ibid*., 74.
41 See Rhoda K Unger, 'Towards a Redefinition of Sex and Gender' (1979) 34:11 *American Psychologist* 1085–1094; Judith Butler, 'Sex and Gender in Simone de Beauvoir's *Second Sex*' (1986) 72 *Yale French Studies* 35–49; Joy L Johnson and Robin Repta, 'Sex and Gender: Beyond the Binaries' in John L Oliffe and Lorraine Greaves (eds), *Designing and Conducting Gender, Sex, and Health Research* (Sage 2012) 17–39; Maria Victoria Carrera, Renee DePalma, and Maria Lameiras, 'Sex/Gender Identity: Moving Beyond Fixed and "Natural" Categories' (2012) 15:8 *Sexualities* 995–1016.
42 Thorpe LJ in the Court of Appeal in *Bellinger v Bellinger* [2001] EWCA Civ 1141; [2002] Fam 150 placed a strong emphasis on psychological gender identity and so did the European Court of Human Rights in the case of *Goodwin v United Kingdom* (2002) 35 EHRR 18.
43 Now repealed by the Equality Act 2010.

education, the provision of housing, goods, facilities and services and stemmed from EU equal treatment directives. The SDA 1975 formed the basis for the application in *White v British Sugar Corporation*,[44] in which the applicant was assigned female at birth (AFAB) but lived as male albeit without any body modification. The applicant identified as male, dressed in male clothing, used a male name and masculine prefix and wanted to be treated as male. He gained employment as an electrician's mate in a factory that involved some work on Sundays, which was prohibited for women.[45] While in employment, he used the male toilets and changing facilities at work. However, rumours about him being female began, and he was dismissed. The industrial tribunal held that he was female for the purposes of the SDA 1975. In determining White's sex, the Chairman of the Industrial Tribunal stated that the dictionary 'defines male as of or belonging to the sex which begets offspring or performs the fecundatory function'.[46] He noted that the dictionary also defines 'female as belonging to the sex which bears offspring'.[47] He stated that in the present case, 'the applicant [. . .] does not have male reproductive organs and there was no evidence that [he] could not bear children'.[48] As a result of this poor determination of legal sex using dictionary definitions, the Industrial Tribunal held that White was female in terms of the SDA 1975, and his dismissal was upheld.

2.2 The 1980s and 1990s

The 1980s and 1990s were not particularly positive times in which to be LGBT. As Chan notes, 'a message was renewed time and again during the 1980s and early 1990s that sexual minorities were not part of society and must not be allowed the room to assert or to have their human rights'.[49] There were a variety of cases and legislative enactments in this period, which both furthered and hindered the quest for LGBT rights. One of the most infamous anti-LGBT measures of the 1980s was the Local Government Act 1988 s.28,[50] which made it illegal for local authorities to promote homosexuality or to promote teaching in local authority-maintained schools 'of the acceptability of homosexuality as a pretended family relationship'.[51] This law was not repealed

---

44 [1977] IRLR 121. Please note that the use of the masculine pronoun here is deliberate to acknowledge and respect the individual's identity despite the law sexing him as female.
45 Factories Act 1961 s.7(2)(f).
46 *White* (n 44) 123.
47 *Ibid.*, 123.
48 *Ibid.*, 123. Note that the Industrial Tribunal used the female pronoun to reflect the individual's legal sex; however, it has been amended here to reflect his gender identity.
49 See Chan (n 6) 130.
50 In Scotland, Clause 2a.
51 Local Government Act 1988 s.28(1).

until 2000 in Scotland[52] and 2003 in England and Wales[53] and, arguably, has had a lasting negative impact on LGBT people.[54]

The first trans case of the 1980s, in the UK courts, was a criminal law case, *R v Tan*,[55] in which someone AMAB but who had transitioned and was living as female was convicted of living off the earnings of prostitution, a crime for which only male persons could be convicted. *Tan* confirmed the *Corbett* test and extended the rule that legal sex is fixed at birth from marriage law into criminal law. *Tan* is interesting because the Court spent some time considering the need to maintain consistency in law in relation to subsequent cases and also the need for certainty in this area of law, which was in distinction to the lack of need for certainty in medicine in relation to an individual's sex.[56] At the time of this case, medicine was continuing its development in this area such that there was flexibility within the medical approach towards trans people to recognise that some individuals identified as members of the opposite sex for reasons not fully known or understood.[57] In addition, as a result of the work of key people in this field, notably Harry Benjamin,[58] it was acknowledged in medicine by the 1980s that the most appropriate treatment for such individuals was not to insist that because their chromosomes, gonads and genitals at birth were congruent, therefore they had to undergo psychological therapies to reconcile mind and body; rather, medicine acknowledged that it was more appropriate to alter the person's physical body, where possible, suitable and required, to correspond with the person's sense of self as male or female.[59] Despite this flexibility in medicine, law continued to maintain the need for consistency between judgements and certainty of legal sex.[60] This divergence of approaches can be explained by the functions and roles of the two systems: the function of medicine was to determine in which sex it was most appropriate

---

52 Ethical Standards in Public Life etc. (Scotland) Act 2000 s.34.
53 Local Government Act 2003 s.122.
54 See Katy Greenland and Rosalind Nunney, 'The Repeal of Section 28: It Ain't Over 'Til It's Over' (2008) 26:4 *Pastoral Care in Education* 243–251.
55 [1983] QB 1053.
56 See *Corbett* (n 25).
57 Questions around the aetiology of gender variance continue now. For an overview of this, see Gray (n 10).
58 For an overview of Benjamin's contribution to this area, see *inter alia* Benjamin (n 14); Harry Benjamin 'In Re: Transsexualism' (1974) 10:2 *The Journal of Sex Research* 173–175.
59 See Gray (n 10).
60 Through this period, the law continued to determine one's legal sex based on biology at birth (based on *Corbett*) and registration in the birth register (based on *X, Petitioner*). It was only in 2005 when the GRA 2004 came into force that an alternative means of determining legal sex was made available. However, it must be noted that the approach in the GRA 2004 is not flexible but rather mandates a very rigid approach to changing one's legal sex. Questions around the ability of the law to provide for a more fluid recognition of one's gender identity are now only just being asked in the second decade of the 21st century.

for the individual to live because the role of medicine was to ease the dysphoria experienced by the patient. Whereas the function of law was to definitively determine as which legal sex one should be classified, because the role of law was to regulate 'the relations between persons, and between persons and the state or community'.[61]

However, although the domestic courts were still adhering to *Corbett* in relation to trans cases, the European Court of Human Rights (ECtHR) began the slow development of SOGI rights, as aspects of private life within Article 8 of the European Convention on Human Rights (ECHR). In 1981, *Dudgeon v United Kingdom*[62] challenged the criminalisation of male homosexual activity in Northern Ireland. The ECtHR held, agreeing with the applicant, that Northern Irish law violated his Article 8 ECHR right to respect for private life.[63] In relation to alleged violations of Article 8 ECHR the ECtHR, in the 1980s and 1990s, found in favour of homosexual applicants a number of times,[64] thus developing the right to respect for one's sexual orientation, but it was not until much later that the ECtHR developed the right to respect for one's gender identity. Indeed, it could be argued that the Court is still to achieve full legal respect for gender identity, as the ECHR protections have proved to be limited to very specific circumstances, as will be shown in the next section.

2.3 The 1980s and 1990s

In relation to trans rights, there was little activity in relation to the law until 1986 when there began a long, ultimately unsuccessful, campaign in the ECtHR brought by transsexual applicants against the UK government.[65] These cases primarily concerned the rights of the applicants under Article 8, in relation to amending birth certificates, and 12 ECHR, in relation to the right to marry.

The facts of *Rees, Cossey* and *Sheffield and Horsham* were very similar. In *Rees*, the applicant was AFAB and lived as male, and in *Cossey* the applicant was AMAB and lived as female as were the applicants in *Sheffield and Horsham*. In each of these cases, the applicants had been diagnosed with gender identity disorder and had been provided with treatment by the NHS in order to align their bodies with their gender identity. *X, Y & Z* concerned three applicants:

---

61 *Corbett* (n 25) 105[D].
62 (1982) 4 EHRR 149.
63 *Dudgeon* (n 62) 168.
64 See *Laskey, Jaggard and Brown v United Kingdom* (1997) 24 EHRR 39; 31 EHRR 33; *Norris v United Kingdom* (1989) 13 EHRR 186; *Lustig-Prean and Beckett v United Kingdom* (1999) 29 EHRR 548; *Smith and Grady v United Kingdom* (1999) 29 EHRR 493.
65 *Rees v United Kingdom* (1987) 9 EHRR 56; *Cossey v United Kingdom* (1991) 13 EHRR 622; *X, Y & Z v United Kingdom* (1997) 24 EHRR 143; *Sheffield and Horsham v United Kingdom* (1999) 27 EHRR 163.

the first was AFAB and lived as male, the second was a cisgender woman with whom the first applicant was in a relationship and the third was the child of the second applicant. The third applicant had been conceived by means of artificial insemination by donor (AID). The first applicant was then denied the ability to register as the child's father because he was not a biological man.[66] The child was allowed to be registered using the first applicant's surname. In each of these cases, the ECtHR held that there were no violations of either Article 8 or Article 12.

Throughout the 1980s and 1990s, the ECtHR was not willing to find in favour of trans applicants when the cases challenged provisions in UK domestic law.[67] In addition to these cases arising in the ECtHR, other cases continued in the UK courts during this time. In January 1996, the case of *J v ST*[68] went before the Family Division of the High Court. This case concerned a marriage between a woman and her husband who had been AFAB but was living as male. The couple married in 1977; however, prior to this, the husband had undergone medical transition. The wife petitioned for divorce in 1994, and it was claimed that it was only during the divorce proceedings that her husband's birth certificate was made available, and that she discovered that her husband had been born female. Therefore, on this basis, rather than divorce, she applied for, and was granted, a decree of nullity. The case does not consider, in depth, how legal sex is determined. However, Russell LJ observed that medical evidence, which provided that there may well be a psychological or brain differentiation reason for trans identity, 'may indeed be correct but that will not do so far as capacity to marry is concerned in England and Wales'.[69] Russell LJ observed the developments in the ECtHR jurisprudence, as discussed earlier, and noted that these 'are not binding upon me but seem, at any rate up to the present, to sustain the law in England and Wales as far as marriage is concerned when dealing with transsexuals'.[70] He continued '[i]t may well be that in many respects a transsexual should be and is treated as having acquired a different gender but not so far as marriage is concerned in this country'.[71] In making this claim, Russell LJ restated the *Corbett* position that sex is fixed at birth based on physiology and ignoring psychology (i.e. ignoring gender identity). The case

---

66 An interesting legal argument around trans peoples' parentage status is currently going through the English courts. See *R (on the application of McConnell v Registrar General for England and Wales* [2020] EWCA Civ 559.
67 However, in one case in the 1990s, the ECtHR was willing to find in favour of a transsexual applicant: *B v France* (1993) 16 E.H.R.R. 1. It has to be noted though that the law in France was such that it was easier to find in favour of the applicant, and the lack of precedent in the ECtHR meant that ultimately this case had no impact on the rights of UK domiciled trans applicants.
68 [1996] 2 FCR 665.
69 *Ibid.*, 676[D]-[E].
70 *Ibid.*, 677[B].
71 *Ibid.*

was then appealed to the Court of Appeal later in 1996,[72] which affirmed the Family Division judgement and restated that the correct test in law was that established in *Corbett*.[73]

Whereas the ECtHR and domestic courts were reluctant to find in favour of trans individuals through the 1980s and 1990s, the employment rights of trans individuals took a particularly positive path. The year 1996 is notable, as it was the year in which the then European Court of Justice (ECJ) delivered its judgement in what has since become one of the landmark trans rights cases. In *P v S and Cornwall County Council*,[74] P was AMAB and transitioned to female. She was dismissed from her job when she informed her employer that she would be undergoing sex re-assignment. P raised an action against her employer based on sex discrimination. The Industrial Tribunal held that the SDA 1975 did not cover P's situation, as there was no sex discrimination since she would have been treated in exactly the same way had she been AFAB and was seeking sex re-assignment to become male. One of the problems faced by the Industrial Tribunal was the question of whether or not the Equal Treatment Directive[75] could apply in the present case, and a preliminary ruling was sought from the ECJ on that matter. The ECJ confirmed that the Equal Treatment Directive applied to those who had transitioned, were in the process of transitioning or were proposing to transition.[76]

In reaching this conclusion, the ECJ held that the general right of all citizens not to be discriminated against was a fundamental human right.[77] It was noted that the protection under the Equal Treatment Directive was not based on one being one sex or the other but also arose in relation to discrimination resulting from one undergoing sex re-assignment,[78] because to treat someone less favourably because they were undergoing sex re-assignment amounted to less favourable treatment between that person and someone of their birth sex,[79] and therefore, this was contrary to the Equal Treatment Directive.[80] The legal position that determined the decision in *White* was overruled by the ECJ's decision in *P v S and Cornwall County Council*, which was subsequently affirmed in the case of *Chessington World of Adventures Ltd v Reed*.[81] Shortly thereafter, the UK government amended the SDA 1975 to expressly prohibit discrimination

---

72 [1998] Fam 103.
73 *Ibid.*, 146.
74 [1996] 2 CMLR 247.
75 76/207/EEC.
76 This is the same as the current protection against discrimination based on gender reassignment in the Equality Act 2010.
77 *P v S and Cornwall County Council* (n 74) [22].
78 *Ibid.*, 20.
79 *Ibid.*, 21.
80 *Ibid.*, 22.
81 [1998] ICR 97.

on the basis of gender reassignment.[82] The Sex Discrimination (Gender Reassignment) Regulations 1999 amended the SDA 1975 by inserting s.2A, which provided that trans people were protected from discrimination in the workplace and in relation to vocational training.

Despite these changes, the employment discrimination cases that followed were of mixed success.[83] Arguably though, these cases were not determined using the *Corbett* test but rather on the basis of EU equal treatment laws. It is argued therefore that the success in employment law cases is as a result of two factors: EU law prohibiting discrimination and the fact that sex was rarely considered to be an essential element of the employment contract.[84] So, to some extent, progress was being made in relation to trans rights but really only in very limited circumstances and only for those who had transitioned, were transitioning or intended to transition. However, the rights were piecemeal and derived from different sources of law, and thereby began to create inconsistency for trans people before UK law; in family law, individuals' gender identity was not recognised at all, whereas in employment law, protection against discrimination began at a pre-medical transition stage when the individual expressed an intention to undergo sex re-assignment. The law, however, did not protect those individuals who identified as non-binary, those individuals who were unable to obtain a diagnosis of GID or those individuals who may have obtained a diagnosis but who determined not to undergo sex reassignment; the protections offered under the SDA only applied to a very specific narrowly defined group of individuals.[85]

3. The 21st Century and the Right to Recognition of One's Gender Identity

The start of the 21st century was key in the development of the law in relation to trans rights. The year 2002 saw the start of two cases – one in the UK courts and one in the ECtHR – which, when combined, put pressure on the UK government to amend the law. In *Bellinger v Bellinger*, both the Family Division[86] and the Court of Appeal[87] refused to recognise gender identity

---

82 Sex Discrimination (Gender Reassignment) Regulations 1999, SI 1999/1102.
83 *Bavin v NHS Trust Pension Agency* [1999] ICR 1192; *Ashton v Chief Constable of West Mercia* [2001] ICR 67; *Chief Constable of West Yorkshire Police v A* [2002] ICR 552; *Chief Constable of West Yorkshire Police v A* [2002] EWCA Civ 1584; [2003] 1 CMLR 25.
84 Although please note the decision in *White* discussed earlier, where the sex of the applicant was considered a genuine occupational qualification under domestic law, thereby making sex an essential element of the employment contract.
85 Martin Mitchell and Charlie Howarth, 'Trans Research Review' *Equality and Human Rights Commission Research Report* (2009) 27; 4.
86 [2002] 3 FCR 733.
87 [2001] EWCA Civ 1141; [2002] Fam 150.

for the purpose of marriage. However, before the *Bellinger* appeal was heard in the House of Lords, the ECtHR held in *Goodwin v United Kingdom*[88] that the UK's continued non-recognition of post-operative trans people amounted to a violation of both Articles 8 and 12 thus firmly acknowledging one's SOGI rights within the ECHR. As a result of *Goodwin*, the House of Lords in the final *Bellinger* appeal[89] issued a declaration of incompatibility under s.4 of the Human Rights Act 1998 providing that English marriage law that refused to recognise post-operative trans peoples' status was incompatible with Article 8 jurisprudence. These developments by the ECtHR and domestic courts in the early 21st century resulted in the enactment of the GRA 2004, which provides that for almost all legal purposes, those who have obtained a full GRC are to be treated as members of the sex opposite to that registered at birth.[90] The GRA 2004 was considered ground-breaking[91] and radical[92] when it was enacted, and at the time it placed 'the UK at the forefront of global transgender law reform'.[93] In one enactment, the UK went from being one of the most resistant states to one of the most progressive in terms of trans rights. The main positive of the GRA 2004 was that it required no body modification to be undertaken before one could apply to obtain a GRC. Thus, one of the most radical aspects of the legislation is that, in theory at least, it recognises that one's gender identity is not necessarily linked to how one appears to others or indeed how one presents oneself. For brevity, the process required in the law to obtain a GRC will not be covered here.[94]

4. Current Climate

4.1 An Overview

As can be seen from the discussion of the development of the law in relation to trans rights, the fact that the GRA 2004 was passed can be seen as a huge step forward. In addition, in relation to sexual orientation rights, the fact that those in a same-sex relationship can marry, enter a civil partnership, adopt,

---

88 (2002) 35 EHRR 18.
89 [2003] UKHL 21; [2003] 2 AC 467.
90 Gender Recognition Act 2004 s.9. Exceptions apply in relation to parentage (s.12), succession (s.15), peerages (s.16) and gender-specific offences (s.20). Section 19 provided an exception applicable to sport, but this was repealed and replaced by a similar provision in s.195 of the Equality Act 2010.
91 Sharon Cowan, 'Looking Back (to)wards the Body: Medicalization and the GRA' (2009) 18:2 *Social and Legal Studies* 247–252, 247.
92 Sheila Jeffreys, 'They Know It When They See it: The UK Gender Recognition Act 2004' (2008) 10:2 *British Journal of Politics & International Relations* 328–345, 328.
93 A Sharpe, 'A Critique of the Gender Recognition Act 2004' (2007) 4 *Journal of Bioethical Inquiry* 33–42, 37.
94 For an overview of this, see Gray (n 10).

undergo fertility treatment as a couple and largely live their private lives with dignity and respect free from state interference would indicate that we have, on the whole, achieved substantive equality for most LGBT individuals in the UK. However, this is perhaps not as accurate as it first appears as recent events have now highlighted.

The proposals of both the Westminster government and the Scottish government[95] to reform the law relating to gender recognition, alongside recent media reports of campaigning against relationship education in primary schools where same-sex relationships are taught to children alongside teaching about single-parent families and opposite-sex relationships,[96] and the recent reports of a straight Pride march in the USA[97] show that there is a tension whereby those of us who identify as LGBT are becoming increasingly the targets of homophobic, biphobic and transphobic comments in the media, online and offline. For those of us who identify as LGBT, there is a growing sense of hostility and fear from some of the community that such anti-LGBT comments and attacks are, not necessarily encouraged, but increasing in frequency, and that there seems little attempt to challenge them. The campaign for reform of the GRA 2004 is an ideal example of this growing hostility towards the, in particular trans, minority. As a supporter for reform of the GRA 2004, these proposals were welcomed and indeed celebrated; however, the consultation and the backlash following the consultation, including the stalling of the reform[98] and the recently reported tension between elected officials at Holyrood,[99] provide a sense that these reforms are at risk of not progressing or indeed being amended in such a way as to remove some of their potential strengths.[100] Indeed, the proposed reforms fall short of what campaigners seek, in particular in relation to non-binary legal recognition and the rights of young people to have their gender identity recognised.

95 See (n 5).
96 See (n 2).
97 See (n 1).
98 Severin Carrell, 'Scotland to Run New Consultations Before Updating Gender Law' *The Guardian*, 20 June 2019. <www.theguardian.com/uk-news/2019/jun/20/scotland-to-run-new-consultations-before-updating-gender-law> (accessed 4 June 2020).
99 Gina Davidson, 'Kate Forbes at Centre of New SNP Row Over Trans Rights' *The Scotsman*, 10 February 2020. <www.scotsman.com/news/scottish-news/kate-forbes-centre-new-snp-row-over-trans-rights-1555422> (accessed 4 June 2020); 'SNP MSPs Criticise Nicola Sturgeon Over Trans Rights' *BBC*, 17 April 2019 <www.bbc.co.uk/news/uk-scotland-47960446> (accessed 4 June 2020); Libby Brooks, 'Several Women "Close to Quitting SNP Over Gender Recognition Plans"' *The Guardian*, 14 October 2019. <www.theguardian.com/uk-news/2019/oct/14/snp-women-close-to-quitting-gender-recognition-proposals-trans-rights-scotland> (accessed 4 June 2020).
100 The Gender Recognition Reform (Scotland) Bill was delayed following the Covid-19 pandemic and not reintroduced during the previous parliamentary term. At the time of writing, there were plans to introduce the Bill in Parliamentary Term 2021/22, but that the Bill would not provide for the recognition of non-binary gender identity and, although welcomed, does not go as far as campaigners would like.

4.2 Understanding the Current Climate

As noted in the preceding discussion, one of the key drivers behind the achievement of LGBT rights has been the human rights narrative developed by NGOs, campaign groups and indeed principally by the ECtHR through the development of SOGI rights within Article 8 ECHR. However, this human rights discourse may also be part of the reason for the current backlash against further reform of the law in this area. Hunt argues that any form of national, or even international, attempt to legislate for the rights of sexual minority groups is 'frequently conceptualised as an attempt to forge innovative forms of citizenship and social equality'.[101] It is this sense of forging 'innovative forms of citizenship and social equality' that might indeed be part of the reason for the backlash against the further development of SOGI rights, in particular those rights for trans people. What is being seen now is a very strong balance, or conflict, of rights: the right to be oneself and be able to live without interference versus the right of others to object, the latter often being expressed as a form of freedom of expression or freedom of religion/belief issue.[102] This conflict of rights can be illustrated by the recent decision of the Employment Appeals Tribunal in *Forstater v CGD Europe*,[103] in which it was held that the belief that biological sex is immutable and cannot be changed and that biological sex cannot be conflated with gender identity amounts to a protected philosophical belief under the Equality Act 2010. Hunt argues that accompanying SOGI rights for LGBT people is a growing restatement of the right to object to such rights acquisition. He claims:

> the liberty to object to such minority sexual rights is frequently advanced in contexts of religious freedom of expression and belief, which, in turn, engage with older conceptions of the civil rights of the citizen which have long been viewed as a bulwark against state-imposed secularism.[104]

So, what we may be witnessing now is a growing anti-LGBT movement deriving from the growth of a conservative Right.[105] Some may argue that this

---

101 Stephen Hunt, 'Christian Lobbyist Groups and the Negotiation of Sexual Rights in the UK' (2014) 29:1 *Journal of Contemporary Religion* 121–136, 122.
102 See the debates in the USA around religious freedom versus the rights of LGBT people. See also Kimberly Saindon, 'Religious Freedom Legislation in Texas Takes Aim at Same-Sex Marriage' (2017) 23 *Texas Journal of Civil Liberties & Civil Rights* 165.
103 [2021] I.R.L.R. 706.
104 Hunt (n 101) 122.
105 Note that this is not to say that all of those who adopt a conservative position oppose SOGI rights, but rather that the main opposition voice against such rights would appear to come from those who adopt a politically conservative outlook; this is particularly evident in the USA. For developments in Europe, see Jelena Dzankic, 'The Rise of the Far Right in Europe: Populist Shifts and Othering' (2017) 55 *Journal of Common Market Studies* 1185.

anti-LGBT movement is religious and a push back against the secularisation of mostly Western society, but this would be an incomplete analysis. What the anti-LGBT rights movement is showing globally is a growth of the conservative Right and an attempt to undermine the 'innovative forms of citizenship and social equality' that Hunt mentions. This is not a particularly new phenomenon, but it has certainly gathered pace in recent years and can be linked with a growth in global right-wing populist politics. Mudde's definition of populism is particularly useful here. He claims that populism is

> an ideology that considers society to be ultimately separated into two homogeneous and antagonistic groups, 'the pure people' versus 'the corrupt elite', and which argues that politics should be an expression of the volonté générale (general will) of the people.[106]

This idea of a corrupt or even liberal elite at odds with the general population of a country appears often in the literature around populism in general[107] but also in relation to the anti-LGBT movement,[108] and it can be situated in the context of globalised human rights. As noted earlier, a lot of the work done in furtherance of LGBT rights was a result of framing the issue as one of basic, global, human rights, much of which was done in the first decade of the 21st century.[109]

However, within the context of global SOGI rights, there are 'oppositional movements' that focus 'on reasserting various forms of heteronormative privilege that refine our understanding of contemporary sexual and gendered landscapes'.[110] When such a movement gathers pace such that minority rights become reframed as a threat in some way to the majority,[111] then there is a risk that, where such populist opinions prevail, 'the basic problem is well known; since a majority can easily trample on the rights of a minority, limitations on its influence are sometimes necessary to protect minority rights'.[112] So, what is needed is for people to continue to acknowledge that LGBT rights, although

---

106 Cas Mudde, 'The Populist Zeitgeist' (2004) 39:4 *Government and Opposition* 541–563, 543.
107 See *Ibid*; Roger Eatwell and Matthew Goodwin, *National Populism: The Revolt Against Liberal Democracy* (Pelican 2018); Conrad Ziller and Thomas Schubel, 'The Pure People" Versus "the Corrupt Elite"? Political Corruption, Political Trust and the Success of Radical Rights Parties in Europe' (2015) 25:3 *Journal of Elections, Public Opinion and Parties* 368–386.
108 Amy L Stone, 'The Impact of Anti-Gay Politics on the LGBTQ Movement' (2016) 10:6 *Sociology Compass* 459–467; Phillip Ayoub, 'With Arms Wide Shut: Threat Perception, Norm Reception, and Mobilized Resistance to LGBT Rights' (2014) 13 *Journal of Human Rights* 337–362.
109 Katherine Browne and Catherine J Nash 'Resisting LGBT Rights Where "We Have Won": Canada and Great Britain' (2014) 13:3 *Journal of Human Rights* 322–336, 324.
110 *Ibid.*, 324.
111 See Ayoub (n 108).
112 Christine Pappas, Jeanette Mendez, and Rebekah Herrick, 'The Negative Effects of Populism on Gay and Lesbian Rights' (2009) 90:1 *Social Science Quarterly* 150–163, 150.

having made huge progress since the 1950s, continue to be fragile and require to be upheld and fought for. For Pappas *et al*, the shift towards right-wing populist ideologies 'increase the likelihood that the majority preferences will prevail. An unfettered majority is likely to trample minority rights, especially if a minority is not viewed positively by society'.[113]

In the UK, at least, it is heartening to know that the position is not as dire as in some other States,[114] but it is worrying given the various protests already discussed elsewhere in this chapter particularly in relation to the further development of laws relating to recognition of gender identity. Additionally, albeit statistically insignificant at this point, the 2019 British Attitude Survey showed that there had been a 2% dip in the British public's acceptance of same-sex relationships.[115] The report also showed that 22% of the UK population were outwardly unsupportive of same-sex relationships to some extent with a further 6% not committing one way or another.[116] Additionally, in relation to thoughts about trans people, the survey showed that 15% were willing to admit to being very or a little prejudiced towards trans individuals,[117] and 6% believe that prejudice towards trans people is rarely or never wrong.[118] What was more striking from this report, and which resonates with the warnings issued by Pappas *et al* mentioned earlier, is that only 34% of the British public believed that prejudice against trans people was mostly or sometimes wrong:[119] the majority therefore either not answering or believing that prejudice against trans people is acceptable. The results of this survey, along with the mobilisation of groups willing to campaign outwardly against LGBT issues,[120] raise the possibility that support for LGBT rights in the UK may have reached a pinnacle in the early 21st century and could be about to change.

This appears theoretical and illusory, but the way in which the campaign for reform of the GRA 2004 has operated in the media to the extent that a growing number of people are now willing to publicly campaign against trans rights — to the extent that there are claims from some that trans women are

---

113 *Ibid.*, 151.
114 In May 2020, the Hungarian parliament voted to end legal recognition of trans people's gender identity – see Shaun Walker, 'Hungary Votes to End Legal Recognition of Trans People' *The Guardian*, 19 May 2020. <www.theguardian.com/world/2020/may/19/hungary-votes-to-end-legal-recognition-of-trans-people> (accessed 4 June 2020).
115 John Curtice, Elisabeth Clery, Jane Perry, Miranda Phillips, and Nilufer Rahim (eds), *British Social Attitudes: The 36th Report* (The National Centre for Social Research 2019).
116 See *Ibid.*, 125.
117 See *Ibid.*
118 See *Ibid.*
119 See *Ibid.*, 126.
120 See, for example, the campaigning by the LGB Alliance, which campaigns against trans issues and has been labelled as transphobic.

not 'real' women, etc.[121] – shows that this threat to the rights of LGBT people is very real. One of the themes of a right-wing populism is of rational people versus the liberal elite, where the 'legal system is seen to persecute traditionalists (rather than protect LGBT people)'.[122] Often, remarks by those seeking to speak out against the furtherance of such rights claim to be upholding freedom of speech and, to some extent, democracy itself. For Korolczuk and Graff, the world is witnessing an important conceptual shift away from global human rights towards a more local illiberal politics – which strangely is itself a global movement – within which 'the key ideologues are self-proclaimed defenders of freedom and democracy, which in their view have been hijacked by liberals and leftists'.[123] Within this framework, LGBT rights are seen as a project of the liberal elite and contrary to the interests of the general population. Korolczuk and Graff claim that this can be termed 'antigenderism', which is 'a coherent ideological construction consciously and effectively used by right-wing and religious fundamentalists worldwide',[124] which 'while selectively borrowing from liberal-Left and feminist discourses, is in fact constructing a new universalism, an illiberal one, that replaces individual rights with rights of the family as a basic societal unit and depicts religious conservatives as an embattled minority'.[125] There is an 'aggressive use of the language of "family values"'[126] within a lot of the anti-LGBT comments at the moment, particularly around the teaching of relationships within primary schools. What we are witnessing is a transnational illiberal agenda being played out locally to the detriment of LGBT individuals through framing us in an ideological fight against traditionalists who are posited as the discriminated against majority merely seeking to protect what is 'normal' from the liberal elite LGBT agenda.[127]

So, SOGI rights, at this point in the 21st century, are at the centre of a transnational right-wing populist movement, which seeks to reassert traditional family values and restate the naturalness of heteronormativity. Unfortunately, this means that the more vocal these anti-LGBT campaigners become, the

---

121 For an excellent response to these issues, see Laura Finlayson, Katharine Jenkins and Rosie Worsdale, '"I'm not transphobic, but . . .": a feminist case against the feminist case against trans inclusivity' <www.versobooks.com/blogs/4090-i-m-not-transphobic-but-a-feminist-case-against-the-feminist-case-against-trans-inclusivity> 17 October 2018 (accessed 4 June 2020).
122 Browne and Nash (n 109) 331.
123 Elzbieta Korolczuk and Agnieszka Graff, 'Gender as "Ebola from Brussels": The Anticolonial Frame and the Rise of Illiberal Populism' (2018) 43:4 *Signs: Journal of Women in Culture and Society* 797–821, 799.
124 Ibid., 798.
125 Ibid.
126 Ibid.
127 Ibid., 799.

more risk there is to rights for LGBT people either stalling,[128] or indeed being eroded.[129]

5. Conclusion

This chapter has shown the development of trans rights in the UK through the initial challenges to registration of births and birth certificates to the final acquisition of the SOGI rights that are enjoyed today. However, as can be seen, there is a challenge not just to the development of these rights beyond what exists now but also to their continued existence and to LGBT peoples' very right to exist and be spoken of. The campaign against teaching children of primary school age that families include single-parent families as well as same-sex families and the campaign against allowing transwomen into women only spaces – indeed challenging whether trans women are 'real' women, whether trans men are 'real' men or indeed whether or not there is such a thing as non-binary identity – along with the (small) decrease in acceptance of same-sex relationships in the latest BSA survey – has highlighted that SOGI rights are fragile and are under attack from a global rise in right-wing populist politics seeking to reassert heteronormativity, and we must therefore remain vocal, and vigilant, in advocating for our rights as LGBT people lest these rights be taken away.

---

128 As was seen with the delay to the reform of the Gender Recognition Act 2004 in Westminster where it now seems very unlikely that such reform will take place.
129 As was seen in Hungary in May 2020 where the parliament voted to remove rights of recognition for trans people.

Chapter 9

In the Name of the People? Plebiscites, Referendums and Same-Sex Marriage

Paul Behrens

1. Introduction

When, on 22 May 2015, the result of the Irish referendum on same-sex marriage was announced, the news were met with delight by members of the LGBT+ community, their friends and allies.[1] With 62% voting in favour,[2] it seemed legitimate to speak of a resounding affirmation of same-sex marriage.

In light of such developments, it is tempting to consider referendums the best way of achieving marriage equality. In fact, some observers compared this option favourably to alternatives that had been pursued in other jurisdictions: in the case of France, for instance, it was noted that same-sex marriage appeared to have been 'imposed by French President Francois Hollande from the top down'.[3]

And yet, this particular aspect of LGBT+ rights invites more discerning consideration. The outcomes of referendums are dependent on temporal and spatial parameters: at another point in time, a referendum in the same country might have led to very different results, and a referendum held in the same year in a fellow European State (Slovenia) did result in a strong majority against same-sex marriage.[4]

Nor could it be said that the use of direct democracy in this field is always free from legal controversy. In Australia, advocates of same-sex marriage themselves brought a court challenge against a 'postal survey' on that matter;[5] in

---

1 Henry McDonald, 'Ireland Becomes First Country to Legalise Gay Marriage by Popular Vote' *Guardian* 23 May 2015; Government of Ireland, 'Referendum Results 1937–2019', 92–93 <www.gov.ie/en/publication/32ea7-1937-2019-referendum-results/>.
2 McDonald (n 1); Government of Ireland (n 1).
3 Dave Keating, 'How Has Ireland's Gay Rights Referendum Changed Activism?' *EU Observer*, 2 November 2015 <https://euobserver.com/health-and-society/130908>.
4 National Electoral Commission of Slovenia, 'Porčilo No 042–3/2015–108', 18 February 2016. <https://web.archive.org/web/20160312010226/www.volitve.gov.si/referendum/ref_zzzdrd_porocilo.pdf>.
5 *Wilkie v The Commonwealth; Australian Marriage Equality v Cormann* [2017] HCA 40.

DOI: 10.4324/9781003286295-12

Costa Rica, the Constitutional Court put a stop to a 2010 initiative for a referendum on civil unions.[6]

Referendums on same-sex marriage thus invite questions that merit more detailed examination. In this chapter, a brief overview of the use of referendums in this field is provided (section 2), followed by a critical evaluation of the reasons commonly named for the employment of referendums – including their apparent contribution to the democratic legitimacy of the decision-making process (3.1), constitutional arguments (3.2) and their perceived ability to provide stable solutions (3.3). But the chapter also raises the question whether judicial decision-making can provide an alternative that avoids some of the difficulties referendums invite – especially in view of the possible lack of expertise of the decision-maker (4.1), their polarising effect (4.2), the problem of settling minority rights through majority decisions (4.3) and the need for the relevant decisions to comply with international law (4.4). The final part (5) offers considerations on the question whether there are difficulties that neither courts nor direct democracy can satisfactorily resolve and suggests solutions which may carry a potential which neither of the other options are able to realise.

2. History and Concepts

Efforts to involve direct democracy in the regulation of same-sex marriage can be traced back to the end of the 20th century. In 2000, California became one of the first jurisdictions in which the legalisation of same-sex marriage was put to the voters.[7] The matter before them was Proposition 22, which would have amended the Family Code to state that 'only marriage between a man and a woman is valid or recognized in California'.[8] The Proposition was adopted with 61.35%;[9] but, as will be seen, this was only the first stage in a complex story.[10]

The extent to which direct democracy plays a part in decision-making depends on the relevant State's constitutional structure. In the USA, for instance,

---

6 Constitutional Chamber of the Supreme Court, application no. 10–008331–007-CO, Decision No. 2010013313 (30 June 2010) <www.tse.go.cr/juris/relevantes/SSC-10-013313.html> and see below at 4.3.
7 The topic of same-sex marriage had, however, arisen in other initiatives before: in Hawaii, an amendment was put to the voters in 1998, under which the constitution of that State would have been changed to allow the legislature to reserve marriage to spouses of the opposite sex. Almost 70% of voters agreed to that amendment. Government of Hawaii, Office of Elections, 'Summary Report', 11 April 1998. <https://files.hawaii.gov/elections/files/results/1998/general/histatewide.pdf> (at 4).
8 Government of California, Legislative Analyst's Office, 'Proposition 22' (2000). <https://lao.ca.gov/ballot/2000/22_03_2000.html>; Todd Steenson, 'United States: Supreme Court Dismisses California's Proposition 8 Same-Sex Marriage Case' *Mondaq Business Briefing*, 9 July 2013.
9 California Secretary of State, Elections and Voter Information, 'Statement of Vote' (2000) <https://elections.cdn.sos.ca.gov/sov/2000-primary/sov-complete.pdf>, at xxx.
10 See below at 3.3.

referendums (despite an initial reluctance of the founders regarding direct democracy)[11] have been part of the legal system of several States, especially from the 20th century onwards, and the appearance of same-sex marriage as a subject of public votes may therefore not seem surprising.[12]

Other States show a great degree of variation in their willingness to resort to direct democracy, and the very possibility of making same-sex marriage the topic of a people's vote does not always exist. The founders of the German Federal Republic, for instance, showed a reluctance similar to that of their American counterparts and envisaged referendums on the federal level only in very limited scenarios.[13]

But the same does not hold true of all States.

Croatia in 2013 held a referendum on a constitutional amendment defining marriage as a union between a man and a woman (resulting in an almost two-thirds majority in favour);[14] Slovakia held a referendum on banning same-sex marriage in 2015;[15] Ireland and Slovenia held referendums in the same year.[16] In a Bermudan referendum in 2016, voters were asked whether they were in favour of same-sex marriages and in favour of civil unions,[17] and a 2019 referendum in Taiwan contained several questions on same-sex marriage, including some advanced by a traditionalist Christian group, asking voters whether they agreed that 'marriage defined in the Civil Code should be restricted to the union between one man and one woman'.[18]

Even this short overview allows reflections on certain aspects of direct democracy, which at least put the initial positive reaction to the Irish referendum in perspective.

For one, the consideration of referendums as a principal way of achieving marriage equality requires repositioning. Referendums can be advanced by both sides on the divide; in more than one instance, a referendum was put forward by those who were opposed to same-sex marriage.[19]

---

11 See, for a discussion of this matter, Franz-Stefan Gady, 'Brexit: The American Founding Fathers Had It Right: Direct Democracy Is a Dead Duck' *The Diplomat*, 25 June 2016.
12 See below at 3.3.
13 Arts 29 and 146 of the German Basic Law (1949 BGBl 1).
14 Elzbieta Kuzelewska, 'Same-Sex Marriage – A Happy End Story? The Effectiveness of Referendum [sic] on Same-Sex Marriage in Europe' (2019) 24 *Bialstockie Studia Prawnicze* 13, 19.
15 *Ibid.*, 15.
16 Above, Section 1.
17 Bermuda, Referendum (Same Sex Relationships) Notice 2016 BR 40/2016. <www.bermudalaws.bm/Laws/Annual%20Laws/2016/Statutory%20Instruments/Referendum%20(Same%20Sex%20Relationships)%20Notice%202016.pdf>.
18 Chao-ju Chen, 'Migrating Marriage Equality Without Feminism: Obergefell v. Hodges and the Legalization of Same-Sex Marriage in Taiwan' (2019) 52 *Cornell International Law Journal* 65, 86; Scott Morgan, 'Same-Sex Marriage Referendums: Taiwan Civil Code to Remain Unchanged' *Taiwan News*, 24 November 2018, 86.
19 See above, at n 18 and below at 3.3.

Secondly, not every referendum relating to same-sex marriage has the same significance: the consequences depend on the relevant constitutional framework. At one end are referendums that may (directly or indirectly) effect a change in the constitution. Examples for this were provided by Proposition 8 in California in 2008, amending the State constitution by providing that marriage was between one man and one woman,[20] and indeed by the Irish referendum in 2015, after the Irish President signed the new law into effect.[21]

In other cases, referendums can change simple (non-constitutional) laws.[22] But direct democracy can also be employed to introduce a bill in the legislature. That was the case in Finland in 2013, when a campaign in favour of same-sex marriage gathered three times the amount of signatures required for a 'citizens' initiative' – a method allowing a particular initiative to be sent to Parliament.[23] The authority to make a decision on the matter thus stayed with Parliament; Parliament retained its right to go against the wishes of the supporters of the initiative.[24]

In some situations, the entirely consultative character of a people's vote is clear from the outset (the Bermudan non-binding referendum on same-sex marriage in 2016 is an example).[25] In the weakest form of a people's vote on the issue, even the wording of the mechanism leaves no doubt about the lack of binding force. The form of direct democracy on which Australia eventually settled in that matter was a 'postal survey', held in 2017, and it is interesting to note that the distance to other forms of voting in that country was further enhanced by the fact that participation in that survey was voluntary[26] (Australia follows, in principle, a system of compulsory voting.).

3. The Ireland Factor: The Lure of the Referendum

3.1 Democratic Legitimacy

The evaluation of the Irish referendum on same-sex marriage in 2015 puts the legitimacy of the decision-making process in sharp focus. In democratic

---

20 Ken Klukowski, 'SCOTUS Considers Same-Sex Marriage, part I: Hollingsworth v Perry' *States News Service*, 26 March 2013.
21 President of Ireland, '2015 Legislation' <www.president.ie/en/the-president/2015-legislation> and see Thirty-Fourth Amendment of the Constitution (Marriage Equality) Act 2015.
22 See above, at n 8.
23 *Agence France Press – English*, 'Finland Takes First Step Towards Legalising Gay Marriage', 28 November 2014. Finland, Ministry of Justice, 'Kansalaisaloite tasa-arvoisesta avioliittolaista' <https://web.archive.org/web/20160111214304/www.kansalaisaloite.fi/fi/aloite/192>.
24 *Ibid.*
25 Michael Kirby, 'The Centenary of Sir Harry Gibbs: Constitutional Methodology, Lawmaking & the Marriage Plebiscite' (2016) 35 *University of Queensland Law Journal* 283, n 49. See above at n 17.
26 Paul Kildea, 'Australia's Same-Sex Marriage Survey: Evaluating a Unique Popular Vote Process' (2020) 46 *Monash University Law Review* 107.

systems, the identification of political arguments in favour of direct participation of the people in such processes would certainly not be a difficult task.

From a legal perspective, the same conclusion cannot be reached with the same ease. The very existence of a right to democracy under international law has courted criticism,[27] although the establishment of its basic foundations is arguably possible. At the very least, the right to self-determination, as enshrined in the International Covenant on Civil and Political Rights (ICCPR) and the International Covenant on Economic, Social and Cultural Rights (ICESCR), embraces a people's right to 'freely determine their political status',[28] a determination that is difficult to realise without the right to take part in elections.[29]

But it would be a further step to derive from that a right to a particular form of democracy, let alone a right to have certain subject matters subjected to a direct vote.

The argument of 'legitimacy' furthermore raises the question whether the people are indeed the only carriers of legitimate decisions within a State. Such reasoning would ignore the fact that, even in democratic States, elements of decision-making are, by necessity, left to others. Quite apart from the fact that a large amount of technical decisions invariably have to be taken by the people's representatives in Parliament, it is also true that governments regularly retain a certain degree of law-making powers (most frequently, in the field of secondary legislation).[30]

While members of Parliament and even members of governments may feel beholden to their particular electorate, a clearer example for carriers of legitimacy who meet with acceptance in democracies but are guided by considerations outside electoral mandates is provided by the judiciary.[31] Where same-sex marriage is concerned, the judiciary certainly has played its role in decision-making processes – a point that became particularly clear in California, where the courts on various occasions took issue with the decision of the voters,[32] as well as in Taiwan, where the Constitutional Court in 2017 found that the ban on same-sex marriage violated the freedom of people to marry as well as the right to equality as guaranteed under the Taiwanese constitution.[33]

Yet even if democratic legitimacy were accepted as the sole factor playing a role in the determination of same-sex marriage, the implementation of that

---

27 For an overview of the discussion, see Cecile Vandewoude, 'The Rise of Self-Determination Versus the Rise of Democracy' (2010) 2 *Goettingen Journal of International Law* 981, 988–991.
28 Art 1 ICCPR (1966); Art 1 ICESCR (1966).
29 Art. 25 ICCPR; see also Paul Behrens, *Diplomatic Interference and the Law* (Hart Publishing 2016) 90.
30 In the UK, more than 3,000 Statutory Instruments are produced every year, Joel Blackwell, 'Delegated Legislation' *Hansard Society* <www.hansardsociety.org.uk/blog/delegated-legislation-frequently-asked-questions>.
31 But see on the point of judicial deference, below at n 93–98.
32 See below at n 52–57.
33 Taiwan Constitutional Court, *J. Y. Interpretation 748* (24 May 2017) at 13 and 16.

concept raises further questions. One of them relates to the composition of the electorate itself. If it is accepted that the decision should rest with the people, then who exactly composes the δημος, i.e. the specific electorate called upon to make the relevant decision?

The fact that the people are, under the ICCPR and the ICESCR, entitled to 'determine *their* political status'[34] appears to give contemporary guise to the Roman maxim *quod omnes tangit, ab omnes tractari et approbari debet* – that which affects everyone is to be deliberated and decided by everyone.[35] If taken as a basis for the legitimacy of determination by the people, that very mandate, however, is not without problems, where referendums on same-sex marriage are concerned. As a minority issue, the claim that same-sex marriage 'affects' the position of the electorate as a whole is not easy to defend. In that regard, it is helpful to keep sight of the fact that, in some fields, human rights law does accept certain restrictions on voting rights, where the alleged bearers of the right were 'less directly or continuously concerned' with the matter at hand.[36]

Even aside from that problem, the determination of the 'people's voice' can be a difficult matter. It is a problem that becomes particularly clear when a referendum has been decided on a very low turnout. If 30% of all eligible voters decide against the establishment of same-sex marriage, would it be right to assume that 'the people' have spoken?[37]

Domestic law sometimes recognises this difficulty and requires a minimum threshold for the referendum to generate any effects. When, for instance, in Slovakia in 2015 a majority of voters expressed themselves against same-sex marriage, the referendum was invalid, as the minimum turnout threshold had not been reached (only 21.4% of qualified voters participated, when the threshold was set at 50%).[38] Similarly, in the Bermudan referendum of 2016, the minimum threshold of 50% was missed, albeit by a much narrower margin (46.89% of all eligible voters participated).[39]

But such requirements do not exist everywhere, and the danger therefore exists that the matter is decided by a section of society that can hardly be said to be representative of 'the people'. In the 2015 Slovenian referendum on a bill

---

34 See above at n 28 (emphasis added).
35 See Gunther Teubner, 'Quod Omnes Tangit: Transnationale Verfassungen Ohne Demokratie?' (2018) 57:2 *Der Staat* 171, 176–177 on the historical derivation of the principle but offering also criticism on its blanket application to the field of democracy.
36 See ECtHR, *Melnychenko v Ukraine*, Application no. 17707/02 (19 October 2004), para 56; ECtHR *Pilav v Bosnia and Herzegovina*, Application no. 41939/07 (9 June 2016), para 44, both in relation to restrictions of voting rights for voters who were not resident in the relevant State.
37 See Kuzelewska (n 14) 19.
38 *Ibid.*, 18; *Agence France Presse – English*, 'Slovak vote on gay marriage, adoption ban a flop', 8 February 2015.
39 Bermuda, Parliamentary Registry, 'Summary' <www.elections.gov.bm/referendum-result/referendum.html?layout=view&kid=5>; US Official News, 'Bermuda Government Attempting to Repeal Marriage Equality', 16 November 2017.

allowing for same-sex marriage, turnout, at 36.38%, was certainly on the low side.[40] That, however, did not affect the validity of the referendum, and the bill was therefore defeated.[41]

The suggestion that it is easy to determine the will of the people appears as strongly founded on a romanticised version of the realities as the suggestion that the people's will can be established as 'settled fact'.

On matters like same-sex marriage, social attitudes are notoriously subject to change.[42] Yet if tools of direct democracy are seen as finding their foundation in the right of the people to determine their fate, then the argument underlying the requirement of the periodicity of elections[43] must, at least to a certain degree, apply here as well: in both cases, the 'people's view' is not necessarily cast in stone; the demographic composition of the electorate undergoes change as well. Subjecting same-sex marriage to changing majorities, however, invites difficulties in its own right – a point that will be revisited below.[44]

3.2 The Constitutional Argument

Depending on the constitutional framework of the State holding a referendum, supporters of a people's vote may be able to invoke a seemingly strong argument in favour of this mechanism. The constitution itself may embody the relevant position, and in some States, constitutional change may indeed only be achieved through a people's vote.

That was the case in the Irish situation: the Irish constitution was considered to contain an implied ban on same-sex marriage; but amendments to the Irish constitution had to be approved by the people.[45]

But even in instances of this kind, closer consideration may result in a more discerning assessment. To those seeking a change to the existing position, the possibility of obtaining the support of a constitutional mandate may appear particularly tempting. But a referendum may of course yield the opposite result, with the effect that the highest law of the political entity now supports the view of the other side on the divide. That was the case when Proposition 102 was put to the voters in Arizona in 2008.[46] The result of that initiative was a new provision in the constitution of the State, which now stated that '[o]nly a

---

40 Kuzelewska (n 14) 18.
41 *Ibid.*, 21, 22.
42 See, for an overview of changing UK attitudes, NatCen, 'Charting Changing Attitudes – Same-Sex Relationships', 27 July 2017. <www.natcen.ac.uk/blog/charting-changing-attitudes-%E2%80%93-same-sex-relationships>. See also below at 3.3.
43 See, eg, Art. 25(b) ICCPR.
44 See below at 3.3 and 4.3.
45 Art. 46(2) Constitution of Ireland (1937).
46 Government of Arizona, 'State of Arizona Official Canvass' <https://web.archive.org/web/20081219172036/www.azsos.gov/election/2008/General/Canvass2008GE.pdf> at 15.

union of one man and one woman shall be valid or recognized as a marriage in this state'.[47]

On the other hand, even the establishment of a new constitutional norm may not necessarily bring the high authority that its proposers envisage. In the aftermath of the Irish referendum, the vote was challenged on the basis that its result would be the adoption of a rule that clashed with other constitutional provisions. While this point was rejected by the Irish Court of Appeal,[48] the possibility of such a result cannot always be dismissed. It gains particular currency in States that recognise entrenched provisions in their constitutions (such as the 'eternity clause' of the German constitution)[49] and where, therefore, the spectre of 'unconstitutional constitutional law' raises its head.[50]

In other situations, the adoption of the new constitutional rule as the outcome of a referendum may in fact run counter to mandates of international law. This is a point that deserves consideration in its own right and to which this chapter will return.[51]

3.3 Stability Achieved Through a People's Vote

The settling of a socially polarising subject matter through a decision by the people may appear an effective way of 'anchoring' the issue within a given society. The outcome of the Irish referendum in 2015 certainly invites the view that same-sex marriage, once it obtained the approval of society, is difficult to remove.

And yet, that view, too, requires more discerning consideration.

The fate of same-sex marriage in California certainly demonstrated that the electorate did not shy away from upsetting an established institution. After the Supreme Court of California in 2008 found that laws against same-sex marriage in that State were in violation of the Californian constitution,[52] same-sex marriages were concluded in California from June of that year.[53] Yet that decision led to a campaign for the adoption, by public ballot, of Proposition

---

47 Article XXX (1) Constitution of Arizona (1910).
48 *Irish Independent*, 'Court of Appeal Dismisses Two Challenges Against Same Sex Marriage Referendum Result', 30 July 2015. <www.independent.ie/irish-news/courts/court-of-appeal-dismisses-two-challenges-against-same-sex-marriage-referendum-result-31416534.html>.
49 Article 79(3) of the German Basic Law provides that certain aspects of the constitution may not be amended.
50 See Michael Lysander Fremuth, 'Patchwork Constitutionalism: Constitutionalism and Constitutional Litigation in Germany and Beyond the Nation State – A European Perspective' (2011) 49 *Duquesne Law Review* 339, 345.
51 See below at 4.4.
52 *In Re Marriage Cases*, 183 P. 3d 384 (Cal. 2008).
53 Jesse McKinley with Carolyn Marshall, and Rebecca Cathcart, 'A Landmark Day in California as Same-Sex Marriages Begin to Take Hold' *New York Times*, 17 June 2008.

8 in November 2008 – a proposition that sought to change the constitution itself by adding to it the phrase that '[o]nly marriage between a man and a woman is valid or recognized in California'.[54] This, too, was challenged in the courts, with the US District Court for the Northern District of California in San Francisco finding, on 4 August 2010, that Proposition 8 was in violation of the (US) constitution.[55] The granting of marriage licences to same-sex couples only resumed in June 2013,[56] after further judicial challenges had been overcome.[57]

For same-sex couples in California, this development meant that they were told in 2000 by the electorate that the Family Code of California did not recognise same-sex marriage.[58] In May 2008, the Supreme Court of California told them that laws against same-sex marriage were in violation of the Californian constitution, but the message from the electorate in November of the same year was the establishment of a constitutional ban on same-sex marriage. Two years later, a federal court ruled that the provision banning same-sex marriage was in violation of the federal constitution, and from June 2013, marriage licences could be obtained again.

Subjecting the regulation of same-sex marriage to a popular vote does bring an element of arbitrariness into play: it gives legitimacy to an electorate that is not bound by the relatively strict parameters (such as compliance with constitutional law) that apply to courts. Coupled with the possibility of further votes on the same issue, it would be difficult to deny the possibility that direct democracy obstructs rather than promotes stability.

Examples from other parts of the United States illustrate that this is not an entirely theoretical consideration. In Arizona, the voters were asked in 2006 to vote on Proposition 107, a suggested amendment to the Arizonan constitution that would have banned same-sex marriage.[59] They voted with 51.8% against it.[60] But when, two years later, the same electorate was asked to vote on Proposition 102 – an amendment stating that '[o]nly a union of one man and one woman shall be valid or recognized as a marriage in this state', they declared their approval of that proposition.[61]

---

54 See Klukowski (n 20).
55 United States District for the Northern District of California, *Perry et al v Schwarzenegger*, No C 09–2292 VRW, Order (4 August 2010). <https://web.archive.org/web/20130316191210/https://ecf.cand.uscourts.gov/cand/09cv2292/files/09cv2292-ORDER.pdf>.
56 Lester Holt et al., 'NBC Nightly News' (transcript), *NBC*, 29 June 2013.
57 For an overview, see Douglas NeJaime, 'Framing (in)Equality for Same-Sex Couples' (2012) 60 *UCLA Law Review Discourse* 184, 194–199.
58 See above at n 8.
59 Judd Slivka, 'Am I Blue?' *Slate Magazine*, 10 November 2006.
60 Steven Spadijer, 'A Hardcore Case Against (Strong) Judicial Review of Direct Democracy' (2012) 31 *University of Queensland Law Journal* 55, 94.
61 See above at n 46.

A similar development took place in Maine, where voters in 2009 opposed a law that would have provided for same-sex marriage[62] but in 2012 allowed for the issuing of marriage licences to same-sex couples.[63]

If the development of same-sex marriage is seen through the lens not only of one State but of the United States as a whole, an even more unsettling picture emerges.

Tools of direct democracy were employed in a variety of States, with the electorate in several States voting in favour, while others voted against it,[64] giving room to the possibility that in the State of residence of one partner in a same-sex relationship, marriage would be denied to them, but in the home State of the other it would be granted.

Stability was brought in only through the seminal judgement by the US Supreme Court in June 2015 in *Obergefell v Hodges*, which required all States to issue marriage licences to same-sex couples,[65] and thus gave the appearance that it 'settled the issue' in a way which decisions of direct democracy had not been able to do.

4. From the Polling Station to the Court Room?

In light of these developments, it may be permissible to ask whether judicial decision-making is to be preferred in the field of same-sex marriage, thus leaving the deliberation to an authority that is not designed to be beholden to an electoral mandate. It is worth noting that in the United States, it was the courts that had first been approached by same-sex couples seeking recognition of their rights,[66] and with the *Obergefell* ruling, it appeared that it was the courts who also had the final word on the matter.

Various arguments have been put forward in favour of the judicial venue, and it is insightful to consider them in the context of alternatives to popular votes but also to subject them to critical analysis.

4.1 The Question of Expertise

On the face of it, a question about the legalisation of same-sex marriage does not seem to make taxing demands on the expertise of the decision-maker: it calls for a binary answer, and its components and consequences do not seem to

---

62 Allison Fetter-Harrott, 'Recognition of Same-Sex Marriage and Public Schools: Implications, Challenges, and Opportunities' (2011) 2 *Brigham Young University Education and Law Journal* 247.
63 Ashley Fetters, 'Same-Sex Marriage Wins on the Ballot for the First Time in American History' *Atlantic Online*, 7 November 2012.
64 Cf. the overview in Todd Donovan, 'Direct Democracy and Campaigns Against Minorities' (2013) 97 *Minnesota Law Review* 1730, 1748–1753.
65 *Obergefell v Hodges*, 576 US 644 (2015).
66 See on this *Baker v Nelson*, 291 Minn. 310, 191 N.W.2d 185 (1971).

be difficult to understand. And yet, as examples in the recent past have shown, there is such a thing as deceptive simplicity, and soliciting a binary answer does not mean that the referendum presupposes a level of expertise that can easily be expected of the average voter.[67]

The question about the required level of expertise and its impact on the democratic system as a whole is not new, but it has been given fresh impetus in recent years.[68] An exhaustive examination exceeds the boundaries of this analysis, but for current purposes, it is illuminating to recall the issues that the European Court of Human Rights (ECtHR) explored in *Oliari*, before it found that the respondent State had a duty to ensure that the applicants had 'a specific legal framework providing for the recognition and protection of their same-sex unions'.[69] Where same-sex marriage is concerned, the relevant considerations can be expected to be at least of similar complexity.[70]

In *Oliari*, the Court's considerations included reflections on the very basis of the right, which the Court derived from the right to private life and family life,[71] an assessment of the 'margin of appreciation' enjoyed by States in implementing their positive obligation under Article 8 and an evaluation on the width of the margin in cases of 'sensitive moral or ethical issues'.[72] The ECtHR also analysed the existing protection that the State provided to same-sex couples and evaluated whether it sufficiently provided for the 'basic needs which are fundamental to the regulation of a relationship between a couple in a stable and committed relationship'.[73] The court also had to investigate whether 'competing interests' of 'the community as a whole' existed and how a fair balance would be struck between them and the interests of the individual.[74]

---

67 The UK referendum on withdrawal from the European Union in 2016 is an example. The question on the ballot paper appeared quite simple ('Should the United Kingdom remain a member of the European Union or leave the European Union?'), UK Government, 'EU Referendum' <www.gov.uk/government/topical-events/eu-referendum/about>. The withdrawal process, however, soon highlighted the fact that issues of high complexity were involved, ranging from the supply of radioisotopes to the difficulty of avoiding a physical border on the isle of Ireland, David Hughes, 'Brexit Puts at Risk the Supply of Vital Medical Radioisotopes, Lords Told' *The Herald*, 12 December 2017; Kit Nicholl, 'Brexit Raises Prospect of Physical Border in Ireland' *IHS Global Insight*, 30 June 2016. In light of that, reports showing that 'What is the EU?' was one of the most googled questions in the aftermath of the referendum, suggest that the question on the ballot paper presupposed a level of knowledge that the average voter may not have had at their disposal. Thomas Tamblyn, 'Following Brexit, "What is the EU?" Becomes One of the Most Searched Terms in the U.K.' *Huffington Post*, 24 June 2016.
68 See, for instance, Jason Brennan, *Against Democracy* (Princeton University Press 2016) 23–53.
69 *Oliari and Others v Italy*, Applications nos. 18766/11 and 36030/11 (21 July 2015), para 185.
70 See on this issue *ibid*, paras 189–194.
71 See *ibid*, para 103, with reference to the Court's earlier case law.
72 *Ibid*, para 162.
73 *Ibid*, para 169.
74 *Ibid*, para 175.

These are points that required penetrating engagement with the legal issues, often under consideration of previous case law and opinions advanced by the government, academics and other observers. But it would be difficult to claim that, at least in their most fundamental shape, questions of existing rights, competing interests, already existing initiatives to protect the relevant rights and the balancing exercise between the interests involved do not play a role in political considerations on these matters as well. Yet to expect this level of analysis from members of the public going to the voting booth at the end of a working day seems an adventurous assumption.

Challenges of this kind may make it tempting to consider, as one of the great advantages of judicial decision-making, that recourse to the required knowledge base – if necessary, with the help of experts – forms part of established processes in this area of governance.

That, however, may attract the criticism that it portrays a somewhat idealised picture of the relevant authority.

In some fields of LGBT matters – such as the area of asylum requests of LGBT persons – the question has, even in the relatively recent past, arisen as to whether the relevant decision-makers were led by the required expertise in the field or by ingrained prejudicial considerations.[75] Where same-sex marriage is concerned, the fact may be recalled that similar concerns materialised following *Andersen v King County*, a US case decided only in 2006, in which the judges upheld a ban in Washington State on same-sex marriage, because

> the legislature was entitled to believe that limiting marriage to opposite-sex couples furthers procreation, essential to the survival of the human race, and furthers the well-being of children by encouraging families where children are reared in homes headed by the children's biological parents.[76]

The flaw in the ruling was soon utilised by critics of the judgement, who, by way of response, filed Initiative 957, for a public vote on the proposal of making the creation of offspring within three years of the conclusion of a marriage a requirement for all marriages in the State of Washington.[77] (The initiative was eventually withdrawn.)[78]

---

75 There is, in particular, a worrying tendency among some courts evaluating claims of homosexual asylum seekers to reduce the concept of homosexuality to particular, stereotypical characteristics. See Frederik Schindler, 'Nicht schwul genug für Deutschland' *Die Welt*, 5 September 2019. <www.welt.de/politik/deutschland/article199702056/Asylbewerber-aus-Russland-Nicht-schwul-genug-fuer-Deutschland.html>.
76 *Andersen v King County*, 138 P. 3d 963 (Wash. 2006).
77 *Newstex*, 'Beget or Begone!' 6 February 2007.
78 Washington, Secretary of State, 'Proposed Initiatives to the People – 2007' <www.sos.wa.gov/elections/initiatives/people.aspx?y=2007>.

In other cases again, judges have shown a deference to other decision-makers, suggesting the possibility that the judiciary may at times give in to the temptation of 'passing the buck' on an issue that was likely to prove controversial in a given society.

It is a point which also raises questions with regard to human rights concerns and which will therefore be revisited in the course of this discussion.[79]

4.2 The Polarising Effect of Referendums

A consideration that casts doubt on the wisdom of referendums on same-sex marriage concerns the effect that the very campaign on the issue can have on society as a whole.

Seen from a wider perspective, this, too, is a problem that has been recognised in the discourse on democracy in general and one that looks back on a certain tradition in political thinking. The worry of division was present even in the founding stages of the United States, leading John Madison to write that the 'tendency to break and control the violence of faction' should be a function of a 'well-constructed Union'.[80]

Yet it is difficult to deny that the implementation of a people's vote on a controversial issue carries considerable potential for the deepening of divisions.

In some countries, the campaign on (and in particular against) same-sex marriage relied at least to a degree on the strengthening of religious discord. When the electorate in Minnesota was faced with a proposed amendment to the Minnesotan constitution on the question of marriage, John Niestedt, the Twin Cities Archbishop, wrote in a letter to priests that it was 'imperative that we marshal our resources to educate the faithful about the church's teachings on these matters, and to vigorously organize and support a grass-roots effort to get out the vote to support the passage of this amendment'.[81] That met with criticism within the Catholic community in Minnesota itself, with Mike Tegeder, a Minneapolis pastor, noting that he considered the letter 'imprudent' and 'divisive'.[82]

Outside religious debate, too, messages advanced in a referendum campaign can be emotive and hurtful to the other side.

In California in 2008, supporters of Proposition 8 suggested to voters that the proposition '*protects our children* from being taught in public schools that

---

79 Below at n 93–98.
80 Sarah Pruitt, 'The Founding Fathers Feared Political Factions Would Tear the Nation Apart' *History.com*, 6 November 2018. <www.history.com/news/founding-fathers-political-parties-opinion>.
81 Rose French and Rachel E Strassen-Berger, 'Bishops Begin Fight for Marriage Vote' *Star Tribune* (Minneapolis), 15 October 2011.
82 *Ibid*. See also, for the papal intervention in the campaign for the Slovenian referendum on same-sex marriage in 2015, Barbara Surk and Sewell Chan, 'Slovenians Deliver Major Setback to Same-Sex Marriage in Referendum' *New York Times*, 21 December 2015.

"same-sex marriage" is the same as traditional marriage' and referred to the possibility that

> TEACHERS COULD BE REQUIRED to teach young children that there is *no difference* between gay marriage and traditional marriage. We should not accept a court decision that may result in public schools teaching our own kids that gay marriage is ok [. . .] [W]hile gays have the right to their private lives, *they do not have the right to redefine marriage* for everyone else.[83]

It is certainly true that the judicial toolkit differs from that of partisan politicians, and in legal culture the language of objective analysis tends to be prioritised over that of emotion (although exceptions exist). The framework of judicial decision-making is predetermined by the law, and while there may be overlaps with the reasoning employed by factions on either side of the political divide, it is not political acceptability within a particular constituency that establishes the mandate that is to be followed. In fact, the impartiality of the relevant tribunal is a feature of the judiciary that is guaranteed under human rights law.[84]

All that suggests a detachment of the judicial process from the passion of political debate that may help the decisions of judges as 'standing above the parties' to gain a wider degree of societal consent.

And yet, the question may be asked whether a judgment by itself can remove contention on an issue on which divisions run deep.

The judgment by the High Court of Botswana in 2019, for instance, which found that a law banning homosexual activities was discriminatory and struck it down,[85] was certainly hailed as a welcome step by LGBT advocates.[86] Yet reservations towards members of the LGBT community were still very much in existence in Botswana – especially among the rural population,[87] and it is questionable whether divisions of this kind disappear thanks to a judicial ruling.

That is not to deny the value of judgments in a society in which the recognition of LGBT rights is still a matter of development and debate. They are capable of exerting an influence in a variety of ways: as a general rule, and unlike

---

83 California Voter Information Guide (4 November 2008), quoted in *Perry v Schwarzenegger* 704 F.Supp.2d 921, 930 (emphasis in original).
84 Art 14(1) ICCPR; Art 6(1) ECHR; Art 8(1) ACHR.
85 *Letsweletse Motshidiemang* v *The Attorney-General* MAHGB-000591–16 (11 June 2019).
86 Rachel Holman, 'LGBT Activists in "Disbelief" After Botswana Strikes Down Laws Criminalising Homosexuality' *France 24*, 11 June 2019. <www.france24.com/en/20190611-botswana-lgbt-disbelief-high-court-strikes-down-laws-criminalising-homosexuality>.
87 Star Awards, *Afrobarometer, Round 7. Survey in Botswana* (2017) 73, where 50% of persons participating in the survey in rural areas noted that they would 'strongly dislike' having homosexuals as neighbours.

referendums, they provide reasoned arguments for their findings, which may in turn aid activists who support the same result in their campaigns.

Most of all, they affirm and clarify particular values for their society and do so with an authority that is often respected across various factions. But in a deeply divided society, the mere existence of a judgment does not per se end the polarising effects of a particular issue; it may rather be the first step on a path which still requires much persuasive effort.

4.3 Rights of a Minority Decided by a Majority

When, in 2010, conservative groups in Costa Rica collected enough signatures to call for a referendum against same-sex unions, their efforts faced an unexpected turn.

The matter was referred by a supporter of CONODIS (the Costa Rican Coalition of Sexual Diversity Organisations and Groups) to the constitutional chamber of the Supreme Court with the claim that the holding of the referendum would violate the Costa Rican constitution.[88] On 10 August 2012, the court did indeed block the referendum,[89] noting that the rights of minorities could not be put into the hands of majorities inclined to deny them.[90]

It is an observation which shines new light on the question of the legitimacy of decision-making processes: where the subject matter concerns the rights of individuals under the jurisdiction of the State, it is clear that it also involves an individual right to the mechanisms of the justice system to enforce their position,[91] and 'the people' therefore cannot be said to be the sole carriers of legitimate authority.

The matter also affects the question of stability. If, on an issue concerning human rights, a referendum were permitted, the possibility exists that individual rights might be affirmed by the judiciary and perhaps even the constitution of the State, but could still be subject to a decision by the electorate. Taken to its logical extreme, even the most fundamental rights could be removed by a simple majority vote.

The result is a legal contradiction: if a certain matter is a right, it does pertain to the individual, and it is correct to state that it exists independently of the votum of a majority. If, however, the matter is subject to majority decision, it may be a boon granted by the people, but it is not a human right.

---

88 Daniel Zueras, 'Costa Rica: Gays United Against Referendum on Civil Unions' *Inter-Press Service*, 9 August 2010.
89 *Thai News Service*, 'Costa Rica: Costa Rica Court Rejects Vote on Same-Sex Civil Unions', 12 August 2010.
90 Constitutional Chamber (n 6) at VI; see also *ibid* at IX.
91 See on this Art 2(3)(a) ICCPR; Art 13 ECHR; Art 25 ACHR.

It is this understanding of same-sex marriage, along with the challenge of dealing with a complex matter,[92] that appears to militate in favour of its determination by the judiciary rather than by popular vote.

Yet the problem outlined above[93] gains particular relevance in this context as well: the difficulty indeed might lie not so much in a lack of expertise on the side of the judges but in their reluctance to take the lead on issues that they perceive to be sensitive in character.

It is a difficulty that was apparent in the *Oliari* case as well. While the ECtHR found that the respondent State had failed in its obligation to provide the above mentioned framework for the recognition and protection of the applicants' same-sex unions,[94] it was more hesitant regarding the alleged violation of the right to marry under Article 12 ECHR. There, it noted, *inter alia*, that marriage had 'deep-rooted social and cultural connotations which may differ largely from one society to another' and that the Court had to be careful 'not rush to substitute its own judgment in place of that of the national authorities' who were 'best placed to assess and respond to the needs of society'.[95]

It is not the finest piece of reasoning ever to emanate from Strasbourg. If prevailing 'social and cultural connotations' within one society are allowed to prevent a determination of the rights of an individual, one may ask what the point of a human rights court is. It is, at any rate, difficult to dispel the impression that the ECtHR was all too keen to pass responsibility for this issue to another authority.

It is not the only occasion on which, in matters of LGBT concern, a court would have sought refuge in deference to other decision-makers. The fact may be recalled that the High Court of Kenya in 2019, dealing with a challenge to sections in the Kenyan Penal Code that criminalised homosexual activities, rejected the petitioners' request that the court not be 'guided by public opinion or majoritarian views'[96] and found that the will of the people as enshrined in the Constitution represented 'societal values, which must always be a factor in considering constitutional validity of a particular enactment where such legislation seeks to regulate conduct, private or public'.[97] As a result, it found that the challenge to the constitutional validity of the relevant sections of the Penal Code was unsustainable.[98]

---

92 See above at 4.1.
93 Above after n 78.
94 Oliari (n 69) para 185.
95 *Schalk and Kopf v Austria*, Application no. 30141/04 (24 June 2010), paras 61, 62; Oliari (n 69) paras 191, 192.
96 *EG & 7 others v Attorney General; DKM & 9 others (Interested Parties); Katiba Institute & another (Amicus Curiae)*, Judgment, 24 May 2019, Kenya Law Reports 2019, 222, para 402.
97 *Ibid*, para 403.
98 *Ibid*, paras 405, 406.

The danger, therefore, of judicial deference, is hardly a theoretical phenomenon and might well count among one of the most significant stumbling blocks in the judicial determination of rights of individuals against prevailing views within their societies.

4.4 Violation of International Law

Just as the outcome of a referendum may violate other provisions of domestic law, including constitutional law,[99] it is entirely possible that it places the relevant State in conflict with obligations that it accepted under international law.

It is this consideration which highlights a potential weakness of the 'constitutional argument' introduced above.[100] Even a referendum resulting in an amendment of the constitution, and even a constitutionally required referendum may still lead to a situation in which the provision that stands at the end of the process violates international law.[101]

In the field of LGBT rights, a referendum which, for instance, asked about the legalisation of homosexual activities in a particular State would, by its very nature, touch on human rights issues; and if its result were the enactment or continuation of legislation that banned same-sex activity, the relevant State would find itself in breach of human rights law as interpreted in the settled practice of the leading human rights bodies.[102]

On the matter of same-sex marriage, the voice of international law is, at the time of writing, less clear. Reference has already been made to the ECtHR's reluctance to identify such a right in Article 12 ECHR;[103] and in *Oliari*, it consequently took the view that the complaint that the right to marry had been violated was 'manifestly ill-founded'.[104]

But there is reason to believe that here, too, the position of the law is subject to change. The ECtHR, it may be recalled, had also found that it 'would no longer consider that the right to marry must in all circumstances be limited

---

99 Above at n 48–50.
100 Above, section 3.2.
101 For treaties, the Vienna Convention on the Law of Treaties (1969) provides, in Art. 27, clarification on the continued applicability of treaty obligations to the relevant State.
102 See Human Rights Committee (HRC), *Toonen v. Australia*, Communication No. 488/1992, U.N. Doc CCPR/C/50/D/488/1992 (31 March 1994), paras 8.1–8.7; ECtHR *Dudgeon v. The United Kingdom*, Application no. 7525/76 (22 October 1981), paras 42–63; Inter-American Court of Human Rights, *Advisory Opinion OC-24/17, Requested by the Republic of Costa Rica* (24 November 2017), para 68.
103 See above after n 94.
104 *Oliari* (n 69) para 194. Cf. also the similar reluctance of the HRC in *Joslin et al v New Zealand*, Communication No. 902/1999, UN Doc CCPR/C/75/D/902/1999 (17 July 2002), para 8.3.

to marriage between two persons of the opposite sex'[105] and highlighted 'the gradual evolution of States on the matter'.[106]

Only two years later, the Inter-American Court of Human Rights (IACHR), in its Advisory Opinion on Gender Identity, and Equality and Non-Discrimination of Same-Sex Couples, went a step further and noted that State parties had to

> ensure full access to all the mechanisms that exist in their domestic laws, including the right to marriage, to ensure the protection of the rights of families formed by same-sex couples, without discrimination in relation to those that are formed by heterosexual couples [. . .].[107]

It found, furthermore, that, '[t]o this end, States may need to amend existing institutions by taking administrative, judicial or legislative measures in order to extend such mechanisms to same-sex couples.'[108]

Same-sex marriage is thus very much a matter whose evaluation can be expected to undergo change in international law and which certainly is the subject of ongoing controversy (not least, because the IACHR adopted a fundamentally different approach to the assessment of the 'consensus of State parties' than the ECtHR).[109]

That, however, means that the potential clash with international law in this field also returns two points to the debate to which reference had been made above. For one, especially if the IACHR is correct in finding that the 'presumed lack of consensus within some countries regarding full respect for the rights of sexual minorities cannot be considered a valid argument to deny or restrict their human rights',[110] the determination of same-sex marriage through a referendum would indeed mean the questionable subjection of a minority right to a majoritarian decision-making process.[111]

Secondly, even if, *arguendo*, it were accepted that referendums on that matter were a legitimate path, the question whether the denial of the right of marriage to same-sex couples affected human rights would not go away and would, these days, almost unavoidably play a part in the relevant campaigns on the matter. However, taking into account the relevant legal aspects whose complexity not only mirrors that of the more general provision of legal protection to same-sex unions[112] but involves additional questions about the divergent opinions

---

105 *Schalk and Kopf* (n 95), para 61; *Oliari* (n 69), para 191.
106 *Oliari* (n 69), para 192.
107 *Costa Rica Advisory Opinion* (n 102), para 229 at 8.
108 *Ibid*, para 228.
109 *Ibid*, paras 83 and 219 and cf *Oliari* (n 69) at paras 162 and 192.
110 *Costa Rica Advisory Opinion* (n 102), para 219.
111 See above at 4.3.
112 See above (n 71–74).

advanced by human rights bodies on these matters and the potential existence of the relevant right under general or regional customary international law, is a task that requires legal analysis to such a degree that it once again raises questions about the level of expertise that can be expected of the average voter.[113] In light of the above considerations, it would not appear unreasonable to prioritise the relevant determination through the judicial authorities of a State rather than the electorate as a whole.

5. Concluding Thoughts

The lure of referendums to settle a matter of social significance is understandable. If the question concerns same-sex marriage, it is, in particular, tempting to see advantages in an outcome that shows that a significant portion of society as a whole supports this institution and gives it its express approval.

Yet, for all their benefits, peoples' votes come with weaknesses that cannot be lightly dismissed.

The fact that the issue, given in particular its legal connotations, is far more complex than may at first appear and requires an expertise and willingness to engage in a form of analysis that cannot reasonably be expected of the electorate, is one of them. The potential lack of stability, especially with regard to those directly affected by the outcome, is another. Most of all, however, it appears increasingly clear that same-sex marriage is not solely a political or social concept but a human right as well. If that is the case, however, subjecting its legality to a public vote involves an irreconcilable contradiction: the matter can be either an enforceable right or a political option. It cannot be both.

These aspects of referendums and plebiscites make it tempting to understand the judiciary as the appropriate authority when it comes to the determination of the status of same-sex marriage in a State.

This, too, comes with difficulties. As recent cases have shown, there is, for one, a real danger that courts are reluctant to fulfil their duty, where socially sensitive matters are concerned and will show undue deference to other decision makers.

But even if a court – as in *Obergefell* – is prepared to confirm the status of same-sex marriage as a right, the fact remains that this particular decision is only one influencing factor within a society, and it appears necessary to guard against the expectation that a judgment, by itself, will bring about fundamental change of societal attitudes. A ruling in Kenya in favour of decriminalisation of same-sex activities or even the establishment of same-sex marriage would have every right to be hailed as a 'landmark decision'. But it is questionable whether it would be enough to effect immediate change in the views of a society, in which, according to a 2015/16 survey, only 14% showed 'tolerance

---

113 See above at 4.1.

for homosexuals' and 72% in 2014/15 declared they would 'strong[ly] dislike' having homosexuals as neighbours.[114]

Alienation of this kind, it appears, can be overcome only by tackling the prevailing prejudices and by removing the barrier of abstraction that separates members of the minority from society as a whole. Dialogue, therefore, continues to play an important role; a court judgment – when seen in isolation – might even be perceived as a 'top-down approach', and thus as carrying the potential of enhancing the existing divisions.

Yet it is at this stage that the various forms of participation by the people in the development of societal issues deserve to be revisited.

For one, dialogue and decision-making are different matters. Leaving the determination of a subject matter to the people appears to be best suited to situations in which the people are directly affected. At the other end of the scale are decisions whose primary effect is limited to a specific group or even to selected individuals. In those cases, the rule of the majority is a poor tool in the decision-making process. If the result has indirect effect on the people, it is appropriate that the people's pathway towards the decision is indirect, too: that they are involved in the consultation process and may indeed be encouraged to engage in it rather than in the eventual determination of the matter at hand.

The involvement of members of the wider society in this way can indeed lead to beneficial results. Discussions especially on issues that still encounter controversy thus allow the weakening of prejudices and may put unfounded fears to rest. The very possibility of meeting same-sex couples and members of support organisations, such as Families and Friends of Lesbians and Gays (FFLAG), carries the potential of removing barriers that previous abstraction had erected.

But in some contexts, consultation also opens the door to more options than referendums. Instead of limiting societal participation to the making of decisions on one issue, consultation can result in the suggestion of new approaches, of initiatives and institutions (such as educational projects) that help bridge divides. The binary choice that referendums impose appears by comparison a crude instrument and one that cannot even be said to be of the greatest democratic value.

Limiting the impact of society to the making of a cross in a polling booth is not necessarily reflective of the values of States whose political systems are meant to represent the thoughts, concerns and hopes of their peoples. Engaging with the people in genuine dialogue is certainly a more time-intensive and costly procedure. But it opens up the creative potential of society and allows for the introduction of original arguments into a debate which make a valuable contribution to the healing of rifts without damaging the rights of the individuals that are primarily affected by the issue at hand.

---

114 Boniface Dulani, Gift Sambo, and Kim Yi Dionne, 'Good Neighbours? Africans Express High Levels of Tolerance for Many, but Not for All' *Afrobarometer Dispatch No 74* (2016) 12, 26.

Chapter 10

The Intrinsic Value of Registered Partnerships and Marriage for Same-Sex Couples, Their Recognition Domestically and at the Strasbourg Court

Helen Fenwick and Andy Hayward

1. Introduction

Across the Western world, securing the right to marry has become one of the primary goals of the LGBT+ community and a key focal point for political and legal activism. Granting same-sex couples access to marriage is viewed as not only demonstrating a state's commitment to the principles of equality and non-discrimination but also as helpful in stimulating beneficial change in societal attitudes towards same-sex relationships.[1]

This drive towards same-sex marriage is often part of a lengthy process that invariably begins with the decriminalisation of homosexual activity between adults, and subsequently involves the conferral of ad hoc legal protections to same-sex couples.[2] Crucially, for this chapter, a further key stage in this process is the creation of a civil or registered partnership regime that confers upon same-sex couples the ability to access a formalised relationship status and a framework of legal protections; a final stage in this process may be viewed as creating availability of marriage equality. But such frameworks are often created in states or receive acceptance by the European Court of Human Rights at Strasbourg, as this chapter documents, at a time when securing marriage equality is not viable on political and/or policy grounds. The value of these registration regimes is highly contested; some critics have viewed them merely as staging posts in the journey to the ultimate destination of marriage,[3] while others have seen them more positively as statuses with an intrinsic value and appeal that endures even in the context of marriage equality.

---

1 See I Lund-Andersen, 'The Danish Registered Partnership Act, 1989: Has the Act Meant a Change in Attitudes?' in R Wintemute and M Andenas (eds), *Legal Recognition of Same-Sex Partnerships: A Study of National, European and International Law* (Hart Publishing 2001).
2 See B Hale, 'Homosexual Rights' (2004) 16 *Child and Family Law Quarterly* 125, 125; K Waaldijk, 'Small Change: How the Road to Same-Sex Marriage Got Paved in the Netherlands' in Wintemute and Andenas (n 1).
3 See P Tatchell, 'Civil Partnerships Are Divorced from Reality' *The Guardian*, 19 December 2005.

DOI: 10.4324/9781003286295-13

While only a minority of states globally permit same-sex marriage at present, this pattern of reform is readily discernible, albeit with great variations as to the situation of a given state within this process.[4] The same path can be traced in the jurisprudence of the Strasbourg Court: same-sex registered partnerships have received some degree of acceptance but in the context so far of a refusal to accept marriage equality, although there are some signs, as will be discussed, that Strasbourg's stance as to same-sex marriage is currently softening.

This chapter will critique that pattern of reform in England and Wales, comparing it with the path currently being traced at Strasbourg. In so doing, this chapter will interrogate the value of civil or registered partnerships as an aspect of the protection of the interests of same-sex couples within England and Wales, and then consider their acceptance within the jurisprudence of the European Court of Human Rights. Noting the divergent views as to the future of same-sex civil partnerships and drawing upon the contribution of Stonewall to these debates, the first part of this chapter explores the academic discourse surrounding that status in England and Wales. In particular, it challenges the arguments advanced as to their superfluous nature following the Marriage (Same Sex Couples) Act 2013 and analyses the problematic trend of eulogising marriage as the 'gold standard' in the formal expression of an interpersonal relationship,[5] although the authors are fully supportive of same-sex marriage. But, it will be argued that since some couples still reject marriage, particularly same-sex couples who have experienced a long history of structural oppression by the Church and state, that necessitates a clearer recognition of the intrinsic value of civil partnerships.[6] Such recognition not only provides support for a well-established method of relationship formalisation for couples with an ideological opposition to marriage, but, as will be argued in the second part of this chapter, it sends a positive message to certain other Council of Europe states considering the introduction of registered partnerships, although they are not yet prepared to accept marriage equality.

The second part of this chapter turns to considering the current stance of the Strasbourg Court as to the recognition of same-sex registered partnerships, and same-sex marriage, under the European Convention on Human Rights (ECHR) framework.[7] The Court has a long history of defending the interests of sexual minorities under the ECHR, and recently certain claims for same-sex

---

4 See JM Scherpe and A Hayward, *The Future of Registered Partnerships – Family Recognition Beyond Marriage?* (Intersentia 2017).

5 See Witness Statements referenced in *Wilkinson v Kitzinger* (No 2) [2006] EWHC 2022 (Fam) [6] (Potter P).

6 K McK Norrie, 'Marriage Is for Heterosexuals – May the Rest of Us Be Saved from It' (2000) *Child and Family Law Quarterly* 363.

7 See H Fenwick and A Hayward, 'Rejecting Asymmetry of Access to Formal Relationship Statuses for Same- and Different-Sex Couples at Strasbourg and Domestically' (2017) 6 *European Human Rights Law Review* 544.

registered partnerships and marriage have come before it, against states offering same-sex couples *no* means of formalising their relationships. It will be found that the Court has shown some recognition of the value of registered partnerships for same-sex couples and is currently showing a willingness to open that non-traditional institution for formalising relationships to such couples under Article 8 (right to respect for private and family life), read alone or with Article 14 (right to non-discrimination within the ambit of another Convention right). But, that stance must be contrasted so far with its reluctance to open the traditional institution of marriage to such couples under Article 12 (right to marry), even read with Article 14. The Court may be said to be following slowly behind the path already traced in England and Wales in terms of accepting same-sex registered partnerships, but its reluctance to take the next step – to recognise marriage equality, as those jurisdictions have done – may be said to represent a marked flaw in its sexual minority jurisprudence.

2. The Civil Partnership Act 2004 and the Drive Towards Same-Sex Marriage

Civil partnerships were introduced through the Civil Partnership Act 2004 and are an opt-in relationship status created following the act of registration by the parties.[8] The scheme was, until very recently, limited to same-sex couples. The rationale behind this move was that different-sex couples had long been able to access religious and civil forms of marriage and, since same-sex marriage was not permitted in 2004, a mechanism was needed to grant same-sex couples some legal recognition of their relationship.[9] The scheme was conceived of as 'marriage in almost all but name' and, with few exceptions, civil partnership and civil marriage are similar in terms of the formalities for creation, legal consequences upon registration and dissolution.[10] Those wishing to register a civil partnership must not be within the prohibited degrees, must be over the age of 16 and cannot already be married or in a pre-existing civil partnership.[11] With a view to pacifying opponents that believed civil partnerships could undermine the institution of marriage or was a disguised form of 'gay marriage', the problematic leitmotif of 'separate but equal' was adopted to describe the way the partnership scheme operated and to signal distinctions.

Following their introduction in December 2005, civil partnerships proved highly popular among the LGBT+ community. In the first three days of the

---

8 See Civil Partnership Act 2004, s. 1(1) and M Harper, S Chevlan, M Downs, K Landells, and G Wilson, *Same Sex Marriage and Civil Partnerships: The New Law* (Jordan Publishing 2014).
9 See Department of Trade and Industry, *Civil Partnership: A Framework for the Legal Recognition of Same-Sex Couples* (Department of Trade and Industry 2003) 13.
10 See *Wilkinson* (n 5) 88 (Potter P) and Hale (n 2) 132.
11 As mandated by the Civil Partnership Act 2004, s. 3(1)(a)–(d).

Act coming into force, there were 1,227 registrations with 1,857 concluded by the end of that year (1,228 concluded between men and 629 between women). The following year saw 14,943 registrations with 9,003 between men and 5,940 between women. As the regime became more established, the total number of civil partnerships entered into each year gradually decreased to around 6,000. This period also saw calls to introduce same-sex marriage, and in 2012, a consultation exercise was undertaken,[12] resulting in the Government stating its commitment to introduction of same-sex marriage.[13] Generating the highest-ever level of responses to a public consultation exercise, the consultation findings revealed both the contentious nature of same-sex marriage for some individuals but also, and of crucial significance for this chapter, clear support for the retention of civil partnerships. Same-sex marriage was introduced in England and Wales through the Marriage (Same Sex Couples) Act 2013; the first ceremonies took place in March 2014.

Unlike other states that phased out their civil partnership regimes following marriage equality,[14] the government sought to evade this issue and created section 15 of the Marriage (Same Sex Couples) Act 2013 to compel the Secretary of State to conduct a review of the future of civil partnerships. This review was conducted in 2014 by the Department for Culture, Media and Sport and generated considerably fewer responses than the earlier Equal Civil Marriage consultation.[15] The exercise ran for a relatively short period of time and produced mixed messages as to the continuing need for civil partnerships. Fifty-five per cent of respondents were against the phasing out of civil partnerships, while only 22% were in favour of extending them to different-sex couples. Without a 'united call for change',[16] and as Stonewall had urged a cautious approach to reform, the government chose to take no further action.[17] Since the consultation exercise was concluded only months after the introduction of same-sex marriage, it is perhaps unsurprising that the results were inconclusive: more time was needed to analyse the uptake of civil partnerships following the availability of same-sex marriage in March 2014. Stonewall considered that there should be a 'long-term' evaluation of the impact of same-sex marriage and the conversion process on the uptake of civil partnerships.[18]

---

12 Government Equalities Office, *Equal Civil Marriage: A Consultation* (Government Equalities Office 2012).
13 HM Government, *Equal Marriage: The Government's Response* (HM Government 2012).
14 See Scherpe and Hayward (n 4) Part I.
15 Department for Culture, Media and Sport, *Civil Partnership Review (England and Wales): A Consultation* (Department for Culture, Media and Sport 2014).
16 Department for Culture, Media and Sport, *Civil Partnership Review (England and Wales): Report on Conclusions* (Department for Culture, Media and Sport 2014) 4.
17 PinkNews, 'Stonewall Says It Will Campaign for Gay Marriage' <www.pinknews.co.uk/2010/10/27/stonewall-says-it-will-campaign-for-gay-marriage> (accessed 19 October 2021).
18 See Department for Culture, Media and Sport (n 16) para 2.26.

A related development that placed the spotlight on the issue of civil partnership reform was a concerted campaign to open up the regime to different-sex couples wishing to access an alternative status to marriage. Via the failure to phase out or extend the civil partnership regime to different-sex couples at the time of introducing same-sex marriage, England and Wales had created a system of asymmetrical access for couples; that is, same-sex couples were able to access both marriage or civil partnership; different-sex couples could only access marriage.[19] That anomalous position was challenged in the courts, resulting in the Supreme Court decision in *R (on the application of Steinfeld and Keidan) v Secretary of State for International Development* ruling that the ban on different-sex civil partnerships constituted discrimination under Articles 14 and 8 of the ECHR.[20] Galvanised by the Supreme Court ruling and supported by the Equal Civil Partnerships campaign, multiple Private Members Bills were introduced into Parliament seeking the extension of the regime. Supported through Parliament by Tim Loughton MP, the Civil Partnerships, Marriages and Deaths (Registration etc.) Act 2019 compelled the Secretary of State to amend the Civil Partnership Act 2004, by way of regulations, so as to permit different-sex civil partnerships. This was achieved through the Civil Partnership (Opposite-Sex Couples) Regulations 2019, which came into force at the end of December 2019 and enabled different-sex couples to access civil partnerships in the same manner as same-sex couples.

3. Interrogating the Value of Civil Partnerships in England and Wales

The introduction of same-sex marriage alongside the deliberations as to the future of civil partnerships revealed a divide in public attitudes. Now that marriage was available for same-sex couples, it was questioned why civil partnerships were still needed, and it is argued that these critiques can be deconstructed into three key arguments.[21] The first argument, centring on progression in terms of legal development, proceeds on the basis that civil partnerships had what Briggs LJ termed in *Steinfeld* an 'essentially transitional purpose, designed to alleviate the disadvantages which then affected same-sex couples, but do not now'.[22] As the key pursuit for LGBT+ activism was the introduction of

---

19 See Fenwick and Hayward (n 7).
20 [2018] UKSC 32. See A Hayward, 'Taking the Time to Discriminate – *R (on the application of Steinfeld and Keidan) v Secretary of State for International Development*' (2019) 41 *JSWFL* 92; A Hayward, 'Equal Civil Partnerships, Discrimination and the Indulgence of Time' (2019) 82:5 *Modern Law Review* 922.
21 See A Hayward, 'Relationships with Status – Civil Partnerships in an Era of Same-Sex Marriage' in F Hamilton and G Noto La Diega (eds), *Same-Sex Relationships, Law and Social Change* (Routledge 2020) 189.
22 [2017] EWCA Civ 81 [172].

same-sex marriage, once that goal was attained there was no need to retain civil partnerships as a status. Indeed, retention of that status could signal that civil partnerships were originally conceived to *segregate* same-sex couples and exclude them from marriage. Support for this progression argument can be seen in the judicial discussion of this area. Writing extrajudicially, Baroness Hale noted that in a country's journey to protect same-sex relationships, '[t]he final steps are taken by family law' and include 'providing for registered civil partnerships, and finally . . . for civil marriage'.[23] The same sentiment can be traced in Parliament and in the debates on the Marriage (Same Sex Couples) Bill, Yvette Cooper MP frequently referred to same-sex marriage as 'the next step for equality'.[24]

The second argument, which will be termed the status argument, involves the contrasting of civil partnership against the more established status of marriage. As marriage possesses a long, rich history and is often positioned within society by politicians and policymakers as the 'gold standard' relationship form, alternatives, such as civil partnerships, are viewed as second rate. Without the perceived social imprimatur possessed by marriage, civil partnerships are seen as an administrative 'construct of statute'[25] or, as Kitzinger and Wilkinson opined, a 'painful compromise between genuine equality and no rights at all'.[26] Echoing the comparisons made in Parliament between the two statuses, Harding remarked that civil partnerships were essentially 'marriage-lite: same great taste, half the respect of regular marriage'.[27] The consequence of this argument is to question why same-sex couples might want the inferior carbon copy of marriage now that the original had become available to them.

The final argument used to evidence the superfluous nature of civil partnerships relates to uptake now that same-sex couples have a choice between two formalised statuses. In England and Wales, following the introduction of same-sex marriage, there has been a notable decrease in civil partnership registrations. This suggests that when couples are faced with a choice, there may exist a preference for marriage. Indeed, in 2013, there were 5,646 civil partnership registrations, but after the introduction of same-sex marriage in 2014, this number decreased to only 1,683. Unsurprisingly, those critical of civil partnerships use these data to demonstrate that in England and Wales, they have now become a 'legacy relationship' applicable to a dwindling number of couples.[28]

---

23 Hale (n 2) 125.
24 HC Deb 5 February 2013, vol 558, col 136.
25 *R v Bala and others* [2016] EWCA Crim 560 [38] (Davies LJ).
26 S Wilkinson and C Kitzinger, 'In Support of Equal Marriage: Why Civil Partnership Is Not Enough' (2006) 8 *Psychology of Women Review* 54.
27 R Harding, '"Dogs Are 'Registered', People Shouldn't Be": Legal Consciousness and Lesbian and Gay Rights' (2006) 15 *Social and Legal Studies* 511, 524.
28 Department for Culture, Media and Sport (n 15) para. 3.10.

The cumulative effect of these arguments is considered problematic for a variety of reasons, but in particular through its effect of undermining the intrinsic value of civil partnerships. If same-sex marriage is viewed as the 'final stop for "full equality" for lesbian and gay men', alternative methods of expressing an interpersonal relationship are subsequently viewed as inferior.[29] Not only does this buttress, and even eulogise, the institution of marriage, it forces assimilation of the infinitely diverse LGBT+ community within an institution long conceptualised as heteronormative. As Norrie has argued in relation to this move, '[e]quality is granted, but only on heterosexual terms'.[30] It is, however, argued that the more recent introduction of different-sex civil partnerships in England and Wales has made an important contribution to this debate and created an opportunity for a critical reappraisal of the value of civil partnerships domestically.

4. Recognising the Value of Civil Partnerships in England and Wales

Recent developments, it is argued, evince a counter-narrative to the view that civil partnerships should become of historical relevance only. It is apparent that, as a jurisdiction, England and Wales are evidencing greater recognition of the institution of civil partnership and acknowledging that couples value choice in the formal expression of their relationships. This can be seen in a variety of ways. First, the pattern of jurisdictions progressing towards same-sex marriage and then abolishing pre-existing civil partnership regimes has started to be offset by countries retaining pre-existing civil partnership regimes. Examples can be found of countries valuing both marriage and civil partnership simultaneously through retaining equal civil partnership regimes upon achieving marriage equality,[31] or extending previously same-sex civil partnership regimes to different-sex couples, thereby creating two statuses open to all couples. For example, Austria introduced marriage equality on 1 January 2019 and simultaneously opened up to different-sex couples the originally same-sex only civil partnership regime, first introduced in 2010. This pattern suggests that the previous model of phasing out civil partnerships following the introduction of same-sex marriage, as exemplified by the Nordic countries, may be giving way to alternative law reform strategies that are underpinned more by offering greater choice and autonomy to couples in terms of the outward expression of their relationships. It can also be viewed as a response to couples wishing to retain their original relationship status following the introduction of

---

29 See N Barker, *Not the Marrying Kind: A Feminist Critique of Same-Sex Marriage* (Palgrave Macmillan 2012) 2.
30 Norrie (n 6) 365.
31 Examples include France, The Netherlands and Belgium.

same-sex marriage. This narrative was particularly prominent when policy-makers in England and Wales were deliberating the future of civil partnerships, and one option, canvassed in the *Future of Civil Partnerships Consultation*, was to phase out civil partnerships. Groups, such as Stonewall and the Peter Tatchell Foundation, were both highly vocal during that process, finding that the phasing out of civil partnerships for same-sex couples would have been met with considerable resistance. Indeed, activist Peter Tatchell believed that such a move would 'provoke an almighty backlash' and 'do catastrophic damage to relations between the Conservative party and LGBT people'.[32] These developments reveal, it is argued, a challenge to the progression argument, to the inevitable marginalisation of civil partnerships or to viewing them as merely a staging post to the final destination of marriage.

Second, as regards the status argument, attitudes as to the significance of civil partnerships for both different and same-sex couples have clearly changed. For example, the judicial discussion of civil partnerships in reported cases evidences a shift from discussing the regime as a somewhat sterile registration process for same-sex couples[33] to seeing it as instead a status or institution expressing commitment.[34] The Department for Culture, Media and Sport remarked in 2014 that civil partnerships had now become a 'well-understood legal institution' that played 'an important role in the lives of many couples'.[35] This sentiment was further reflected in the consultation responses and empirical research into the lived experiences of couples in civil partnerships.[36] Stonewall's then Interim Chief Executive, Paul Twocock, acknowledged the important value that some couples ascribe to civil partnerships and indicated that abolition would 'imply that civil partnerships are now less valued than a marriage and somehow irrelevant'.[37] Thus, civil partnerships have become part of the fabric of LGBT+ lives, acknowledged as a significant outward expression of a relationship.

Third, while it is clear that the availability of same-sex marriage has clearly affected the civil partnership rate, 2016 saw the first annual increase in registrations. In that year, 890 civil partnerships were formed in England and Wales, representing an increase of 3.4% compared with the previous year.[38]

---

32 See: <http://equalcivilpartnerships.org.uk/2018/02/campaign-responds-reports-government-u-turn-civil-partnerships-opposite-sex-couples/> (accessed 19 October 2021).
33 See *Ghaidan v Godin-Mendoza* [2004] UKHL 30 [96].
34 See *Bull v Hall* [2013] UKSC 73 [26] and *Radmacher v Granatino* [2010] UKSC 42.
35 Department for Culture, Media and Sport (n 15) para 1.4.
36 See A Jowett and E Peel, '"A Question of Equality and Choice": Same-Sex Couples' Attitudes Towards Civil Partnership After the Introduction of Same-Sex Marriage' (2017) 8 *Psychology and Sexuality* 69.
37 Stonewall, 'Abolishing Civil Partnerships Is Not an Option' <www.stonewall.org.uk/cy/node/72816> (accessed 19 October 2021).
38 Office for National Statistics, *Civil Partnerships in England and Wales: 2016* (Office for National Statistics, 26 September 2017).

Then, 994 civil partnerships were registered in 2019 representing an increase of 4.0% from 956 in 2018 and an increase of 9.5% from 908 in 2017.[39] The conversion statistics are perhaps more revealing when rejecting the aforementioned arguments as to the need for civil partnerships. Conversion from civil partnership to marriage is currently permitted by section 9 of the Marriage (Same Sex Couples) Act 2013. It has the effect of backdating a marriage to the point in which the parties first entered their original civil partnership. At present, only one in eight civil partnerships has been converted to marriage,[40] and, as noted by Tim Loughton MP, 'more than 80% of same-sex couples who have committed to a civil partnership do not think that they need to or want to convert that into marriage'.[41] The views of Stonewall are yet again informative: they noted that this pattern was attributable to the desire of couples 'to maintain the integrity of the day they made their commitment to each other in a civil partnership'.[42]

At a domestic level, then, it is argued that, despite being a newly created registration regime, civil partnerships clearly serve an important expressive function for couples and are a desired status when parties are wishing to formalise their relationships. Moreover, the rationales motivating a couple to choose a civil partnership over marriage, or vice versa, are varied and personal to the parties concerned. But, the pattern of reform of the position of sexual minorities discussed earlier has now culminated in providing that choice in an era of marriage equality. The position now reached in England and Wales, which is characterised by personal autonomy and choice, must be contrasted with the position in a number of other ECHR Member States, and at Strasbourg. With a view to interrogating how far the intrinsic value of registered partnerships has received recognition and to considering why the pace of Strasbourg-driven reform is so slow, this second part therefore explores the rationales behind the reluctant, even paradoxical, stance of the Court in this context.

5. The Strasbourg Stance as to Civil (Registered) Partnerships and Same-Sex Marriage

This second part of this chapter considers challenges at the Strasbourg Court from same-sex couples, often supported by activist groups, to the lack of methods of formalising their relationships in a number of Member States. The Court can be credited, as is well-documented, with a number of legal changes

---

39 Office for National Statistics, *Civil Partnerships in England and Wales: 2019* (Office for National Statistics, 22 September 2020).
40 See J Haskey, 'Civil Partnerships and Same-Sex Marriages in England and Wales: A Social and Demographic Perspective' (2016) *Family Law* 44; J Haskey, 'Perspectives on Civil Partnerships and Marriages in England and Wales: Aspects, Attitudes and Assessments' (2021) *Family Law* 816.
41 HC Deb, vol 635, col 1142 (2 February 2018).
42 Stonewall (n 37).

recognising various aspects of the interests of sexual minorities.[43] But, this part will argue that the current approach of the Strasbourg Court in this context shows tensions between two conflicting demands: it is seeking both to protect sexual minorities, but also its own authority, by relying on the consensus doctrine (crudely – finding that a majority of Member States protect a certain interest) to avoid determinations likely to lead to open conflict with a number of Member States. In respect of homophobic hate crimes and bans on public manifestations of support for sexual minorities,[44] the Court has recently shown a robust determination to provide protection for such minorities, partly on the basis that there is no consensus among the Member States supporting such practices. But, in strong contrast, in the context of formalisations of same-sex relationships, there are signs that 'East'/'West' divisions between the Member States are having some inhibitory impact on its judgements, accommodated mainly via consensus analysis. It will be found that as a result of reliance on such analysis, the Court has demonstrated a lack of willingness to recognise fully the intrinsic value of both registered partnerships and marriage for same-sex couples and a reluctance to confront homophobia robustly in this context. This part will therefore consider the basis for its strong reluctance to open marriage to same-sex couples and its restrained stance until 2021 even in respect of same-sex registered partnerships, as well as the probable position as further claims for such relationship formalisations come before it.

5.1 The Role of Consensus Analysis

Discrimination against same-sex couples is manifest in the refusals of a number of the contracting states to allow them to enter a registered partnership or marriage. It might be thought that this was precisely the type of situation that the Court was set up to address, but its reliance on the consensus doctrine has had some inhibiting impact on its response in this context.[45] The term 'consensus' is often taken to denote identifying common ground between the laws of a majority of Member States in relation to the domestic protection for particular rights, but it can also refer to a *trend* towards occupying such ground.[46] In general, if discrimination on particular protected grounds, including sexual orientation, is

---

43 See P Johnson, *Homosexuality and the European Court of Human Rights* (Routledge 2013) Chap 2; *Dudgeon v United Kingdom* (1980) 3 E.H.R.R. 40; *Smith and Grady v United Kingdom* (2001) 31 E.H.R.R. 24; *Perkins and R v UK* Applications nos. 43208/98; 44875/98.
44 See *Alekseyev v Russia* (App. No.4916/07), Judgment of 21 October 2010.
45 See P Laverack, 'The Indignity of Exclusion: LGBT Rights, Human Dignity and the Living Tree of Human Rights' (2019) 2 *European Human Rights Law Review* 172, 182.
46 See L Wildhaber, A Hjartarson, and S Donnelly, 'No Consensus on Consensus? The Practice of the European Court of Human Rights' (2013) 33 *Human Rights Law Journal* 248; K Dzehtsiarou, 'Does Consensus Matter? Legitimacy of European Consensus in the Case Law of the European Court of Human Rights' (2011) *Public Law* 534.

alleged under Article 14 ECHR, the scrutiny accorded to the state's justification will be strict *unless* no consensus on the matter is apparent among the Member States.[47] Further, lack of consensus among the Member States means that the margin of appreciation widens, as an aspect of the subsidiarity principle,[48] so the *scope* of the right in question can be narrowly interpreted.[49] In other words, the existence of a consensus will be taken into account in determining that a state which has not provided domestic protection answering to the potential obligation in question has over-stepped its margin of appreciation.[50] Or, under a lack of consensus the justification put forward for discrimination under Article 14, or for failing to introduce a rights-protecting measure, is not closely scrutinised, so the demands of proportionality are much more readily satisfied.[51]

A majority of the Member States have not introduced same-sex marriage; therefore, since no consensus on such marriage is currently available, the margin conceded to a particular state is very wide. States failing to introduce such marriage are under no ECHR obligation to do so: due to the lack of consensus, the Court has not accepted that the right to marry under Article 12 covers same-sex couples.[52] But, conversely, since a consensus on accepting same-sex registered partnerships is currently identifiable, a narrow, or possibly no, margin will be conceded to the state in question, which is not aligned with the majority, as discussed further as follows.

5.2 The Rapidly Changing Picture Across Contracting States as to State Formalisations of Same-Sex Unions

A number of efforts have been made by same-sex couples, often supported by LGBT activist organisations, to achieve formal legal recognition of their

---

47 See *Abdulaziz v United Kingdom* (1985) 7 E.H.R.R. 471 [90]-[91]; *DH and others v Czech Republic* (2008) 47 E.H.R.R. 3 [196]; *EB v France* (2008) 47 E.H.R.R. 21 [93].
48 See D McGoldrick, 'A Defence of the Margin of Appreciation and an Argument for Its Application by the Human Rights Committee' (2016) 65(1) *International and Comparative Law Quarterly* 21, 28.
49 See as to the Court's general stance *Goodwin v United Kingdom* (1996) 22 E.H.R.R. 123 [103]; *Bayatyan v Armenia* (2012) 54 E.H.R.R. 15 [108]. See further: A Legg, *The Margin of Appreciation in International Human Rights Law: Deference and Proportionality* (Oxford University Press 2012); E Bates, 'The UK and Strasbourg: A Strained Relationship – The Long View' and H Fenwick, 'Protocol 15, Enhanced Subsidiarity and a Dialogic Approach, or Appeasement in Recent Cases at Strasbourg against the UK, Both' in Ziegler et al. (eds), *The UK and European Human Rights – A Strained Relationship* (Hart 2015).
50 See *Schalk and Kopf v Austria* (2011) 53 E.H.R.R. 20 [58].
51 See: *Rees v United Kingdom* (1987) 9 E.H.R.R. 56 [37]; *Cossey v United Kingdom* (1991) 13 E.H.R.R. 622 [234]; *Evans v United Kingdom* (2007) 43 E.H.R.R. 21 [77]; *Fretté v France* (2004) 38 E.H.R.R. 21 [41]; *ABC v Ireland* (2011) 53 E.H.R.R. 13 [232]. In the sexual minority context see *Tomás v Spain* (2017) 65 E.H.R.R. 24.
52 See in particular *Oliari v Italy* (2015) 65 E.H.R.R. 957 and P Johnson, 'Same Sex Marriage and Article 12 of the ECHR' in C Ashford and A Maine (eds), *Research Handbook on Gender, Sexuality and the Law* (Edward Elgar Publishing 2020).

relationships via Strasbourg claims under the ECHR for same-sex registered partnerships and same-sex marriage. The position as to state formalisations of same-sex unions has changed with very striking rapidity over the last 20 years among the Member States,[53] but the spread of such formalisations across the states has been uneven: some 'East'/'West' divisions between the Member States have emerged on this matter. At the present time, the majority of states, including all the 'Western' ones, have introduced same-sex marriage[54] and/or forms of registered partnership schemes for same-sex couples.[55] But, a number of 'Eastern' states have shown no or little inclination to introduce such schemes, in some instances evincing a steadfast refusal to do so,[56] while a number of them have also recently enshrined a ban on same-sex marriage in their Constitutions.[57] While a number of predominantly Western European Member States introduced same-sex registered partnership schemes around 9–30 years ago, usually phasing them out following the subsequent introduction of same-sex marriage, some Western states introduced them much more recently,[58] after certain 'Eastern' states – Slovenia, the Czech Republic and Hungary – had already done so. Certain states on either side of the East/West 'divide', including Estonia and Italy, only introduced registered partnership schemes covering same-sex couples in the last few years,[59] while in some inequality is perpetuated since different-sex couples can access marriage *or* a registered partnership, while same-sex couples can only access a registered partnership.[60] Change in certain 'Eastern' states may be imminent: some have brought forward Bills in the last few years to introduce same-sex registered partnerships, which have not yet passed.

5.3 Claims at Strasbourg for Formalisations of Their Relationships from Same-Sex Couples

The first step towards recognising an ECHR right to formal recognition of their relationships for same-sex couples, taken in *Schalk*,[61] was to recognise same-sex

---

53 For a comparative analysis, see Scherpe and Hayward (n 4); K Boele-Woelki and A Fuchs, *Same Sex Relations and Beyond – Gender Matters in the EU* (Intersentia 2017).
54 See *Fedotova and others v Russia* (2021) ECHR 225 [29]. See JM Scherpe, 'Formal Recognition of Adult Relationships and Legal Gender in a Comparative Perspective' in Ashford and Maine (n 52).
55 See *Fedotova* (n 54).
56 No same-sex partnership scheme has been considered at a legislative level in Armenia, Azerbaijan, Moldova, Turkey and Russia.
57 Such bans exist in the Constitutions of Armenia, Bulgaria, Croatia, Georgia, Hungary, Latvia, Lithuania, Moldova, Montenegro, Poland, Serbia, the Slovak Republic and the Ukraine. See H Fenwick, 'Same Sex Unions at the Strasbourg Court in a Divided Europe: Calling the Legitimacy of the Court into Question?' (2016) 3 *European Human Rights Law Reports* 249.
58 Italy (2016), San Marino (2018).
59 Both in 2016. Croatia introduced registered partnerships in 2014.
60 That is the position in Andorra, Greece, Cyprus and Estonia. See D Lima, 'Registered Partnerships in Greece and Cyprus' in Scherpe and Hayward (n 4).
61 *Schalk* (n 50).

couples as 'families' under Article 8 read with 14 since they 'are just as capable as different-sex couples of entering into stable committed relationships',[62] but that finding did not form the main basis for the determination as to the meaning of 'family'. The Court relied instead on the changing consensus as to the broadening of the concept of 'family' in Member States. Article 9 of the EU Charter of Fundamental Rights was also relevant since its wording potentially offers a non-exclusionary concept of marriage and family.[63]

But, while recognising the applicant couple's need for 'legal recognition and protection of their relationship',[64] the Court also established that nevertheless they should be debarred from accessing marriage under Article 12[65] due to the lack of a consensus on the matter.[66] The Court also dismissed the claim to access same-sex marriage under Article 8 since the obligation did not arise under the more specific Article.[67] Its reluctant stance on that issue, and its failure to give weight to the value of dignity,[68] can readily be compared with the more robust one taken by the Inter-American Court of Human Rights, which has found that the American Convention on Human Rights requires states to recognise 'a specific mechanism to govern relationships between persons of the same sex', encompassing recognition of same-sex marriage.[69] In so finding, the Court observed that the lack of consensus on the matter among relevant states could *not* justify the rejection of such marriage. As Dominic McGoldrick observes, that stance may have arisen since the 'impression that sexual orientation rights is a 'Western' conspiracy against non-Western States'[70] is less apparent in such states, contrasting with the stances of certain 'Eastern' Council of Europe states.

Strasbourg's exclusionary interpretation of Article 12 has been upheld consistently since *Schalk* on the basis of a continuing lack of consensus in the Member States as to the availability of same-sex marriage. At the time when *Schalk* was decided, only eight states of the Council of Europe allowed same-sex marriage,[71] and at the present time there is still no consensus on the matter.[72]

---

62 *Ibid.*, 94.
63 The terms 'men and women' used in Article 12 are absent.
64 *Schalk* (n 50) 99. That was confirmed by the Grand Chamber in *X v Austria* (2013) 57 *European Human Rights Reports* 14.
65 See *Hämäläinen v Finland* (App. No.37359/09), judgement of 16 July 2014 at [74].
66 *Schalk* (n 50) 58.
67 *Ibid.*, 101.
68 For criticism, see Laverack (n 45) 182.
69 See Advisory Opinion OC-24/17, IACtHR Series A, 24 (2017).
70 D McGoldrick, 'The Development and Status of Sexual Orientation Discrimination Under International Human Rights Law' (2016) 16 *Human Rights Law Review* 613, 660–661.
71 *Schalk* (n 50) 58.
72 See *Oliari* (n 52) 192 and *Orlandi v Italy* (App. No.26431/12), judgement of 14 December 2017, 204–205. See further F Hamilton, 'Same sex marriage, consensus, certainty and the European Court of Human Rights' (2018) 1 *European Human Rights Law Reports* 33; Johnson (n 52); P Johnson and S Falcetta, 'Sexual Orientation Discrimination and Article 3 of the ECHR: Developing the Protection of Sexual Minorities' (2018) 43:2 *European Law Review* 167.

However, the Court's reluctance to take the next step, by accepting marriage equality, may be diminishing: in *Orlandi v Italy*,[73] the Court left open the possibility that if the consensus strengthens in the future, it might be prepared to recognise a right to marry for same-sex couples under Article 12.[74]

But, there is already a consensus among the Member States as to the availability of same-sex registered partnership schemes, so the Court has shown more receptivity to recognising a right to such a partnership under Article 8 read alone or with 14. In *Vallianatos*,[75] the applicants, who were in same-sex unions, challenged their exclusion from the registered partnership scheme introduced in Greece for different-sex couples, under Article 8 read with 14. The Court found that same-sex couples need recognition of their relationship and civic benefits just as different-sex couples do.[76] The government sought under Article 14 to justify the exclusion of same-sex couples from the scheme on the basis of the need to make provision for unmarried different-sex couples with children. In evaluating that justification, the Court found that of the 19 states authorising some form of registered partnership, only Lithuania and Greece reserved it exclusively to different-sex couples; nine Member States provided for same-sex marriage and 17 for forms of same-sex civil partnership.[77] Therefore, in assessing the proportionality of the means chosen with the aims pursued, the Court conceded only a narrow margin of appreciation to the state, finding as a result that proportionality demands under Article 14 did not merely require that the measure chosen was in principle suitable to achieve the aim in question: it also had to be shown to be *necessary*, in order to achieve that aim, to exclude same-sex couples from the category of civil unions. Given that the scheme differentiated between same- and different-sex couples who did *not* have children, it was found that the government had failed to justify the difference in treatment since the goals it was seeking to attain did not *necessitate* excluding same-sex couples from the civil union scheme. Accordingly, a breach of Article 14 read with 8 was found.

In *Oliari v Italy*,[78] the Court took a further and highly significant step: it was confronted with a situation resembling that in *Vallianatos* but in which *no* registered partnership scheme had been introduced, even for different-sex couples. Three same-sex couples, supported by various activist organisations, complained under Article 8 read alone or with 14, that Italy did not allow them access to a legal framework for formalising their relationships in the form of either marriage or a registered partnership, so they were being discriminated

---

73 *Orlandi* (n 72).
74 *Ibid.*, 204–205.
75 *Vallianatos v Greece* (2014) 59 *E.H.R.R.* 12.
76 *Ibid.*, 81.
77 *Ibid.*, 91–92.
78 *Oliari* (n 52).

against as a result of their sexual orientation. The Court decided the matter solely on the basis of the existence and scope of a positive obligation under Article 8(1) to introduce registered partnerships for same-sex couples, affording them a legal framework protecting and recognising their relationships, since the protection related, it was found, to central, not peripheral, needs of the applicants.[79] The Court, however, did not decide to impose a positive obligation to introduce a new legislative framework largely on a basis of principle, founded on notions of the inherent value of such a framework for same-sex couples. Instead, it viewed the notion of 'respect' for private and family life under Article 8(1) as a flexible one, finding that the requirements denoted by the term would vary considerably from case to case:

> The notion of "respect" is not clear-cut, especially as far as positive obligations are concerned: having regard to the diversity of the practices followed and the situations obtaining in the Contracting States, the notion's requirements will vary considerably from case to case.[80]

It identified *two* localised factors in particular that influenced its findings as to those requirements. The first comprised the 'conflict between the lived social reality of the applicants, and 'the law, which gives them no official recognition',[81] finding 'there is amongst the Italian population a popular acceptance of homosexual couples . . . and support for their recognition and protection'.[82] The second factor concerned the 'unheeded' calls of the Italian courts to introduce a legal framework[83] providing same-sex couples with such recognition.[84]

In determining the scope of the positive obligation, the Court considered the balance to be struck between the interests of the applicants and those of the community. The margin of appreciation conceded was not specified with any clarity, although impliedly it was narrowed due to the consensus among the Member States on the matter as regards the importance to be attributed to the ability of the individual to access a registered partnership: the Court noted that a 'thin majority' of Member States (24 out of 47) had by mid-2015 already legislated to introduce forms of same-sex registered partnerships.[85] The Court took account of the absence of a counter-vailing community interest

---

79 *Ibid.*, 169.
80 *Ibid.*, 161.
81 *Ibid.*, 173.
82 *Ibid.*, 181.
83 *Ibid.*, 183–185.
84 *Ibid.*, 45.
85 *Ibid.*, 178. The Court also took account of the global trend towards state recognition of same-sex unions. See: H Fenwick and A Hayward (n 7); A Hayward, 'Same-Sex Registered Partnerships – A Right to Be Recognized?' (2016) 75 *Cambridge Law Journal* 27; Fenwick (n 57).

put forward by the Italian government, while making the significant finding that providing access to a registered partnership related to the 'core protection of the applicants as same-sex couples'.[86] The government merely relied on its margin in arguing that time was needed to achieve general recognition of 'this new form of family'.[87] But, the Court found that the margin would not cover that position, given that the Italian Constitutional Court had repeatedly called for a juridical recognition of the relevant rights and duties of same-sex unions, but the government had not responded.[88]

The Court proceeded therefore to find a breach of Article 8 but found the claim for same-sex marriage under Article 12 inadmissible. The couples' claims under Article 12 in respect of access to marriage were found to be manifestly ill-founded,[89] following the Court's established stance on that matter, based mainly on the lack of a consensus among the Member States as to the introduction of same-sex marriage, following the findings in *Hämäläinen v Finland*.[90] It also declined to consider Article 14, leaving the discriminatory dimension unrecognised.[91]

Post-*Oliari*, the relevant consensus strengthened somewhat as to acceptance of same-sex registered partnership schemes, and it was expected that eventually Strasbourg would find that the positive obligation recognised under Article 8 in *Oliari*[92] should be extended to Member States even where one or both of the particular local factors present in Italy were absent. That eventually occurred in *Fedotova and Others v Russia*:[93] the Court took a further step, following *Oliari*, in finally finding a clear positive right to a form of formalisation of same-sex unions under Article 8(1), where such couples have *no* means of having their relationship recognised by law. Three same-sex couples sought to claim a right to same-sex marriage in Russia, on the basis that only one form of formalisation of relationships is available in Russia – marriage – which is not open to same-sex couples. All three couples applied on a number of occasions unsuccessfully to the Register Office locally to have their marriages registered. The requests were dismissed by reference to Article 1 of the Russian Family Code, which states that the regulation of family relationships is based on 'the principle of a voluntary marital union between a man and a woman'.

Unsurprisingly, given Strasbourg's current stance on same-sex marriage under Article 12, the claims were brought to Strasbourg under Articles 8 and

86 *Ibid.*, 177–178.
87 *Ibid.*, 176.
88 *Ibid.*, 185.
89 *Ibid.*, 194.
90 *Hämäläinen* (n 65) 74.
91 *Oliari* (n 52) 188.
92 *Ibid.*, 185.
93 (2021) ECHR 225.

14 only, for a means of formalising the couples' relationships in Russia via a form of registered partnership. The key stumbling block for the claim, based on the preceding discussion, appeared to be that the Court in *Oliari* had referred to a discordance between social reality in Italy and the legal position as to formalisation of a same-sex union, as determinative of the reach of positive obligations under Article 8(1). So, it appeared to have accorded to itself the possibility, where such discordance did not exist, or did not exist to the same extent in a Member State, of avoiding a finding that the Article had been breached. Such a discordance would clearly be unlikely to be discerned in Russia (and some other Eastern European states), where it would be much harder for a same-sex partnership to live openly as a couple since a much higher percentage of the population is opposed to recognition of same-sex unions than in Italy.[94] As to the second factor from *Oliari*, the Russian courts had dismissed the applicants' challenges to the Register Offices' decisions,[95] and so their stance had affirmed the state's rejection of the introduction of registered partnerships for same-sex couples.

The Court in *Fedotova* did *not*, however, rely on the first or second factors identified in *Oliari* as having a role in determining the scope of the requirement under Article 8 to provide same-sex couples with a means of formalising their relationships. It focused only on the first, noting that the Russian government had pointed out that the majority of Russians did not approve of same-sex unions,[96] but it refused to allow that factor to influence its judgement. Accordingly, the Court found that 'it would be incompatible with the underlying values of the Convention, as an instrument of the European public order, if the exercise of Convention rights by a minority group were made conditional on its being accepted by the majority', relying on *Alekseyev v. Russia*,[97] *Bayev and Others v. Russia*[98] and *Beizaras and Levickas v. Lithuania*.[99] Further, the Court found that the respondent government had a margin of appreciation in terms of choosing 'the most appropriate form of registration of same-sex unions taking into account its specific social and cultural context (for example, civil partnership, civil union, or civil solidarity act)'. But, Russia had overstepped that margin, because 'no legal framework capable of protecting the applicants' relationships as same-sex couples has been available under domestic law'.[100]

---

94 See e.g. the Pew Research Center Study (2018) <www.pewforum.org/2018/10/29/eastern-and-western-europeans-differ-on-importance-of-religion-views-of-minorities-and-key-social-issues> p. 12 (accessed 19 October 2021).
95 Under article 1 of the Russian Family Code.
96 *Fedotova* (n 93) 52.
97 *Alekseyev* (n 44) 81.
98 (2017) ECHR 207 [70].
99 (2020) ECHR 19 [122].
100 *Fedotova* (n 93) 56.

This decision completes the journey described here, undertaken by the Court, towards finding that same-sex couples have a right to formal recognition of their unions in law. States retain choices as to the nature of the formalisation to be adopted, but, impliedly, the choice could not be one that failed to provide the couples with a number of civic and other benefits, although the precise range of such benefits to be accorded will no doubt be the subject of future claims. It is reasonable to conclude that the right in question has finally been accorded clear recognition because the Court found that the two relevant factors to be taken into account were the adverse impact on the applicants of lack of such recognition and the burden that providing it would impose on the state. It is hard to imagine situations in particular states, in which an applicant would fail to demonstrate such an adverse impact or where the respondent state could plausibly claim that the burden of providing such recognition would be too great. Russia's attempts to identify such burdens were summarily dismissed.[101]

5.4 Future Strasbourg Claims from Same-Sex Couples

Post-*Fedotova* and *Oliari* same-sex registered partnerships may spread further across the Member States, aside from the most intransigent ones; Russia itself is unlikely to comply with the *Fedotova* ruling in the near future. While a number of 'Eastern' states include bars in their Constitutions to same-sex marriage, their Constitutions usually, not invariably, also include provisions on non-discrimination.[102] Domestic courts or legislatures could therefore find that they require the introduction of same-sex registered partnerships, but not marriage, in an effort to avoid perpetuating discrimination based straightforwardly on sexual orientation. Courts or legislatures in some 'Eastern' states would not, however, be likely to favour formal recognition of same-sex unions,[103] and in such states popular acceptance of formal same-sex unions would be likely to be much less apparent than in Italy. So, despite *Fedotova*, the struggle to introduce such unions is likely to continue in some states for a number of years.

---

101 *Ibid.*, 54, 55.
102 E.g. in 2009 the Slovenian Constitutional Court found that Article 22 of the Registration of Same Sex Partnerships Act violated the right to non-discrimination under Article 14 of the Constitution on the ground of sexual orientation: see Equal Rights Trust, <www.equalrightstrust.org/news/constitutional-court-slovenia-upholds-equal-rights-same-sex-partners> (accessed 19 October 2021).
103 See e.g. *Position of the 'Iustitia' Association of Polish Judges and 'THEMIS' Association of Judges and the Cooperation Forum of Judges on the New National Council of the Judiciary*, 17 November 2018. <www.aeaj.org/media/files/2018-11-17-92-Position-Polish%20Judges%20Association.pdf> (accessed 19 October 2021).

6. Strasbourg Appeasement of Majorities, Evading Confrontation with Homophobia

The tendencies towards 'East'/'West' divisions as to acceptance of formalised same-sex unions identified in this part place the Court in a sensitive position. While the principle has been recently reinforced that the Court's protection for the Convention rights is subsidiary to the protection provided by the state,[104] reliance on the Court is still required to protect vulnerable minorities who fail to receive protection for their Convention rights domestically, including in the domestic courts.[105] As the Court pointed out in *Alekseyev v Russia*, the exercise of Convention rights by a sexual minority in a particular state cannot depend on their acceptance by the majority.[106] But, reliance on consensus analysis linked to the width of the margin of appreciation conceded to a state has the capacity to allow popular opinion in a *number* of Member States to affect the protection offered to sexual minorities adversely.[107] As discussed, if a clear majority of states provide legal protection for such minorities, the Court will be emboldened to follow suit, conceding a narrow margin of appreciation to the state and tending to find a violation as in *Fedotova*. But, until there is a consensus on same-sex marriage, the Court has demonstrated that it will not recognise a right to contract such a marriage under Article 12 read with 14.[108]

The use of consensus analysis sits uncomfortably, especially in this context, with the Court's approach to protecting minorities and especially to the relevance of majority values in a single state: it has found that majoritarian support in a state should not be relied on to narrow down the scope of the substantive protection of a Convention guarantee, whereas it could enable that scope to be broadened.[109] That could be seen as consistent with the findings in *Oliari* since the wider ambit ascribed to Article 8 in that instance was found to encompass acceptance of a positive obligation to introduce same-sex registered partnerships, due to popular support for such an innovation in Italy. But, conversely, as discussed, *lack* of such support in some 'Eastern' states could argue for a more restrained ambit, as accepted via the first factor found relevant to the notion of 'respect' in *Oliari*, but contrary to the findings on that point in *Bayev*. That argument was put on behalf of the applicants in *Oliari*: 'empirical evidence ... showed that lack of recognition of same-sex couples in a given state

---

104 See Protocol 15 that came into force on 1 August 2021 and *Council of Europe Explanatory Report on Protocol 15*. <www.echr.coe.int/Documents/Protocol_15_explanatory_report_ENG.pdf> (accessed 19 October 2021). See further Bates (n 49); Fenwick, in Ziegler et al., (n 49) and McGoldrick (n 48).
105 See e.g. *L and V v Austria* (2003) 36 E.H.R.R. 55; *Alekseyev* (n 44); *Bączkowski and Others v Poland* (2009) 48 E.H.R.R. 19.
106 *Alekseyev* (n 44) 81.
107 See McGoldrick (n 70) 666.
108 See *Oliari* (n 52) 192 and *Orlandi* (n 72) 204–205; see further Hamilton (n 72).
109 See *Bayev* (n 98) 70.

corresponded to a lower degree of social acceptance of homosexuality . . . by simply deferring normative choices to the national authorities, the Court would fail to take account of the fact that certain national choices were . . . based on prevailing discriminatory attitudes against homosexuals'.[110]

The Court has accepted that a lack of state protection and recognition of same-sex relationships relates to an especially intimate aspect of private and family life; it has already found that the availability of same-sex registered partnerships relates to 'core' interests of same-sex couples and to 'facets of an individual's existence and identity'.[111] So, in a state in which there is little discordance between social reality and the law, or no acceptance of the argument for such partnerships by the domestic courts due to the climate of homophobia, the risk of acquiescing to prejudice against sexual minorities was expected to lead the Court eventually to rely on a strengthened European consensus to find that an 'outlier' state had over-stepped its narrowed margin of appreciation. That eventually occurred in *Fedotova*: its findings that the Court should not allow majority homophobia to determine the treatment of minorities in *Alekseyev* were finally applied in the context of formalisation of same-sex unions. Further, but – it appears – only on the basis of a strengthening consensus, it seems probable that it will eventually find that Article 12 read with 14 encompasses same-sex marriage.

7. Conclusions

This chapter has found that civil or registered partnerships represent a non-traditional formalised relationship status, but that that in itself does not undermine their value. In one respect, it enhances that value. The very fact that such partnerships do not represent traditionalism accords them value due to their non-heteronormative, largely secular, non-patriarchal status. However, this chapter has not sought to argue that, therefore, such partnerships are more appropriate for same-sex couples than is marriage, or that they should merely be viewed as a 'lighter touch' status, representing a staging post on the way to achieving marital status. Same-sex couples should not be viewed as a homogenous group, just as different-sex couples cannot be. Therefore, the traditional status and nature of marriage should not be viewed as providing an argument for excluding same-sex couples from that relationship status. Rather, this chapter has argued for equality of access to *both* formal relationship statuses:[112] registered partnerships should be available to same-sex couples only in the context of the availability *also* of same-sex marriage – otherwise, a ghettoisation of such couples into the non-traditional status only occurs. It is therefore strange to find that a

---

110 *Oliari* (n 52) 113.
111 *Ibid.*, 177; *Orlandi* (n 72) 206.
112 See further Fenwick and Hayward (n 7).

Court set up partly to protect the interests of minorities is so far from accepting that it should protect equality of access to both statuses. Paradoxically, while the Court has had a significant influence in terms of furthering the protection of homosexual individuals in the UK,[113] it has now been entirely outstripped in terms of refusing to countenance homophobia by the Westminster and Scottish Parliaments in the context of ensuring equality of formal relationship statuses. But, as further claims for equal marriage arise, the Court should take greater account of its core mission to protect a vulnerable minority and of the current struggles of LGBT activists to combat homophobic denials of such access in the contracting states.[114]

---

113 See *Dudgeon* (n 43); *Smith and Grady* (n 43); *Lustig-Prean and Beckett v United Kingdom* (2000) 29 ECHR 548.
114 See L Hodson, 'Activists and Lawyers in the ECtHR: The Struggle for Gay Rights' in D Anagnostou (ed), *Rights in Pursuit of Social Change: Legal Mobilisation in the Multi-Level European System* (Oxford University Press 2014).

Chapter 11

Changing Perceptions of Homosexuality as Revealed by the Law of Defamation in Scotland

Kenneth McK. Norrie

1. Introduction

The law of defamation, in Scotland as elsewhere, is designed to protect reputation, that is to say, the esteem in which an individual is held by other people.[1] Now, reputation is a concept that is very much based on social values. It 'is inherently public and only exists to further or hinder one's status in a community'.[2] As such, reputation can be enhanced or destroyed as society embraces new values or abandons old ones. So, it is no surprise that the definition of 'defamation', the legal wrong of damaging the esteem in which an individual is held, relies on a protean standard, captured in the words of the classic test laid down for English law, which has been applied by the Scottish courts for the past 85 years: a statement is of a defamatory nature if the words used would tend to lower the subject 'in the estimation of right-thinking members of society generally'.[3] The Scottish statutory formulation of the test is that 'the statement . . . causes harm to the person's reputation (that is, if it tends to lower the person's reputation in the estimation of ordinary persons)'.[4] This test is designed to base the standard on community values rather than on the values held either by the subject of the statement or its maker. Its strength lies in its

---

1 The two interests that reputation encompasses are (i) the personality interest in self-esteem and (ii) the economic interest in commercial reputation: K Norrie, 'The Scots Law of Defamation: Is There a Need for Reform?' in NR Whitty and R Zimmermann (eds), *Rights of Personality in Scots Law: A Comparative Perspective* (Duke University Press 2009) 435. Scotland was unusual in that an injury to personality sounded in damages even though the words were communicated to no one other than their subject, but that rule will be changed when s.1(2) of the Defamation and Malicious Publication (Scotland) Act 2021 comes into force.
2 Gregory K Davis, 'A Bottom Up Approach to LGB Defamation: Criticizing Narratives of Public Policy and Respectability' (2014) *The Dukeminier Awards Journal of Sexual Orientation and Gender Identity Law* 1, 11.
3 *Sim v Stretch* [1936] 2 All ER 1237, 1240 per Lord Atkin. The most recent acceptance that this represents the law of Scotland is found in *Wildcat Haven Enterprises CIC v Wightman* 2020 SLT 473, per Lord Clark at para. 21.
4 Defamation and Malicious Publication (Scotland) Act 2021, s.1(4)(a).

DOI: 10.4324/9781003286295-14

being an objective standard against which statements that cause offence to an individual can be judged and in being flexible enough to accommodate the changing values of a vibrant and shifting culture. But, being a *legal* standard, it is the judges who determine what right-thinking members of society, or ordinary persons, think: whether any particular statement is capable of bearing a defamatory meaning is quintessentially a question of law and not of fact.[5]

These characteristics of the *Sim v Stretch* test mean that defamation actions offer a valuable mechanism to test the temper of the times. In other words, an exploration of how the test has been applied over a long period allows us to trace changing social attitudes to particular personal characteristics. As we will see, the cases often reveal broader social attitudes as well.

This chapter seeks to explore the developing social and judicial attitudes to the characteristic of homosexuality through the lens of defamation actions in the Scottish courts. The time frame examined will span the 200 years that separate the case of the Drumsheugh school mistresses in Regency Edinburgh, where the judges regarded the accusation of lesbian behaviour with naked abhorrence, and the action against the politician Kezia Dugdale, where it was the attribution of anti-gay sentiment that was regarded as 'toxic'. We will see a paradigm shift from right-thinking people dissociating themselves from homosexuals to right-thinking people dissociating themselves from homophobes, although that shift manifested itself only at the very end of the period being examined.

2. A Time of Witchcraft

In 1819, the House of Lords gave the final judgement in the case of *Pirie and Woods v Cumming Gordon*, affirming the Court of Session's award of damages against the defender 'for having spread sundry reports of a nature tending to the ruin of [the pursuers'] establishment'.[6] Earlier proceedings in the Court of Session are not reported in the law reports, but they have been commented upon in numerous accessible sources.[7]

The defender was the grandmother and sponsor of a girl[8] whom she had placed at a girls' school run by two mistresses in Drumsheugh Gardens in Edinburgh. She repeated to other parents with girls at the school the allegation

---

5 K Norrie, *Defamation and Related Actions in Scots Law* (Butterworths 1995) 13.
6 *London News*, 21 July 1819.
7 The judgements and transcript of proceedings, held in the Advocates Library, were extensively researched by Professor Lillian Faderman for her book *Scotch Verdict* (William Morrow & Co 1983). The case is also fully discussed by the well-known legal antiquarian William Roughead in his article 'Closed Doors: Or, the Great Drumsheugh Case' 1929 JR 91 and in his book *Bad Companions* (Duffield and Green 1931). And it is the subject of a chapter by the present author in JP Grant and EE Sutherland (eds), *Pronounced for Doom: Early Scots Law Tales* (Avizandum Publishing 2013).
8 She was the offspring of the defender's son who had impregnated a serving girl while in India.

made by her granddaughter that the school mistresses were found on a number of occasions in a sexual embrace. The daughters were removed and the school ruined. When the mistresses sued, it was assumed without question that the allegation against them was of a defamatory nature; indeed, it was deemed by the judges to be defamatory of the most outrageous sort conceivable.

The focus of the legal dispute in the case was whether the allegations were true (for publishing the truth is not capable of founding an action for defamation),[9] and this turned on the judges' assessment of the credibility of the witnesses, in particular the schoolgirl whose words had been spread by her grandmother, the defender. In the Inner House Lord Justice Clerk Hope found the allegations so scandalous as to be, literally, incredible:

> I never saw a case so disgusting . . . These ladies were accused of gross immorality and shameful indecency. The description of their behaviour is so gross, brutish, beastly and absurd that I could not give it the slightest credit.[10]

Lord Boyle thought that while possibly occurring elsewhere, female sexuality expressed without a male was simply unheard of in Scotland:

> One cannot but help be sensitive to the fact that however well known the crime here charged may be amongst Eastern nations, this is the first instance on record of such an accusation having ever been made in this country.[11]

Lord Meadowbank opined that since sexual 'excitements' in women must be 'calculated to excite the venereal appetite and prepare for the admission of the male sex [organ]' an accusation of such excitements in the all-female environment at issue must perforce be untrue.[12] He had earlier expressed himself 'disposed to believe that the crime in question . . . was equally imaginary with witchcraft, sorcery or carnal copulation with the devil'.[13] Now, he castigated those of his brethren who saw confirmation of the truth in the very extraordinariness of the allegations: 'It is apparent that such an imputation operates upon the moral feelings as the imputation of witchcraft did upon the religious feelings of our ancestors: to them too the charge was evidence of its own truth'.[14]

---

9 In fact, this was accepted unequivocally only some decades later, in *McKellar v Duke of Sutherland* (1859) 21 D 222.
10 Faderman (n 7) 232–233.
11 *Ibid.*, 239.
12 *Ibid.*, 66.
13 *Ibid.*, 65.
14 *Ibid.*, 258.

But, these judges were in a minority, and the four other judges who heard the witnesses believed the schoolgirl and found that, the statements being true, the school mistresses had not lost any justified reputation. However, on a review of that decision in 1812, the court subsequently found that the defamation had indeed been made out, primarily because the evidence of the defender's granddaughter was tainted by the fact that she was half-Indian – 'wanting', in Lord Meadowbank's words, 'in the advantages of legitimacy and of a European complexion and therefore all the more dependent on the favour of [the defender]'.[15] She had been brought up by Indian domestics and, in Lord Meadowbank's words, 'it is an historical fact and matter of notoriety that the language of the Hindoo female domestics turns chiefly on the commerce between the sexes'.[16] So, she alone in the school had the capacity to invent stories beyond the ken of respectable Scottish schoolgirls. Seven years later, the House of Lords affirmed the verdict in the school mistresses' favour.[17]

That mere allegations of homosexuality retained over 100 years later their power to taint the innocent, as allegations of witchcraft once did was made clear when the legal historian William Roughead came to write on the Drumsheugh case in the 1920s. He felt obliged to dissociate himself from something so unspeakable as lesbianism and asserted that nothing would have induced him to write on the case had he thought there to be any substance at all to the allegations.[18] Roughead, as the majority judges had, put the blame squarely on the 'half-caste' schoolgirl, describing her background in language, doubtless unexceptional at the time, but breathtakingly racist to today's reader.[19]

We see the same level of taint attached to homosexuality in the next Scottish case, in which that characteristic was at issue. In *AB v XY*,[20] an employer, on discovering two of his clerks together in the office toilet, summarily dismissed them, saying that 'there was only one inference to be made'; he subsequently informed the rest of his staff that the two men had been dismissed using the words, 'they left without a shred of character; they are not men, they are beasts'.[21] This was accepted to be an implication of sodomy and gross indecency. Now, both of course were criminal offences at the time and no distinction required to be made as to where the defamation lay – in the imputation of criminality or of immorality. The legal question before the Inner House was

---

15 *Ibid.*, 258.
16 *Ibid.*, 153.
17 See (n 6).
18 William Roughead, 'Closed Doors: Or the Great Drumsheugh Case' 1929 *JR* 91, 107.
19 She was, in Roughead's words, a 'half-caste', 'Asiatic', 'daughter of the Philistines' who 'imported into the Water of Leith the bane which she had gathered on the banks of the Ganges'. It was not, he surmised, that she had no heart but 'that she had, and one to match her complexion': 1929 *JR* 91, 100–101.
20 1917 SC 15.
21 *Ibid.*, 16.

whether both statements were made in situations of privilege, and there was no dispute, either that the words used by the defender bore the innuendo or that that innuendo was actionable as defamation. The action was dismissed on the basis that the statements had indeed been made in a situation of privilege, and that malice (an additional element that has to exist in cases of privilege) was absent. Truth was not pleaded as a defence, probably because the defender knew he could not prove what had actually happened behind the closed toilet door. Lord Dundas struggled to find sympathy for the pursuers:

> It is to be regretted that the future careers of these two young men may be hampered by what has occurred. But it seems to me that, if this should be so, they have mainly themselves to blame. Their conduct, assuming the truth of their own averments, appears to have been amazingly foolish; they have augmented the publicity of the matter by raising these (as I think, ill-founded) actions; and gravely accentuated the scandal by the mode in which, for obvious tactical purposes, the innuendoes have been stated on their records.[22]

Lord Salvesen pointed out:

> The only consolation that can be afforded the pursuers is that, as the defender has not asked an issue of justification [truth], it must be assumed that the charge is untrue, and it cannot therefore be repeated by others without their exposing themselves to an action of damages for defamation.[23]

These statements suggest, I think, that the judges regarded the allegation as far more serious than an accusation of merely criminal behaviour. Indeed, the very fact that the parties were anonymised in the law report confirms this, for that is an indulgence not normally shown to innocent people charged but acquitted of crimes. A sexual orientation that differed from the norm was such an outrage to decent society that the mere making of the allegation could cause irreparable damage to the subject – irrespective of its truth or otherwise.

There was no anonymity in the next British case, which was raised in the English court, but the damage that the allegation could cause (if with a different focus) is no less great. In *Kerr v Kennedy*,[24] Mrs Innes Margaret Kerr sued Lady John Kennedy who had told an acquaintance that Mrs Kerr was a lesbian. Now, lesbian sexual activity, unlike male homosexual activity, was not a criminal act, so the defamation could only be founded on the basis of immorality. Although the allegation itself was in relation to a state of being rather

---

22 *Ibid.*, 21.
23 *Ibid.*, 22.
24 [1942] 1 KB 409.

than to a specific act, Asquith J found from the word 'lesbian' an inescapable implication of 'unchastity'.[25] The values of society at the time were startlingly revealed by the judge's identification of the loss caused by the allegation: damages were due, said he, 'since [the allegation] is calculated to bring [the plaintiff] into social disfavour and, as the phrase runs, to damage her prospects in the marriage market and thereby her finances'.[26] The only difference between opposite-sex and same-sex sexual activity, he said, was 'that the imputation of the latter is, if anything, more wounding, more likely to excite abhorrence on the part of average reasonable people, more likely to spoil the victim's prospects of marriage'.[27] So, while lesbianism raised no implications of criminality, as male homosexual activity would, it was peculiarly harmful to women at a time when their marriage prospects were a real economic asset. Mrs Kerr was awarded £300.

Fifteen years later, the Wolfenden Report was published,[28] but the law reports themselves reveal little evidence of any change in social attitudes towards homosexuality. That the very severity of the allegation rendered it incredible, the point made by the Lord Justice Clerk in 1812, was a phenomenon seen even as late as 1959, at the end of a decade notorious for a substantial increase in the prosecutions of men for homosexual offences. An action for defamation was raised by Liberace,[29] a popular pianist famed for his sequined outfits and effeminate mannerisms, against the *Daily Mirror*, which had published a piece by its gossip columnist, William Connor (who wrote under the by-name 'Cassandra'),[30] describing the pianist as 'the summit of sex – the pinnacle of masculine, feminine and neuter. Everything that he, she or it can ever want', and as a 'deadly, winking, sniggering, snuggling, chromium-plated, scent-impregnated, luminous, quivering, giggling, fruit-flavoured, ice-covered heap of mother love'.[31] An innuendo of homosexuality, particularly from the word 'fruit' (an American slang term of the time for gay man) was made out, and Liberace robustly denied the allegation in the witness box. The jury rejected the defence of truth, and the plaintiff received £8,000 damages: as he later gleefully put it, he 'cried all the way to the bank'.[32]

---

25 *Ibid.*, 413.
26 *Ibid.*, 411.
27 *Ibid.*, 412.
28 *Report of the Committee on Homosexual Offences and Prostitution* 1957 Cmnd 247 (HMSO, London).
29 A short report of *Liberace v Daily Mirror* may be found in the *Times* 18 June 1959: for a more detailed discussion, see J Wilson, 'Behind the Candelabra, in Front of the Bench' (2013) 163 *NLJ* 30.
30 Made famous by his febrile attack on PG Wodehouse for the latter's radio broadcasts while a prisoner in Germany during the war.
31 Wilson (n 29) 30.
32 Liberace claimed this as a catchphrase after the case in his 1973 *Liberace: An Autobiography*, but he had used it earlier in response to negative reviews: see Ben Yagoda, 'Crying All the Way to the Bank' in *Lingua Franca* blog posted 11 July 2013. <www.chronicle.com/blogs/linguafranca/crying-all-the-way-to-the-bank> (accessed 29 September 2021).

There is no challenge in any of these 20th century cases to the understanding that an allegation of homosexuality was in and of itself a serious defamation. Given the nature of the *Sim v Stretch* test, and the attitudes of society at the time, any other view would be met with bemusement. Gay people (like witches) were perceived to be horrid, monstrous beings, living nightmare lives, and not unthreatening and talented people like Liberace, respectable lady school-teachers and hard-working office clerks.

3. Questioning Old Truths

By the 1990s, it was becoming apparent that the deeply ingrained social antagonism towards gay and lesbian people was softening, as their visibility in the media and popular culture increased. This change in attitude was particularly noticeable amongst younger members of society, and it is no coincidence that the first stirrings of change in the way defamation claims involving allegations of homosexuality played out were in cases brought by well-known singers with a much younger fan base than the likes of Liberace – although their desire to protect their reputations among their fan base was no less keen than his. Reports in a music magazine had (wrongly) suggested that the actor and singer Jason Donovan was gay, and he was awarded the preposterous sum of £200,000[33] in 1992.[34] Robbie Williams, a popular singer, settled a similar claim for an undisclosed amount in 2005.[35] Interestingly, neither singer claimed that he had been directly harmed by being identified as gay: both indeed loudly resisted asserting that right-thinking people would (or should) be unwilling to associate with gay people. Instead, they sought to draw an innuendo of hypocrisy, both singers having previously publicly denied being gay. Although structuring their claim this way looks as if it is taking some of the sting out of an assertion of homosexual abomination, in truth it goes little further than the celebrities claiming: 'there's nothing offensive in being gay, but I am offended if you call me one'.[36] Structuring the claim as an allegation of hypocrisy contains the very homophobia the claimants would seem to have been seeking to avoid, for if hypocrisy is claiming to be something better than you are, then to be offended at being accused of falsely claiming heterosexuality is to assert an actual superiority over homosexuals.

---

33 English courts are (or were then) notoriously generous in their assessment of damages for defamation, a tendency statute has since reined in somewhat. The Australian Donovan would be better, today, to sue in Australia, which can lay claim to having taken England's mantel as the world's 'haven for libel tourism': see J Larkin, 'False Havens: Assessing New Developments in the Libel Tourism Debate' (2019) 11 *Journal of Media Law* 82.
34 *Donovan v The Face* (1992) unreported. See Ursula Smartt, *Media Law for Journalists* (Sage 2006) 177.
35 *The Telegraph*, 7 December 2005.
36 See D Knight, '"I'm Not Gay: Not that There's Anything Wrong with That!" Are Unwanted Imputations of Gayness Defamatory?' (2006) 37 *VUWLR* 249.

Perhaps we should not read too much into the 'celebrity' cases, motivated almost certainly more by commercial than personal considerations (although commercial interests are another way of testing social attitudes and are of course equally protected by the law of defamation). But, from the late 1990s, a number of Scottish cases suggest that the unquestioned acceptance of the defamatory nature of allegations of homosexuality was beginning to break down. The first hint of this was in the 1997 Outer House decision of *Prophit v BBC*,[37] where proof before answer was allowed in a claim for damages for defamation when, in the radio comedy programme 'The News Quiz', reference was made to a 'lesbian nun' in the context of a news report concerning the pursuer, a nun accused of fraud. Judge Coutts declined to exclude the allegation of lesbianism from the case on the ground that it clearly implied unchastity and homosexuality. Although the judge refused to consider 'as a matter of law whether a suggestion of lesbianism remains defamatory these days',[38] it is nonetheless significant that the question was raised at all: in the earlier cases, no such defence could even have been conceived. This new questioning of old truths was occurring elsewhere at the same time. The Supreme Court of New South Wales, where the test of defamatoriness is analogous to that used in English law,[39] similarly no longer took it as read that an allegation of homosexuality was necessarily defamatory but, as in *Prophit*, the court declined to find that it was not.[40] And in 1998, the English High Court refused to accept that an allegation that the actors Tom Cruise and Nicole Kidman (then married to each other) were both gay was not in itself defamatory in law.[41]

Yet, the balance shifted a year later in the Scottish case of *Quilty v Windsor*,[42] where a prisoner had written a letter of complaint to the Scottish Prison Service, alleging that a prison warder was unfit for his job for various reasons, including that he was homosexual. The warder sued for defamation and the defender argued, inter alia, that the imputation of homosexuality could not be seen as defamatory. The major legal issue in the case was, as in *AB v XY*, one of privilege (on which rock the claim similarly foundered), but for our purposes the interest lies in the fact that the judge, for the first time in a Scottish court,

---

37 1997 SLT 745.
38 *Ibid.*, 748.
39 In *Radio 2UE Sydney Pty Ltd v Chesterton* [2009] HCA 16, paras. 5–6, the High Court of Australia pointed out that Australian courts tend to interpret the phrase 'right-thinking members of society generally', as used in *Sim v Stretch*, to mean 'fair minded people', or 'ordinary, reasonable people', as does the Scottish statutory formulation (above n 4).
40 In *Horner v Goulburn City Council* (1997) NSW Lexis 2220, at 2225, quoted in Knight (n 36), Levine J stated that 'I do not consider that it can conclusively be said that even towards the end of this century's last decade that there can be, among ordinary members of the community, a view that to say of a person that that person is in a homosexual relationship is not disparaging or is not likely to lower that person in the estimation of such people'.
41 *Cruise v Express Newspapers*, affirmed by the Court of Appeal at [1999] QB 931.
42 1999 SLT 346.

declared himself unpersuaded that a mere allegation of homosexuality would meet the *Sim v Stretch* test.[43] Lord Kingarth said: 'I am inclined to agree with counsel for the first defender that merely to refer to a person as being homosexual would not now generally at least be regarded – if it ever was – as defamatory per se'.[44] The judge qualified his conclusion by stating that the action might have been allowed to proceed (had it been pleaded with greater specificity) on the basis of an innuendo that the warder's sexual orientation interfered with his work, that is to say, if homosexuality was a proxy for some genuinely damaging accusation. That in itself is, however, troubling. A tendency to use homosexuality as a proxy for other disparaging things, such as infidelity, hypocrisy or unprofessional behaviour, can be traced, Knight suggests, to the same underlying prejudice that is still often faced by gay and lesbian people today,[45] and he quotes Kirby J in the High Court of Australia offering this resistance to a definitive conclusion that allegations of homosexuality were no longer defamatory:

> The day may come when, to accuse an adult of consenting homosexual activity is . . . generally a matter of indifference. However, it would ignore the reality of contemporary Australian society to say that that day has arrived for all purposes and all people. At least for people who treat their sexuality as private or secret, or people who have presented themselves as having a different sexual orientation, such an imputation could, depending on the circumstances, still sometimes be defamatory.[46]

To me, this is a benign but doctrinally misconceived attempt to use the law of defamation as a mechanism to protect the right of privacy (and it is not out of the question that this is the true explanation for the outcome in the *Liberace* case), or as a means of protecting people from the social prejudice that still existed against gay people. Be that as it may, the timing of the Scottish cases (the late 1990s) is not accidental and reflects increasing ambivalence in the law's general response to homosexuality. By the late 1990s, the law was beginning to accommodate changing social attitudes, beyond the decriminalisation

---

43 This was not a particularly Scottish development. Social mores had become much more international (at least in the developed Western world) as the media and travel opportunities became so. In 1996, it was accepted in the New Zealand Court of Appeal, *Television New Zealand Ltd v Quinn* [1996] NZLR 24, 60, per McGechan J that 'homosexuality or lesbianism might be viewed less seriously now than 20 years ago'. Other Commonwealth cases from around this time are discussed by Knight (n 36). US decisions on the point are explored in Randy M Fogle, 'Is Calling Someone Gay Defamatory? The Meaning of Reputation, Community Mores, Gay Rights and Free Speech' (1993) 3 *Law and Sexuality: A Review of Lesbian and Gay Legal Issues* 165.
44 1999 SLT 346, 355.
45 Knight (n 36) 267.
46 *John Fairfax Publications Pty Ltd v Rivkin* (2003) 201 ALR 77(HCA), para. 140.

of less than 20 years previously. The year 1999 saw two watershed decisions that transformed LGBT law: the domestic case of *Fitzpatrick v Sterling Housing Association*,[47] which held (if by a narrow 3–2 majority) that the survivor of a same-sex couple could succeed to a tenancy as a member of the deceased tenant's 'family'; and the European Court of Human Rights case of *Da Silva Mouta v Portugal*,[48] which held for the first time that sexual orientation came within Article 14 of the European Convention on Human Rights and was therefore an illegitimate ground upon which to discriminate. Yet, this accommodation was limited, and the law was not yet ready completely to jettison its hostility towards homosexuality. As the old century drew to a close, there was still an unequal age of consent to sexual activity, no employment protection, no prohibition on goods and services discrimination and virtually no family law recognition for same-sex relationships beyond, after *Fitzpatrick*, tenancy inheritance. And of course, 'section 28' (of the Local Government Act 1988), the notorious provision that prohibited the 'promotion of homosexuality', remained on the statute book. If judges took their assessment of how the right-thinking member of society would regard homosexuals from the legal position of gay people and same-sex couples,[49] then it is by no means obvious that they would conclude, at the turn of the millennium, that right-thinking views had changed sufficiently that an allegation of homosexuality could no longer be deemed to be defamatory.

4. A New Reality for a New Century

But, the first decade of the 21st century tilted the legal balance very much in favour of equal rights for gay and lesbian people. 'Section 28' was repealed (in Scotland) in 2000,[50] the same year that an equal age of consent to sexual activity was achieved;[51] employment protection was granted in 2003;[52] civil

---

47 [1999] 4 All ER 705.
48 [2001] 31 EHRR 47.
49 Fogle (n 43) above, proposes that the legal situation of gay and lesbian people should be the sole determinant of how right-thinking people are assessed to view homosexuality. That argument rather underplays the spectrum of protections that any one legal system may offer to gay and lesbian people and does not suggest a 'tipping point' of protections, which, when they exist, mean that the courts must accept that right-thinking people will regard an allegation of homosexuality as not demeaning. Davis (n 2), criticises that approach as a 'top-down' approach, which starts by asking how the state views homosexuality and, by focusing on formal rather than substantive provisions, preferences what the law says to the reality of people's experiences. He prefers a 'bottom-up' approach, which starts by asking what harm is actually done to the plaintiff in the community in which he or she lives. That, too, is problematic insofar as it might require the courts to give imprimatur to views that the law itself would reject.
50 Ethical Standards in Public Life etc. (Scotland) Act 2000, s.34.
51 Sexual Offences (Amendment) Act 2000, s.1(3).
52 Employment Equality (Sexual Orientation) Regulations 2003 (SI 2003/1661).

partnership for same-sex couples was created in 2004;[53] cohabitation rights were extended to same-sex couples in 2006;[54] discrimination in the provision of goods and services was prohibited in 2007;[55] adoption was opened to same-sex couples in 2009,[56] as was parenthood for both partners in same-sex couples after infertility treatment and surrogacy.[57] The law itself clearly no longer regarded gay and lesbian people (and their relationships) with abhorrence nor treated them as second-class citizens. Although there was some political opposition to all of these legal developments, there is little doubt that they reflected (and contributed to) the substantial change in social attitudes in that decade.[58]

As such, by the end of the first decade of the new millennium, allegations of homosexuality or homosexual behaviour could no longer logically continue to be regarded as in all circumstances, such as would lower the subject in the estimation of right-thinking members of society. Social attitudes had moved on sufficiently that, as Knight put it in 2006, any court's 'conclusion that imputations of gayness are defamatory effectively defames gays, perpetuating asserted assumptions that gays are less worthy than straights'.[59]

The first unequivocal acceptance of that by a Scottish court came a matter of months after the Scottish Government announced its intention to open marriage to same-sex couples. In *Cowan v Bennett*,[60] the pursuer sued on the basis of unwanted 'bantering' in a businessmen's network by the defender (a known 'joker'), which consisted of persistently drawing attention to and making fun of the pursuer's (perceived) homosexuality. None of the other members of the network took this tiresome behaviour as constituting a serious allegation that the pursuer was gay, which, it was accepted, he was not. The pursuer argued that nevertheless the comments had the effect of lowering his reputation in the eyes of other members of the network. The defender, whose behaviour and attitudes we would certainly describe today as homophobic, argued that society had moved on from the earlier cases, and that it could no longer be said that an allegation of homosexuality would damage a person's reputation in the eyes of

---

53 Civil Partnership Act 2004, Part 3.
54 Family Law (Scotland) Act 2006.
55 Equality Act (Sexual Orientation) Regulations 2007 (SI 2007/1263).
56 When the Adoption and Children (Scotland) Act 2007 came into force.
57 Human Fertilisation and Embryology Act 2008.
58 The British Social Attitudes Survey recorded a fall in the number of people who considered same-sex relationships to be always or mostly wrong from 48% in Scotland and 46% in England in 2000, to 27% in Scotland and 29% in England in 2010; those who considered same-sex relationships to be not wrong at all rose from 29% in Scotland and 34% in England in 2000 to 50% in Scotland and 44% in England in 2010: *British Social Attitudes 28 (2011/12 edition)*, table 2.6.
59 Knight (n 36) 269.
60 2012 GWD 37–738 (Sheriff McGowan at Dunfermline 5 November 2012). See R Whelan, 'Case Comment: *Cowan v Bennett*' (2013) *JR* 557.

right-thinking people. This defence was accepted by Sheriff McGowan, who dismissed the action as irrelevant. He said this:

> Assuming, for the sake of argument that I had found it to be established that the words complained of were capable of being taken to actually mean that the pursuer was homosexual, is such an imputation defamatory? In other words, did the words used, with their assumed imputation of homosexuality on the part of the pursuer, tend to lower the plaintiff in the estimation of right-thinking members of society generally, or be likely to affect a person adversely in the estimation of reasonable people generally? . . .
>
> This is a question of fact, but it appears to me that an imputation of homosexuality cannot generally be regarded as calculated (i.e. likely) to harm the reputation of a person, save perhaps in very special circumstances. As Mr McPhate put it, times have moved on. Homosexuality is not illegal. On the contrary, the rights of homosexuals are widely protected by the law. There are many people in public life in Scotland and the UK who are openly homosexual. Looked at in that way, it is difficult to see how an imputation of homosexuality could be defamatory. This is not an innovative view: *Quilty v Windsor* 1999 SLT 346, cited at *Gloag and Henderson*, 12th edition, para.30.05 and *Stair Memorial Encyclopaedia*, Obligations, para.490.[61]

The view expressed was probably more innovative than the sheriff asserts, at least insofar as it is used as the basis of the decision. The comments in *Quilty* were obiter to the actual decision, and the reference to the *Stair Memorial Encyclopaedia* was to a piece I wrote in 1995, which might be rather partial and, marginally early, was at the time probably aspirational argument rather than settled law. But, there is a clear development from *Quilty*. In that case, allegations of homosexuality were said to be 'not generally' defamatory; in the present case, they would become so only in 'very special circumstances'. An example of such circumstances might be *Prophit v BBC*, which involved an imputation of homosexuality that was damaging to the pursuer's reputation because of her membership of a particular religious order where homosexuality was frowned upon as sinful.

But, the law of defamation has a remarkable capacity to play tricks on the mind. We are pleased at the result in *Cowan v Bennett* while at the same time thinking the wrong man won. With the Drumsheugh school mistresses, we are delighted they won their case, even though we probably hope (and secretly believe) that at least some of the allegations against them were true. Two hundred years ago, the only protection against homophobia

---

61 2012 GWD 37–738, paras. 106–107.

was hiding one's sexuality; that was barely less true 50 years ago. Today, the protections are much greater, but they are not to be found in the law of defamation.

5. Homophobia as the New Homosexuality

The defender in *Cowan v Bennett* was clearly guilty of homophobia, and the case called him out for that – but homophobia that falls short of hate crime[62] is no legal wrong, and the disparaging behaviour in this case, although here directed towards a straight man, remains the lived experience of too many LGBT citizens today. Nevertheless, the case is clear evidence of the judiciary recognising the shift in social attitudes, which now holds that the mockery of gay and lesbian people is as unacceptable in polite society as homosexuality itself was at the time of the Stonewall Riots 50 years ago, and less. In a commentary on the Drumsheugh case, published in 2013, I expressed the hope that one day someone would sue for defamation on being called a homophobe rather than being called a homosexual.[63] And so it came to pass, exactly 200 years after the Drumsheugh school mistresses celebrated the final outcome in their case.

Stuart Campbell is a widely followed political blogger,[64] who in a 'tweet'[65] responded to a speech given by the Scottish Conservative MSP Oliver Mundell at the Conservative Party Conference in March 2017 with the following unkind words: 'Oliver Mundell is the sort of public speaker that makes you wish his dad had embraced his homosexuality sooner'.[66]

The reference was to Mr Mundell's father, the Conservative MP and (then) Secretary of State for Scotland David Mundell who, a year earlier, had come out as gay having previously been married to a woman and having three children, including Oliver. The then-leader of the Labour Party in Scotland, Kezia Dugdale, responded to this tweet in a newspaper article, published by the *Daily Record*. She said this: 'I was shocked and appalled to see a pro-independence blogger's homophobic tweets during the Tory conference'.

Campbell sued Dugdale on the basis that her words suggested that he had expressed homophobic views. The attribution to him of anti-gay sentiments was, he averred, defamatory:[67] right-thinking members of society

---

62 See the Hate Crime and Public Order (Scotland) Act 2021, s. 1.
63 Grant and Sutherland (n 7) 104.
64 His website 'Wings Over Scotland' claims to be 'The World's Most-Read Scottish Politics Website'.
65 A short and pithy commentary made on social media.
66 *Campbell v Dugdale* 2020 SC 27, para. 5.
67 It is interesting to note, but not the main focus of this chapter, that the attribution of unpopular views had previously been sued upon in Scotland under the civil wrong of verbal injury, in particular *convicium*, or holding the pursuer up to public hatred, contempt and ridicule, as opposed to the

would be less likely to associate with him if he were to be exposed as a homophobe. Now, the major legal issue in the case was the extent to which Dugdale's comments amounted to 'fair comment' (an absolute defence).[68] That turned on whether she (a) was expressing an opinion, formed from his tweet, that Campbell was homophobic, or (b) was directly accusing him of being homophobic in fact. The distinction is sometimes subtle,[69] but it is legally crucial since everyone is free to express their opinions so long as honestly held, even if factually inaccurate; no one, on the other hand, is free to state facts that are not true just because they believed them to be true. For our purposes, however, that point is less important than the question of whether an allegation of factual homophobia can be said to be defamatory at all. Both parties accepted that an accusation of being a homophobe would indeed tend to lower the subject in the estimation of right-thinking members of society, just as previously an accusation of being a homosexual would have done. At first instance, Sheriff Ross endorsed the view 'that to be called homophobic in modern Scotland is a serious imputation on character and would lower a person in the estimation of society'[70] and on appeal the Inner House of the Court of Session explicitly agreed: 'The sheriff was right to regard an accusation of homophobia as a serious one in contemporary society'.[71] The Inner House also held that referring to the pursuer as homophobic was a direct defamatory statement rather than a matter of innuendo.[72]

That point settled, the court turned to the main point of contention in the case – whether Dugdale's words amounted to 'fair comment'. Was the article an allegation of fact ('Campbell is homophobic') or a comment ('Based on Campbell's statements, it is fair to conclude that he is homophobic')? The Inner House agreed with the sheriff that they were comment. And the comment was 'fair' in the legal sense of being a comment that could be rationally made from the stated facts, even if others would come to a different conclusion. That ended the case, in the defender's favour.

---

civil wrong of defamation. See for example *Paterson v Welch* (1893) 20 R 744 and the discussion of *convicium* in Norrie, *Defamation and Related Actions in Scots Law* (Butterworths 1995) 38–41.
68 Now the statutory defence of 'honest opinion': Defamation and Malicious Publication (Scotland) Act 2021, s. 7.
69 See *Telnikoff v Matusevitch* [1992] 2 AC 343; *Joseph v Spiller* [2011] 1 AC 852.
70 2019 SLT (Sh Ct) 141, para. 43.
71 2020 CSIH 27, para. 47. A year later, the Northern Irish High Court agreed that such an allegation would result in people thinking 'the worse of the plaintiff' and so defamation was established when the First Minister of Northern Ireland was accused (again in a 'tweet') of, amongst other things, being homophobic: *Foster v Jessen* [2021] NIQB 56, para. 38.
72 *Campbell v Dugdale* 2020 SC 481, para. 35. Sheriff McGowan, in earlier proceedings reported at 2019 SLT (Sh Ct) 89, had treated the case as one of innuendo.

Sheriff Ross had concluded his judgement with some remarks on what level of damages would have been appropriate, and for our purposes they are worth repeating:

> A further point relates to the seriousness of the defamation. The article used the term 'homophobic' which has, as both Mr Campbell and Mr Kavanagh explained, a particularly toxic association. It bears comparison with 'racist' or 'holocaust denier'.[73]

But, even although the allegations were 'toxic', it did not follow that the pursuer would have been entitled to substantial damages had he succeeded. Sheriff Ross pointed out that Campbell 'has chosen insult and condemnation as his style. He has received these in return . . . I do not accept that he can dismiss the feelings and reputations of his opponents cheaply, but receive a high valuation of his own'.[74] So, notwithstanding the highly damaging nature of the defamation, this particular pursuer would have received, had the defence of fair comment been rejected, damages of £100. On this (obiter) point, the Inner House disagreed with the sheriff and held that an allegation of homophobia was significantly more serious and potentially damaging: in their view, had liability been established, a more appropriate award would have been £5,000. It is interesting to compare this to *Foster v Jessen*[75] where the High Court in Northern Ireland awarded £125,000, although that reflected not only the damage to the political standing of the plaintiff but also the fact that the allegation of homophobia was only one of several defamatory allegations made by the defendant.

It is significant that the pursuer in *Campbell v Dugdale*, a blogger who thrives on insult and robust criticism of others, felt he had to sue when someone criticised him in this particular manner. Either he is an example of that exceptionally thin-skinned type of person who is unable to take the medicine they are happy to dole out to others, or he considers that an allegation of homophobia is so far beyond the pale that he had no choice but to sue in order to vindicate his honour. He claimed the latter: he stated that it was 'a disgraceful thing' to be homophobic,[76] and the sheriff did 'not doubt him when he says he is horrified at being called homophobic'.[77] However, just as in the past when allegations of homosexuality would be particularly serious for individuals holding particular positions (such as the nun in *Prophit v BBC*), the allegation of homophobia may well be perceived as particularly harmful to those

---

73 2019 SLT (Sh Ct) 141, para. 86.
74 *Ibid*, para. 97.
75 [2021] NIQB 56.
76 2019 SLT (Sh Ct) 141, para. 9.
77 *Ibid*, para. 33.

holding high political office – such as the plaintiff in *Foster v Jessen*[78] but unlike a rebarbative political commentator. That in itself indicates a sensitivity to the allegation for those who seek public approval and support, giving confirmation that homophobia is the new homosexuality: a toxic allegation that attracts the condemnation of an appalled society and which would unquestionably render right-thinking (fair-minded) members of society less willing to associate with the subject.

6. The Wider Context

It is legitimate to question whether any of this matters terribly much. After all, few claims for defamation are ever made in Scotland (where damages, when awarded, are traditionally modest), and not all allegations of homophobia will be defamatory. A person may be proudly, even defiantly, homophobic, and their right to express their opinion will, in the present state of the law, be protected under Article 10 of the European Convention on Human Rights (ECHR). It is, however, worth remembering that that protection is limited to views that are worth protecting and are not incompatible with human dignity.[79] Some views are so unconscionable that they are not worth protecting, and any complaint about their restriction will fall foul of Article 17 of the Convention. In *Pastörs v Germany*,[80] the European Court of Human Rights found the punishment of a German *Land* MP's expression of his views to be justified because the applicant (convicted under a domestic law criminalising Holocaust denial) was seeking 'to use his right to freedom of expression with the aim of promoting ideas contrary to the text and spirit of the Convention'.[81] Now, there is authority for the view that regarding homosexuality as a sin is 'not a belief that is unworthy of recognition'[82] – it is not so incompatible with the values of the European Convention that Article 17 will deprive it of all ECHR protection. Although an Employment Tribunal held that the view that homosexuality was contrary to God's law and nature (and that no Jewish people were gassed in concentration camps) was not a philosophical belief for the purposes of the

---

78 Although her party had been vigorously opposed to the opening of marriage in Northern Ireland to same-sex couples, as First Minister, it was her duty to respect the Rule of Law, including respect for the law on same-sex marriage: the High Court accepted that for an individual to espouse homophobic views would therefore be incompatible with that individual holding the office of First Minister or Deputy First Minister of Northern Ireland: [2021] NIQB 56, para. 37.
79 See *Campbell & Cosans v UK* (1982) 4 EHRR 293, para. 36; *R (Williamson) v Secretary of State for Education and Employment* [2005] 2 AC 246; *Grainger v Nicholson plc* [2010] 2 All ER 253 (EAT).
80 Appl. 55225/14, 3 October 2019.
81 *Ibid*, para. 46.
82 *Re Christian Institute's Application for Judicial Review* [2008] IRLR 36, per Weatherup J, para. 50. In *Foster v Jessen* [2021] NIQB 56 McAlindin J said at para. 36: 'as Northern Ireland becomes a more secular society, there must be room or accommodation for an individual to hold such traditional religious views without being automatically classed as homophobic'.

Equality Act 2010,[83] the UK Supreme Court in 2018 held that the espousal of the belief that marriage should remain limited to opposite-sex couples was protected under both Articles 9 and 10 of the ECHR.[84] The mere expression of anti-gay sentiment, whether in the form of an insistence on the 'sinfulness' of gay sex, or of an insistence that marriage should exclude same-sex couples is therefore likely to continue for some time to be protected by the (undeniably important) right to express unpopular views.

However, the more homophobia is seen as being incompatible with human dignity, the closer it comes to something like Holocaust denial – the quintessential belief that is denied all respect by the application of Article 17.[85] Yet, Sheriff Ross, quoted earlier, explicitly likened being called a homophobe to being called a racist or Holocaust denier. No court has yet accepted that opposition to same-sex marriage is inherently homophobic,[86] in the way that the expression of white, or Arian, supremacy (manifested in, say, disapproval of miscegenation) is inescapably racist. But, more and more people are coming to believe this, and opposition to same-sex marriage may well be moving from a legitimate political belief to one that is necessarily contrary to the text and spirit of the ECHR. The real importance of *Campbell v Dugdale* is that it not only expands the law's understanding of homophobia to include laughing at, and not just inciting hatred towards, gay people, but it also moves homophobia beyond the unpopular and towards the unacceptable. If this defamation case colours how courts see the nature of homophobia in discrimination cases too, such as *Lee v Ashers Baking Company Ltd*,[87] then it will have served a wider social function than defamation cases are normally capable of doing. Its long-term effect on the place of gay and lesbian people in modern Scotland may yet prove to be profound.

---

83 *Ellis v Parmagan Ltd* [2014] WL 10246833, para. 26.
84 *Lee v Ashers Baking Company Ltd* [2020] AC 413.
85 *Forstater v CGD Europe* [2021] IRLR 706 (EAT).
86 This was indeed explicitly denied by the judge in *Foster v Jessen* (n 82) above.
87 See above (n 84).

Chapter 12

'Lewd, Disgusting and Offensive'
A Critical Discourse Analysis of the Law Lords' Ideologies Toward Homosexuality Between 1967 and 2004

Sean Becker

1. Introduction

Homosexual sexual acts between males were legalized in England and Wales with the coming into force of the Sexual Offences Act 1967. The impetus for the Act came from the Wolfenden Report published in 1957 by a committee of academics and politicians, which recommended that homosexual acts be decriminalized.[1] Although the Act was an important step forward in the history of LGBTQ rights in England and Wales, the intention of Parliament was not to fully embrace homosexuality by recognizing its place in society. Rather, the Act was used to control homosexual practices by confining them to the private sphere of the individual.[2] Section 1 of the Act permitted homosexual intercourse only in *private*, between *no more than two* consenting males, who both had attained the *age of 21*. All homosexual behavior that did not fall within these very narrowly defined margins remained illicit and punishable under criminal law. Indeed, following the decriminalization of homosexual acts, the numbers of arrests and convictions for homosexual offenses rose, with the length of imposed sentences likewise increasing.[3]

Scholarship has focused predominantly on Parliament and the Wolfenden Report, leaving the judiciary's role in maintaining the (homophobic) *status quo* largely unexplored. This is especially surprising, considering that law is 'one of the most important mechanisms through which the normative "truths" of sexuality are established', propagated and maintained.[4] This mechanism works

---

1 Committee on Homosexual Offences and Prostitution, *Report of The Committee on Homosexual Offences and Prostitution* (HL 1957–10) 115.
2 Kate Gleeson, 'Freudian Slips and Coteries of Vice: The Sexual Offences Act of 1967' (2008) 27:3 *Parliamentary History* 393, 409.
3 Jeffrey Weeks, *Coming Out: Homosexual Politics in Britain, from the Nineteenth Century to the Present* (Quartet Books 1977) 176; Antony Grey, 'Privacy and the Outsider: Address to the Parliamentary Civil Liberties Group' in *Speaking Out: Writings on Sex, Law, Politics and Society 1954–95* (Continuum 1997) 22.
4 Paul Johnson, '"An Essentially Private Manifestation of Human Personality": Constructions of Homosexuality in the European Court of Human Rights' (2010) 10:1 *Human Rights Law Review* 67, 72.

DOI: 10.4324/9781003286295-15

through the production of case law and the practice of legal citation.[5] As there is no body within England and Wales with greater judicial authority than the House of Lords,[6] it is their judgments that this chapter will analyze.

This analysis aims to deconstruct the discursive production of ideology present in the House of Lords judgments in order to reveal the homophobic ideology embedded within the Law Lords' speeches. It is hypothesized that both analyzed judgments exhibit homophobic opinions and attitudes, which give expression to an underlying ideology of homophobia. Notably, this analysis focuses exclusively on *male homosexuality*, as female homosexuality was never criminalized in England and Wales.[7]

Section 2 offers an overview of the theoretical framework utilized herein, while section 3 provides a summary of the House of Lords' judgments. The substantive analysis of said judgments is undertaken in section 4. Lastly, section 5 offers a conclusion and ponders on two general insights derived from the chapter's findings.

2. Theoretical Framework

This chapter follows the analytic paradigm of critical discourse analysis,[8] which in itself does not adhere to a homogenous method[9] but is more properly characterized as a critical *attitude* or *perspective* within discourse studies.[10] Rather than being discipline-oriented CDA focuses on specific problems, each problem requiring a particularized approach, including a problem-specific set of goals, data and methods.[11] As such, CDA's multidisciplinary nature can be applied to a variety of disciplines, including law.[12]

Transcending 'traditional' discourse study, CDA concerns itself with how discourse both shapes and is shaped by socio-cultural structures.[13] CDA analyzes how certain discourse *reflects* social structures within a specific culture and

---

5 See *Ibid*.
6 Since 2009 the Supreme Court.
7 Rebecca Jennings, *A Lesbian History of Britain: Love and Sex Between Women Since 1500* (Greenwood World Publishing 2007) 109–114.
8 Hereafter: CDA.
9 Bryan Jenner and Stefan Titscher, *Methods of Text and Discourse Analysis* (Sage 2000) 144.
10 Teun A van Dijk, 'Critical Discourse Studies: A Sociocognitive Approach' in Ruth Wodak and Michael Meyer (eds), *Methods of Critical Discourse Studies* (3rd edn, Sage 2016) 63.
11 Marianne Jørgensen and Louise Phillips, *Discourse Analysis as Theory and Method* (Sage 2002) 60; see *van Dijk* (n 10) 63.
12 Francesca Ammaturo, 'Europe and Whiteness: Challenges to European Identity and European Citizenship in Light of Brexit and the 'Refugees/Migrants Crisis' (2018) 22:4 *European Journal of Social Theory* 548; see *Johnson* (n 4).
13 Peter Teo, 'Racism in the News: A Critical Analysis of Newspaper Reporting in Two Australian Newspapers' in Michael Toolan (ed), *Critical Discourse Analysis: Critical Concepts in Linguistics* (Routledge 2002) 363; see *Jenner* and *Titscher* (n 9) 146.

society at a specific point in time while simultaneously *influencing* these same structures. Hence, CDA is sensitive to how discourse is both *constituted* by and *constitutive* of society.

The origins of CDA lie in Marx's ideas on social theory and organization, which in turn influenced the ideas of more contemporary CDA forerunners, such as Antonio Gramsci and Louis Althusser, who both emphasize the importance of ideology in maintaining and bolstering modern societies' social structures.[14] Such understanding of social structures relies on a neo-Marxist conception of ideology, which in turn makes up the basis of contemporary CDA.[15] Ideology, so understood, is the instrument by which unequal power relations between social groups are produced and maintained.[16] However, the abstract notion of ideology in itself is not capable of directly causing such effects. It is rather through discourse that ideologies are conveyed, effectuated and maintained.[17] In CDA, analyzing discourse is thus considered a way to unmask the ideologies that underlie the socio-cultural structures of a given society as well as groups within that society.[18] While CDA directs its focus principally 'on the role of discourse in the reproduction processes of ideologies', discourse analysis is not the *only* means by which ideologies can be analytically revealed.[19] Leaving aside the non-verbal means of discovering ideologies, this chapter will solely analyze discourse, by making use of van Dijk's concept of ideology under the socio-cognitive approach.

2.1 Ideology Under the Socio-cognitive Approach

Van Dijk defines ideology as 'the *basis of the social representations shared by members of a group*. This means that ideologies allow people, as group members, to organize the multitude of social beliefs about what is the case, good or bad, right or wrong, *for them*'.[20] Ideologies are thus nothing more than 'clusters of beliefs in our minds'.[21] To properly define ideologies, it is necessary to deconstruct the preceding definition, beginning with the social dimension of ideologies followed by a closer examination of the concept of beliefs.

2.1.1 Social Dimension

According to van Dijk's definition, part of what makes an ideology an ideology is that it possesses a social dimension. In other words, ideologies are *ipso*

---

14 See *Teo* (n 13) 363.
15 See *Jenner* and *Titscher* (n 9) 145.
16 See *Jørgensen* and *Phillips* (n 11) 63.
17 See *Teo* (n 13) 364.
18 See *Teo* (n 13) 365; see *van Dijk* (n 10) 70.
19 Teun A van Dijk, *Ideology: A Multidisciplinary Approach* (Sage 1998) 191.
20 *Ibid.*, 8 (emphasis in original text).
21 *Ibid.*, 26.

facto shared by members of an ideological group.[22] Conversely, if an 'ideology' is unique to an individual, that is, if it is not shared by anyone else, it cannot – according to van Dijk's conception – be an ideology.

2.1.2 Beliefs: The Building Blocks of Ideologies

Van Dijk refers to beliefs as 'the building blocks of the mind'.[23] While, according to the socio-cognitive approach all ideologies are clusters of beliefs, only clusters of certain *types* of beliefs make up ideologies. Important in this context is the distinction between *factual beliefs* and *evaluative beliefs*. Factual beliefs are those beliefs, which are shared by a collective – be it a community, culture, institution or group – and which are perceived by this collective to be 'true' based on certain criteria of truthfulness.[24] Another term for this specific category of beliefs is *knowledge*. According to van Dijk's definition, knowledge is not defined by an absolute criterion of truthfulness but rather varies based on the specific criteria of truthfulness applied by a certain collective.

If the category of factual beliefs is entirely contingent on the applied criteria of truthfulness, then the problem arises that nothing can ever be perceived as objectively true. Van Dijk addresses this by introducing a further distinction, which he calls cultural knowledge and group knowledge. Cultural knowledge, or C-knowledge, are factual beliefs 'shared by all or most members of epistemic communities or cultures'.[25] Group knowledge, or G-knowledge, on the other hand, are factual beliefs only held by one or more groups within a culture, which do not make up all or most of that epistemic community or culture.[26]

The other type of beliefs are *evaluative beliefs*, which are defined as beliefs that, rather than being assumed to be factually 'true', inform groups and thereby the members of that group of what is good or bad, right or wrong, moral or immoral, fair or unfair, etc.[27] These types of beliefs help people evaluate certain situations. Van Dijk also calls evaluative beliefs *opinions*. Like knowledge, opinions can be divided into C-opinions and G-opinions, although opinions usually take the form of G-opinions.[28] In other words, opinions are generally more divided across an epistemic community than knowledge.

How, one might ask at this point, does one get from opinions to ideology? Remembering van Dijk's aforementioned definition, ideologies are clusters of beliefs – to be more accurate, clusters of predominantly evaluative beliefs (i.e. opinions). These clusters of evaluative beliefs are subordinate to specific

---

22 *Ibid.*, 32.
23 *Ibid.*, 19.
24 *Ibid.*
25 See *van Dijk* (n 10) 69; *van Dijk* (n 19) 41.
26 See *van Dijk* (n 19) 41.
27 *Ibid.*, 33.
28 *Ibid.*, 41.

'Lewd, Disgusting and Offensive' 167

ideologies. In other words, ideologies function as headings under which clusters of opinions are organized schematically.[29]

However, the general and abstract nature of opinions calls for a further subcategory of beliefs. Van Dijk calls these 'clusters of domain-specific social opinions of a group' (i.e. less abstract) *attitudes*.[30] Van Dijk's concept of attitudes differs from the general understanding of attitudes as 'personal opinions' in that they are not personal to an individual but rather shared by a group holding a particular ideology.[31] To use one of van Dijk's own examples, within a feminist ideology, one may identify more general opinions about gender inequality, as well as more specific attitudes about unequal pay, workplace harassment or job discrimination.[32] This example illustrates the difference in hierarchy between opinions and attitudes.

Under the socio-cognitive approach, the mental representation of ideologies is structured in a tripartite manner. Figure 12.1 visually depicts this structure:

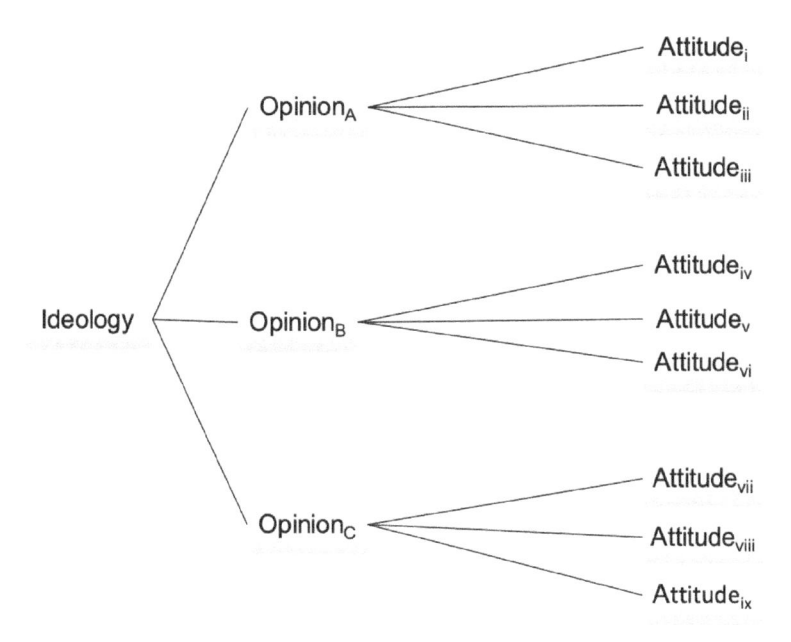

Ideology → Opinion$_A$ → Attitude$_i$, Attitude$_{ii}$, Attitude$_{iii}$

Ideology → Opinion$_B$ → Attitude$_{iv}$, Attitude$_v$, Attitude$_{vi}$

Ideology → Opinion$_C$ → Attitude$_{vii}$, Attitude$_{viii}$, Attitude$_{ix}$

Figure 12.1

29 See *van Dijk* (n 10) 69.
30 See *van Dijk* (n 19) 33.
31 *Ibid.*, 43.
32 *Ibid.*, 33.

2.2 Discursive Production of Ideology

Recalling the basic principle of CDA that discourse functions ideologically, the illustrated structure becomes important as a figurative road map for analyzing how specific ideologies are expressed through discourse. Using van Dijk's theoretical conception of ideology, it is possible to identify not only direct expressions of ideology within discourse but also the *indirect* ways in which ideologies may be expressed through written texts, by identifying the more general opinions and more specific attitudes that are constituent to an ideology.[33] Specifically, van Dijk identifies four ways ideologies can be (re)produced through discourse, which are relevant to the analysis of legal judgments.

2.2.1 Direct Expression

Ideological propositions are at times expressed directly in text or talk. This form of discursive production is the most straightforward way in which ideology can '"get into" actual text and talk'.[34] The author[35] principally takes on the role of the group member by expressing ideological statements with reference to a collective 'we'. Direct expression can be distinguished from the other forms of discursive production in that the formulations of ideologies remain on an abstract and general level and make use of generic expressions and concepts, rather than specific ones.[36]

2.2.2 Instantiated Direct Expression

Ideological propositions can also be expressed in less general terms. This is the case when the abstract and general concepts of an ideological statement are replaced by the specific variables of the discursive context.[37]

2.2.3 Direct Expressions of Ideological Attitudes

It is also possible to directly express the constituent elements of ideologies.[38] These types of expressions convey the attitudes controlled by an ideology rather than the ideology itself. Accordingly, an additional step is necessary to identify the ideology, which underlies the attitude expressed. Van Dijk uses this term

---

33 *Ibid.*, 193.
34 *Ibid.*
35 The concept of discourse includes both written and spoken expressions. For reasons of clarity and space, this section will, however, only refer to written text, as the material analyzed in this chapter is in written form.
36 See *van Dijk* (n 19) 239.
37 *Ibid.*, 240.
38 *Ibid.*

to refer to both *direct* and *instantiated* expressions of attitudes.[39] Moreover, this type of discursive production of ideology can also apply to the expression of opinions (i.e. more general evaluative beliefs).

2.2.4 Event Model Expression

Because the majority of discourse concerns *specific events or experiences*, ideologies and attitudes are oftentimes applied to particular personal situations.[40] As this form of ideological expression is the most abstracted from the actual ideology, it is the most elaborate to analytically deconstruct. Peter Teo describes this process of analytic deconstruction as 'gradually chip[ping] away at the layers of discourse to reveal the construction of a[n] . . . ideology embedded within [. . .].'[41] Ideologies, opinions and attitudes can all take the form of *event model expression*, provided they are instantiated.

3. The Cases

This chapter focuses on two judgments of the House of Lords. The judgments were selected based on a preliminary search via Westlaw UK, with the search terms 'homosexual!', 'gay' and 'sodomy'. Only judgments by the House of Lords relating to criminal law between 27 July 1967 and 1 May 2004 were considered. The start date reflects the day on which homosexual acts were legalized in England and Wales with certain restrictions.[42] The end date reflects the day on which these restrictions were repealed.[43] An initial search yielded 31 judgments, which in turn were assessed for pertinence. Judgments that only mentioned the search terms in passing (i.e. not as material to the judgment) were excluded from the refined list of cases. In the end, two cases in which the homosexuality of the parties was material to the substance of the judgments were found.

3.1 Knuller v DPP (1972)

In *Knuller Ltd. v Director of Public Prosecutions*,[44] the appellants were directors of a publishing company that circulated a biweekly magazine titled *International Times*, more commonly known by its acronym 'IT'. The respondent was the Director of Public Prosecutions (i.e. the state).

---

39 *Ibid*.
40 *Ibid*.
41 See *Teo* (n 13) 366.
42 Sexual Offences Act 1967, c 60, s 1 (27 July 1967).
43 Sexual Offences Act 2003, c 42, Sch 7, para. 1 (1 May 2004).
44 Hereafter: *Knuller*.

At first instance, the appellants had been convicted of two counts, namely (1) *conspiracy to corrupt public morals* and (2) *conspiracy to outrage public decency*. The first count of conspiracy to corrupt public morals was stated in the indictment by the prosecution as follows:

> Knuller (Publishing, Printing and Promotions) Ltd., [and multiple individuals] conspired together [. . .] to induce readers [of the magazine IT] to meet those persons inserting such advertisements [situated under a column headed 'MALES'] for the purpose of sexual practices taking place between male persons and to encourage readers thereof to indulge in such practices, with intent thereby to debauch and corrupt the morals as well of youth as of divers other liege subjects of Our Lady the Queen.[45]

The second count of conspiracy to outrage public decency read:

> Knuller (Publishing, Printing and Promotions) Ltd., [and multiple individuals] conspired together and with persons inserting lewd, disgusting and offensive advertisements in issues of a magazine entitled "IT" [. . .], by means of the publication of the said magazine containing the said advertisements to outrage public decency.[46]

On appeal by the appellants, the Court of Appeal dismissed their appeals against conviction.[47] Upon further appeal, the case moved in front of the House of Lords.

The five Law Lords presiding over the case were Lord Reid, Lord Morris of Borth-Y-Gest,[48] Lord Diplock,[49] Lord Simon of Glaisdale[50] and Lord Kilbrandon. The House of Lords dismissed the appeal on the first count and allowed the appeal on the second; Lord Diplock dissenting on the former and Lord Morris dissenting on the latter.

Table 12.1 Graphical representation of whether the Law Lord dismissed (X) or allowed (✓) the appeal.

	Count 1	Count 2
Lord Reid	X	✓
Lord Morris	X	X
Lord Diplock	✓	✓
Lord Simon	X	✓
Lord Kilbrandon	X	✓

45 *Knuller*, 481–482 (Lord Simon of Glaisdale).
46 Ibid., 491.
47 see *R v Knuller (Publishing, Printing and Promotions) Ltd. and Others* [1971] 2 Q.B. 179.
48 Hereafter: Lord Morris.
49 Lord Diplock was a member of the committee that published the Wolfenden Report in 1957.
50 Hereafter: Lord Simon.

3.2 R v Brown (1994)

The case *R v Brown [1994]* 1 AC 212[51] involved a group of sadomasochists, the appellants, who had been convicted at first instance for *assault occasioning actual bodily harm* under section 47 of the Offences Against the Person Act 1861. Three of the five appellants had also been convicted of *inflicting bodily injury* contrary to section 20 of the Act. These convictions were upheld by the Court of Appeal, whose decision the appellants appealed before the House of Lords.[52]

The events that occasioned the convictions were 'sadomasochistic homosexual activities carried out consensually by the appellants with each other and with other persons'.[53] Although the charges in themselves are not directly connected to the sexual orientation of the appellants, a substantial proportion of the Law Lords' speeches in *Brown* mentioned the appellants' homosexuality, not only in passing but also materially to their judgments.

Presiding over the case were Lord Templeman, Lord Jauncey of Tullichettle,[54] Lord Lowry, Lord Mustill and Lord Slynn of Hadley. The majority dismissed the appeal, with Lord Mustill and Lord Slynn of Hadley dissenting.

Table 12.2 Graphical representation of whether the Law Lord dismissed (X) or allowed (✓) the appeal.

	Appeal against conviction
Lord Templeman	X
Lord Jauncey	X
Lord Lowry	X
Lord Mustill	✓
Lord Slynn of Hadley	✓

4. Analysis

In the following sections, the re-occurring themes within the judgments will be explicated and analyzed in order to lay bare the homophobic attitudes that they display. In particular, the analysis will focus on the themes of *self-control*, *decriminalization vs. legalization* and *corruption*.

---

51 Hereafter: *Brown*.
52 *Brown*, 230 (Lord Templeman).
53 *Brown*, 230 (Lord Jauncey of Tullichettle).
54 Hereafter: Lord Jauncey.

4.1 Sexual Self-Control

In Western society sex and sexuality, in many regards, is about self-control. In our everyday lives the sexual impulses, which come to us naturally, must be controlled and regulated. Those who fail to regulate their impulses are ostracized by society and, in some instances, may even be punished by criminal law. Adultery and rape are two such examples. Thus, '[t]he sexual instinct must be brought under control or "harnessed" to the proper ends of society'.[55]

Within this conception of sexuality, there traditionally existed a *sexual double standard*: a two-pronged set of societal expectations regarding females and males' sexual behaviour.[56] This double standard expected males to be 'sexually active, assertive and take sexual initiative', while expecting females to be 'sexually reactive, [. . .] submissive and passive'.[57] As such, females were viewed as the 'gatekeepers' of (male) sexuality.[58] Many of scholars writing in the 1950s, 1960s and even 1970s (i.e. from the time of the *Knuller* judgement) supported such views.[59]

According to these scholars, male sexual desire is kept in check in two ways. Firstly, his own ability to control and regulate his omnipresent sexual impulses. Secondly, the female's role as the counterpart to the libidinous male. What happens then when the female is taken out of the equation and replaced with a male? In line with this heteronormative cultural stereotype, absent the female's bridling of the male's libido, males will give in to their sexual impulses far more frequently. Simultaneously, because *every* male is *always* ready to have sex, there is no more need for self-control either.[60]

Some, like the sociologist Steven Seidman, went as far as saying that this lack of self-control, characteristic of homosexuals, made them choose to have sexual intercourse with another man until the point of physical exhaustion;[61]

---

55 Carl F Stychin, *Law's Desire: Sexuality and the Limits of Justice* (Routledge 1995) 130.
56 Ine Vanwesenbeeck, 'Doing Gender in Sex and Sex Research' (2009) 38:6 *Archives of Sexual Behavior* 883–898.
57 Peggy MJ Emmerink, 'Gendered Sexuality: Exploring Dynamics of the Sexual Double Standard', Ph.D. Utrecht University 2017 154.
58 Letitia A Peplau, Zick Rubin, and Charles T Hill, 'Sexual Intimacy in Dating Relationships' (1977) 33:2 *Journal of Social Issues* 86–109.
59 see e.g. Winston Ehrmann, *Premarital Dating Behavior* (Henry Holt and Company 1959); Gilbert R Kaats and Keith E Davis, 'The Dynamics of Sexual Behavior of College Students' (1970) 32:3 *Journal of Marriage and the Family* 390–399; Ira L Reiss, *The Social Context of Premarital Sexual Permissiveness* (Holt, Reinhart and Winston 1967); Michael George Schofield, *The Sexual Behavior of Young People* (Little, Brown & Co. 1965); Robert C Sorenson, *Adolescent Sexuality in Contemporary America* (World Publishing 1973).
60 This is an example of heteronormative discourse (i.e. discourse which regards heterosexuality as the natural normal) while rendering 'all other forms of human sexual expression pathological [and] deviant' (Gust A Yep, 'From Homophobia and Heterosexism to Heteronormativity' (2002) 6:3–4 *Journal of Lesbian Studies* 163, 167).
61 Steven Seidman, *Embattled Eros* (Routledge 1992) 159.

an 'immoral act', which if they possessed enough self-control they never would commit. Others saw in the alleged lack of self-control among homosexuals an attribute shared by a number of groups, related to each other by immorality: 'Gays, prostitutes and addicts are not in control of their desires or do not allow their desires to be controlled, and this makes them perverse and threatening agents of pathology'.[62]

4.1.1 Discourse Around Self-Control in Knuller

In *Knuller* references to self-control – or rather the lack thereof – are embedded within the Law Lords speeches.

Firstly, the term 'indulge in' is used an entirety of 12 times throughout the Law Lord's speeches in relation to homosexual acts. All five Law Lords use the term. The Merriam-Webster's Collegiate Dictionary defines the word 'indulge' as 'to take *unrestrained* pleasure in'.[63] Hence, the word 'indulge' indicates a lack of restraint or self-control. Moreover, the phrasal verb 'indulge in', defined as 'to become involved in (something, especially something that is considered *wrong* or *improper*)',[64] adds a moral dimension to the activity that is indulged in. Thus, the phrase 'indulge in' implicitly characterizes homosexual acts as lacking in both self-control as well as morality. The abundant usage of the phrase by the Law Lords highlights the firmness of this characterization.

Secondly, Lord Reid, Lord Morris[65] and Lord Diplock[66] use examples that associate homosexuality with other groups allegedly characterized by lack of self-control: prostitutes and addicts. Lord Reid, when discussing the legalization of homosexual acts by section 1 of the Sexual Offenses Act 1967, writes: 'But there is a material difference between merely exempting certain conduct from criminal penalties and making it lawful in the full sense. *Prostitution* and *gambling* afford examples of this difference'.[67] Within the quoted passage, Lord Reid draws a comparison between homosexual acts, prostitution and gambling, essentially grouping these three activities as equally 'immoral' pursuits.

When speaking of prostitution the Law Lords – in line with the heteronormative discourse they employ – are referring to female prostitution. Female prostitutes, under the traditionalist view, upset the natural state of women as the 'gatekeepers' of male sexuality. They also defy the 'natural' characteristics

---

62 James W Jones, 'Discourse on and of AIDS in West Germany' in John C Fout (ed), *Forbidden History: The State, Society, and the Regulation of Sexuality in Modern Europe* (The University of Chicago Press 1992) 364–365.
63 Merriam-Webster, Inc. 'Indulge' in *Merriam-Webster's Collegiate Dictionary* (Merriam-Webster 2003) 637.
64 *Ibid.*, 638 (Emphasis added).
65 *Knuller*, 460 (Lord Morris).
66 *Knuller*, 460 (Lord Morris; emphasis added).
67 *Knuller*, 457 (Lord Reid; emphasis added).

that were associated with (younger) women as being sexually inhibited and having an underdeveloped interest in coitus.[68] Thus, the prostitute's uninhibitedness (i.e. lack of self-control) was seen as equally immoral as it was unnatural. Gambling, aside from raising moral questions,[69] is an activity with a high addictive potential. By comparing homosexuality with gambling, Lord Reid implies that, much like a chronic gambler has lost all self-control to resist her addiction, the homosexual has no self-control over his sexual desires. This parallel between gambling and homosexuality is further amplified in the summing up of the appellants' arguments, in which homosexuals are referred to as 'addicts' of homosexual sex.[70]

Thirdly, Lord Morris implies that homosexuality is a *choice* that can be restrained from:

> a casual perusal of the advertisements reveals that it could not rationally be held that they were only so addressed [to those who already indulged in homosexual conduct] or directed: in the second place, it is a fallacy to assume [. . .] *that someone cannot be corrupted more than once.*[71]

This quote asserts that anyone can be 'corrupted' by advertisements soliciting intercourse between two males, implying that, rather than being biologically pre-determined, homosexuality is something that each person can decide to indulge in or not. Furthermore, a male does not choose once and for all to be a homosexual; rather, every time he engages in homosexual acts, he is consciously choosing this 'immoral' lifestyle anew. Lord Morris implies that since homosexuals are in control of their homosexuality, their 'indulgence' in homosexual acts can only stem from a lack of self-control.

Social science research has consistently found that 'individuals who believe that a homosexual orientation results from social learning and/or a *conscious choice* that *remains within one's control* statistically have higher levels of homophobia than those who believe that a homosexual orientation results from biological and psychosocial influences'.[72] Moreover, high levels of homophobia have

---

68 Alfred C Kinsey and Wardell Baxter Pomeroy, *Sexual Behavior in the Human Female* (Saunders 1953) 353–354.
69 Lino A Graglia, 'Government Promotion of Moral Issues: Gambling, Smoking, and Advertising' (2008) 31:1 *Harvard Journal of Law & Public Policy* 69.
70 *Knuller*, 441.
71 *Knuller*, 461–462 (Lord Morris; emphasis added).
72 Christopher W Blackwell, 'Belief in the "Free Choice" Model of Homosexuality: A Correlate of Homophobia in Registered Nurses' (2007) 3:3 *Journal of LGBT Health Research* 31, 32; see also: Gregory M Herek, 'The Psychology of Sexual Prejudice' (2000) 9:1 *Current Directions in Psychological Science* 19–22; Gregory M Herek, 'Gender Gaps in Public Opinion About Lesbians and Gay Men' (2002) 66:1 *Public Opinion Quarterly* 40–66; Mikael Landén and Sune Innala, 'The Effect of a Biological Explanation on Attitudes Towards Homosexual Persons. A Swedish National Sample Study' (2002) 56:3 *Nordic Journal of Psychiatry* 181–186; Nuray Sakalli, 'Application of the

been correlated to the belief that homosexuals are in control of their homosexuality.[73] Lord Morris showcases both stances in his speech in *Knuller*.

4.1.2 Discourse Around Self-Control in *Brown*

Initially, it may appear unclear whether, when addressing the topic of self-control, the Law Lords are referring to sadomasochism or homosexuality, or both. All three Law Lords who dismiss the appeal in their speeches convolute the term 'sadomasochism' with the addition of the term 'homosexuality'. Lord Templeman speaks of 'sado-masochistic homosexual encounters',[74] Lord Jauncey uses the terms 'homosexual sado-masochism'[75] and 'homosexual sadomasochistic activities'[76] and Lord Lowry refers to the acts as 'sado-masochistic homosexual activity' and 'homosexual sadomasochism'.[77] The use of such terminology does not only serve a descriptive purpose. It is explicitly connecting the practice of sadomasochism to homosexuality. Moreover, in the dissenting speeches of Lord Mustill and Lord Slynn of Hadley, who both call on their learned colleagues to not base their judgments on moral grounds, the word 'sadomasochism' is not once semantically coupled with the word 'homosexuality'. This factor further underlines the majority opinions' overt decision not only to comment on the practice of sadomasochism in general, but particularly on homosexual sadomasochism. As such, homosexuality and sadomasochism are inseparably intertwined within the Law Lords' speeches.[78]

Similar to *Knuller*, the Law Lords imply that homosexuals are characterized by a lack of sexual self-control. Such implication is discernible when Lord Lowry speaks of 'the [high] probability that some sado-masochistic activity, under the *powerful influence of the sexual instinct*, will get out of hand and result in serious physical damage to the participants'.[79] Lord Lowry considers the homosexuals' sexual instinct to be so powerful that all caution is thrown to the wind, resulting in injury or worse. Lord Jauncey underlines this view when he sarcastically remarks, 'there was, of course, no referee present such as there would be in a boxing or football match'.[80] His comment implicitly asserts that

---

Attribution-Value Model of Prejudice to Homosexuality' (2002) 142:2 *The Journal of Social Psychology* 264–271.
73 M Herek and John Capitanio, 'Black Heterosexuals' Attitudes Toward Lesbians and Gay Men in the United States' (1995) 32:2 *Journal of Sex Research* 95–105.
74 *Brown*, 230 (Lord Templeman).
75 *Brown*, 245 (Lord Jauncey of Tullichettle).
76 *Ibid.*, 246.
77 *Brown*, 255 (Lord Lowry).
78 This finding applies not only to the reoccurring theme of self-control but also to the two other themes of decriminalization and corruption.
79 *Brown*, 255 (Lord Lowry; emphasis added).
80 *Brown*, 238 (Lord Jauncey of Tullichettle).

without a third-party monitoring, there is no restraint to the sexual desires of homosexual sadomasochists, whose lack of self-control will ultimately lead to bodily harm or worse.

4.2. Decriminalization vs. Legalization

This section focuses on the recurrent discursive theme of decriminalization vs. legalization. Whereas legalization means that a behavior and all its surrounding activities are fully legal, decriminalization means only that the behavior that is decriminalized will not be punishable under criminal law. The surrounding activities remain unlawful. For instance, when a drug is decriminalized, a person will not be criminally charged for using that drug. However, the production and sale of the drug remain illicit, and anyone who engages in such activity will be charged with a criminal offense. By contrast, to legalize a drug means to officially allow not only its use but also its production and sale.[81]

The relevance of the Law Lords' classification of homosexual acts as merely decriminalized lies within what such classification implies. The classification of homosexual acts as decriminalized points to the underlying opinion that homosexuality remains 'immoral', even if some aspects of it have been decriminalized. Particularly, a very narrow interpretation of the statute decriminalizing homosexual acts allows for surrounding activities to be interpreted as remaining illicit, whereas a broad interpretation would lead to the opposite outcome. Hence, if the Law Lords display a restrictive interpretation of laws on homosexuality, this can be taken as an indication of the opinion that homosexual acts are immoral.

4.2.1 Discourse Around Decriminalization in Knuller

Three of the five Law Lords apply the distinction between decriminalization and legalization to homosexual acts, unanimously finding that the fact that homosexual acts have been decriminalized does not mean that the surrounding activities have attained the status of lawful activities. Lord Reid remarks, 'there is a material difference between merely exempting certain conduct from criminal penalties and making it lawful in the full sense', from which he concludes:

> I find nothing in the [Sexual Offenses] Act [1967] to indicate that Parliament thought or intended to lay down that indulgence in these practices is not corrupting. I read the Act as saying that, even though it may be corrupting, if people choose to corrupt themselves in this way that is their affair and the law will not interfere. But *no licence is given to others to encourage the practice.*[82]

---

81 For a more in-depth discussion, see: Douglas Husak. 'Four Points About Drug Decriminalization' (2003) 22:1 *Criminal Justice Ethics* 21, 22.
82 *Knuller*, 457 (Lord Reid; emphasis added).

Lord Morris concurs with Lord Reid's characterization, stating:

> What section 1 of the [Sexual Offenses] Act [1967] does is to provide that certain acts which previously were criminal offences should no longer be criminal offences. But that does not mean that it is not open to a jury to say that to *assist or to encourage* persons to take part in such acts may be to corrupt them.[83]

Lastly, Lord Simon echoes his learned colleagues' assertions:

> although Parliament decided that homosexual acts in private between persons over the age of 21 should no longer be offences either at common law or by statute, *it does not appear that Parliament was even neutral in its attitude towards such conduct*.[84]

By applying the decriminalization–legalization distinction to homosexual acts and interpreting the Sexual Offenses Act 1967 very narrowly, the Law Lords take the stance that, while homosexual acts may be *tolerated* by the law, any surrounding activities, including solicitation and mere encouragement, are still punishable under criminal law.

Such expression of tolerance without moral acceptance mirrors the recommendation made by the Committee on Homosexual Offences and Prostitution in the Wolfenden Report, which gave the impetus for Parliament to pass section 1 of the Sexual Offenses Act 1967. The report distinguishes between criminal law and private morality; a distinction Lord Reid is cautious to uphold when he writes 'if people choose to corrupt themselves in this way that is their affair and the law will not interfere'.[85] Moreover, the emphasis in the Wolfenden Report lies on 'a realm of *private* morality and immorality'.[86] Hence, like the Law Lords, the report suggests that as soon as homosexual acts transcend the very limited private sphere of the individual the criminal law must intervene by enforcing moral standards. These parallels between the discourse on decriminalization in *Knuller* and the Wolfenden Report further evidence the Law Lords' opinion that homosexuality is immoral.

More direct proof that the Law Lords regard homosexuality as immoral is given in the following passages of Lord Reid's speech:

> I hold that opinion the more strongly in this case by reason of the nature of the subject-matter we are dealing with. I said in *Shaw's case [1962] A.C. 220*, 275 and I repeat that Parliament and Parliament alone is the proper authority to change the law with regard to the punishment of *immoral acts*.[87]

---

83 *Knuller*, 460 (Lord Morris; emphasis added).
84 *Knuller*, 484 (Lord Simon; emphasis added).
85 *Knuller*, 457 (Lord Reid).
86 See *Committee on Homosexual Offences and Prostitution* (n 1) 24.
87 *Knuller*, 455 (Lord Reid; emphasis added).

Lord Reid is implying that the acts subject to this appeal (i.e. homosexual acts and their solicitation and encouragement) are immoral. What is more, he uses rhetorical devices to put special emphasis on this statement, underlining the importance and firmness of this particular opinion. Firstly, Lord Reid uses *parallelism* ('*I said* in Shaw's case [. . .] and *I repeat*') to emphasize that he is being consistent in his statement. Secondly, he makes use of *amplification* ('Parliament and Parliament alone') to underline that the judiciary is not competent to settle questions of morality.

4.2.2 Discourse Around Decriminalization in Brown

Nearly three decades after the decriminalization of homosexual acts, not much in the Law Lords' discourse around decriminalization had changed. They still emphasize that '[h]omosexual activities performed in circumstances which do not fall within section 1(1) of the Act of 1967 remain unlawful'.[88] Lord Templeman adds that 'Parliament has retained criminal sanctions against the practice, dissemination and encouragement of homosexual activities'.[89] Such reliance on Parliament is both a way for the Law Lords to shift responsibility to the legislative branch as well as to appear neutral while passing off their own beliefs as 'what Parliament has said'. Lord Jauncey provides a good example of this:

> When Parliament passed the Sexual Offences Act 1967 which made buggery and acts of gross indecency between consenting males lawful it had available the Wolfenden Report [. . .] which was the product of an exhaustive research into the problem. If it is to be decided that [sado-masochistic homosexual activities] are injurious neither to [individuals] nor to the public interest, then it is for Parliament with its accumulated wisdom and sources of information to declare them to be lawful.[90]

Lord Jauncey characterizes 'buggery and acts of gross indecency between consenting males', then, as well as homosexual sadomasochism, now, as 'problems', thereby implicitly expressing a negative attitude toward such practices. He then goes on to interpret section 13 of the Sexual Offenses Act 1956, which criminalizes *indecency between men*, and section 1(7) of the Sexual Offenses Act 1967, which decriminalizes indecency between men *in private*, narrowly:

> Your Lordships were referred to no material which suggested that Parliament, when enacting the Act of 1956 had in contemplation the type of activities engaged in by the appellants [. . .] The activities of the appellants

---

88 *Brown*, 234 (Lord Templeman).
89 *Ibid.*, 234.
90 *Brown*, 246 (Lord Jauncey of Tullichettle).

thus went far beyond the sort of conduct contemplated by the legislature in the foregoing statutory provisions and I consider that they were unlawful even when carried out in private.[91]

Lord Lowry concurs with Lord Jauncey's approach of interpreting the Sexual Offenses Act 1967, such that the current instances of homosexual sadomasochism do not fall within the ambit of what the Act has decriminalized:

> If in the course of buggery, as authorised by the Act of 1967, one participant, either with the other participant's consent or not, deliberately causes actual bodily harm to that other, an offence against section 47 has been committed. *The Act of 1967 provides no shield.*[92]

By this narrow interpretation, the Law Lords perpetuate the narrative that while the law *tolerates* certain homosexual acts done in private, it does not morally approve of homosexuality nor accept homosexual practices *en masse*. This moral disapproval is powerfully demonstrated in Lord Lowry's speech when he refuses to 'encourage the practice of homosexual sado-masochism, [. . .] by withdrawing the legal penalty and giving the activity a judicial imprimatur'.[93]

Interestingly, expressions of the opinion that homosexuality is immoral cannot be found in the speeches of the Law Lords who have interpreted the laws on homosexuality narrowly. Rather, this opinion is indicated in the dissenting speeches of Lord Mustill and Lord Slynn of Hadley, who call on their learned colleagues to 'leav[e] aside repugnance and *moral objection*' in deciding the case.[94] Specifically, Lord Mustill writes:

> the issue before the House is not whether the appellants' conduct is *morally right*, but whether it is properly charged under the Act of 1861. When proposing that the conduct is not rightly so charged I do not invite your Lordships' House to *endorse it as morally acceptable*. Nor do I pronounce in favour of a libertarian doctrine specifically related to sexual matters. Nor in the least do I suggest that *ethical pronouncements* are meaningless, that there is no difference between right and wrong, that sadism is praiseworthy, or that *new opinions on sexual morality* are necessarily superior to the old, or anything else of the same kind. What I do say is that these are questions of *private morality*; that the standards by which they fall to be judged are not those of the criminal law; and that if these standards are to be upheld the individual must enforce them upon himself according to his *own moral standards*.[95]

---

91 *Ibid.*, 247.
92 *Brown*, 256 (Lord Lowry; emphasis added).
93 *Brown*, 255.
94 *Brown*, 274 (Lord Mustill; emphasis added).
95 *Ibid.*, 273.

In this rather lengthy passage, Lord Mustill carefully emphasizes that he does not endorse the opinion that homosexual sadomasochism is morally acceptable, but that it is a matter of private morality. This echoes the Wolfenden Reports' recommendation while simultaneously implying, like the Wolfenden Report and his colleagues in *Knuller*, that homosexuality remains immoral even if the law does not criminalize it. Moreover, Lord Mustill implies that the majority opinion's faulty ruling is based on their moral rejection of homosexual sadomasochism.

4.3 Corruption

The third re-occurring discoursive theme in the two judgments is that of *corrupting*. A critical analysis of the discourse around corruption reveals three underlying homophobic beliefs: the aforementioned opinion that homosexuality is immoral, the opinion that homosexuality spreads like a virus and the constituent attitude that homosexuals especially target minors to engage in sexual acts with.

The attitude that homosexuals target especially minors is born out of the same cluster of specific beliefs under which the attitude that homosexuals lack self-control is organized. Specifically, homosexuals are perceived as being so obsessed with sex that they lack the self-control to refrain from molesting minors.[96] Moreover, as minors themselves lack the self-control of adults, they are seen as 'easy targets' for 'homosexual predators'. According to this view, homosexuality was considered to spread like a 'corruptive contagion'.[97] This homophobic opinion, which took on an almost conspirative character, perceived homosexuality as a metaphorical virus, leading to an irrational fear that homosexuality causes 'the very destruction of family and civilization itself'.[98] Homosexuals, thus, were perceived as agents of contagion who target minors, whom they seek to engage in homosexual acts with. The alleged result is the spreading of the 'homosexual virus' across all of society.

4.3.1 Discourse Around Corruption in Knuller

Firstly, the opinion that homosexuality is immoral is expressed indirectly through the Law Lords' characterization of the activities charged as corrupting and debauching of public morals. The fact that the charge in the first place connects solicitation of homosexuality with the corruption of public *morals* is the best example of this presumed connection between homosexuality and

---

96 Richard D Mohr, *A More Perfect Union: Why Straight America Must Stand Up for Gay Rights* (Beacon Press 1994) 2.
97 Ibid.
98 Ibid.

immorality. Indeed, not a single Law Lord questions the capacity of the adverts to corrupt public morals, as this passage from Lord Morris' speech demonstrates: 'The learned judge left it to the jury to decide whether the advertisements would induce males and encourage males to indulge in homosexual acts'.[99] Here, Lord Morris is responding to the criticism voiced by the appellants that the trial judge had not adequately instructed the jury as to the requirements of the charge of 'conspiracy to corrupt public morals'. Lord Morris dismisses this criticism. Reconstructed as a syllogism, his argument is as follows:

(P1) If the trial judge instructed the jury that it is up to them to decide

whether the acts charged were corrupting to public morals, then the instructions of the trial judge to the jury were adequate.

(P2) The trial judge instructed the jury that it was up to them to decide

whether the acts charged would induce and encourage males to engage in homosexual acts.

(P3) To induce and encourage males to engage in homosexual acts is

corrupting to public morals.
Therefore (from (P1), (P2) and (P3)),

(C) The instructions of the trial judge to the jury were adequate.

The deconstruction of this argument reveals an implicit assumption (P3) in his reasoning. Rather than arguing that the jury must additionally decide whether inducing males to engage in homosexual acts satisfies the requirement of 'corrupting public morals', he automatically assumes that it does. Lord Kilbrandon is less subtle than his learned colleague:

> the corrupting and depraving which are here alleged do not arise from the articles themselves. They arise from the whole apparatus of liaison organised by the appellants. The subject-matter of the conspiracy was [. . .] the *introduction of males to one another for sexual gratification.* [. . .] Th[is], not the publication of the article, constituted the corruption and the depravity.[100]

Lord Kilbrandon candidly proclaims that the 'introduction of males to one another for sexual gratification' was what in fact 'constituted the corruption' of public morals. The opposite of public morals are public 'immorals'.[101]

---

99 *Knuller*, 462 (Lord Morris).
100 *Knuller*, 497 (Lord Kilbrandon; emphasis added).
101 Jonathan Law, 'Public Morals' in *A Dictionary of Law* (Oxford University Press 2018).

Hence, anything that has the potential to corrupt public morals must in itself be immoral. The assumptions expressed by Lord Morris and Lord Kilbrandon, which equate inducing homosexual acts to the corruption of public morals, are instantiated expressions of the homophobic opinion that homosexuality is immoral.

Secondly, although research has yielded no findings in support of a link between homosexuality and pedophilia,[102] such link is repeatedly implied in the Law Lords' speeches. Lord Reid writes:

> It is not disputed that a great many copies found their way into the hands of *young students and schoolboys*, but no point is made by the prosecution that it was likely that males under 21 would reply to the advertisements.[103]

Since the prosecution did not make a point regarding the appeal of the adverts to minors, Lord Reid does not discuss this point in his speech. However, he does choose to specifically mention that no such point was made, instead of omitting any reference to this fact altogether. Hence, while Lord Reid does not directly address the presumed link between homosexuality and pedophilia, he does so indirectly.

Lord Kilbrandon, for his part, chooses to be more vocal about the attitude toward homosexuals as pedophiles, stating:

> When one of the accused admitted – or perhaps boasted – in the witness-box that his publication was read by some *10,000 schoolboys*, it could only be some person utterly ignorant of the world of adolescence who would fail to appreciate the *inevitable consequences*.[104]

The 'inevitable consequences', which Lord Kilbrandon assumes here are that schoolboys will answer to the adverts and be corrupted into homosexual acts by pedophilic homosexuals.

Even Lord Diplock who is alone in allowing the appeal on the first count does not manage to entirely avail himself from the homophobic attitude of homosexuals as pedophiles. He states that while he cannot find support for the convictions on either count to stand, 'the defendants might well have been guilty of [. . .] inciting or procuring the commission of the statutory offence of doing acts of gross indecency with male persons under the age of 21.'[105] With this sentence, Lord Diplock endorses – by instantiated expression – the view that homosexuals more often than not target minors for sexual purposes.

---

102 See e.g. Kurt Freund et al., 'Pedophilia and Heterosexuality vs. Homosexuality' (1984) 10:3 *Journal of Sex & Marital Therapy* 193–200; Kurt Freund, Robin Watson, and Douglas Rienzo, 'Heterosexuality, Homosexuality, and Erotic Age Preference' (1989) 26:1 *Journal of Sex Research* 107–117.
103 *Knuller*, 454 (Lord Reid; emphasis added).
104 *Knuller*, 497 (Lord Kilbrandon; emphasis added).
105 *Knuller*, 481 (Lord Diplock).

4.3.2 Discourse Around Corruption in Brown

In contrast to *Knuller*, the opinion that homosexuality is immoral is replaced by an increase in expressions of the opinion that homosexuality spreads like a virus. This, undoubtedly, is a result of the appearance of HIV/AIDS. In 1972, at the time of the *Knuller* judgment, HIV/AIDS, although already existent on the African continent, had not yet spread to the UK. It was not until 1981 that the first AIDS-related death was registered in the UK.[106] And even then, medical professionals did not exactly know what was causing the immunosuppression, terming it *gay cancer*,[107] *gay compromise syndrome* (GCS)[108] or *gay-related immune deficiency* (GRID),[109] due to it being found predominantly in homosexual males. The correlation between AIDS and homosexuality within the Western world appeared, for people holding homophobic ideologies, to be a confirmation of the opinion that homosexuality spreads like a virus, only that now the virus was not merely figurative anymore. The *human immunodeficiency virus* (HIV), in this view, stood literally for the *virus* that was homosexuality, while AIDS was seen as the consequence of the immorality that results from homosexual acts. This view of homosexuality as a life-threatening 'virus' is reflected in MP Rhodes Boyson's comment from 1987 on the 'gay plague': 'The current fashion for the flouting of homosexuality and lesbianism is both *anti-family* and *anti-life*'.[110]

The Law Lords' speeches in *Brown* feature direct expressions of this opinion. For instance, Lord Lowry writes:

> considering the danger of infection, with its *inevitable threat of Aids*, I am not impressed by the argument that this threat can be discounted on the ground that, as long ago as 1967, Parliament, subject to conditions, legalised *buggery*, now a well known *vehicle for the transmission of Aids*.[111]

Lord Mustill, on his part, remarks: 'what is currently the *principal cause* for the transmission of this scourge [AIDS], namely consenting *buggery between males*, is now legal'.[112]

---

106 RM Du Bois et al., 'Primary *Pneumocystis carinii* and Cytomegalovirus Infections' (1981) 318:8259 *The Lancet* 1339; Jaymi McCann, 'The Timeline: Aids' *The Independent* (2011). <www.independent.co.uk/life-style/health-and-families/features/the-timeline-aids-2292352.html>.
107 Matt Cook, 'From Gay Reform to Gaydar: 1967–2006' in Matt Cook (ed), *A Gay History of Britain: Love and Sex Between Men Since the Middle Ages* (Greenwood World Publishing 2019) 196.
108 Robert O Brennan and David T Durack, 'Gay Compromise Syndrome' (1981) 318:8259 *The Lancet* 318 1338–1339.
109 GA Oswald et al., 'Attempted Immune Stimulation in the "Gay Compromise Syndrome"' (1982) 285:6348 *BMJ* 1082–1082.
110 Rhodes Boyson, *Daily Express*, 17 March 1987 (emphasis added).
111 *Brown*, 255–256 (Lord Lowry; emphasis added).
112 *Brown*, 274 (Lord Mustill; emphasis added).

Both Law Lords state that AIDS is directly correlated with homosexual acts: spreading homosexuality equalled spreading of AIDS. Indeed, according to Lord Templeman, even the most careful and diligent exercise of homosexual sadomasochism 'could not have removed the danger of infection'.[113] From this perspective, the only way to stop the spread of AIDS is to stop the spread of homosexuality. However, since the law permits homosexual intercourse, the Law Lords had to find other ways to restrict the spread of homosexuality. This is where the attitude that homosexuals target especially minors comes into play.

Explaining 'the function of criminal law in relation to homosexual behaviour', Lord Templeman quotes the Wolfenden Report: 'to preserve public order and decency, to protect the citizen from what is *offensive* or *injurious*, and to provide sufficient safeguards against exploitation and corruption of others, particularly those who are *specially vulnerable because they are young*, [. . .]'.[114] Essentially, he is calling homosexual acts both offensive – in that they are immoral – and injurious – in that they spread AIDS amongst the population. Especially minors, who, under this view, made 'easy targets' for homosexuals, had to be protected by the law. As such, Lord Templeman is expressing three homophobic beliefs at once, namely (1) the opinion that homosexuality is immoral, (2) the opinion that homosexuality spreads like a virus and (3) the attitude that homosexuals target especially minors.

Moreover, Lord Templeman, quoting Lord Lane C.J. in the Court of Appeal case, describes how one of the appellants targeted and achieved the corruption of a minor:

> [one of the appellants] had befriended K. when the boy was 15 years old. He met him in a cafeteria and, so he says, found out that the boy was interested in homosexual activities. He introduced and encouraged K. in 'bondage affairs.' He was interested in viewing and recording on videotape K. and other teenage boys in homosexual scenes.[115]

Lord Jauncey likewise quotes a passage from Lord Lane C.J.'s speech. One of the lines both Law Lords quote is: 'It is some comfort at least to be told, as we were, that K. has now it seems settled into a normal heterosexual relationship'.[116]

The fact that both Law Lords 'take comfort' in the fact that K. has reverted to a 'normal' heterosexual orientation demonstrates a heteronormative discourse in which homosexuality is characterized as unnatural and immoral. Moreover, it points to the homophobic attitude that homosexuality is a choice, which, when chosen correctly, can be refrained from with enough self-control.

---

113 *Brown*, 236 (Lord Templeman; emphasis added).
114 *Ibid.*, 233.
115 *Ibid.*, 235.
116 *Brown*, 235 (Lord Templeman), 245 (Lord Jauncey).

Returning to the evidence for the attitude that homosexuals especially target minors, Lord Jauncey states:

> the possibility of *proselytisation* and *corruption of young men* is a *real danger* even in the case of these appellants and the taking of video recordings of such activities suggests that secrecy may not be as strict as the appellants claimed to your Lordships. If the only purpose of the activity is the sexual gratification of one or both of the participants what then is the need of a video recording?[117]

Lord Jauncey implies that the fact that the appellants video recorded some of the homosexual sadomasochistic acts is evidence that the appellants were not only targeting minors to proselytize and corrupt, but that they also intended to maximize the effectiveness of their pedophilic recruiting efforts by reaching a larger viewership. Similarly, Lord Mustill asserts:

> As the evidence in the present case has shown, there is a risk that strangers (and *especially young strangers*) may be *drawn into* these activities at an early age and will then become *established in them for life*. This is indeed a *disturbing prospect* [. . .].[118]

In essence, Lord Mustill asserts that the fact that homosexuals especially target minors is so dangerous because the earlier a person is 'infected' with homosexuality, the longer he can spread the 'virus', both literally and figuratively, and such spread 'cannot be regarded as conducive to the enhancement or enjoyment of family life or conducive to the *welfare of society*'.[119] Lord Jauncey concurs, stating that it would be contrary to *public interest* to hold homosexual sadomasochistic acts to be lawful.[120] These assertions reveal the opinion that homosexuality spreads like a virus that has the potential to destroy society as we know it.

5. Conclusion

This chapter has argued that the House of Lords between the years 1967 and 2004 displayed a homophobic ideology, which was given expression through a number of homophobic attitudes and opinions contained in the Law Lords' speeches on matters relating to homosexuality. Beyond the importance of documenting such *institutional homophobia*,[121] two valuable insights can be taken from the findings of this chapter.

---

117 *Brown*, 246 (Lord Jauncey of Tullichettle; emphasis added).
118 *Brown*, 275 (Lord Mustill; emphasis added).
119 *Brown*, 255 (Lord Lowry; emphasis added).
120 *Brown*, 246 (Lord Jauncey).
121 Warren J Blumenfeld, *Homophobia: How We All Pay the Price* (Beacon Press 1992) 5.

Firstly, ideologies only change very slowly, much slower than the law. Not only do the speeches in *Brown* contain the same homophobic beliefs expressed in *Knuller* more than two decades prior, but the discursive themes used to convey these beliefs are shockingly similar. By contrast, especially since the mid-1980s laws and public policy around homosexuality had begun to slowly but surely change. Driven most significantly by local councils, these changes aimed at expanding the legal protection and rights of homosexuals within their local communities.[122] The law in such instances seems to function as a forerunner, which heralds the beginning of a new ideology. Although it can only be speculated which ideological shifts may occur in the future, the ideology of transphobia perhaps will be the next target of such law reform.[123] In any case, the findings of this chapter show that the law does not always function as a barometer of society's dominant ideology, but it can also be the first step in ringing in a new, more progressive one. As Alfred Simpson said: 'law is the product of its social context, yet the social context is itself in part a product of law'.[124]

Secondly, the analysis of the Law Lords judgments demonstrates that perceptions of sexual morality are in a constant state of change. Which sexual practices are morally acceptable is 'historically contingent and socially constructed'.[125] From today's perspective, it is almost impossible to imagine members of a body as powerful as the House of Lords letting their judgments be influenced so strongly by specific notions of sexual morality. But, that is exactly what occurred in *Knuller* half a century and *Brown* a quarter of a century ago.

At least some comfort can be taken from the fact that not all Law Lords fell prey to such moral-based reasoning. As Lord Simon says in *Knuller*, 'public decency must be viewed as a whole; and I think the jury should be invited, where appropriate, to remember that they live in a *plural society*, with a *tradition of tolerance towards minorities*, and that this atmosphere of toleration is itself part of public decency'.[126] The findings of this chapter should remind legal scholars, practitioners and judges not to pass judgment in sexual matters all too quickly based on notions of (im)morality; it is unbecoming of the rational thinking that makes for a good legal mind.

---

122 See *Cook* (n 107) 193.
123 Libby Brooks, '"A Monumental Change": How Ireland Transformed Transgender Rights; Since 2015, Ireland Has Allowed People to Change Gender by Self-Declaration. Now The UK Is Considering Following Suit" *The Guardian*, 15 January 2018; Julian Norman et al., '"Shifting Sands": Six Legal Views on the Transgender Debate' *The Guardian*, 19 October 2018.
124 Alfred WB Simpson, 'Analysis of Legal Concepts' (1964) 80:4 *Law Quarterly Review* 535.
125 Sharon Cowan, 'The Pain of Pleasure: Consent and the Criminalisation of SM "Assaults"' in James Chalmers, Fiona Leverick, and Lindsay Farmer (eds), *Essays in Criminal Law in Honour of Sir Gerald Gordon* (Edinburgh University Press 2019) 140.
126 *Knuller*, 495 (Lord Simon; emphasis added).

Part 3

The Continued Struggle for Equality

LGBT Students, Identity and Language

Chapter 13

Living Identity

Perspectives from the Fields of Education and Language

Sean Becker and Paul Behrens

The surge in support for the Black Lives Matter movement in May of 2020 led to considerable backlash by conservatives in the USA against the prospect of students being taught *critical race theory* (CRT) in public high schools.[1] Their concern: fear that children are being 'indoctrinated' with 'left-wing ideology'.[2] The discourse around CRT provides a good example of the universally acknowledged impact and importance of education, not just on the topic of race, but on all topics involving social, political and cultural issues, including LGBT rights.

In fact, in the mid 1980s, the same type of debate was passionately led in the UK over the 'promotion of homosexuality'.[3] In 1988, the Thatcher government introduced Section 28 under the Local Government Act 1988. The clause banned the promotion of homosexuality in British schools and by local authorities – some commentators noted that it 'meant in practice that teachers were prohibited from discussing even the possibility of same-sex relationships with students'.[4] While Section 28 was repealed in 2001 and 2003,[5] respectively, the teaching of an LGBT inclusive curriculum is by no means a moot issue in Europe.

In June of 2021, Hungary passed legislation, echoing Russia's infamous 2013 law that bans the dissemination of 'propaganda of nontraditional sexual

---

1 See e.g. Sophia Ankel, 'Virginia's New Republican Governor, Who Banned Critical Race Theory in Schools, Is Launching a Tip Line for Parents to Report Their Kids' Teachers' *Business Insider*, 25 January 2022.
2 Thomas F Berner, 'Indoctrinating Kids in Critical Race Theory' *The Wall Street Journal*, 19 July 2021; Jarrett Stepman, 'Parents Wise Up About Critical Race Theory' *New York Post*, 23 January 2022.
3 Joe Sommerland, 'Section 28: What Was Margaret Thatcher's Controversial Law and How Did It Affect the Lives of LGBT+ People?' *The Independent*, 25 May 2018.
4 Ibid.
5 See s. 122, Local Government Act 2003, c. 26. (This was the last vestige of s. 28 Local Government Act 1988); Section 28 was repealed in Scotland in 2001 by s. 34, Ethical Standards in Public Life etc. (Scotland) Act 2000 asp 7.

DOI: 10.4324/9781003286295-17

relations'[6] among minors.[7] The Hungarian law, which went into effect in July 2021,[8] forbids teachers from including content deemed to promote homosexuality and gender reassignment in the curriculum.[9] Prime Minister Orbán's government claims that the legislation protects children and leaves choices on sexual education up to parents.[10] What Orbán's government neglected to consider, however, is the impact the legislation may have on LGBT students and teachers. As the law essentially bans an entire field of discourse, it severely restricts the language available to teachers. Language, however, plays a large role in shaping societal values. As the LGBT rights activist Rita Mae Brown once said, 'Language is the road map of a culture.'[11] By exploring the relationship between education, language and the LGBT community, much insight can be gained from society's stances on LGBT relevant topics.

The chapters in this section are dedicated to the fields of education and language.

Chapter 14 (Capaldi and Sykes) highlights the detrimental consequences a consistent lack of visibility of LGBT experiences and lives in the curriculum presents for both students and staff, by focusing on the campus environment in higher education, specifically on student and staff learning and teaching experiences.

Exploring the emerging themes of institutional facilities and administration; harassment, bullying and transphobia; inclusion and exclusion; and representation in the curriculum, Chapter 15 (Regan) surveys transgender students' experiences to garner a better understanding of the needs of this student group.

Based on a decade of interviews, Chapter 16 (Adams) examines the use of language in the Arabian Peninsula to create a shared experience and engage in community building among LGBT persons in that region and the way it helps to overcome cultural barriers in the process.

---

6 Human Rights First, *The Spread of Russian-Style Propaganda Laws: Fact Sheet*, n.d., <www.humanrightsfirst.org/sites/default/files/HRF-Fact-Sheet-Spread-of-Anti-LGBT-laws.pdf> (accessed 25 January 2022).
7 Graeme Reid, 'Political Homophobia Ramps Up' *Human Rights Watch*, 13 August 2021.
8 Gergely Szakacs and Alicja Ptak, 'As Hungary's Anti-LGBT Law Takes Effect, Some Teachers Are Defiant' *Reuters*, 8 July 2021.
9 *CNN World News*, 'Hungary's Parliament Passes Anti-LGBT Law Ahead of 2022 Election', 15 June 2021.
10 *See* (n 9).
11 Jonathan Patterson, *Villainy in France (1463–1610): A Transcultural Study of Law and Literature* (Oxford University Press 2021) 282.

Chapter 14

Embedding LGBT Equality in the Curriculum and the Classroom

Eleanor Capaldi and Amanda Sykes

1. Introduction

While there has increasingly been investigation and research into the experiences of LGBT+ (lesbian, gay, bisexual, transgender, plus further identities represented by this acronym)[1] students on university campuses in the UK, and even more so in the USA, termed 'campus climate', there has been comparatively little investigation into core elements of the university experience, which form the focus of our research project – the curriculum and the classroom. Mark Connolly suggests this neglect is in part due to assumptions that classroom settings are 'value-neutral' in that the pursuit of learning and knowledge is objective and separate from concerns outwith the classroom.[2] Such assumptions can play a part in this sizeable component of student and staff experiences being overlooked and underestimated in the role they can play to encourage and enable equality and inclusion. While it may be uncomfortable to think about, universities, despite being places of learning and critical enquiry, have not always been welcoming to marginalised identities, including LGBT+. The structures that have shaped the environment in which staff work and students learn are deep rooted and have to be continually addressed. Thankfully, initiatives, both legal and grassroots, both in and outside the university, have been counteracting this history to create an environment in which LGBT+ students and staff have as equitable a chance to pursue and succeed in their research interests and careers as their peers.

In a study of 'non-traditional' college students, defined by the metric of non-white non-male, including at that time 'gays and lesbians', it was found that

---

1 The acronym to represent diverse identities has evolved over time. The + symbol signifies identities, including, but not limited to queer, pansexual, intersex and asexual. When an acronym is used in connection with a cited source, it reflects the acronym used in that source. This project was commissioned under the acronym 'LGBT'.
2 M Connolly, 'Issues for Lesbian, Gay, and Bisexual Students in Traditional College Classrooms' in VA Wall and N Evans (eds), *Toward Acceptance: Sexual Orientation Issues on Campus* (University Press of America 2000) 111.

DOI: 10.4324/9781003286295-18

'when validation is present, students feel capable of learning; they experience a feeling of self worth and feel that they, and everything that they bring to the college experience, are accepted and recognized as valuable'. Conversely, 'lacking validation, students feel crippled, silenced, subordinate, and/or mistrusted'.[3] There is a power and authority inherent in the classroom setting. Therefore, what is spoken about LGBT+ people and how, whether positive or negative, alongside what is absent, can signal to students and staff what is considered normal or un/acceptable. If an environment is seen to be unwelcoming, individuals may hide their sexuality or gender identity to avoid repercussions. The impact of 'concealing a non-heterosexual orientation is associated with more emotional distress, such as depression, than is disclosing this orientation'.[4] Attempting to conceal stigmas can disrupt social interactions, the mechanisms of trying to hide a concealable stigma enacted by 'increased self-monitoring and impression management, behavioural performance deficits, increased social avoidance and isolation, and the increased importance of feedback in shaping behaviour'.[5] It is therefore demonstrable that environments that are unwelcoming to LGBT+ people place pressures upon these individuals, which require additional energy and effort from LGBT+ people to navigate such environments.

The legal landscape has progressed in Scotland, with rights granted for same-sex marriage, adoption and the repeal of Section 28 of Chapter 9 of the Local Government Act 1988, which prohibited the 'promotion' of homosexuality in schools. However, a key Stonewall report examining hate crime in the UK from 2018 found that the number of LGB people who experienced a hate crime based on their sexual orientation has risen 78%, from 9% to 16% between 2013 and 2017. During 2017, 41% of trans people had experienced a hate crime or incident. Additionally, young people were found to be at greatest risk: 56% of trans young people aged 18–24 and 33% of LGB people aged 18–24 experienced a hate crime based on their sexual orientation or gender identity in the same period. When LGBT individuals are also BAME or disabled, incidences of crime enacted upon them increase, with a third of BAME LGBT people experiencing hate crime or incident compared to one in five white LGBT people, and 27% of LGBT disabled people compared to 17% of non-disabled LGBT people.[6] Efforts to reform the Gender Recognition Act are ongoing and uncertain. The most recent announcement at the time of writing regarding gender options on

---

3 L Rendon, 'Validating Culturally Diverse Students: Toward a New Model of Learning and Student Development' (1994) 19:1 *Innovative Higher Education* 44.
4 J Pachankis, 'The Psychological Implications of Concealing a Stigma: A Cognitive Affective Behavioural Model' (2007) 133:2 *Psychological Bulletin* 328, 334.
5 *Ibid.*, 335.
6 Stonewall, LGBT in Britain – Hate Crime and Discrimination, 2017, 8. <www.stonewall.org.uk/lgbt-britain-hate-crime-and-discrimination>.

the next Scottish census is that they will not include non-binary identities.[7] Meanwhile, intersex individuals are currently not explicitly protected in the Equality Act (although one must not be discriminated against based on your gender or perceived gender).[8]

In 2011, the Higher Education Academy stated: 'The basic principle that attitudes, barriers and other forms of discrimination rather than individual characteristics or deficits are the cause of disadvantage can and should be universally applied.'[9] When students are no longer required to divert attention to address comments in the classroom, to protect or hide their identity for fear of the response or to educate others (students and staff) during their education, only then do they have the same access as their heterosexual cisgender peers.

1.1 Scotland

Our University of Glasgow research follows a study conducted within the university's Psychology Department, which demonstrated a discrepancy in student learning experiences between LGBT and cisgender and heterosexual peers, supporting a call for further research.[10] In 2018, Stonewall released its national LGBT University Report, in which they found one in seven LGBT students (14%) had been the target of negative comments or conduct from a member of university staff in the last year due to their sexual/gender identity (which rises to more than one-third of trans students at 36%), 24% for BAME LGBT students and 22% for LGBT disabled students.[11] Even larger numbers of LGBT students were the target of negative comments or conduct *from fellow students*, at 33%, increasing to 60% for trans students. They also discovered high percentages of LGBT students having to hide, or being encouraged to hide, their sexual or gender identity, revealing that one in five are not out to their parents. A welcoming university environment could, and should, be a safe environment where LGBT+ students can be at ease without fear of discrimination or judgement.

---

7 Scotgov, Scotland's Census 2021 Equality Impact Assessment Results v1.0 January 2020, 2020, 17 <www.gov.scot/binaries/content/documents/govscot/publications/impact-assessment/2020/01/scotlands-census-2021-equality-impact-assessment/documents/scotlands-census-2021-equality-impact-assessment-results-v1-0/scotlands-census-2021-equality-impact-assessment-results-v1-0/govscot%3Adocument/scotlands-census-2021-equality-impact-assessment-results-v1-0.pdf>.
8 The protected characteristics are age, gender reassignment, being married or in a civil partnership, being pregnant or on maternity leave, disability, race including colour, nationality, ethnic or national origin, religion or belief, sex and sexual orientation, Equality Act 2010.
9 H Morgan and A Houghton, 'Inclusive Curriculum Design for Higher Education' (2011) *Higher Education Academy* 8.
10 J Bohan and A Sykes, *LGBT- University Campus Climate and Representation in the Course Curriculum* (University of Glasgow 2016).
11 Stonewall, LGBT in Britain – University Report, 2018, 2 <www.stonewall.org.uk/lgbt-britain-university-report>.

A number of campus climate studies have taken place in the USA, where advancement towards equality has taken longer in some respects compared to the UK.[12] Despite being home to the Stonewall Inn Riots of 1979 in New York, which marked a significant turning point in the fight for equal rights, individual states, which have no explicit LGBT anti-discrimination laws, have been introducing 'exemption laws', invoking religious reasons to refuse LGBT people service from individuals, businesses and healthcare providers.[13] In 2018, only 19 states and the District of Columbia explicitly prohibited discrimination based on sexual orientation and gender identity in employment, housing and public accommodation.[14] Only after the initial research period, in June 2020, did the Supreme Court rule that discrimination based on sex should include sexual orientation and gender identity.[15] Despite these variations, research undertaken around US colleges has revealed results similar to those of our own survey in terms of the impact of exclusion/inclusion on the learning experience. The findings of these reports towards curriculum inclusion therefore have their basis in comparable student experience, and so we consider these alongside our own suggestions.

Higher Education Institutions (HEIs) in Scotland have a commitment to public sector equality outcomes regarding equality in the curriculum, ensuring a fair environment for all students. In a Scottish specific context, Hazel Marzetti of the Social and Public Health Science Unit at the University of Glasgow explored LGBT+ student HEI experiences. In interviews with LGBT+ identified students, Marzetti found that while 'it would be beneficial to include more queer subject matter in the curriculum . . . their discussion had to be carefully managed'.[16] Part of this includes shifting thinking to see the need for inclusion of LGBT+ identities in coursework, while another element includes enabling access to resources while providing robust support for teaching staff so that they may deliver content confidently, including responding to discussions the content might broach.

The TransEdu project at the University of Strathclyde, led by Drs. Matson Lawrence and Stephanie McKendry, specifically looks at the experiences of

---

12 See *Rendon* (n 3); *Connolly* (n 2); C Connell, *School's Out: Gay and Lesbian Teachers in the Classroom* (University of California Press: USA 2014); S Crowley, C Bertram, and S Massey (eds), *Beyond Progress and Marginalisation* (Peter Lang Publishing 2010).
13 Human Rights Watch, All We Want Is Equality, 2018 <www.hrw.org/report/2018/02/19/all-we-want-equality/religious-exemptions-and-discrimination-against-lgbt-people> (accessed 18 June 2019).
14 Human Rights Watch, United States: State Laws Threaten LGBT Equality, 2018 <www.hrw.org/news/2018/02/19/united-states-state-laws-threaten-lgbt-equality> (accessed 18 June 2019).
15 D Rushe, 'US Supreme Court Rules Employers Cannot Discriminate Against LGBTQ+ Workers' *The Guardian*, 15 June 2020 <www.theguardian.com/law/2020/jun/15/supreme-court-civil-rights-law-lgbtq> (accessed 20 June 2020).
16 H Marzetti, 'Proudly Proactive: Celebrating and Supporting LGBT Students in Scotland' (2017) 23:6 *Teaching in Higher Education* 710.

trans and non-binary people in Further and Higher Education. They found that 86% of respondents had encountered barriers in study or work relating to their trans status or identity.[17] In the breakdown of 15 areas of educational experience, 25% attributed barriers to teaching and learning – the fourth highest aspect. Within the curriculum, barriers and challenges encompass '... difficulties with peers, teaching staff, curriculum content, and placements', where in particular external providers were not in step with institutional values.[18] Differences were also observed across subjects of study, as 'students enrolled on professional courses, including Medicine, Nursing, Social Work, Counselling, and Teaching, reflected on the dearth of curriculum content pertaining to trans people in the training of future practitioners'. And when trans people were discussed in learning and teaching contexts, the content was all too often inaccurate and outdated, and in some cases even offensive and potentially harmful.[19]

The Scottish charity LGBT Youth Scotland explores experiences of education in its report *Life in Scotland for Young People*.[20] They found that while trans students were more likely to rate their university experience as good now (60% compared to 37% in 2012)[21] and that incidents of bullying decreased compared to those in school and Further Education, 14% of LGBT young people and 28% of trans young people still experienced bullying at university, with 94% of all LGBT young people saying bullying negatively affected their education, and 63% of LGB and 68% of trans people saying bullying had negatively affected their educational attainment.[22] While it is not possible to discern from these results where individual incidents of bullying at university took place, we do know from our own survey results that negative comments, teasing and bullying have taken place in the classroom, as also recorded in reports from the National Union of Students (NUS)[23] and Sheffield Hallam University.[24] Conversely, creating through the curriculum an environment, which strongly signals that LGBT+ lives are accepted while supporting students in the face of such comments or behaviour in the classroom, means the educational experience and student attainment can be impacted positively.

---

17 S McKendry and M Lawrence, *Trans Edu Scotland: Researching the Experience of Trans and Gender Diverse Applicants, Students and Staff in Scotland's Colleges and Universities* (University of Strathclyde 2017) 7.
18 See *Ibid.*, 11.
19 See *Ibid.*, 12.
20 LGBT Youth Scotland, Life in Scotland for Young People, 2017 <www.lgbtyouth.org.uk/media/1354/life-in-scotland-for-lgbt-young-people.pdf>.
21 See *Ibid.*, 5.
22 See *Ibid.*, 20.
23 National Union of Students, Education Beyond the Straight and Narrow LGBT Students' Experience in Higher Education (London 2014) 30.
24 E Formby, *From Fresher's to Finals* (Sheffield Hallam 2015).

Due to the passing of inclusive education recommendations and regulations, school pupils in Scotland and England will also, from 2021 and 2020, respectively, begin to experience LGBTI-inclusive curricula.[25] It is important, given this government-backed integration of LGBTI identities in primary and high school curricula, that students do not fall off a 'cliff edge' of inclusion, and that the university allows for a continuation of the space, validation and active acceptance of these identities in the curriculum and the classroom. For the vast majority of current and prospective students, and for those who will not be able to experience LGBT+-inclusive education in their schooling, the university will offer a much-needed space for, and valuable experience of, the inclusion of diverse identities.

1.2 Staff

Each year, the Equality and Diversity Unit at the University of Glasgow launches a staff-wide survey, which anonymously records the identities and experiences of LGBT+ staff across the University of Glasgow. Over time, there has been an increase in the number of declarations of sexual orientation in the survey. However, it is of ongoing concern that even in the anonymised survey, which boasts higher declaration results, in 2018–2019, 8.8% of respondents still selected 'prefer not to say' (seeing a 2.3% *increase* since 2017–2018), while 32.8% left the category unmarked.[26] This marks a change from 2012 to 2013, when answers of 'prefer not to say' were lower at 4.4%, but responses of not known/blank responses totalled 50.1%.[27]

Previous research has shown a pervasiveness of fear surrounding 'coming out', which can lead to LGBT+ people hiding their identity.[28] Even with progression in legal protections and social attitudes within Scotland and the UK, these changes are recent, and there are considerations to be made on a micro level of the attitudes of individuals. Recent research undertaken at the University of Glasgow shows that while LGBT+ and non-LGBT+ students reported low levels of anti-LGBT+ prejudice (where higher scores = more positive attitudes and lower scores = more negative attitudes), a portion of non-LGBT+ identified students (1%) demonstrated strongly negative attitudes towards both their LGBT+ colleagues and towards the existence of University of Glasgow LGBT+ Equality policies, with 4.5% of respondents recording the lowest score (1 = strongly disagree to 5 = strongly agree).[29]

---

25 Scottish Government, LGBTI Education, 2018 <www.gov.scot/news/lgbti-education/> (accessed 24 April 2019); Stonewall, Historic Announcement on LGBT Education in England's Schools, 2019 <www.stonewall.org.uk/node/132831> (accessed 24 April 2019).
26 Staff Equality Monitoring Report 2017–2018 (University of Glasgow 2018) 11.
27 See *Ibid.*, 9.
28 See *LGBT Youth Scotland* (n 20), 23.
29 (n = 1,110; LGBT+ students = 356, non-LGBT+ students = 754), Evangelista, Lido, Swingler, Bohan, 2019.

In addition, there is a sense of precarity around gains in policy and progressions in attitudes in a context of recent increases in LGBT hate crime,[30] the detrimental impact of anti-trans rhetoric in the British media[31] and a rise in social conservatism.[32] This could, in part, explain why people are reluctant to share their identity for fear of how they may be treated.

1.3 Students

Higher Education Statistics Authority (HESA) began to record student data relating to gender identity, sexual orientation, religion or belief in the academic year 2012–2013.[33] This was to ensure they monitored equal opportunities following the newly introduced Equality Act 2010. The categories of sexual orientation (bisexual, gay man, gay woman, heterosexual, other and information refused) and gender identity (does gender identity match that assigned at birth) are designated optional.[34] Currently, HESA record the following categories defined as 'sex': female/male/other,[35] so, in turn, UK universities are only required to record these too. As will become clear in our own survey results, the diversity of gender and sexual identity contains more multitudes than such categories allow.

HESA offers data sets on disability, ethnicity, age and sex on its webpage 'Who's Studying in HE'. However, it does not share information gathered on sexual orientation or gender identity. In discussions of inclusion in Higher Education, the term itself cannot be relied upon as necessarily synonymous with LGBT+ identities. We strongly suggest the experiences of LGBT+ students should be considered alongside groups affected by discrimination and inequality when discussing inclusion and equality.

2. Survey Results

Our survey was extended to all University of Glasgow students and staff, of all identities, LGBT+ as well as cisgender heterosexual. The responses totalled 950.

---

30 See Stonewall (n 6).
31 R Humphrey, ' "I Think Journalists Sometimes Forget that We're Just People": Analysing the Effects of UK Trans Media Representation on Trans Audiences' (2016) 56 *Gender Forum: An Internet Journal for Gender Studie*s 23, 32.
32 According to the Global Populism Database, the number of populist leaders has more than doubled since the early 2000s; see P Lewis, C Barr, S Clarke, A Voce, G Levett, and P Guitiérrez, 'Revealed: The Rise and Rise of Populist Rhetoric' *The Guardian*, 6 March 2019 <www.theguardian.com/world/ng-interactive/2019/mar/06/revealed-the-rise-and-rise-of-populist-rhetoric> (accessed 14 May 2019).
33 Information received per email from HESA on 16 September 2019 (on file with the author).
34 HESA, Sexual Orientation, 2018. <www.hesa.ac.uk/collection/c18051/a/sexort> (accessed 12 March 2019).
35 HESA, Sex Identifier, 2018 <www.hesa.ac.uk/collection/student/datafutures/a/student_sexid> (accessed 12 March 2019).

Of these, 664 were students, representing all Colleges, and 264 staff (22 did not stipulate whether they were staff or student, and of those, 13 did not provide answers beyond identifying information). The categories of sexual identity offered within the survey were lesbian, gay woman (results combined with 'lesbian'), gay man, bisexual, queer, pansexual and asexual. The categories of gender identities offered within the survey were female, male, non-binary, queer, trans man and trans woman.[36] In total, 482 students and 85 staff identified as LGBTQPA.[37]

2.1 Identity and the Classroom

We asked students, 'To what degree do you think that heterosexuality is assumed in the teaching you receive?' Of all respondents, 48% thought that heterosexuality was assumed in their teaching, all or most of the time.[38] A further 27% thought it was assumed sometimes. When students were asked, 'To what extent are non-binary identities included in your course?', inclusion rates were extremely low: 51% of all respondents said non-binary identities were included 'not at all', with a further 31% saying 'insignificantly' (in total: 82%).

The experiences of LGBT+ identified people can vary from their cisgender heterosexual counterparts. For example, when we asked students if they had ever deliberately concealed their sexual orientation or gender identity to a tutor/lecturer/supervisor or other staff member to avoid negative consequences, 23% LGBT+ said 'frequently' or 'sometimes', while 14% additionally said 'yes – rarely', while 96% of cisgender heterosexuals said 'no'.

When younger people are more likely than older respondents to identify as pansexual, asexual, queer, and identify as non-binary,[39] as reflected in our results, the student population is only becoming more diverse. Assumption of heterosexuality and binary identities centres these identities and positions them as default and expected. The presumptions, which place anyone who does not fall into the default categories of heterosexual or binary into a position where they have to 'come out', are in opposition to this supposed ideal. It can neither be assumed that those who are out as LGBT+ in the classroom are necessarily out, or able to be out, to their family at home. An inclusive classroom where LGBT+ identities are brought in from the margins can have a role to play, as a part of the broader campus environment, in supporting students as they develop as people as well as academically.

---

36 The survey added the option for those choosing male or female to add whether their gender matched that assigned at birth.
37 Lesbian, gay, bisexual, trans, queer, pansexual and asexual. No staff self-identified as trans in the survey, although three respondents chose not to answer or identified as 'other'.
38 All report results on file with the author.
39 Government Equalities Office, National LGBT Survey (2018) 15.

2.2 Classroom Climate

In relation to comfort in contributing to discussions in the classroom, 42% of LGBT+ students said they are uncomfortable raising LGBT issues in the classroom, while in comparison 66% of heterosexual people are comfortable. The level of comfort of gay men is 62%, which corresponds to a result from the NUS LGBT survey, which found that gay men were more confident than heterosexual women in the classroom,[40] indicating an impact of gender and sexual orientation.

Sixty-nine per cent of LGBT+ students are comfortable speaking in class generally, but this drops to 44% when they speak about LGBT issues, a decrease of 25%. This lack of ease in speaking about LGBT+ issues can translate to less participation from LGBT+ students, potentially impeding their learning as they miss out on a valuable part of the learning process, and an intrinsic component to the format of many classes on which students can be assessed.

Within the classroom, homo/bi/transphobia (HBT) still occurs. In our survey, 13% of LGBT+ students reported witnessing or being the subject of HBT in the classroom, while 4% of heterosexual students reported this. This indicates a discrepancy in the observation of such incidents when they do occur. When asked what kind of HBT such incidents fell into, the main kinds were name calling, 52%, and outing (revealing someone's sexual orientation or gender identity without permission), 19%. Instances of harassment, intimidation and threat of physical violence and one incident of assault were reported. Students could provide additional examples to this question, and of these, misgendering (not calling students by their correct pronouns) returned significant results. If taken as its own category, misgendering would have appeared second to name calling, before 'other'. The perpetrators were reported to be students 84% of the time and staff 23%. This demonstrates a need to equip staff with the information and resources to de-escalate and respond to scenarios in the classroom in which LGBT+ identities or people are specifically targeted by fellow students. When asked if lecturers address or challenge HBT in the classroom, 34% of students said 'rarely' or 'never', with a further 37% reporting 'not often'. Simultaneously, 88% of staff who work in the classroom told us they felt very or moderately equipped to respond to such circumstances. This indicates a further discrepancy between the experiences of students and perception of staff in their responses to HBT in the classroom. Staff told us how important they felt it to respond to these situations. Of those who felt equipped, they were so because the subject matter of their courses directly related to LGBT+ content, or they had experience outside of work, through activism, being friends with and having family members who were LGBT+ or identifying this way themselves. Based on our results, staff, feeling able to deal with incidents when they occur,

---

40 See *LGBT Youth Scotland* (n 20) 20.

is not necessarily translating into the experience of LGBT+ students who have witnessed or been the subject of these incidents. However, staff responses also suggest that familiarity with LGBT+ knowledge, and involvement with the LGBT+ community, helps people to feel better able to respond.

2.3 Curriculum

We asked students, To what extent are LGBT identities included in your course? Sixty per cent of students said 'insignificantly' and 'not at all', with a further 24% selecting 'moderately'. We asked staff a yes/no variation of the question: Do you include LGBT identities in your curriculum? Of this, the breakdown was as follows:

Table 14.1 'Do you include LGBT identities in your curriculum?' Answer by College.

	Yes	No
College of Arts	74%	26%
College of Social Sciences	51%	49%
College of Medical, Veterinary and Life Sciences (MVLS)	24%	76%
College of Science and Engineering	7%	93%

The number of teaching staff who chose to answer in MVLS and Science and Engineering was small (17 and 29, respectively). In addition to a low response in these Colleges, 31% of all teaching staff who answered told us they were 'not very', or 'not at all', equipped to include LGBT+ identities as part of their teaching. Institutional guidelines and the commitments to equality and diversity by professional bodies[41] signal that there is an awareness of and even sectoral requirements towards LGBT+ inclusion, but asking people to be actively inclusive needs to be followed by supportive, consistent, action, and as such a planned outcome of this project is a workshop on creating an inclusive curriculum and classroom. With this in mind, it is a reassuring sign that 73% of all teaching respondents said they would be willing to review their curriculum content to make it more LGBT+ inclusive.

When LGBT+ identities are included in the curriculum, the response from students is extremely positive. Words and phrases used frequently in

---

41 British Sociological Association, 'We are aware of the need to pay attention to all aspects of difference and diversity, not least because differences occur within as well as between groups' (British Sociological Association, Equality, Diversity and Inclusion, 2019. <www.britsoc.co.uk/Equality-Diversity/> (accessed 18 June 2019); Institute of Physics, 'We want to build a thriving, diverse physics community and play our part in solving the STEM skills shortage by ensuring that people, no matter their background or where they live, have access to world-class physics education and training.' (Institute of Physics, 'Unlocking the Future' (2020) <https://beta.iop.org/strategy?_ga=2.192952676.875823953.1595415409-1290990227.1595415409> (accessed 22 July 2020).

open response boxes from students were 'motivated', 'comfortable', 'safer', 'included', 'engaged', 'improved performance', 'more enjoyment' and 'taking part more'.

For example, a student wrote, 'My performance was positively affected when it came to offer(ing) discussion points on the notion of LGBT identities. I felt that I had a chance to explain this topic from my personal point of view. Generally, it feels like you are finally given a voice, and you do not have to be afraid of speaking out.' There were some worries, which appeared, relating to the content of discussions that might transpire as a result of these mentions and how these might be navigated. A student said, 'I feel more included with the work, yet uncomfortable with the platform this gives other people in lectures and seminars to broadcast their ignorance in the name of "discussion", especially when discussing gender identity and transphobia.' A cisgender heterosexual identified respondent commented that, 'I think I learned to discuss LGBT (identities) in a sensitive manner. There are still things I am learning, and the last thing I want to do is offend anyone. Talking about it in class gave me the right vocabulary and the chance to ask questions I was unsure of.'

We are confident that the results from our survey demonstrate that LGBT-inclusive education is beneficial for all.

3. Recommendations

Across the majority of staff, there is a strong urge to be inclusive. When an overall outlook on teaching is one of critical questioning, this translates to better inclusion of LGBT+ identities and those beyond the 'default' identities of cisgender, male, white, heterosexual and able bodied.

DeSurra and Church created a model for considering the inclusiveness of the curriculum and classroom, based on a scale of explicit marginalisation, implicit marginalisation, implicit centralisation and explicit centralisation.[42] The categories of scale range from explicit marginalisation (e.g. overt homophobic messages and behaviours from the instructor or students that go unchallenged, omitting LGBT+ people when the discussion would warrant it), implicit marginalisation (e.g. invisibility, indifference and ignorance; heterosexual examples predominate), implicit centralisation (e.g. challenging an overtly homophobic comment, disclosing heterosexist assumptions of course readings, although significant structural changes in course content and instructional strategies have not yet occurred) and explicit centralisation (e.g. transmits messages that clearly inform students that marginalised perspectives, including LGBT+ people, will be actively integrated throughout the course). In explicit centralisation,

---

[42] CJ DeSurra and KA Church, 'Unlocking the Classroom Closet: Privileging the Marginalized Voices of Gay/Lesbian College Students' Papers Presented at the Meeting of the Speech Communication Association, 1994.

teaching staff are unequivocal in their efforts to centre minority perspectives, not only refraining from using heterosexist terms but actively seeking to introduce examples of LGBT+ terminology and viewpoints.[43] The language used in the DeSurra and Church model is relevant to current discourse, in a 'de-centring' of previously dominant voices and perspectives and a 're-centring' of those marginalised. This approach can be productive when attempting to reintegrate numerous silenced histories and perspectives.

Long-lasting inclusion involves a shifting of perspective, a critical pedagogy, 'one that explicitly sees the purpose of education as the opportunity to critically interrogate privileged perspectives that are manifest in every discipline . . .'.[44] It is a move towards demonstrating the value of LGBT+ identities as much as any others.

A College of Arts student told us, 'In other modules not specifically LGBTQ+, I find they are often added as an after-thought – queer-specific material included in extensive reading lists, rather than ever being required readings, or added as one power point slide amongst other "minority" identities, such as BAME or disability.' This type of 'add-on' approach, for example, placing a slide at the end of a class, optional reading or a week at the end of a course to mention LGBT+ identified people, intentionally or otherwise, can indicate that LGBT+ identities are not worth as much time or focus as the 'main' identities (cisgender and/or heterosexual). LGBT+ identities are, while connected, seen as separate, 'other'.[45] As LGBT+ identities possess the same inherent value and worth as any other sexual or gender identity, they should be reflected as such.

There are a number of methods through which LGBT+ identities can be included in the curriculum and the classroom (some of these are drawn from examples provided by teaching staff within our survey), such as use of LGBT+-specific case studies/scenarios or clinical examples, required readings, set exams and assignments (only allowing LGBT+ identities in student-led open essays or dissertation topics without any prior LGBT+ inclusion may not best support students in exploring these themes), class discussion – with support offered to LGBT+ students if H/B/transphobic comments are made, using queer theory, using same sex family representation, referring to one's own (same sex) partner (when comfortable doing so), including pronouns in class introductions (this normalises not being able to assume someone's gender identity and lifts pressure on trans and/or non-binary people from having to counter or correct someone else's assumptions), ensuring placement providers reflect University of Glasgow Equality standards.

---

43 Fuller versions of these updated descriptions of categories can be found in VA Wall and NJ Evans, *Toward Acceptance: Sexual Orientation Issues on Campus* (University Press of America 2000) 120.
44 *Ibid*.
45 Creating an environment of inclusion across a course would create a context where a dedicated unit to address specific issues could be tenable without 'othering' LGBT+ identities.

These examples indicate initial steps to approaching diversifying a curriculum and classroom environment. Examples of existing good practice at the University of Glasgow include an active re-design of a module to incorporate LGBT+ perspectives and materials, based on hearing an early conference presentation on the project, and a collaborative video on trans health between MVLS, the NHS and My Genderation, a filmmaking group run by and for trans and non-binary people. The research undertaken for this project showed that efforts to be inclusive of LGBT+ identities exist across the university, albeit in isolation. However, we are hopeful that showing these existing practices side by side will encourage and support staff in knowing they are not alone in their efforts to be LGBT+ inclusive, and that they are some of many making commitments to do so.

4. Conclusions

It is clear from our research that there are gaps in the curriculum and in the classroom relating to LGBT+ identities. Our survey demonstrated that the student population is comprised of a broad spectrum of identities, including lesbian, gay, bisexual, transgender, queer, pansexual, intersex and asexual, which is not reflected wholly by institutional and governing bodies' data gathering. Students told us they would like to see more LGBT+ inclusion, but commented that when it was added on this did not always feel like it had been thought through. Staff told us that where they were not being inclusive they would like to be but needed to know how they could do this. Some responses were disappointing, in stating there was no relevance in the inclusion of LGBT+ identities, particularly from the sciences. Recognising the impact of how we include and discuss LGBT+ identities on students' experiences, academic performance, attendance and well-being, in addition to diversifying research and teaching, can address this. In the course of this chapter, we have explored how inclusion in the curriculum and/or the classroom, when implemented, can positively impact on the student experience. In not having to divert energy to hiding or having to defend their identity, this enables students to focus on what they are in the classroom to do – learn. For students and staff of all identities, efforts to make the classroom environment, and the curriculum, more representative, and nuanced in that representation, contribute to providing LGBT+ students as equitable a chance as their cisgender heterosexual peers to succeed while equipping students of all identities to go out into a complex world and thrive.

Chapter 15

Investigating the Experiences of Transgender Students in Higher Education in the UK – Pilot Study

Lynne Regan

1. Introduction

1.1 Terminology

'Transgender' is an umbrella term for those whose gender identity and/or gender expression does not match the sex they were assigned at birth, or who do not conform to conventional gender identity binaries of man or woman. Within this chapter, I will use the term 'trans', an inclusive shorthand term used to reflect the full spectrum of identities within this, including but not exclusive to transgender, transsexual, genderqueer, gender fluid, non-binary and gender non-conforming.

1.2 The Relevance of the Study

Negotiating the university environment can be difficult for many students, but for those who identify as transgender, there can be additional hurdles to face. This study took place at a time when the experiences of trans people were becoming more visible through national, international and social media. There appears to be an increase in the number of people in the UK identifying as transgender, and the UK Gender Identity Clinic in London reported an 'unprecedented rise in referrals in the last year . . . [outstripping] the number of available first appointments by a factor of 2 to 1' with an estimated 201 referrals made in December 2018 and an 18-month wait for first appointments.[1] By October 2020, the waiting time for first appointments had risen to 33–36 months, and as of September 2021, there were 9,667 people on the waiting list with first appointments being offered to people referred in October 2017.[2] With university often being the first experience of real

---

1 Gender Identity Clinic, 'Waiting Times' (2018) <https://gic.nhs.uk/appointments/waiting-times/> (accessed 28 February 2019).
2 Gender Identity Clinic, 'Waiting Times' (2021) <https://gic.nhs.uk/appointments/waiting-times/> (accessed 26 September 2021).

DOI: 10.4324/9781003286295-19

independence for young people, it may also be a place where young trans people feel they can be themselves for the first time, as they navigate an environment free of family and friendship ties from the past. Employing a critical theoretical framework, this pilot study used an Internet survey to explore the challenges that trans students in one higher education institution face with key findings around institutional facilities and administration; harassment, bullying and transphobia; inclusion/exclusion; and representation in the curriculum.

1.3 Rationale

In my role within Student Services at a UK university, I recognise there are areas of transgender policy and procedure that could be improved. The aim of my research is to investigate the experiences of trans students in Higher Education (HE) in respect of support services, institutional administration, peers, academics and curriculum, social experience and facilities, with a view to creating a better understanding of the needs of this student group.

Trans people are becoming increasingly visible in public life, and this has embedded trans issues into popular culture; such increased visibility has enabled some change to take place: 'where once there was *pure* ignorance and prejudice of trans issues, now we see *informed* prejudice and discrimination, which is more easily addressed through the courts and legislature'.[3] Despite this, gender identity is one of the 'least discussed and under-researched phenomenon within post-compulsory education'.[4]

The main purpose of my research is to identify obstacles encountered by trans students in HE, and identify institutional policy and procedure changes that could address areas of concern. The questions driving my research are:

- What are the experiences of trans students in HE in respect of support services, institutional administration, peers, academics, curriculum, social experience and facilities?
- How well are Higher Education Institutions (HEIs) supporting trans students, including the development and implementation of trans student policy?

This chapter focuses solely on the pilot study, which used an Internet survey to explore the challenges that trans students in one higher education faced. The full study will also include one-to-one interviews with students and a document analysis of HEI policies and procedures.

---

3 S Stryker and S Whittle, *The Transgender Studies Reader* (Routledge 2006) xii.
4 T Hafford-Letchfield et al., 'Transgender Students in Post-Compulsory Education: A Systematic Review' (2017) 86 *International Journal of Educational Research* 1.

Beemyn[5] proposed that it is often at college that students first have the opportunity to question their assigned gender, as they are away from the confines of family and childhood friends. From my experience working with students in HE, I have observed that it is often a student's first real experience of independence and a time when boundaries are pushed as they discard the constraints of school and family life. This gives students an opportunity to identify in a way that they feel most comfortable, as they are mostly away from people who have known them as they have grown up. For these students, being able to experiment with how they feel in a safe environment is a key factor, and one that HEIs need to ensure is available to them. However, in contrast to the time in which Beemyn was writing (2003), it is possible that there are also now more students who are already living in their acquired gender when they arrive at university, and these students may encounter different issues, such as being able to live their lives without being outed, and again, clear and consistent HEI policy and practice is important for this to happen.

1.4 Transgender Law and Current Political Issues in the UK

1.4.1 UK Law

Under the Equality Act 2010,[6] which includes gender reassignment as a 'protected characteristic', universities along with other public sector organisations are required by the Public Sector Equality Duty to endeavour to eliminate discrimination and advance equality of opportunity, moving towards the prevention of discrimination, harassment and victimisation. In a university environment, to support trans students, this may include updating student records to reflect name and/or gender changes, provision of appropriate toilets and changing rooms and ensuring equality of education. It will involve ensuring policies and procedures include a commitment to trans equality, providing staff training, creating safe working and social spaces for trans students and challenging inappropriate/transphobic behaviour.

1.4.2 Current Political Issues in the UK

One area of concern for trans people is the challenging process involved in changing legal gender, as set out in the Gender Recognition Act 2004.[7] Although this Act does not require people to have undergone surgical

---

5 B Beemyn, 'Serving the Needs of Transgender College Students' (2003) 1:1 *Journal of Gay & Lesbian Issues in Education* 40.
6 Equality Act (2010) c. 15, s. 7.
7 Gender Recognition Act (2004), c. 7.

procedures or hormone therapy, it does require people who wish to legally change their gender to provide two medical reports evidencing a diagnosis of gender dysphoria; provide documentation that proves they have lived in their acquired gender for at least two years; submit a 'statutory declaration of their intention to live in their acquired gender until death'; and if married, either obtain the consent of their spouse or end their marriage. Acquiring a Gender Recognition Certificate (GRC), although not a requirement, is costly (£140 at the time of writing).[8] There is also no option currently for people who identify as non-binary (i.e. identifying as neither male nor female). It is noted that pro-trans law and social policy focus on 'binary conceptualisations of the body',[9] whereby gender fluidity is further 'silenced'.

In 2018, the UK Government undertook a consultation[10] to identify people's views on how best to reform the process. One of the main issues of contention is the current pathologisation of transgender identification through the requirement for psychiatrists to 'diagnose' gender dysphoria. The consultation closed on 22 October 2018, after which responses would be analysed and a report would be published, indicating what action the Government intends to take.[11] At the time of writing, this report has not yet been made available.

1.5 Emerging Themes

Findings from the literature review identified four main themes: institutional facilities and administration; harassment, bullying and transphobia; inclusion/ exclusion; and representation in the curriculum.

1.5.1 Institutional Facilities and Administration

The theme of institutional facilities and administration is one that has been mentioned in most of the literature reviewed and, in my opinion, is possibly the easiest for HEIs to address, as it relates to physical and administrative changes that can be made and that are visible. This theme covers areas, such as changing names/gender on electronic records, the provision of suitable toilet and changing facilities and alternative gender options on forms and systems.

Research by Seelman into the experiences of transgender students and staff from colleges and universities in Colorado, USA[12] discussed improvements

---

8 <www.gov.uk/apply-gender-recognition-certificate/how-to-apply>.
9 S Hines, 'Trans★ Policy, Politics and Research: The UK and Portugal' (2018) 38:1 *Critical Social Policy* 39.
10 <www.gov.uk/government/consultations/reform-of-the-gender-recognition-act-2004>.
11 Government Equalities Office, *Reform of the Gender Recognition Act – Government Consultation* (Government Equalities Office 2018).
12 KL Seelman, 'Transgender Individuals' Access to College Housing and Bathrooms: Findings from the National Transgender Discrimination Survey' (2014) 26:2 *Journal of Gay & Lesbian Social Services* 202, 203.

that could be introduced to address issues of marginalisation and victimisation of transgender students, gained directly from empirical data gathered from transgender students. This research consisted of interviewing 30 individuals (staff, students and academics) who identified as transgender, of which 19 were students. The aim of the research was to identify what institutional policy and procedure changes would be required to address these areas of concern.

In respect of institutional facilities and administration, the report identified a need for improved procedures for recording names and gender and simplified processes for requesting changes, including designation of a 'preferred name', as well as physical changes to facilities, such as toilets, changing rooms and on-campus housing, to make them more inclusive.

In Marzetti's study of seven LGBT students in Scotland,[13] it was identified that non-binary students in particular found the lack of gender-neutral toilets on campus challenging. In addition, Storrie and Rohleder's study of five participants from universities across Wales and the East, South East and West of England[14] recommended a need for policies to be consistent across HEIs, and that these should include procedures for transitioning students to change their names and pronouns easily, as well as ensuring the inclusion of trans students in discussion when planning changes to facilities and policies.

Similar research[15] from Goldberg and Kuvalanka used focus groups totalling seven students to investigate the specific experiences of non-binary college students in the USA with regards to identity. They reported on concerns raised regarding a lack of clarity in how to change names and pronouns on the university computer systems, as well as knowing that until a name had been changed legally, their birth names would be used on legal documentations, such as degree certificates.

Research by the National Union of Students (NUS)[16] revealed that a lack of gender-neutral toilets and facilities on campus was a major issue that could lead to trans students avoiding using them or feeling unsafe doing so. The research also reported difficulties with updating records, such as changing their names in the register, and that this could lead to trans students being 'outed' to tutors or classmates. Lack of a third gender option and a lack of gender-neutral facilities

---

13 H Marzetti, 'Proudly Proactive: Celebrating and Supporting LGBT+ Students in Scotland, Teaching in Higher Education' (2018) 23:6 *Teaching in Higher Education* 702, 710, 713.
14 R Storrie and P Rohleder, '"I Think If I Had Turned Up Sporting a Beard and a Dress Then You Get in Trouble": Experiences of Transgender Students at UK Universities' (2018) *Psychology & Sexuality* 5, 6, 7, 10.
15 A Goldberg and K Kuvalanka, 'Navigating Identity Development and Community Belonging When 'There Are Only Two Boxes to Check': An Exploratory Study of Nonbinary Trans College Students' (2018) 15:2 *Journal of LGBT Youth* 121, 122, 126.
16 L Acciari, *Education Beyond the Straight and Narrow: LGBT Students' Experience in Higher Education* (NUS 2014) 5, 6, 37.

were also barriers reported by students in research for TransEdu Scotland,[17] which, in addition, reported trans students' fear of being outed by ineffective administrative processes, after navigating the challenging administrative and bureaucratic systems to change their names and/or genders on university records. Stonewall[18] research stated that one in six trans students reported feeling unable to use the toilet they felt comfortable with at university.

1.5.2 Harassment, Bullying and Transphobia

Harassment, bullying and transphobia are concerns for trans people from all areas of life. A study looking at the impact of discrimination, violence and exclusion commissioned by Stonewall[19] noted that of 871 trans participants across England, Scotland and Wales, 41% had experienced a hate crime or incident because of their gender identities in the 12 months prior to the survey, with younger trans adults (aged 18–24) at higher risk with 53% having experienced such occurrences.

Harassment, bullying and transphobia can take many forms, including physical violence, verbal abuse, discrimination when accessing services and microaggressions such as mis-gendering, showing intrusive curiosity or asking about *real* names or *preferred* pronouns.

Beemyn[20] proposed that it is often at college that students first have the opportunity to question their assigned gender, as they are away from the confines of family and childhood friends. However, the study also suggested that many gender-variant students choose to remain 'closeted' in fear of negative response and rejection. Seelman's report[21] recommended institutional change to support transgender students, including creating a campus LGBT centre (despite having previously noted that even within the LGB community, trans students faced isolation and discrimination), developing policies to address transphobia on campus and creating a group for transgender and gender-questioning students.

A study by one institution in Scotland[22] noted that the university was failing to protect LGBT+ people on campus from harassment and discrimination. They included in their description areas, such as verbal abuse and transphobic comments, physical abuse and sexual abuse, commenting that halls of residence and social spaces were the most likely places where such harassment would

---

17 S Mckendry and M Lawrence, *Researching the Experience of Trans and Gender Diverse Applicants, Students and Staff in Scotland's Colleges and Universities* (TransEdu Scotland 2017) 8.
18 CL Bachmann and B Gooch, *LGBT in Britain University Report* (Stonewall 2018) 5, 8.
19 CL Bachmann and B Gooch, *LGBT in Britain Trans Report* (Stonewall 2018) 8.
20 See Beemyn (n 5).
21 See Seelman (n 12).
22 See Marzetti (n 13).

occur. Research by Storrie and Rohleder[23] suggested that trans students are frequently 'objectified and othered', describing examples of students being asked inappropriate questions about being trans. The same study also reported the increased risk of transphobic abuse within drinking spaces at university.

McGlashan and Fitzpatrick[24] described a critical ethnographic study undertaken in New Zealand with six secondary school pupils who identified as transgender or non-binary, to explore how these students negotiated their identities in school and how the school supported them, particularly looking at how gendered pronouns were used. The ethnographic approach used by the researchers enabled them to gather locally contextualised data, which they then theorised in relation to the wider trends in education and society around trans youth and gendered pronouns. One of the findings of the report was that when, in a group they were asked to share their names and pronouns, non-binary pupils were less comfortable with having to 'come out' as non-binary to their trans peers by not having a gender to allocate to themselves. This identified that even within a group of trans people, there are power relations at work, which may make the situation feel less inclusive to those involved. Although conducted within a school setting, this research is important in highlighting the need within university administration for alternative gender options on forms and documents, and the investigation of power relations within the trans student community is something that I have not found in any other UK-based research.

Similar research from Goldberg and Kuvalanka[25] investigated the experiences of non-binary college students in the USA with regard to identity. They used focus groups to gather qualitative data from seven undergraduate students who identified as non-binary. One of the key findings here was that participants considered gender identity to be fluid over time and across context, with one participant describing how disconcerting it can be, to have to share pronouns with someone they have just met and potentially have to defend their name and pronoun, and another commented on how at times, it is easier to be less truthful in order to manoeuvre through the situation more smoothly.

Results from Sheffield Hallam University of a small consultation of 28 LGBT+ HE students[26] reported that misnaming and misgendering trans students were a particular issue, but that this could be symptomatic of a lack of awareness amongst peers and academics, something also borne out in Storrie and Rohleder's research,[27] which described trans students experiencing often

23 See Storrie and Rohleder (n 14).
24 H McGlashan and K Fitzpatrick, '"I Use Any Pronouns, and I'm Questioning Everything Else": Transgender Youth and the Issue of Gender Pronouns' (2018) 18:3 *Sex Education* 246.
25 See Goldberg and Kuvalanka (n 15).
26 E Formby, *From Freshers' Week to Finals: Understanding LGBT+ Perspectives on, and Experiences of, Higher Education* (Sheffield Hallam University 2015) 10, 15, 29.
27 See Storrie and Rohleder (n 14).

unintentional 'micro-aggressions', including being misgendered, especially where there were conflicting gender signals, such as their physical presentation not matching their gender identity. The latter was research specifically into the experiences of trans students in the UK and although small-scale, it provided good examples feeding into the emerging theme of harassment, bullying and transphobia.

The NUS survey[28] asked participants questions about feeling safe on campus and found that only 20.6% of trans student respondents felt 'completely safe' compared to 43% of heterosexual respondents and 36.7% of LGB+ students. One in three trans students reported that they had experienced bullying and/ or harassment on campus, and most of the trans student respondents reported not knowing how or where to report transphobic abuse.

Stonewall research[29] asked 522 LGBT students, of whom 17% (88) said they identified as trans, about their experience at British universities. This reported that 36% of trans students had faced negative comments and conduct from university staff, and 60% had faced negative comments and conduct from other students; 7% of trans students who responded to the survey reported having been physically attacked by a student or staff member at university within the last year because of being trans. The identification in this study of trans students experiencing comments/harassment from staff suggests that although the behaviour of students may not always be directly under the control of HEIs, especially in social spaces, staff behaviour is a key issue that needs to be addressed. This study is important, as having been undertaken with students in UK universities it provides a base from which to discuss such issues with students in my own study in order to fill the gap in academic research into this subject.

A study at Newcastle University in the UK[30] sought to improve inclusivity for trans staff and students, who were interviewed about their interaction with others, negotiation of spaces and processes of the university and experiences of transition. They discussed how trans staff and students felt uncomfortable about being misgendered, particularly with regard to power relations, whereby students did not feel they could correct staff who misgendered them, and similarly postgraduate students did not feel they could correct their supervisors.

1.5.3 Inclusion/Exclusion

University is often seen as a space where people can feel able to be themselves, away from the constraints of family and childhood friends. For trans students,

---

28 See Acciari (n 16).
29 See Bachmann and Gooch (n 18).
30 P Hopkins, G Mearns, and C Bonner-Thompson, *Transgender Experiences of Newcastle University 2018* (Newcastle University 2018) 6.

this can be a place where they are first able to freely express their identity, so it is important that university is inclusive to this student group. In Storrie and Rohleder's survey of six participants from UK universities,[31] trans students identified attending university as being a key point in their gender transition, a place where they could make a 'new start' as a trans person, amongst people who had not known them in their previous gender presentation.

Similarly, research from Goldberg and Kuvalanka,[32] investigating the experiences of non-binary college students in the USA, noted that the students interviewed felt that college offered a place where they could explore their gender identity more fully than they were able to at school, as well as providing them with a community of peers who had shared experiences or questioning gender identity. The fact that these two research articles, one from the USA and one from the UK, share this finding, was worth investigating further to look at how many trans students now express this feeling. With trans individuals becoming more visible in society in the UK, particularly in the last couple of years, more students are now transitioning during compulsory education years. Given this change, it is important to investigate whether trans students still view HE as a key place for exploring their gender identity more freely.

Storrie and Rohleder[33] reported that the opportunity for activism within student societies, whereby students can be involved in challenging institutional discrimination and supporting change, helped trans students to feel more included and allowed them to forge relationships with others who understood their issues. This research is particularly valuable, as it was exclusively composed of trans participants, and the use of semi-structured interviews enabled the researchers to bring to the interview a set of common themes whilst also enabling the students to participate in a way that would provide additional information.

However, university can also be exclusionary to this student group. A recent study in Scotland described 'institutional cisheteronormativity'[34] to portray how society in general, and in this case university education, is orientated around a presumption of cisgender, heterosexual identities. Research participants illustrated how their university acknowledged LGBT+ student issues at a superficial level only, hosting events during LGBT History Month but not openly supporting students or understanding the issues they face. One trans participant described how transphobic comments by peers during a class discussion on trans identities had gone unchallenged by staff. The timeliness of this research makes its results valuable with regard to providing an area for further research.

31 See Storrie and Rohleder (n 14).
32 See Goldberg and Kuvalanka (n 15).
33 See Storrie and Rohleder (n 14).
34 See Marzetti (n 13).

According to the NUS survey,[35] compared to LGB and heterosexual respondents, fewer trans students felt confident to speak up in class and fewer felt included in group learning activities, with one in ten trans students responding that they never feel comfortable to speak up in class. Fifty-one per cent of trans students who responded to the survey said they had considered dropping out of their course, and two-thirds of these reported feelings of not fitting in.

Stonewall research[36] reported that 52% of trans students felt they had been excluded by other students in the last year and that one in seven trans students had either dropped out or considered dropping out of a course because of harassment or discrimination. This will provide a good basis on which to base my own research into this area, which appears lacking in UK academic literature.

1.5.4 Representation in the Curriculum

Many universities are currently looking at inclusion of Black, Asian and minority ethnic (BAME) students in the curriculum after student campaigns, such as 'Why is my curriculum white?' argued that teaching should be more representative of the modern world with regard to non-white communities in the UK.[37] It can be argued that as a main component of university life is the curriculum, LGBT issues and in this case, trans issues, should also find representation in the curriculum.

After a small number of consultation events with a total of 28 LGBT+ students, Formby[38] suggested that this is not the case and that students felt 'forgotten' within the content of their learning, or if included this felt 'tagged on' or, at times, inaccurate. Formby's research is useful in that it is recent and UK-based, and although from LGBT+ without data as to how many of the 28 identified as trans, its report from one participant who described an example used in a statistics class as gender being a binary statistic because all participants are either male or female, is a good example of cisheteronormativity in teaching.

Similarly, in Marzetti's small UK research study[39] of seven LGBT students, one trans participant had reported that when trans identities were discussed in their course, the discussion had evoked comments from their peers that had made them feel uncomfortable, but that this had gone unchallenged by staff. In as much as this identifies an issue of non-representation in the curriculum, it also identifies a potential need for better staff awareness of how to support the needs of trans students. This research did distinguish between

---

35 See Acciari (n 16).
36 See Bachmann and Gooch (n 18).
37 M Hussain, *Why Is My Curriculum White?* National Union of Students (2015) <www.nus.org.uk/en/news/why-is-my-curriculum-white/> (accessed 5 January 2019).
38 See Formby (n 26).
39 See Marzetti (n 13).

LGB and trans students, with two out of the seven students identifying as trans, but I feel this is another gap in UK-based research that can be bridged by my own study.

NUS research that drew on a national online survey of over 4,000 respondents from 80 HEIs in the UK (of which 3% of participants were trans) and focus groups, including one specifically with trans students, discussed representation in the curriculum. When asked to score on a scale of 1–10 whether they saw trans experiences and history reflected in their curriculum (where 1 meant strongly disagree and 10 meant strongly agree), trans participants scored an average of 2.47.[40]

The NUS report acknowledged that some subject disciplines were 'better' than others at including LGBT representation in the curriculum, noting that humanities subjects received the highest scores with science, technology, engineering and mathematics (STEM) subjects receiving the lowest. They suggested that even within the STEM subjects, courses such as medicine or health sciences could improve, and within the humanities subjects, more still could be done to improve representation by diversifying the authors cited and including critical theories, such as queer and gender studies, into the curriculum.

In a survey of trans staff and students at Newcastle University,[41] it was noted that some participants felt that transgender issues were rarely discussed in the curriculum, and recommendations in the report included integration of trans issues into the curriculum in all disciplines.

2. Research Design and Methodology – Pilot Study

2.1 Introduction

The literature reviewed identified four key themes: institutional facilities and administration; harassment, bullying and transphobia; inclusion/exclusion; and representation in the curriculum. It is these themes that will be addressed in the research.

The questions driving my research are:

- What are the experiences of trans students in HE in respect of support services, institutional administration, peers, academics and curriculum, social experience and facilities?
- How well are HEIs supporting trans students, including the development and implementation of trans student policy?

---

40 See Acciari (n 16).
41 See Hopkins et al. (n 30).

2.2 Summary of Data Collection

The aim of the pilot study was to explore the first of the research questions with a small number of participants to ensure the methods were fit for purpose. A combined approach to analysis that used qualitative data from surveys to provide context and background to qualitative data from interviews was planned.

2.3 Internet Survey

The Internet survey model was chosen in preference to ethnography, case study or action research, due to the sensitive nature of the research topic and to allow the target participants to take part anonymously. An Internet survey would provide quantitative data and relevant demographic information. The Internet survey would include mainly closed questions, based on the findings of other research with one opportunity for the participants to expand on their answer.

Limitations to collecting Internet survey responses were considered. Given the sensitivity of the topic, participants might be more likely from those target students who are 'out' rather than those who are not; there may also be some degree of bias in the sample, with those more interested in the political agenda or those who have experienced more serious incidents of discrimination more likely to participate. However, as critical theory involves owning a clear bias towards the point of view of the marginalised or oppressed group, this method does match well with the theoretical approach. Another limitation of an Internet survey in particular could be that those from a higher socioeconomic status may be more likely to participate due to ease of computer and Internet access, as those relying on HEI computers may not feel comfortable completing the survey in shared study areas on campus.

For the pilot study, the link to the Internet survey was shared with trans students at a single university through contact with the Student Union; LGBT+ student societies; a peer support group for trans students; the Student Equality, Diversity and Inclusivity Officer; and the LGBT+ Staff Network. At the end of the survey, there was a link that participants could follow if they wished to take part in the one-to-one interviews. The main study aims to roll out the project to as many UK HEIs as possible.

The questions were constructed in order to provide data relating to the four main themes identified in the literature review: institutional facilities and administration; harassment, bullying and transphobia; inclusion/exclusion; and representation in the curriculum. The targeted population for the pilot study was trans students at a single university. Demographic questions included what their academic course of study was, how they described their gender identity and what pronouns they used.

One of the main hurdles identified was gaining access to the target group. Trans students do not always declare their gender identity and are not obliged to do so, and even if they have declared it on university records, universities are legally bound not to share this information. It made sense that the main route initially was through the Student Union as well as through any LGBT+ or transgender groups on campus. However, this would only reach those students who participate in these groups. In order to capture more participants, the university student group as a whole would need to be contacted. Facebook and Twitter were identified as good methods, as well as through the university online intranet/information pages.

2.4 Interviews

It was planned that the second part of the research would use informal conversational interviews to provide a far greater insight into the lived experiences of participants and which would shape the main focus of the research, as this qualitative approach would allow them to discuss their experiences in greater detail, outside of the defined questions of the Internet survey. Within critical theory, the aim is to prioritise the voices and needs of the oppressed/marginalised group, and as such, interviews would allow participants to have a greater degree of control over the agenda and what they think is important. As a cisgender researcher, I feel it is essential that the trans student is given a voice, which can indicate what the real issues are, rather than those issues conceived from a cisgender existence. However, none of the surveyed students opted to take part in interviews. This will form part of the main study, discussed briefly at the end of this chapter.

2.5 Documentary Analysis

The second part of the research question, 'How well are HEIs supporting trans students, including the development and implementation of trans student policy?', will be completed during the main study. It will be partly explored using the participant responses to the survey questions and interview analysis, which will identify where participants feel their HEIs have met their needs. However, to examine this question in more detail, part of the main study will also include a descriptive research method of documentary analysis to make an in-depth study of the policies currently in place at UK HEIs with regard to support for trans students, to identify how/whether the policies meet the needs of this group.

2.6 Ethics

I followed British Educational Research Association (BERA) 2011 ethical guidelines and completed the Open University Human Research Ethics Committee (HREC) application form. Requirements were met, and permission to commence data collection for the pilot study was granted.

3. Data Analysis of the Pilot Study

3.1 Introduction

This section seeks to analyse the results of the pilot study and identify relationships with the research questions, literature reviewed and theoretical framework.

3.2 Internet Survey

3.2.1 Demographics

Nine people responded to the survey invitation; one declined to take part and the other eight fully completed the survey. The eight students represented seven different courses of study: two from Computer Science, and one each from Social Anthropology, Classical and Archaeological Studies and Drama, Drama and Theatre Studies, Law, Comparative Literature and Criminology. Four students identified as male; four students identified as non-binary. Five students used the pronouns he/him/his/himself; three used the pronouns they/them/theirs/themselves.

It was interesting to note that no participants identified as female. No robust data of the LGBT population in the UK currently exist, although there are moves by the Office for National Statistics to include sexual orientation and gender identity in the 2021 census.[42] The National LGBT Survey, an online survey launched by the UK government in July 2017[43] reported that of 108,000 respondents, 13% were trans, and of these, 6.9% identified as non-binary, 3.5% were trans women and 2.9% were trans men. However, the results also showed a difference in identification between younger trans respondents and older trans respondents – 57% of the trans respondents aged under 35 identified as non-binary compared to 36% of those 35 and over; more younger respondents identified as trans men, with 26% of trans respondents under 35 being trans men compared to 10% aged 35 and over and 17% of trans respondents under 35 being trans women compared with 54% of those aged 35 and over. The report also notes that this fits with the referral figures to the children and adolescent gender identity services, stating that 69% of referrals in 2016–2017 were for young people assigned female at birth (1,400 of 2,016 referrals). The Gender Identity Development Service website's referral figures for 2017–2018 show a greater percentage again, with 1,806 of 2,519 referrals (72%) having been assigned female at birth.[44]

3.2.2 Institutional Facilities and Administration

Six participants had requested a change of name to be made to their university record. Of these, five felt the information had filtered down to the

---

42 Office for National Statistics *Gender identity update – An update to our 2009 Trans Data Position Paper, detailing changes and progress around the topic of gender identity* (no date) <www.ons.gov.uk/methodology/classificationsandstandards/measuringequality/genderidentity/genderidentityupdate> (accessed 27 March 2019).
43 Government Equalities Office *National LGBT Survey: Summary Report* (2019) <www.gov.uk/government/publications/national-lgbt-survey-summary-report/national-lgbt-survey-summary-report#contents> (accessed 27 March 2019).
44 Gender Identity Development Service (GIDS) *Number of Referrals* (2019) <http://gids.nhs.uk/number-referrals> (accessed 27 March 2019).

relevant academics (e.g. seminar leaders). All six participants reported not having been given the opportunity to change their university email addresses, where these included their names or initials. Only two of the eight participants had requested a gender change to be made to their university records.

Results showed that the majority of the participants did not feel that academic and administrative staff were knowledgeable enough about trans issues:

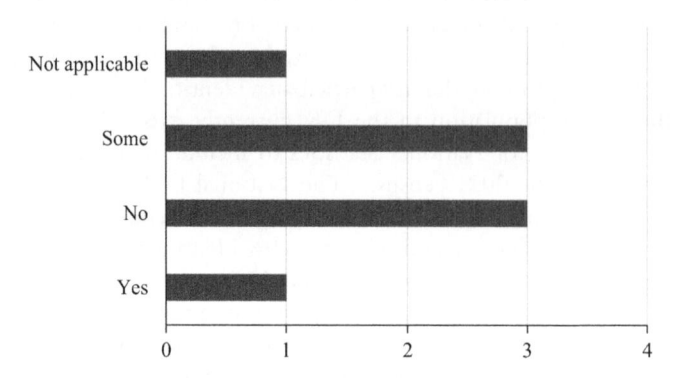

Figure 15.1 Do you feel administrative staff you have had contact with are knowledgeable enough about trans issues?

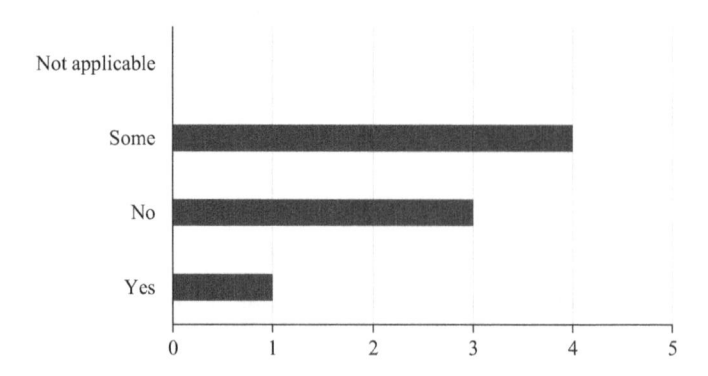

Figure 15.2 Do you feel academic staff you have had contact with are knowledgeable enough about trans issues?

Administration was, however, one of the main points mentioned in the one open question in this pilot survey, in which participants were asked to describe where the university has been particularly positive in supporting trans students. Statements included:

The ease of changing ID cards without legal proof was very supportive. This change applies to all records besides the ones applicable for the diploma certificate. I am aware this change had to be fought for by the previous trans officer who left the university a few years ago. The options for Mx instead of Mr and Ms, is pleasant, although people otherwise struggle to use gender neutral language in everyday life.

Storrie and Rohleder's small-scale study of five participants from universities across Wales and the East, South East and West of England[45] had recommended a need for policies that include procedures for transitioning students to change their names and pronouns easily, to be consistent across HEIs. It appears that at the pilot study university, although changing names was reported as a reasonably easy task, the fact that email addresses cannot be changed could be problematic. This will be something that can be taken further in the main study, where comparisons with the results of the pilot study can be made.

Some gender-neutral/trans-inclusive facilities (e.g. toilets and changing rooms) were reported:

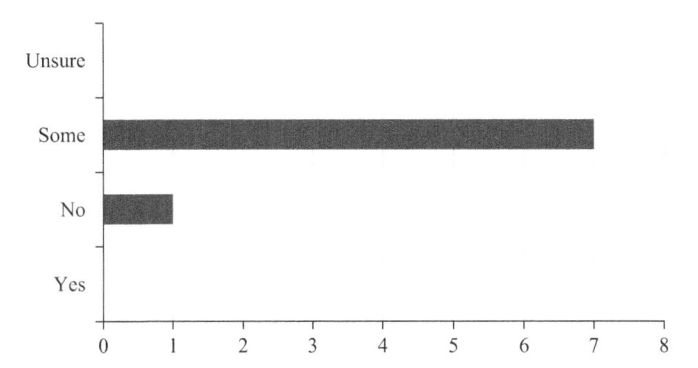

Figure 15.3 Does the university have gender-neutral or trans-inclusive facilities (e.g. toilets and changing rooms)?

Research discussed earlier by the NUS[46] revealed that a lack of gender-neutral toilets and facilities on campus was a major issue that could lead to trans students avoiding using them, or feeling unsafe doing so. Research for Stonewall[47] also stated that one in six trans students reported feeling unable to use the toilet they felt comfortable with at university. It can be identified that the pilot

---

45 See Storrie and Rohleder (n 14).
46 See Acciari (n 16).
47 See Bachmann and Gooch (n 18).

study university appears to be making moves to provide such facilities, but that more could be done, particularly as one of the students appeared unaware that there were any such facilities available.

3.2.3 Harassment, Bullying and Transphobia

Six out of the eight participants reported being aware of transphobic violence, bullying or harassment on campus; one had experienced this themselves:

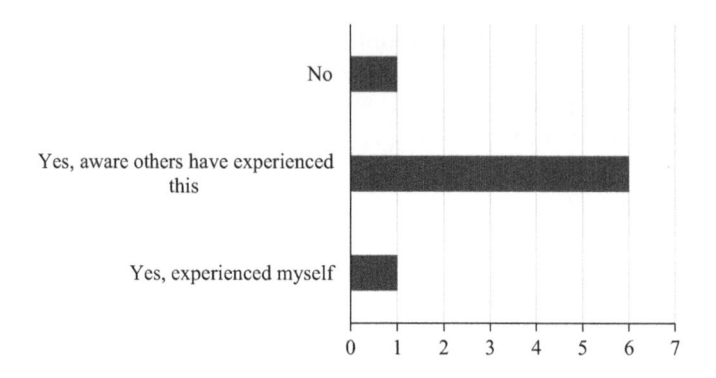

Figure 15.4 Have you experienced or been aware of transphobic violence, bullying or harassment on campus?

Research by the NUS[48] highlighted that 21% of trans student respondents felt completely safe on campus (in comparison to 37% of LGB students) and that one-third of trans participants had experienced bullying or harassment on campus. The fact that seven out of the eight participants in the pilot study had either experienced or were aware of transphobic violence/harassment suggests that this is something that is potentially not being managed by the university and an area for improvement with regard to policy and procedure.

3.2.4 Inclusion/Exclusion

Stonewall research[49] reported that 52% of trans students felt they had been excluded by other students in the last year. In the pilot study, all participants were aware of an LGBT+ society at the university, but of these none felt well-supported:

---

48 See Acciari (n 16).
49 See Bachmann and Gooch (n 18).

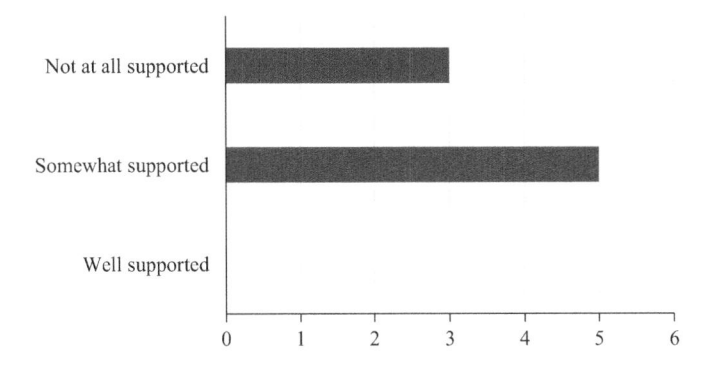

Figure 15.5 How well supported do you feel by the LGBT+ student society?

However, seven out of the eight were aware that the Student Union has a dedicated Trans Officer, and six reported knowing that the university has someone they can turn to regarding trans-specific issues (e.g. trans group and dedicated staff member). The open question asking about instances where the university had been particularly positive in supporting trans students included a student including having a specific Trans Officer role as part of the Student Union within this response.

McKinney[50] described LGBT that groups were more supportive of LGB issues, providing only superficial support for transgender students. It appears at the pilot study university that despite having a dedicated Trans Officer, trans students still felt under-supported by the LGBT+ student society. However, the fact that this university is reported to have someone the students could turn to regarding trans-specific issues is a positive finding.

The responses in the pilot study regarding inclusion in the social side of university life were mixed:

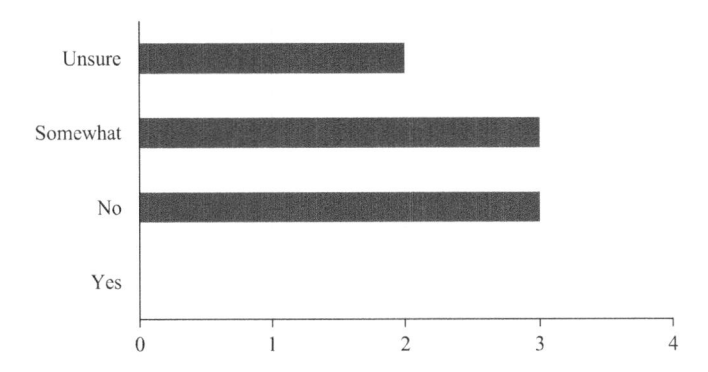

Figure 15.6 Do you feel represented in the social side of university life?

50 JS McKinney, 'On the Margins: A Study of the Experiences of Transgender College Students' (2005) 3:1 *Journal of Gay & Lesbian Issues in Education* 72.

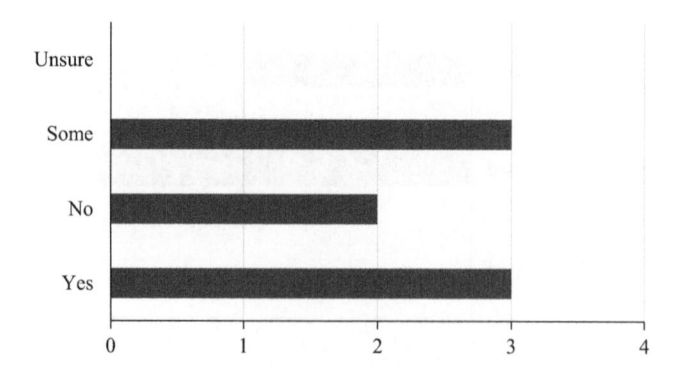

Figure 15.7 Do you feel welcome/comfortable to join university clubs/societies?

Most felt that at least some of their peers were knowledgeable about trans issues:

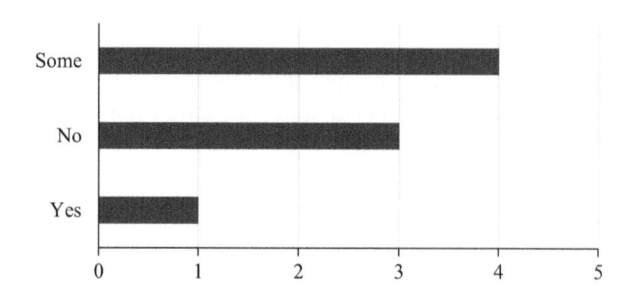

Figure 15.8 Do you feel that your peers are knowledgeable enough about trans issues?

3.2.5 Representation in the Curriculum

The results appeared to reflect this as a concern in that 50% of participants said they did not feel represented in the curriculum, with the other 50% reporting feeling only 'somewhat' represented; all participants felt that trans representation in the curriculum was at least somewhat important:

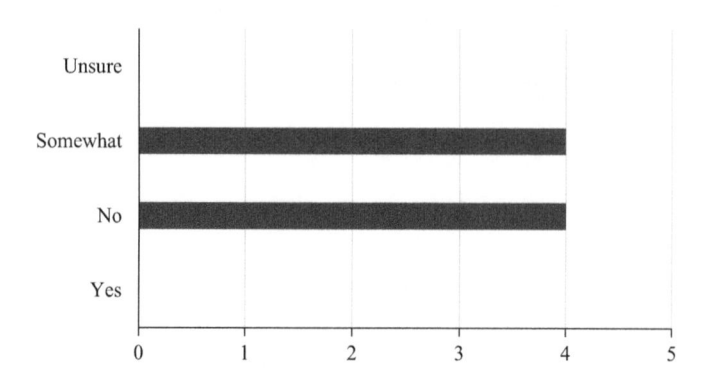

Figure 15.9 Do you feel represented in the university curriculum?

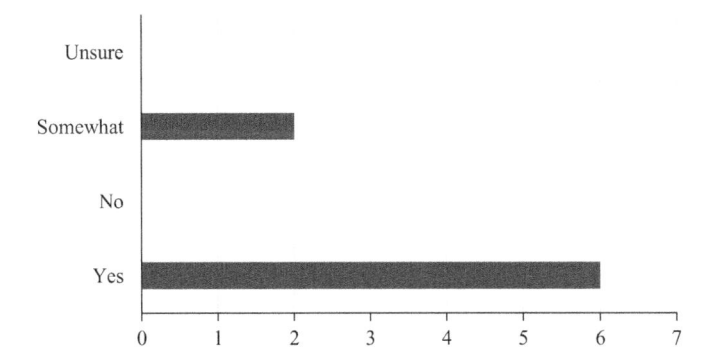

Figure 15.10 Do you feel trans representation in the university curriculum is important?

As discussed previously, Formby[51] argued that as a main component of university life is the curriculum, LGBT issues should be represented. Changing the curriculum is a challenging area, and I hope my main study will help to provide evidence that can be used at senior levels within UK institutions to improve this.

4. Looking Ahead to the Main Study

The initial study enabled me to evaluate the methodology and methods to be used and to begin to consider how these may need to be adapted for the main study.

With no interview participants recruited by the end of the pilot study, I reconsidered the data collection methods, considering expanding the Internet survey for the main study to include more open questions. However, it is acknowledged that too many open questions may result in a drop-out of participants, if this makes the survey too long or involves too much typing. The option of taking part in a one-to-one interview will still be made available to all survey participants as, even if participant numbers are low, the depth of qualitative information this will provide will be worthwhile for the purpose of analysis.

In addition, I will be modifying some of the questions in the existing pilot study survey before proceeding to the main study. For example, the question that asks, 'Have you experienced or been aware of transphobic violence, bullying or harassment on campus?' will be split in order to consider the difference between experiencing this directly and being aware of it happening, and also to distinguish between physical violence, bullying and other forms of harassment, including a question about micro-aggression issues, such as misgendering.

---

51 See Formby (n 26).

Furthermore, the question that asks, 'Does the Student Union have a dedicated Trans Officer?' will be taken further to identify whether and how this is, or is not, of benefit. The questions regarding the gender identity and pronouns of the participants will be moved to the end of the survey, where additional demographic questions will also be added in order to identify intersectionality between transphobia and, for example, racism and/or ableism, which critical theory identifies as interconnected.

Working from a critical theory perspective, subjectivity is also important, and my own positionality needs to be considered as having an influence on the data, which are seen as constructed, rather than being a researcher observing natural occurrences, as would occur with a more positivist approach. It is therefore not possible to eliminate bias and seek an objective truth, minimising my own effect on the data. Having designed the study, I am not a 'disinterested observer' – the subject is important to me and so is trying to make a positive change for this student group. However, it is important that I consider my own position as a cisgender researcher and identify potential problems that this may produce. My research questions do not come from personal experience and may not be addressing the needs of the trans student community. It has therefore been an important part of designing the research survey that the input of trans students has been sought, to ensure the way questions are worded is suitable. I may also experience challenges with regard to participants' expectations of my intentions as a cisgender researcher. I will need to reflect upon how my own cisgender privilege may affect my approach to the study and my relationships with participants, how I have negotiated that and how my identity may shape how I interpret and frame my results. I must be attentive to my own assumptions about gender throughout the research.

The main study will also explore the research question, 'How well are HEIs supporting trans students, including the development and implementation of trans student policy?', looking at a selection of HEI trans student policies in light of the guidance from the Equality Challenge Unit,[52] which sets out to help HEIs meet their legal responsibilities, ensure policies and procedures meet the needs of trans people and provide support to trans staff and students.

5. Update on the Main Study

The main study has now been completed, with 166 survey responses and seven interview transcriptions from trans students at HEIs across the UK having been collected and analysed. For more information, please contact the author.

---

[52] E Pugh, *Trans Staff and Students in Higher Education Revised 2010* (Equality Challenge Unit 2010) 11.

Chapter 16

Queerly Fluent/Fluently Queer

On (Re)Creating Shared Identities in Second and Third Languages Among Migrant LGBTQ Populations in the Arabian Peninsula

Gaar Adams

1. Introduction: The Arabian Peninsula and Its Residents

The six countries comprising the regional intergovernmental union known as the Gulf Cooperation Council (GCC) – Bahrain, Kuwait, Oman, Qatar, Saudi Arabia and The United Arab Emirates – share a host of notable attributes extending well beyond just a desert climate on the Arabian Peninsula. Historically, each of the six relatively young countries – only Saudi Arabia was established before the turn of the mid-20th century – relies on petroleum-based industries; collectively, they boast nearly a third of the world's identified oil reserves.[1] Economically, each country prospers: the International Monetary Fund includes all six in a global list of top 30 countries ranked by gross domestic product per capita, with Qatar sitting at the very top.[2] And looming perhaps largest in the world's imagination are these countries' aggressive plans for their respective wealth: similar, ambitious strategies to accumulate soft power by building elaborate cultural institutions, investing in mammoth tourism infrastructure projects and hosting unprecedented global entertainment and sporting events.

But, each of these large-scale events and projects – from the $US1 Billion Dubai Creek Tower[3] set to become the world's tallest upon its completion

---

1 BP Statistical Review of World Energy, June 2016 <http://oilproduction.net/files/especial-BP/bp-statistical-review-of-world-energy-2016-full-report.pdf> (accessed 1 November 2018).
2 International Monetary Fund GDP Per Capita, Current Prices, 2019 <www.imf.org/external/data mapper/PPPPC@WEO/THA/KWT/COM/QAT/ARE/SAU/BHR/SYR/YEM/SDN/MAR/JOR/LBY/IRN> (accessed 1 August 2019).
3 'Emaar Properties Completes Dubai Creek Tower Phase 1' *Zawya*, 7 April 2019 <www.zawya.com/mena/en/business/story/Emaar_Properties_completes_Dubai_Creek_Tower_Phase_1-ZAWYA20190407104512/> (accessed 4 August 2019).

DOI: 10.4324/9781003286295-20

in 2021 to the recently announced 10,000 square-mile 'smart city' of Neow in Saudi Arabia with the eye-watering price tag of US$500 billion[4] – requires a scale of labor unavailable in such a sparsely populated region. In order to support these mega-projects and their associated rapid urbanization, the countries of the GCC collectively host one of the most significant migrant labor populations on the planet, with Saudi Arabia alone housing the second largest number of migrants in the world,[5] despite a population ranked only 40th globally.[6]

With multiple state agencies often authorized to admit migrant workers[7] and a growing international spotlight on human rights, current exact figures on migrant populations released by the GCC countries themselves are increasingly rare, but a 2005 survey by the Population Division of the United Nations[8] included all six in the top ten of countries worldwide with the highest percentage of international migrants. Another study analyzing this decade's GCC statistics showed that only Saudi Arabia and Oman had national populations larger than their foreign migrant populations; in Qatar, migrants made up an astounding 90% of the in-country population.[9] Although the largest migrant groups in the region hail from the Indian subcontinent – namely India, Pakistan, Bangladesh and Sri Lanka – and Southeast Asia, these populations are truly global, with significant numbers also from places as disparate as urban centres in the Philippines, ports along the Iranian coast and farms in rural Upper Egypt, as well as countries throughout Europe and the Americas. Amidst all this diversity, perhaps the starkest figure to consider: the majority of people living in the Arabian Peninsula are navigating a country – and, almost as frequently, also a culture and a language – that is not their own.

---

4 James Vincent, 'Robot Cage Fights and Flying Taxis: Leaked Documents Reveal Saudi Arabia's Plans for Its Next Megacity' *The Verg*, 26 July 2019 <www.theverge.com/2019/7/26/8931389/saudi-arabia-mega-city-neom-plans-futuristic-dystopian-ai-robot-fake-moon> (accessed 1 August 2019).
5 United Nations, International Migration Report, 2017 <www.un.org/en/development/desa/population/migration/publications/migrationreport/docs/MigrationReport2017_Highlights.pdf> (accessed 4 November 2018).
6 United National Population Division, World Population Prospects, 2017 <www.un.org/en/development/desa/population/migration/publications/migrationreport/docs/MigrationReport 2017_Highlights.pdf> (accessed 4 August 2019).
7 Mohammed Ebrahim Dito, 'GCC Labour Migration Governance' (21 September 2008) UN Doc POP/EGM-MIG/2008/7 <www.un.org/en/development/desa/population/events/pdf/expert/14/P07_Dito.pdf> (accessed 6 August 2019).
8 United Nations Population Division, International Migration in GCC Countries, 2007 <www.un.org/en/development/desa/population/migration/events/docs/IttMig_170407.pdf> (accessed 12 October 2018).
9 Gulf Labour Markets, Migration, and Population Programme, 2016 <https://gulfmigration.org/gcc-total-population-percentage-nationals-foreign-nationals-gcc-countries-national-statistics-2010-2016-numbers/>.

1.1 The LGBTQ Community: A Persecuted and Prosecuted Minority

In addition to these notable historic, economic and emigrational commonalities, the countries comprising the Arabian Peninsula also share another important attribute, a distressing legal one: their national governments enforce some of the most restrictive and repressive LGBTQ legislation in the world. Of the six, United Nations states that actively impose the death penalty around the world, two (Saudi Arabia and Yemen) are in the Arabian Peninsula; of the five other countries where the death penalty is not currently regularly practiced but still codified in law, two more (Qatar and the United Arab Emirates) are also in the Peninsula.[10] Same-sex relations are punishable by imprisonment and deportation in all seven of Peninsula's countries except for Bahrain, although LGBTQ residents there still report discrimination, 'state sponsored homophobia' and arrests,[11] including for a wide array of vague, tangential offenses ranging from cross-dressing to 'enticing' same-sex behavior under penal code morality laws.[12]

Despite recent sensational media reports regarding plans to 'medically screen' for homosexuals attempting to work in the region,[13] LGBTQ migrant populations do of course exist throughout the Arabian Peninsula. Indeed, in the face of both high-profile arrests – including a massive public jailing of 213 people in Kuwait City in 2013[14] and a public beheading of five men who confessed to homosexual acts under torture[15] in Saudi Arabia in 2019 – as well as incarcerations and other legal punishments that go unreported or are contained to local media, queer migrants from across the globe still live, work and often thrive in the region.

---

10 International Lesbian, Gay, Bisexual, Trans and Intersex Association, A World Survey of Sexual Orientation Laws: Criminalisation, Protection and Recognition, 2017 <https://ilga.org/downloads/2017/ILGA_State_Sponsored_Homophobia_2017_WEB.pdf> (accessed 2 September 2018).
11 International Lesbian, Gay, Bisexual, Trans and Intersex Association, A World Survey of Sexual Orientation Laws: Criminalisation, Protection and Recognition, 2019 <https://ilga.org/downloads/ILGA_State_Sponsored_Homophobia_2019.pdf> (accessed 1 August 2019).
12 Bahrain Penal Code, 1973 <www.unodc.org/res/cld/document/bhr/1976/bahrain_penal_code_html/Bahrain_Penal_Code_1976.pdf> (accessed 2 August 2019).
13 Habib Toumi, 'Gays to Be Barred from Entering Gulf' *Gulfnews*, 7 October 2013 <https://gulfnews.com/world/gulf/kuwait/gays-to-be-barred-from-entering-gulf-1.1240199> (accessed 5 September 2018).
14 JK Trotter, 'Kuwaiti Police Sweep Cafes, Arrest 215 People for Being Gay' *The Atlantic*, 14 May 2013 <www.theatlantic.com/national/archive/2013/05/kuwaiti-police-sweep-cafes-arrest-215-people-being-gay/315272/> (accessed 4 August 2019).
15 Tamara Qiblawi and Ghazi Balkiz, 'Saudi Arabia Said They Confessed. But Court Filings Show Some Executed Men Protested Their Innocence' *CNN*, 26 April 2019 <https://edition.cnn.com/2019/04/26/middleeast/saudi-executions-court-documents-intl/index.html> (accessed 9 August 2019).

1.2 Methodological Approach and Goals: From New Languages to New Voices

Over the span of a decade, I interviewed over 500 such people: LGBTQ migrants who – for the span of a few months or nearly a lifetime – have called a country in the Arabian Peninsula 'home'. From the start of 2009 – when I arrived in the Yemeni capital of Sana'a while it was abuzz with anger about the barber who raped and killed a child[16] – to the end of 2018, when I left the UAE shortly after Indian migrant workers were celebrating their homeland's legalization of homosexuality,[17] I interviewed LGBTQ migrants living in each country in the Arabian Peninsula from a wide swath of socioeconomic, educational, religious and cultural backgrounds. I also engaged in participant observation and took an inductive approach to listening, speaking with and documenting LGBTQ voices, stories and lived experiences across the region, where I became acquainted with dozens of interlocutors and met hundreds more through snowball sampling who migrated to the Gulf for a wide variety of social, economic, political and lifestyle factors.

This research seeks to inform a narrative nonfiction book I am writing for a general audience that interweaves these archival interviews of LGBTQ migrant stories in the Arabian Peninsula with my own story of meeting a man in the United Arab Emirates in 2012 who would become my husband after six years of navigating the perils of building a relationship in a country where same-sex relations are illegal.

While acknowledging the nuanced but too-scant academic publishing on the Arabian Peninsula's informal urbanism 'beyond the city as spectacle',[18] it is worth noting that much empirical research on migrant stories in the region is limited to one country, and almost none of it acknowledges – let alone delves into – queer stories or attempts to consider the realities or implications of queer migration to, in or on the region.

The aim of this chapter – three case studies of queer migrants in the Arabian Peninsula – is twofold: to investigate the ways in which language, language acquisition and legal subversion play into queer community-building and queer migrants' relationships to their home, each other and themselves and also to

---

16 'Execution of Yemeni Child Killed Captured on Camera' *The Telegraph*, 7 July 2009. <www.telegraph.co.uk/news/worldnews/middleeast/yemen/5765664/Execution-of-Yemeni-child-killer-captured-on-camera.html> (accessed 9 August 2019).
17 'Campaigners Celebrate as India Decriminalizes Homosexuality' *The Guardian*, 6 September 2018 <www.theguardian.com/world/2018/sep/06/indian-supreme-court-decriminalises-homosexuality> (accessed 9 August 2019).
18 Yasser Elsheshtawy, 'Where the Sidewalk Ends: Informal Street Corner Encounters in Dubai' (2013) 31:4 *Cities* 31, 382–393.

interrogate popular narratives in Western media's cultural representation of the region as a 'sterile and morally destitute'[19] nouveau riche land devoid of cultural vibrancy.

2. The Yemeni Athlete in Abu Dhabi

In 2016, I met 23-year-old Yemeni fitness instructor Ahmed[20] who worked at a gymnasium in downtown Abu Dhabi. As a teenager living in southern Yemen – a place where he described feeling unable to meet or access any gay community for fear of being caught by his conservative Muslim family – he longed to travel abroad. When his family moved to the UAE just before he enrolled in university, Ahmed eagerly looked forward to living in what he labeled as 'finally, a real city'.

While studying in his third year at university, Ahmed met a young Sri Lankan man at a cafe who would become his boyfriend, although they initially struggled to carry on a clandestine relationship due to the fact that both of their living arrangements included sleeping in close proximity to religious family members who strongly disapprove of homosexuality.

After graduating and upon securing a job two years later, Ahmed attempted to gain more personal freedom by securing a flat to live in away from his family, but he described feeling shocked at the beginning this search:

> There were signs all over the city for flat-shares but all people only wanted other people of the same nationality. Everything was divided by country: 'Pakistani bachelor only.' 'Indian executive bachelors only.' 'Filipino family only.' I was scared that I could not find any place to live because people only want to speak their language and most of the Yemenis I knew lived with their families only.

After explaining his predicament to his boyfriend, the two men decided to move in together. Although they both harbored a great deal of early trepidation about technically breaking the UAE's laws on unmarried couples living together and premarital sex,[21] they decided – as long as they kept a spare single bed so as not to arise suspicion from their 'annoying Egyptian landlord' – their

---

19 Alex Proud, 'Who in Their Right Mind Would Want to Visit Dubai?' *The Telegraph*, 19 October 2019 <www.telegraph.co.uk/men/thinking-man/11936981/Who-in-their-right-mind-would-want-to-visit-Dubai.html> (accessed 8 August 2019).
20 Name changed to preserve anonymity.
21 Abu Dhabi Judicial Department, 2011, UAE Penal Law, s. 5, art. 312, para. 3. <www.adjd.gov.ae/sites/Authoring/AR/ELibrary%20Books/E-Library/PDFs/Penal%20Code.pdf> (accessed 3 September 2018).

living situation would not create the same level of suspicion as a heterosexual couple. Ahmed delighted in relaying this:

> No one had any problems with us because they did not know we're a gay couple living together. They thought we are only friends. My friend who is a girl and knows about [my boyfriend] makes jokes that it is easier to live together if you are gay.

Ahmed also spoke with a measure of pride about feeling that he and his boyfriend are part of establishing a larger queer community across the national and racial divides that he sees as pervasive across the city. Although they do not have a large flat, they now host regular gatherings for their queer social group of about 20 homosexual men and women from seven countries. 'We are mixing here in a way that some heterosexual people are not,' he said.

2.1 Analysis: Queering the City

Ahmed's dream of living in what he classified as a 'real city' since identifying his same-sex desires as a young man mirrors the metropolitan aspirations of many in the LGBTQ community since 'urban centres have been conducive to homosexual expression, whether integrated into or transgressive against social norms'.[22] Although he was able to find a measure of that expression early on in his nascent relationship, it was only upon attempting to extricate himself from the stifling nature of his devout family's watchful eyes that he faced an unexpected hurdle on his path as a migrant to 'break out of the strictures imposed elsewhere:'[23] his experience of segregation in the city's housing market.

Ethnic segregation in the Gulf has been noted elsewhere, including the 'economic practices and cultural attitudes [that] reinforce the exclusionary or hierarchising nature of the legal and immigration system'.[24] For Ahmed, at its most tangible, this segregation took the form of exclusionary flat-share signs and an inability to locate a viable living situation as a young adult living independently for the first time.

But, it was his homosexuality – a characteristic that might seem like a dangerous liability in most circumstances in the UAE – that allowed him to overcome and participate in 'queering urban spaces' in which he could begin 'building an emancipatory public and emerge from the shadows of a mainstream society

---

22 Robert Aldrich, 'Homosexuality and the City: An Historical Overview' (2004) 41:9 *Urban Studies* 1719–1737.
23 Alan Collins, *Cities of Pleasure: Sex and the Urban Socialscape* (Taylor and Francis 2013) 93.
24 Sharon Nagy, 'Making Room for Migrants, Making Sense of Difference: Spatial and Ideological Expressions of Social Diversity in Urban Qatar' (2006) 43:1 *Urban Studies* 119–137.

which hitherto denied and negated urban-societal reality'.[25] Even further, it is this very queerness that is allowing others to also emerge from the shadows and into the mixed social group they are building – a group that is also changing the very fabric of the city.

3. A Keralite Tailor in Riyadh

On the western edge of Riyadh, Saudi Arabia, I met Abdul Rahman,[26] a 43-year-old man from Thiruvananthapuram, India, in December 2011. He had moved from the southern Indian state of Kerala six years earlier to work as a tailoring shop's master cutter in the Saudi capital. During the initial part of our earliest conversation, Rahman expressed that his motivation to move to Riyadh was to become a financial success story and join the roughly 10% of Keralans who work abroad.[27] It was only as our conversation progressed that he admitted that he had been engaging in physical relationships with men since adolescence and also had been struggling to reconcile these actions with his devout Muslim upbringing.

After acknowledging that he was spending increasing time on a popular Malayalam-language online message board that facilitated anonymous same-sex sexual encounters, he decided to move to Saudi Arabia with the hope that living in what he felt was the most devout Muslim country – and one intolerant of same-sex desire – might stop the homosexual actions and fantasies that were leading to feelings of torment and guilt and which he thought were distracting him from finding a wife and having children, major goals for his immediate future.

Although he felt that he was initially praying more after his relocation to Riyadh, Abdul Rahman nonetheless began a sexual relationship with a male Jordanian customer three months after his move. Abdul Rahman describes inner turmoil both in regard to his actions as well as his identity:

> In the beginning, I felt anger and shame that I could feel things in my heart for a man. [In Thiruvananthapuram], I did not like the word 'Kundan'[28] I did not like thinking of myself as one of these people. But I knew I liked that part [that was physical].

---

25 Y Doderer, 'LGBTQs in the City, Queering Urban Space' (2011) 35:2 *International Journal of Urban and Regional Research* 431–436.
26 Name changed to preserve anonymity.
27 K Zachariah and S Irudaya, 'Kerala's Gulf Connection: CDS Studies on International Labour Migration from Kerala State in India' in KC Zachariah, KP Kannan, and S Irudaya Rajan (eds) (2002) 62:4 *The Journal of Asian Studies* 1311–1313.
28 Malayalam slang for 'homosexual'.

Abdul Rahman estimated that the men began to spend several nights a week together a month after meeting, at which point the Jordanian man, Tariq,[29] added Abdul Rahman to a WhatsApp group composed of his gay friends living in Riyadh and Jeddah. Initially, Abdul Rahman was confused by the group's banter but began to view the communication differently as time passed and the messages continued:

> I did not always understand all the jokes, but they always said the word 'mithli'[30] for each other. In Malayalam, I would not call myself this but [Tariq] said it was not a bad thing. It was normal for them to use it; it was no problem and after that, I began slowly, slowly to feel lighter. I was also feeling better about [the relationship].

Although Rahman's partner has since returned to Jordan, they have maintained a platonic online relationship, and Rahman has even met some of those in the WhatsApp group which now includes nearly 30 men from Jordan, India, Pakistan and Nepal. He has even found two more men from Kerala living in Riyadh to add to the group and relishes the community: 'Sometimes we translate for each other online or when we meet. But even if you don't understand everything, it is nice to be in the group, so I don't feel alone.'

3.1 Analysis: The 'Gay International' and Self-Identification

Abdul Rahman is a study in human complexity: he felt shame about his homosexual actions, moved across the world to inhibit his ability to act on those impulses and then continued to pursue homosexual relations while also continuing to pine for a wife and children.

In his seminal work 'Desiring Arabs', Joseph Masaad rails against Western gay rights activists, a group he coins the 'Gay International' for flattening human sexuality – particularly in the Middle East – into a binary and 'transforming sexual practices into identities'.[31]

Much space could be given to queer and gender theory in hypothesizing Abdul Rahman's 'true' sexuality: self-loathing homosexual, situational homosexual or bisexual, or MSM, a phrase coined in 1994 by epidemiologists for 'men who have sex with men' to better capture the reality of sexual behavior and identity during the campaign to destigmatise HIV.[32] But, what is clear is that Rahman was initially uncomfortable with labels.

---

29 Name changed to preserve anonymity.
30 Arabic slang for 'homosexual'.
31 Joseph Massad, *Desiring Arabs* (University of Chicago Press 2008) 195.
32 M Glick, BC Muzyka, LM Salkin, and D Lurie, 'Necrotizing Ulcerative Periodontitis: A Marker for Immune Deterioration and a Predictor for the Diagnosis of AIDS' (1994) 65:5 *Journal of Periodontology* 393–397 <www.ncbi.nlm.nih.gov/pubmed/7913962> (accessed 4 September 2019).

It was only when he was exposed to them through online chat and memes that his negative feelings around queer linguistics began to shift. It was exposure to the process of language reclamation or 'the phenomenon whereby a stigmatised group re-values an externally imposed negative label by self-consciously referring to itself in terms of that label'[33] – that allowed him to feel more at ease with names and phrases he had previously considered derogatory or shameful.

During our last in-person meeting in Jeddah in 2017, Abdul Rahman was still looking for a wife, still pursuing sexual relationships with men, still not labeling himself, but was more comfortable with being considered by both himself and others as part of a queer community. Upon relocating to Jeddah in 2016, he even found two more men to add to the WhatsApp group.

4. The Filipino Waitress in Al Ain

The 35-year-old Sarah[34] moved to Al Ain, the quiet, inland UAE border town with Oman, in 2010 from an impoverished suburb on the outskirts of Manila, the sprawling capital of the Philippines. Like many of the non-Muslim non-native English-speaking migrants I interviewed, Sarah described a litany of challenges in adjusting to a new culture – from relatively small everyday culinary challenges ('the food doesn't have the same good flavor as my home!') to the larger linguistic challenges of operating in a new language.

Sarah's decision to work in the UAE came in the wake of hearing stories from a cousin who would periodically return to Manila from his lucrative work as a nurse in Doha. Before she decided to move, she spoke with a gay acquaintance who also worked in hospitality in the UAE in order to hear what it would be like to live there as a gay man. Soon after her arrival, however, she came to terms with her identity as a transgender woman.

In addition to having to reckon with her gender identity in a new country, Sarah also described initially feeling disillusioned with how small her new home felt and admitted to expecting something more akin to the media images and stories she had heard from acquaintances in larger cities, like Dubai and Manama, Bahrain.

After eight months of difficulty adjusting to the UAE as well as her own inner feelings about her gender identity, Sarah developed a physical and emotional relationship with an Omani man who regularly patronised the restaurant where she worked. She described the relationship's early period and its effect on her:

> None of [our colleagues] know [that we are gay] so he meets me after I am finishing my shift and we drive outside the city and talk. English is no

---

33 A Galinsky, C Wang, J Whitson, E Anicich, K Hugenberg, and G Bodenhausen, 'The Reappropriation of Stigmatizing Labels' (2013) 24:10 *Psychological Science* 2020–2029.
34 Name changed to preserve anonymity.

good for him, and also no good for me, but it is better than my Arabic, so we speak [in English] together like this. We sometimes watch Hollywood movies, and sometimes he likes me to teach him a little Swardspeak[35] . . . I like we are both learning things.

As their relationship progressed, Sarah's boyfriend began to express an interest in learning more about her native language, Tagalog. Sarah felt that as his interest in Tagalog increased, their relationship grew even stronger, and her boyfriend began to ask to meet her gay and transgender Filipino friends living in the UAE. She lightly boasted about a relationship that she views to be furtive and intellectually curious in equal measure:

We have many things undercover! One time, we went to a wig shop and I asked him [in Tagalog] to buy one wig for me! He told [the shopkeeper] that he needed to buy one for his wife! . . . His friends don't know he is speaking better English now, or he is speaking Tagalog to me. This is only for us and God to know.

The other secret that only Sarah and her boyfriend know is that she now yearns to present as a woman in public, a decision she was initially concerned he wouldn't accept. Happy to be building a larger LGBTQ community in Al Ain, she sees transgender acceptance as the next frontier in the region but regards her boyfriend's lack of reticence as evidence that attitudes are already slowly changing. She hopes that beginning to transition more publicly within the safety of her own community may have a ripple effect for the larger population: 'soon [being transgender] won't be [seen as] a problem for just one in a million people.'

4.1 Analysis: Secret Languages/Secret Intimacies

Sarah described her early experiences in the UAE as being marked by the dual challenges of contending with the secret of her sexuality and also dealing with adjustments: recalibrating her expectations of the city to which she relocated as well as reconceptualizing her own gender identity.

But, Sarah chronicled how another secret – this time a linguistic one – became an unexpected path forward in navigating the challenges that her new home presented.

Her motivation in teaching her boyfriend Swardspeak is much like the motives of those utilizing its cant slang contemporary in the UK, Polari, who 'required and desired some form of secret language, working simultaneously

---

35 A historic argot used primarily by gay men in the Philippines.

to affirm the secret unity of the outcast, and by "speaking in tongues" to hide from the larger, hostile world'.[36]

Although it is Swardspeak, so often theorised as 'secretive' because – as one Filipino scholar put it – it 'conceivably [helps] women and gays get away with murder and a smile tucked in between their lips';[37] for Sarah and her boyfriend, it is actually English that operates in the same manner as a coded language; they are both able to speak a second language together beyond the purview of others who might suspect their queerness. The same could be theorised about Sarah's boyfriend learning Tagalog – it is in this new ability to converse in another language hidden from most of his own Arabic-speaking community that provides him both secrecy and a window into finding a wider queer community.

As for Sarah's other challenges, at least one of them – feeling that Al Ain was initially too small – has been alleviated as she described gaining a richer social circle with her boyfriend. However, any potential resolution for her other challenge – living as a transgender woman in the UAE – still feels some distance off: despite some hope in 2016 about a highly publicised law seeming to allow gender reassignment surgery to move forward in-country, the three transgender Emiratis who catalyzed the nascent movement had their case rejected by the Federal Supreme Council on 31 December 2018.[38] But, that won't necessarily stop Sarah or the region's queer community. As Sarah herself said with a smile: 'Sometimes I feel almost like a secret. But I wake up, and I am still here.'

5. Conclusion

In the face of so many daunting and seemingly insurmountable challenges: linguistic foreignness; socioeconomic and racial segregations as all-too familiar realities; and the pervasive threat of imprisonment, deportation or death for engaging in same-sex relations, it is perhaps both surprising and unsurprising that so many queer migrants are not just living but thriving in the Arabian Peninsula.

After all, from contemporary social theory on 'queering the city' to the demonstrated vitality of Swardspeak, it is queer people across the breadth of eras and cultures who have demonstrated unique ways to avoid legal reprisal, communicate their emotional needs and physical desires and build a robust and vital community – so often in secret – time and time again.

And while the anecdotes, feelings and examples of Ahmed, Abdul Rahman, Sarah and their respective communities are only a small window into a much

---

36 J Green, 'Language: Polari' (1997) 39:1 *Critical Quarterly* 127–131.
37 J Garcia, *Philippine Gay Culture* (Hong Kong University Press 2009) 111.
38 Shireena Al Nowais, 'Transgender Emiratis Have Case Rejected by UAE High Court' *The National*, 7 January 2019 <www.thenational.ae/uae/health/transgender-emiratis-have-case-rejected-by-uae-high-court-1.810021> (accessed 4 September 2019).

larger reality in the Arabian Peninsula, the buoyancy that they maintain should at the very least also demonstrate that a region so often derided as 'fake' or 'plastic' is in fact a complex home to a kaleidoscope of intersecting subcultures and subversion, and that its queer population should not continue to be erased or ignored in either academic discourse or media depictions.

As I finish writing my larger work on these queer migrant communities while in the year of the 50th anniversary of the Stonewall Riots, I pause to remember how these demonstrations so inspired me as a closeted 18 year old who moved to the 'Big City' of New York after a stifling childhood in rural Midwest America. And then I dream about how the actions of these queer communities in the Arabian Peninsula – in ways both too small and too profound to fully imagine – are already affecting the next generation of queer migrants moving to the Arabian Peninsula, a place still erroneously dismissed as devoid of culture.

Part 4

Between Disenfranchisement and Inclusion

The LGBT Community and the Medical Sector

Chapter 17

Changing Science and the Science of Change

Medical Perspectives

Paul Behrens and Sean Becker

Few areas are as representative for challenges and progress in LGBT matters as their relationship with the medical field. At the time of Stonewall, homosexuality was still pathologised in several States; conversion 'therapy' was widely practiced. But there were also early signs of a more accepting approach: in 1973, the American Psychiatric Association decided that homosexuality 'per se' was no longer to be seen as a 'psychiatric disorder' and removed the relevant diagnosis from the Diagnostic and Statistical Manual.[1] International progress took longer, but in 1990 the World Health Organization removed homosexuality as an illness.[2]

By that time, another development had taken place, which, in a tragic way, made the LGBT community subject of consideration by the medical profession. In 1981, the first cases of a viral illness were observed, which seemed to affect in particular men who had sex with men (MSM). The new illness heralded the beginning of a crisis of staggering dimensions,[3] but would also put societal reactions in relief. Discrimination played its role, starting with the names given to the disease, such as 'gay-related immunodeficiency disease' ('GRID'),[4] until the more neutral 'acquired immune deficiency syndrome (AIDS)' came to be used. In the early stages of the epidemic, the suspicion of being gay could suffice for people to be expelled by their landlords or to lose their jobs.[5]

---

1 *New York Times*, 'The A.P.A. Ruling on Homosexuality'. 23 December 1973; Jack Drescher, 'Out of DSM: Depathologizing Homosexuality' (2015) 5 *Behavioral Sciences* 565.
2 European Council, '17 May: International Day Against Homophobia and Transphobia', 17 May 2017 <www.consilium.europa.eu/en/documents-publications/library/library-blog/posts/17-may-international-day-against-homophobia-and-transphobia/>; *BBC News*, 'Transgender No Longer Recognised as a "Disorder" by WHO', 29 May 2019 <www.bbc.co.uk/news/health-48448804>.
3 In the United States alone, the cumulative number of deaths due to AIDS exceeded 100,000 by 1990, Foundation for AIDS Research, 'HIV/AIDS: Snapshots of an Epidemic' <www.amfar.org/thirty-years-of-hiv/aids-snapshots-of-an-epidemic/>.
4 See Lawrence K Altman, 'Clue Found on Homosexuals' Pre-Cancer Syndrome' *New York Times*, 18 June 1982.
5 André Picard, 'How the Advent of AIDS Advanced Gay Rights' *The Globe and Mail*, 15 August 2014; see also Andrew Anthony, '"We Were so Scared": Four People Who Faced the Horror of Aids in the 80s' *The Observer*, 31 January 2021.

Yet the suffering of LGBT persons also told a human story, and arguably, especially when personalities such as Rock Hudson contracted the virus, perceptions of the LGBT community began to change. That is not to say that discriminatory treatment disappeared. The situation in many African States today evokes memories of the experience of LGBT persons in the Western hemisphere in the 1980s, and the fear of stigma is still capable of preventing MSM with the human immunodeficiency virus (HIV) from seeking the medical help they need.[6] It is a sad observation on the 21st century that, while HIV, from a scientific perspective, need no longer be a death sentence, death by dint of social stigma is as much of a possibility as it has ever been.

The medical issues that are of relevance to the LGBT community today cover a wide field. Some concerns are not new: the high occurrence of depression among gay men has long been the subject of medical debate, as have approaches to potential explanations.[7] Other issues, while not new, have entered public debate only more recently, such as the availability of assistance under healthcare plans of transition treatment for transgender persons. Discrimination in the medical field has not entirely disappeared either, as evidenced, for instance, by States that still exclude gay donors from their blood donation system.[8]

A particularly worrying matter is the fact that conversion 'therapy' is, in wide parts of the world, still carried out and is, in a large number of cases, done by '[m]edical and mental health providers'[9] – a surprising development in view of the international condemnation that these practices have evoked.[10] At the time of writing, efforts are ongoing in several jurisdictions, including Scotland, to outlaw these methods.

For LGBT members of the medical profession, coming out in the days of Stonewall often took courage, and LGBT acceptance in the profession was not a foregone conclusion. LGBT doctors, nurses, dentists, veterinary surgeons and other healthcare workers were at times confronted with traditionalist perceptions by their peers, but they also had to deal with patients whose views on LGBT matters were based on social stereotypes.[11] At the same time, a comparison with Stonewall days cannot avoid the conclusion that, at least in some

---

6 Picard (n 5).
7 Cf on the minority stress model, Carrie Lee et al., 'Depression and Suicidality in Gay Men: Implications for Health Care Providers' (2017) *American Journal of Men's Health* 911, 912.
8 *The Economist*, 'Which Countries Prohibit Gay or Bisexual Men from Donating Blood?' 14 June 2021.
9 UN Independent Expert on Protection against Violence and Discrimination Based on Sexual Orientation and Gender Identity, *Practices of So-Called 'Conversion Therapy'*, Report to the Human Rights Council, 1 May 2020, A/HRC/44/53, at para 28 (with reference to a submission by the LGBT Foundation).
10 See *ibid.*, para 20.
11 See e.g. European Union News, 'Two Thirds of LGBT Doctors Suffer Discrimination' (News release by the British Medical Trade Union), 18 February 2017.

fields, progress has been made. Visibility has arguably led to greater understanding and acceptance. The establishment in the United States of GLMA: Health Professionals Advancing LGBTQ Equality;[12] in the UK of GLADD (The Association of Gay and Lesbian Doctors and Dentists) and BVLGBT+ (British Veterinary LGBT+); and, internationally, the World Professional Association for Transgender Health (WPATH)[13] are exemplary for that. Difficulties notwithstanding, the voice of LGBT persons in the medical profession is increasingly heard.

The chapters in this part are dedicated to the very intersection of LGBT matters and the medical field.

Chapter 18 (Kelsall-Knight and Sudron) discusses experiences made by LGBT mothers in the healthcare system and analyses the fact that LGBT parents may be reluctant to access healthcare for their children for fear of discrimination. It outlines the importance of practiced inclusivity and in particular of inclusive terminology.

Chapter 19 (Behrens) deals with the topic of conversion 'therapy' and explores the confrontation with human rights law, which these practices typically invite. It traces the ongoing development towards their criminalisation and critically analyses challenges that legislation on this topic is likely to encounter.

---

12 GLMA. Health Professionals Advancing LGBTQ Equality, 'History' <www.glma.org/index.cfm?fuseaction=Page.viewPage&pageId=532>.
13 www.wpath.org/about/mission-and-vision.

Chapter 18

Disenfranchisement in British Healthcare

Being a Lesbian Non-Biological Mother

Lucille Kelsall-Knight and Ceri Sudron

1. Introduction

Lesbian, gay, bisexual, transgender (LGBT) parents are fearful of discrimination and a lack of acceptance when accessing healthcare for their children.[1] Despite government recommendations, policy and law, stories of inappropriate questioning and parental exclusion point towards the prevalence of homophobia in the National Health Service (NHS).[2] Lesbian mothers report ingrained homophobia and a heteronormative culture, which leaves them unable to 'fit' into the box of motherhood, and they are therefore disenfranchised in healthcare.[3]

This paper draws upon self-narratives from a wider study that has raised various commonalties around being a non-biological mother and the rhetoric, language and behaviours encountered within British healthcare.

2. Background

Family demographics have altered significantly due to legal changes in recent British history, including an increase of LGBT parents.[4] In 2018, one in eight of all adoptions within England were of children placed with same-sex parents;

---

1 Rose Chapman et al., 'Nursing and Medical Students' Attitudes, Knowledge and Beliefs Regarding Lesbian, Gay, Bisexual and Transgender Parents Seeking Healthcare for Their Children' (2012) 21:7–8 *Journal of Clinical Nursing* 938, 938; Linda Shields et al., 'Lesbian, Gay, Bisexual, and Transgender Parents Seeking Health Care for Their Children: A Systematic Review of the Literature' (2012) 9:4 *Worldviews on Evidence-Based Nursing* 200, 201.
2 Ruth Hunt, Katherine Cowan, and Brent Chamberlain, *Being the Gay One: Experiences of Lesbian, Gay and Bisexual People Working in the Health and Social Care Sector* (Stonewall 2015) 6; Catherine Somerville, *Unhealthy Attitudes: The Treatment of LGBT People Within Health and Social Care Services* (Stonewall 2016) 8.
3 B Hayman, L Wilkes, E Halcomb, and D Jackson, 'Marginalised Mothers: Lesbian Women Negotiating Heteronormative Healthcare Services' (2013) 44:1 *Contemporary Nurse* 120.
4 L Mellish, S Jennings, F Tasker, M Lamb, and S Golombok, *Family Relationships, Child Adjustment and Adopters' Experiences* (BAAF 2013) 5; Susan Golombok et al., 'Adoptive Gay Father Families: Parent-Child Relationships and Children's Psychological Adjustment' (2014) 85:2 *Child Development* 457.

DOI: 10.4324/9781003286295-23

however, there are no real statistics available regarding the number of LGBT-headed families.[5] Due to these legal changes with regard to same-sex parenthood, public opinion has often been controversial, which – when voiced in a healthcare setting – could have an effect on the emotional health and wellbeing of children and their parents.[6]

There is little research specific to LGBT parents' experiences of accessing healthcare for their children.[7] This small-scale qualitative study, therefore, sought to ascertain the experience of non-biological lesbian mothers accessing healthcare for their children. The assumptions made about them and their family constellation by healthcare professionals working in a heteronormative culture steered these mothers towards a feeling of disenfranchisement within the British healthcare system.

3. Method

A narrative inquiry approach was chosen, which allows the researcher and participant – through storytelling – to gain awareness of critical incidents and values that are of importance to the individual.[8] This then allows the social, political and cultural environment to be put into context.

3.1 Participants and Setting

The authors were participants in the pilot study, self-define as lesbian and are both non-biological mothers. A non-biological mother is one who has not conceived her child through surrogacy or in vitro fertilisation (IVF), and therefore shares no DNA with the child. This relationship can be through adoption or through a same-sex relationship where the mother did not carry the child but her partner did.

Two interviews were conducted with three participants, all of whom were non-biological mothers (two were a married couple with adopted children and one non-biological mother due to IVF with her partner), aged 36–45 years from two families. All participants were educated to master's degree level and

---

5 Department for Education, Main Report: Children looked after in England including adoption: 2017 to 2018, 2018, 2. <https://assets.publishing.service.gov.uk/government/uploads/system/uploads/attachment_data/file/757922/Children_looked_after_in_England_2018_Text_revised.pdf>; Nicola Hill, *The Pink Guide to Adoption for Lesbians and Gay Men* (BAAF 2012) 11.
6 See Mellish et al. (n 4) 4; see Golombok et al. (n 4).
7 E Perrin and H Kulkin, 'Pediatric Care for Children Whose Parents Are Gay or Lesbian' (1996) 97:5 *Pediatrics* 630; Ruth McNair et al., 'Lesbian Parents Negotiating the Health Care System in Australia' (2008) 29 *HealthCare for Women International* 92; K Mikhailovich, S Martin, and S Lawton, 'Lesbian and Gay Parents: Their Experiences of Children's Healthcare in Australia' (2001) 6:3 *International Journal of Sexuality and Gender Studies* 1812; see Shields et al. (n 1) 200.
8 M Montello, *Narrative Ethics: The Role of Ethics in Bioethics* (Special Report: Hastings Centre 2014) 3.

were registered healthcare professionals working full time at the time of the interviews. Two informants were born in the United Kingdom, one was born in the Netherlands. All are British citizens.

4. Data Collection

Convenience sampling was conducted for recruitment.[9] The first researcher made contact with a colleague to ascertain if she would be interested in contributing. Therefore, as a result of the interview and the collaborative elements, both became part of the research team. Two interviews were conducted via Skype: the first established consent, and the second facilitated a discussion of critical incidents that had happened when accessing healthcare for their children.

5. Analysis

Two frameworks for analysis were employed: Webster and Mertova critical event analysis and Clandinin and Connelly thematic analysis.[10] The audio files were transcribed, and the transcripts were read and listened to multiple times to appreciate the content and context. The content was then coded using broadening, burrowing and re-storying, which allowed commonalities to be developed.[11] The analysis was discussed, reviewed and revised throughout the analysis stage, and four commonalities were identified.

6. Ethical Considerations

Ethical approval was obtained from the University of Wolverhampton prior to recruitment.

7. Findings

Lesbian non-biological mothers experienced various professionals' attitudes when traversing healthcare. Positive and negative experiences were identified during data analysis, and four commonalities emerged: (1) attitudes and managing healthcare experiences, (2) acknowledgement of sexual orientation, (3) professional standards and (4) family constellation.

---

9 D Polit and C Beck, *Nursing Research: Principles and Methods* (7th edn, Lippincott Williams and Wilkins 2004) 258.
10 L Webster and P Mertova, *Using Narrative Inquiry as a Research Method: An Introduction to Using Critical Event Narrative Analysis in Research on Learning and Teaching* (Routledge 2007) 72; DJ Clandinin and FM Connelly, *Narrative Inquiry: Experience and Story in Qualitative Research* (John Wiley 2000) 138.
11 See *Ibid*.

7.1 Attitudes and Managing Healthcare Experiences

Managing healthcare interactions and the attitudes of some staff members could be difficult at times for the non-biological mothers. Inclusivity was apparent in some consultations; however, a significant number resulted in feelings of marginalisation, insignificance and being 'less of a mother'.

> I think it was just . . . you feel like this second-class citizen because you didn't give birth . . . some people think they have this automatic right to talk about you . . . in that negative manner.
>
> (Participant 3)

> [A]nd I've been visiting them [the children in a hospital setting] almost constantly for three days before anybody said do you want to cuddle with skin to skin . . . and she [nurse] recognised me as their parent, at that point . . . and nobody else had up until that point, I was just basically . . . I felt like I was the milkman because I brought the milk . . . brought the milk and the clean clothing.
>
> (Participant 2)

7.2 Acknowledgement of Sexual Orientation

The requirement of relationship justification and the need to repeatedly 'come out' was an issue faced multiple times when attending with their children.

> I think that's it though, when the two of us go together . . . I mean . . . it's a long time . . . since I had had to walk into a room and announce my sexuality . . . .. But since we've had the children, we walk in together and people go . . . 'and you are?' oh we're both mum, we're together and this is our son.
>
> (Participant 1)

> . . . but I think also it's also that assumption isn't it . . . where you have to justify who you are . . . you have to tell them [health professionals] how to refer to you and do they do that with straight couples or do they just assume that it's Mummy and Daddy.
>
> (Participant 2)

7.3 Professional Standards

Professionalism was an issue highlighted. Due to the researchers being registered healthcare professionals, they possessed knowledge of the applicable codes of practice. They felt that professional standards were not always followed, challenging the inclusiveness of the NHS.

> [S]he [doctor] was just so abrupt and uncaring and just lack[ed] compassion . . . y'know whatever her feelings . . . it didn't come across that she

was in a caring profession and there to make things ok for the children . . . certainly not for our son.

(Participant 3)

I've been to so many patients in my career that you just accept what they tell you, from trans patients to gay families to everything and the NHS Constitution states that you should treat everyone . . . not the same, but equally. So yeah I didn't realise how much it upset me at the time and it has made me more angry, but now it almost aggrieves me, for in the NHS there are still people that can't see beyond the normal boundary if you know what I mean, or what they perceive as normal.

(Participant 2)

7.4 *Family Constellation*

The concept of diverse family constellations often leads to uncertainty over appropriate terminology and ascribed 'gender roles', highlighting a struggle for healthcare professionals with constellations that deviate from the perceived 'norm'.

I think it's just y'know for her I don't think it was a normal family structure and I think she didn't know how to deal with it . . . whether that's the fact we've got two adopted children or because we're two women . . . or a combination of both of those.

(Participant 3)

If you are not the biological mum, to then somehow be marginalized or lessened by being told that you are not the parents and I mean, when they wrote sperm donor on [the medical notes] they also . . . they wrote I was the father and I mean how ridiculous was that.

(Participant 2)

8. Discussion

The findings showed that non-biological lesbian mothers often have to tread a complex and heteronormative path within healthcare.[12] The mothers experienced heteronormative views of family constellations and parentage from healthcare professionals and a lack of inclusivity and honour for the professional code of conduct. These findings and a feeling of marginalisation are mirrored by Hayman et al.[13] Inappropriate questioning from healthcare professionals can

---

12 Rose Chapman et al., 'A Descriptive Study of the Experiences of Lesbian, Gay and Transgender Parents Accessing Health Services for Their Children' (2012) 21 *Journal of Clinical Nursing* 1134; see Chapman et al. (n 1) 940; see Shields et al. (n 1) 201.
13 See Hayman et al. (n 3) 120.

be attributed to a poor awareness of routes to parenthood, which then triggered the mothers to respond protectively in defence of their family, role and identity, ultimately leading to a feeling of disenfranchisement and alienation, as echoed in the work of Hayman *et al*, whereby 'sister' or 'friend' was used in preference to 'mother', and inappropriate delving into paternal location and conception methods occurred.[14] Despite the challenges of non-acknowledgement of motherhood from healthcare professionals, the non-biological mothers did perceive themselves as being equal to their biological counterparts and felt that the healthcare professionals should mirror such expectation.[15]

The findings, however, also showed that despite the remaining rhetoric of heteronormativity in healthcare, there are pockets of positive affirmation of lesbian non-biological motherhood. These should be applauded and encouraged as 'gold standard' patient care.

9. Conclusion

Positive and negative interactions with healthcare professionals were experienced by the non-biological lesbian mothers in this study. Whilst there may be people who hold prejudicial views, progression within the United Kingdom is apparent due to an increase in understanding and acceptance. There is evidence of disenfranchisement for non-biological mothers; however, the pockets of good practice suggest greater understanding of the needs of non-biological mothers and their children, which in turn may lead to the dissolution of the heteronormative culture that exists within healthcare. Further research is planned through the larger study, which will help inform clinical practice with regard to this marginalised group of parents.

---

14 See *Ibid*.
15 General Medical Council, *Good Medical Practice* (GMC 2014) Sections 54 and 59; Health and Care Professions Council, *Standards of Proficiency: Paramedics* (HCPC 2014) Standards 5 and 6; Nursing and Midwifery Council, *The Code* (NMC 2015) Sections 1 and 20.

Chapter 19

False Therapy, Real Harm
Aspects of Conversion Practices and Their Evaluation

Paul Behrens*

1. Introduction

The term 'conversion practices' or 'conversion therapy' denotes methods that seek to change, suppress or eliminate the sexual orientation, gender identity or gender expression of a person.[1] Such practices seem to hail from an earlier age, and at the time of the Stonewall Riots, they were certainly widely performed.[2] But even today, they have not disappeared: when the Independent Expert on Protection against Violence and Discrimination Based on Sexual Orientation and Gender Identity ('Independent Expert') issued his 2020 Report on the topic, he referred to surveys showing that they were carried out 'in at least 68 countries'.[3] In 2016, the Southern Poverty Law Centre listed ten 'ex gay groups' in the United States, the majority of which advocated or performed conversion practices, and noted that there were 'many other smaller, similar groups, as well as uncounted individual practitioners'.[4] In the United Kingdom, it was reported in 2018 that a church in Liverpool offered gay people 'the chance to "cure" themselves of their homosexuality through a relentless prayer session involving three days without food or water'.[5] Even exorcisms have not disappeared from the scene: as late as 2010 did a charity helping young LGBT

---

* This chapter is based on two submissions, which the author made to the Scottish Parliament on this topic: *The Need for Legislative Action on Conversion Therapy* (13 August 2021) and '*Conversion Therapy': Criminalisation and Accompanying Legislative Measures* (31 August 2021). It is written in a private capacity.
1 See on this clause 1(a) of the Prohibition of Conversion Therapies Bill 2018 (Ireland) ('the Irish Bill').
2 David Carter, 'What Made Stonewall Different' 16:4 (August 2009) *Gay and Lesbian Review Worldwide* 11–13.
3 See Independent Expert on Protection against Violence and Discrimination Based on Sexual Orientation and Gender Identity, *Practices of So-Called "Conversion Therapy"*, Report to the Human Rights Council, A/HRC/44/53 (1 May 2020) ['Independent Expert'], para 24.
4 Mark Potok et al., *Quacks. 'Conversion Therapists', the Anti-LGBT Right, and the Demonization of Homosexuality* (Southern Poverty Law Centre 2016) 38–44.
5 Josh Parry, 'This Is the Reality of Gay "Cure" Conversion Therapy Taking Place in Liverpool' *Liverpool Echo*, 3 July 2018.

DOI: 10.4324/9781003286295-24

homeless people in the UK report of victims who had to flee exorcisms that were planned in order to rid them of their 'gay demons'.[6]

Internationally, conversion practices have drawn critique by medical associations,[7] while in the UK, several health organisations agreed in a memorandum that 'the practice of conversion therapy' was 'unethical and potentially harmful'.[8] Such condemnation is also mirrored in the views of various UN treaty bodies.[9]

This chapter investigates the phenomenon of conversion practices and explores the evaluation such methods have received in particular by States dealing with that problem in an effort to provide support structures for the victims. Section 2 deals with the phenomenon of conversion practices itself, the impact they have on the affected persons and their human rights as well as legislative measures adopted to address this conduct. Section 3 explores the difficulties that arise when States seek to address the relevant practices in their laws and focuses on aspects such as the role of consent of the victim, the impact of criminalisation on freedom of religion, the scope of a prohibition on conversion practices which covers transgender persons and the difficulty of forms of conduct that appear to fail to reach a threshold of significance. Section 4 examines the advantages of measures that go beyond the criminalisation of the principal perpetrators, such as the comprehensive support system envisaged under the law of Victoria, Australia, the potential offered by wider educational initiatives, the possibility of a denial of State support to organisations involved in conversion practices and the establishment of an offence covering failures in the supervision of the principal perpetrators. Section 5 provides concluding thoughts on these matters and reflects on the difficulties and opportunities likely to arise in legislation on conversion practices.

The term 'conversion therapy' is not free from controversy: 'therapy' indicates a process of healing and is inappropriate where efforts are concerned that seek to change sexual orientation or gender diversity – neither of which are illnesses. In this chapter, the preferred term is therefore that of 'conversion practice(s)' – a name that had been used inter alia in the law of Malta on that matter.[10]

2. The Phenomenon of Conversion Practices and State Reactions

Conversion practices are carried out by various providers: in a 2019 survey of LGBT persons in the UK, 19% of those who had undergone conversion

---

6 ILGA World, *Curbing Deception. A World Survey on Legal Regulation of So-Called 'Conversion Therapies'* (ILGA World 2020) 43–44. See also Independent Expert (n 3), para 53.
7 *Ibid.*, para 20.
8 British Psychological Society et al., 'Memorandum of Understanding on Conversion Therapy in the UK, Version 2' (October 2017) <www.bacp.co.uk/media/11738/mou2-reva-0421.pdf>.
9 Independent Expert (n 3) paras 59–74.
10 S. 2 Act No. LV [Affirmation of Sexual Orientation, Gender Identity and Gender Expression Act] 9 December 2016 ('the Maltese Act').

practices stated that a 'healthcare provider' or 'medical professional' had performed them; for 16%, it had been a relative or guardian; for 51%, a 'faith organisation or group'.[11] The techniques vary, too: in the same survey, it was noted that they 'can range from pseudo-psychological treatments to, in extreme cases, surgical interventions and "corrective" rape'.[12]

While persons subjected to conversion practices include adults and minors, a global 2019 survey suggests that 36.9% of those who had to undergo such change efforts were under 18 years of age; a further 45.2% were between 18 and 24 years old.[13]

The damaging effects of conversion practices on the health of their victims are reported to include, in addition to 'often significant physical pain and suffering' also 'significant loss of self-esteem, anxiety, depressive syndrome, social isolation, intimacy difficulty, self-hatred, shame and guilt, sexual dysfunction' and 'symptoms of post-traumatic stress disorder'[14] – as well as suicidal ideation.[15]

These consequences suggest that such practices can impact on a range of human rights. An exhaustive examination of all relevant rights is outside the scope of this chapter, but they certainly include the right to personal development, which, in the system of the European Convention on Human Rights (ECHR), is embraced by Article 8 (right to respect for private life).[16] The European Court of Human Rights (ECtHR) expressly referred to 'gender identification [...] sexual orientation and sexual life' as falling within the scope of that article.[17]

Conversion practices will regularly also have an effect on the right to health. In that regard, the UN Committee on Economic, Social and Cultural Rights noted in 2016 that a 'clear violation' of the rights of LGBT and intersex persons

---

11 UK Government, Equalities Office, National LGBT Survey: Summary Report (updated February 2019) <www.gov.uk/government/publications/national-lgbt-survey-summary-report/national-lgbt-survey-summary-report>.
12 *Ibid*. See also Christopher Romero, 'Praying for Torture: Why the United Kingdom Should Ban Conversion Therapy' (2019) 51 *George Washington International Law Review* 201, 209–210.
13 Amie Bishop, *Harmful Treatment. The Global Reach of So-Called Conversion Therapy* (OutRight Action International 2019) 42.
14 Independent Expert (n 3) para 55 with further references. See also, on potential harmful consequences, Jack Drescher, 'Ethical Concerns Raised When Patients Seek to Change Same-Sex Attractions' (2002) 5:3–4 *Journal of Gay & Lesbian Psychotherapy* 181, 192–193; Douglas C Haldeman, 'Therapeutic Antidotes: Helping Gay and Bisexual Men Recover from Conversion Therapies' *ibid*., 117, 118–120; Sanam Assil, 'Can You Work It: Or Flip It and Reverse It: Protecting LGBT Youth from Sexual Orientation Change Efforts' (2015) 21 *Cardozo JL & Gender* 551, 564–565.
15 Peer Briken et al., *Gutachten im Auftrag der Bundesstiftung Magnus Hirschfeld (BMH) zur Fragestellung von so genannten Konversionsbehandlungen bei homosexueller Orientierung* (Hamburg 2019) 25. See also Romero (n 12) 213–214.
16 ECtHR, *Pretty v United Kingdom* (Application no. 2346/02), Judgment, 29 April 2002, para 61.
17 *Ibid*.

to sexual and reproductive health existed where regulations required that 'they be "cured" by so-called "treatment"'.[18] The right to 'the highest attainable standard of physical and mental health' is enshrined in Article 12(1) of the 1966 International Covenant on Civil, Economic, Social and Cultural Rights (ICESCR). Certain health-related rights are likewise recognised under the ECHR system, in particular, the right to physical integrity and the right to personal autonomy, both within the scope of Article 8 ECHR.[19]

In 2019, the UN Special Rapporteur on Torture also noted that so-called 'conversion therapy', given the fact that it is capable of inflicting 'severe pain or suffering', can amount to torture or other cruel, inhuman or degrading treatment or punishment.[20] Beyond that, the Independent Expert observed that conversion practices are 'by their very nature degrading, inhuman and cruel and create a significant risk of torture'.[21] He also found that conversion practices are 'per se discriminatory', since they 'target a specific group on the exclusive basis of sexual orientation and gender identity, with the specific aim of interfering in their personal integrity and autonomy'.[22]

Where children are involved, the interests enshrined in the 1989 Convention on the Rights of the Child (CRC) require consideration, including the protection of children 'from all forms of physical or mental violence, injury or abuse' as well as from 'neglect or negligent treatment' (Art. 19(1) CRC), the need to preserve their identity (Art. 8(1) CRC) and their freedom from 'torture or other cruel, inhuman or degrading treatment or punishment' (Art. 37(a) CRC). In that regard, the UN Committee on the Rights of the Child urged States to take 'effective action to protect all lesbian, gay, bisexual, transgender and intersex adolescents from all forms of violence, discrimination or bullying by raising public awareness and implementing safety and support measures'.[23]

---

18 United Nations, Economic and Social Council, Committee on Economic, Social and Cultural Rights, *General Comment No. 22 (2016) on the Right to Sexual and Reproductive Health*, E/C.12/GC/22 (2 May 2016), para 23.
19 See ECtHR *Glass v United Kingdom* (Application no. 61827/00), Judgment, 9 March 2004, para 70; ECtHR, *VC v Slovakia* (Application no. 18968/07), Judgment, 8 November 2011, para 138.
20 United Nations, Special Rapporteur on Torture and Other Cruel, Inhuman or Degrading Treatment or Punishment, *Relevance of the Prohibition of Torture and Other Cruel, Inhuman or Degrading Treatment or Punishment to the Context of Domestic Violence* (12 July 2019), A/74/148, para 49; and see Romero (n 12) 214–219.
21 Independent Expert (n 3), para 83. See on this Article 7 of the International Covenant on Civil and Political Rights (ICCPR) and Article 3 ECHR.
22 Independent Expert (n 3) para 59.
23 Committee on the Rights of the Child, *General Comment No. 20 (2016) on the Implementation of the Rights of the Child During Adolescence*, CRC/C/GC/20 (6 December 2016) para 34. See also Ignatius Yordan Nugraha, 'The Compatibility of Sexual Orientation Change Efforts with International Human Rights Law' (2017) 35 *Netherlands Quarterly of Human Rights* 176, 183–189; Assil (n 14) 566–569, 577–579.

In light of such violations, it is understandable that criminalisation has at times been employed to address conversion practices. But there are additional aspects that can inform the legislative rationale.

For one, conversion practices not only concern the directly affected parties; they also exert a harmful societal influence. The very pathologisation of gender identity and sexual orientation conveys the message that LGBT persons fall short of a desirable standard, and thus facilitates their stigmatisation and discrimination.[24]

The impact of conversion practices on the reputation of health and medical services is likewise of concern. Society relies on the fact that the performance of services that are suggested with the appearance that they reflect recognised medical treatments is based on true representations. In that regard, conversion practices also affect the public interest in the prohibition of pseudo-medical treatments.

And yet, at the time of writing, criminalisation has taken place only in certain States. Among EU members, only two have resorted to such a prohibition (Malta and Germany).[25] Yet criminalisation is under debate in various jurisdictions: in Ireland, the relevant law is at Committee Stage in the Seanad;[26] in Canada, the House of Commons in June 2021 approved a bill that would provide for criminalisation;[27] New Zealand on 30 July 2021 introduced a corresponding bill.[28] Efforts to ban conversion practices are also under way in all constituent parts of the United Kingdom;[29] yet draft legislation has not yet been introduced.

With regard to the conduct in question, both the German and Maltese Acts ban the performance of conversion practices,[30] as do the Irish[31] and the Cana-

---

24 See also Bundestag-Drucksache (BT-DS) 19/17278 [19 Feb 2020] <https://dserver.bundestag.de/btd/19/172/1917278.pdf>, paras 11 and 17.
25 European Parliament, *Declaration of the EU as an LGBTIQ Freedom Zone* (11 March 2021) 2021/2557(RSP), P9_TA(2021)0089, at K.
26 The Irish Bill <https://data.oireachtas.ie/ie/oireachtas/bill/2018/39/eng/initiated/b3918s.pdf>.
27 House of Commons (Canada), Bill C-6, An Act to Amend the Criminal Code (Conversion Therapy) (22 June 2021) <https://parl.ca/Content/Bills/432/Government/C-6/C-6_3/C-6_3.PDF> ('the Canadian Bill').
28 Conversion Practices Prohibition Legislation Bill [New Zealand] <www.legislation.govt.nz/bill/government/2021/0056/latest/LMS487197.html>.
29 See, for England and Wales, Harry Farley, Eleanor Lawrie, 'What Is Conversion Therapy and When Will It Be Banned?' *BBC Online*, 11 May 2021 <www.bbc.co.uk/news/explainers-56496423>; for Northern Ireland, Colm Kelpie, 'Gay Conversion Ban: Therapy Is a "Humiliating and Harmful Practice"', *BBC Online*, 20 April 2021 <www.bbc.co.uk/news/uk-northern-ireland-56802428>; for Scotland, Scottish Government, *Programme for Government 2021–22* (Edinburgh 2021) 50 <www.gov.scot/publications/fairer-greener-scotland-programme-government-2021-22/documents/>. For Wales, see also Welsh Government, 'The Welsh Government Announces New Support Package for Pride', *Impact News Service*, 29 June 2021.
30 s. 2(1) of the Gesetz zum Schutz vor Konversionsbehandlungen vom 12. Juni 2020 (BGBl. I S. 1285) ('the German Act'); ss. 3(a)(i) and 3(a)(ii) of the Maltese Act.
31 cc. 2(a)(i) and 2(c)(i) of the Irish Bill.

dian bills[32] and the Victorian Act.[33] In addition to that, three further acts tend to be criminalised: the offering of such practices; arranging them or making a referral to another person to perform conversion practices; and advertising them.[34] The removal of a person from the relevant territory for the purposes of performing conversion practices on them is criminalised only in certain jurisdictions.[35]

3. The Evaluation of Conversion Practices Under Criminal Law: Challenges and Debate

While conversion practices have encountered international condemnation,[36] it is also true that a ban on the relevant conduct is not inevitably supported by all sectors of society.[37] Legislative initiatives in this field can therefore still encounter difficulties and invite an assessment of the relevant aspects of the practices and their consequences that are slated for criminalisation. The exact nature of these challenges depends on various parameters, including the particular societal context and the shape that debate on these practices has taken that far. But the difficulties that have arisen in the codification of pertinent laws as well as existing criticism in jurisdictions in which such a ban is being discussed allow for the indication of issues that are likely to form the topic of debate in efforts to subject conversion practices to legal evaluation.

3.1 The Question of Consent

A particular point of consideration is likely to be the role of the consent of the recipient of conversion practices. In existing laws on conversion practices, consent either receives express mention or retains a position whose significance is clarified through the context of the law.

The German law thus prohibits 'conversion treatment' on persons who have not yet reached the age of 18 years but also on adults whose consent for the performance of conversion practices is impaired,[38] with the grounds for

---

32 c. 5 of the Canadian Bill.
33 s. 9 of the Change or Suppression (Conversion) Practices Prohibition Act 2021 No. 3 of 2021 ('the Victorian Act').
34 ss. 3(a)(iii); 3(b)(i); 3(b)(ii); 3(iii) of the Maltese Act; s. 3 of the German Act; s. 13 of the Victorian Act; ss. 2(a)(ii); 2(c)(ii) of the Irish Bill.
35 See s. 9 Sexuality and Gender Identity Conversion Practices Act 2020, A2020–49 [Australian Capital Territory]; s. 12 of the Victorian Act; c. 3(5) of the Irish Bill.
36 See above at n 9, 18, 20; Independent Expert (n 3), para 20.
37 See, for the UK context, Harriet Sherwood, 'C of E Bishop Backs Prosecution of Those Who Defy "Gay Conversion" Ban' *Guardian*, 9 June 2021; Conor Matchett, 'Conversion Therapy a "Form of Torture", MSPs told' *Scotsman*, 7 September 2021.
38 s. 2(2) of the German Act.

impairment further outlined in the Explanatory Note.[39] Yet this also means that, where such impairment does not exist and consent has been given, conversion practices can still be performed. The Maltese Act, similarly, prohibits conversion practices when committed in a forced or involuntary manner,[40] but also when committed against a vulnerable person, with 'vulnerable person' being defined as persons under the age of 16 years, persons 'suffering from a mental disorder' and persons who are 'considered by the competent court to be particularly at risk' when certain conditions are taken into account.[41] Here, too, conversion practices could therefore be performed on persons who have given consent and are not deemed 'vulnerable persons'.

What these regulations reveal is the fact that 'consent' as a decisive factor for criminalisation has its limitations – otherwise, the lawmakers could have allowed it to stand as the sole border marker between permitted and criminalised conduct.[42] As it is, they grant protection also to certain persons who may have given consent. (And even with regard to this extended circle, controversy did not abate: the definition of 'vulnerable persons' has certainly courted debate.)[43]

Apart from that, the question of 'autonomous decisions' may itself require discerning assessment – especially in view of persons who experience conversion practices at the hands of faith organisations with which they have strong connections.[44] What is more: the fact must be taken into account that the protection of the immediate victims is not the only rationale for criminalisation. If that were the case, there would be no reason why an LGBT person could not, for instance, request a prayer meeting by the entire community to provide 'treatment', or even practices in front of the congregation that, were it not for the existence of consent, would be considered humiliating.[45] Yet, in situations of that kind, a clear message is sent out to the congregation at large that a certain sexual orientation or gender diversity falls short of expected standards – a message that thus allows the discriminatory character of conversion practices to materialise.

---

39 BT-DS 19/17278 (n 24) 2 and 17.
40 s. 3(a)(ii) of the Maltese Act.
41 s. 3(a)(i) and s. 2 at 'vulnerable person' of the Maltese Act.
42 On further difficulties regarding 'informed consent', see Michael Schroeder, 'Ethical Issues in Sexual Orientation Conversion Therapies: An Empirical Study of Consumers' (2002) 5:3–4 *Journal of Gay & Lesbian Psychotherapy* 131, 140–145.
43 See, on the controversy about the age limit in the German law, Bundestags-Drucksache 19/18768 (23 April 2020), 16, Änderungsantrag 2 (Left Party); <www.bundesgesundheitsministerium.de/fileadmin/Dateien/3_Downloads/Gesetze_und_Verordnungen/GuV/K/Konversionstherapienverbot_bf_Beschlussempfehlung_GE_AfGesundh.pdf> and *ibid*, 18, Änderungsantrag 1 (Green Party); BT-DS 19/17278 (n 24) 25, 28, 29. On the difficulty of restricting criminalisation to practices performed on minors, see James Taglienti, 'Therapists Behind Bars: Criminalizing Gay-to-Straight Conversion Therapy' (2021) 59:1 *Family Court Review* 185, 188.
44 Cf Butler-Sloss in *Re T (Adult: Refusal of Treatment)* [1993] Fam. 95, 120.
45 Cf Independent Expert (n 3), para 52.

Not every jurisdiction in which criminalisation was contemplated felt the need to exclude victims who had provided consent. The Irish Bill makes no such distinction: under its provisions, it would be unlawful for any person to perform conversion practices 'on a person'.[46] By so doing, the draft legislation also carries advantages with respect to the principle of legal certainty. The Irish Bill is comprehensive and simple: any form of conversion practices is prohibited – regardless of the person of the victim.

3.2 The Impact of Criminalisation on Freedom of Religion

When the possibility of a law against conversion practices was discussed in England and Wales, concern was voiced that religious ministers might be put 'in jeopardy when they preach, and church members [. . .] when they pray for each other'.[47] From a legal perspective, these difficulties relate to the impact that criminalisation may have on freedom of religion (a right recognised under Article 9 ECHR).

Freedom of religion, however, is not an unlimited right. Its 'internal dimension' – the right to 'hold any religious belief and to change religion or belief' is indeed held to be 'absolute and unqualified';[48] its 'external dimension', however – the right to manifest one's beliefs 'in worship, teaching, practice and observance' – has the capacity of having an impact on other persons;[49] and it is for that reason that the ECHR accepts certain restrictions to this aspect of the right.[50] Such restrictions are possible where they are prescribed by law and seek to protect a legitimate aim (including the rights of others).[51] In the parallel situation of freedom of expression – a right with similar restrictions –,[52] the ECtHR did consider State interference, where certain homophobic statements were involved, as serving the legitimate aim of protecting the reputation and rights of others.[53]

The relevant interference must be 'necessary in a democratic society' to protect the legitimate interest.[54] In this regard, the State has to strike a 'fair balance between the competing interests at stake'.[55] Where the criminalisation of conversion practices is concerned, the fact has to be taken into account that

---

46 c. 2(a)(i) of the Irish Bill.
47 Sherwood (n 37), with reference to the Evangelical Alliance.
48 ECtHR, *Eweida and Ors v United Kingdom* (Applications nos. 48420/10, 59842/10, 51671/10 and 36516/10), Judgment, 15 January 2013, para 80.
49 *Ibid.*
50 Art. 9(3) ECHR. See also Art. 18(3) ICCPR for the corresponding provision under that treaty.
51 Art. 9(3) ECHR and see Art. 18(3) ICCPR.
52 See Art. 10(2) ECHR; Art. 19(3) ICCPR.
53 ECtHR, *Vejdeland and Others v Sweden* (Application no. 1813/07) Judgment, 9 February 2012, para 49.
54 Art. 9(2) ECHR; similarly Art. 19(3) ICCPR.
55 ECtHR *Polat v Austria* (Application no. 12886/16), Judgment, 20 July 2021, para 91.

the holding of opinions is not outlawed – nor even the expression of views, however offensive, about LGBT persons. Conversion practices constitute a problem that is more severe. By their very nature, they accord LGBT persons lesser 'value' than their heterosexual and cisgender peers and work towards the destruction of those characteristics that mark their existence as a human group. The intended harm is therefore significant, while the impact of criminalisation on religious communities as a whole remains small – it is limited to the relevant acts that have an impact on LGBT persons.

Less restrictive means that would promise the same degree of effectiveness are not available. Information campaigns, as the German government noted, are not sufficient: in spite of the already existing warnings by scientific and psychotherapeutic associations against 'conversion treatment', the relevant practices are still being carried out.[56] Laws against conversion practices in the United States tend to focus on healthcare providers as perpetrators only,[57] which avoids the conflict with religious freedom altogether but is, for the same reason, an inadequate tool to counter the danger posed by conversion practices.[58]

It therefore does not appear that a ban on conversion practices constitutes undue interference with freedom of religion. The proportionality assessment lends, in this regard, further strength to the recommendation by the UN Special Rapporteur on Freedom of Religion or Belief in 2020 that States ensure that their 'legal protections for individuals to manifest their religion or belief [. . .] do not have the effect of denying [. . .] LGBT+ persons the right to non-discrimination or other rights'.[59]

3.3 The Application of the Law to Transgender Persons

A comprehensive ban on conversion practices that also covers efforts to change gender identity can likewise be expected to be a contentious issue: the lack of progress of legislation against conversion practices in England and Wales that far, for instance, has been explained by objections raised inter alia by 'gender-critical feminists and anti-trans groups'.[60]

---

56 BT 19/17278 (n 24), 12.
57 Bishop (n 13) 21.
58 See, on this point, Christy Mallory et al., *Conversion Therapy and LGBT Youth* (The Williams Institute 2018) 3 <https://williamsinstitute.law.ucla.edu/publications/conversion-therapy-and-lgbt-youth/>; BT-DS 19/17278 (n 24) 12. The inadequacy of such restricted measures is particularly clear when faith groups occupy a prominent place among providers of conversion practices, see above, at n 11.
59 Special Rapporteur on Freedom of Religion or Belief, *Gender-Based Violence and Discrimination in the Name of Religion or Belief*, A/HRC/43/48 (24 August 2020), para 76(a) and (f).
60 Tara John, 'Anti-Trans Rhetoric Is Rife in the British Media. Little Is Being Done to Extinguish the Flames' *CNN Wire*, 9 October 2021.

The existing laws on conversion practices do indeed tend to embrace methods that seek to change a person's 'gender identity'.[61] It is, however, at that point that the development of human rights law and aspects of the contemporary transgender debate can show a considerable degree of deviation.

As early as 1992 did the European Court of Human Rights in *B v France* find that the difficulties that the transsexual applicant encountered due to the lack of recognition of her gender in official documents had led to a situation, which was 'not compatible with the respect due to her private life'.[62] Ten years later, in *Goodwin*, the Court cast doubt on the 'chromosomal element' as being of 'decisive significance' for the legal attribution of gender identity.[63] In 2001, the ECtHR had already noted that Article 8 also embraced a right 'to identity and personal development' and that 'elements such as *gender identification*, name and sexual orientation are important elements of the personal sphere' that were protected by that provision.[64]

In view of these considerations, it would be difficult to reach any conclusion other than that gender identity is, under human rights law, seen in the same context as sexual orientation. The protective scope of the right to identity extends to this aspect of human existence and the need for its protection, as apparent in laws against conversion practices, is as strongly indicated in this case as in the case of practices targeting sexual orientation.

3.4 The Problem of 'de minimis' Infractions

A particular difficulty discussed in various jurisdictions may be described as the problem of '*de minimis*' conduct. In other words – should criminalisation proceed even when the relevant acts appear to have only minimal impact on the victims?

It is that question which comes into play when, for instance, the Bishop of Manchester, while generally supporting a ban on conversion practices, noted that he 'was not referring to "gentle, non-coercive prayer"'.[65] In Germany, a *de minimis* exclusion made it into the law: for parents and guardians, the law

---

61 See s. 2 of the Maltese Act at 'conversion practices'; s. 5(1)(a) of the Victorian Act; s. 1(1) of the German Act; see also c. 1 of the Irish Bill at 'conversion therapy'.
62 ECtHR, *B v France* (Application no. 13343/87), Judgment 25 March 1992, in particular paras 59, 62, 63.
63 ECtHR, *Christine Goodwin v United Kingdom* (Application no. 28957/95), Judgment 11 July 2002, para 82.
64 ECtHR, *PG and JH v United Kingdom* (Application no. 44787/98), Judgment 25 November 2001, para 56. Emphasis added.
65 Sherwood (n 37).

envisages criminalisation only if the practices amount to a 'gross neglect' of the duty of care or upbringing.[66]

Such exemptions have encountered criticism.[67] In Germany, the Federal Council advocated the complete removal of this exception, noting that conversion practices on children or young persons constituted severe interference with their physical and psychological integrity.[68]

Another problem of *de minimis* exceptions lies in the difficulty that attaches to the identification of parameters for their assessment. A certain subjectivity is unavoidable: the same practice may in the case of one victim be found to qualify as 'significant' but may be assessed quite differently in the case of another victim, inviting arbitrariness into the decision-making process.

It is a better approach to abandon efforts of resolving this difficulty at the level of substantive law and to address it instead in relation to criminal procedure. Criminalisation does not always mean that prosecution must follow, nor would that invariably be in the interests of the victims. There is therefore room for the inclusion of a measure of discretion: for instance, by making official investigation dependent on the decision of the victim and allowing *proprio motu* investigations by the prosecution only where this is indicated by the public interest in them. The advantage of this lies in the fact that in cases that appear to fall below that threshold, room is given to the victim's autonomy, allowing for investigation if, but only if, the victim considers this the appropriate course of action.

4. Criminalisation and Beyond: Towards a Comprehensive Law on Conversion Practices

Criminalisation certainly sends out a message of solidarity with the victims, but it does not by itself address the support requirements that arise in situations of that kind. Persons affected by conversion practices may need additional services, which are not embraced by the tools of criminal law – a point which has been addressed in arguably the most comprehensive manner by the State of Victoria, Australia (see 4.1) but which can be helpfully supplemented by wider educational initiatives (4.2) and a general ban on State support for organisations engaging in conversion practices (4.3). But even with regard to criminalisation itself, there is room for measures, which, while not typically included in existing laws on conversion practices, can helpfully contribute to the ending of such practices, especially where they are carried out in organisations marked by hierarchical relationships (4.4).

---

66 s. 5(2) of the German Act.
67 See Sherwood (n 37) regarding the Bishop of Manchester's position.
68 BT-DS 19/17278 (n 24), 25 and 26.

4.1 A Comprehensive Support System: The Victorian Commission

In addition to criminalisation, the Australian State of Victoria included in its law on conversion practices a 'Civil Response Scheme' whose regulation is impressive.[69] At the core of the Scheme is a raft of functions given to the Victorian Equal Opportunity and Human Rights Commission ('the Commission'), which also has the necessary powers to perform these tasks.[70] It can thus direct persons affected by conversion practices to 'appropriate support services' but also support victims 'to voluntarily report' such practices to the police.[71]

In addition to this, the Commission is obliged to receive reports about alleged conversion practices (which can be made by any person).[72] It has the power to request further information[73] and may adopt a number of options, including the offer of targeted education to persons or organisations reported to have engaged in these practices but also the offer of the 'facilitation of an outcome in relation to the matters in the report'.[74] It may, however, also refer the issue to other institutions, including the Ombudsman or the Victoria Police.[75] The Commission's response to reports 'should be informed by the needs and wishes of persons affected' by the conversion practices.[76]

The Commission may also, under certain circumstances, conduct an investigation into matters relating to the Victorian Act, which raise 'an issue that is serious in nature or indicates' conversion practices that are 'systemic or persisting'.[77] It has power to compel the provision of information or documents and to compel the attendance of a person to answer questions.[78] The outcome of such an investigation can be an agreement with a person about action required to comply with the Act, the acceptance of an enforceable undertaking (a written statement by which persons undertake to take certain actions or refrain from taking certain actions to comply with the Act) and the issuing of a compliance notice to a person (a notice setting out the date by which a person must take or refrain from taking specified actions).[79]

The particular benefit of this system lies in the fact that the Commission thus takes on many of the tasks which victims would otherwise have had to initiate

---

69 Part 3 of the Victorian Act.
70 s. 17 of the Victorian Act, in conjunction with s. 4, at 'Commission' and s. 4(1) of the Equal Opportunity Act (Victoria) (2010), at 'Commission'.
71 s. 17(1)(g) and (h) of the Victorian Act.
72 *Ibid.*, ss. 24(1) and 21(a).
73 *Ibid.*, s. 26.
74 *Ibid.*, ss. 28(1)(a) and (b).
75 *Ibid.*, s. 29.
76 *Ibid.*, s. 25(b).
77 *Ibid.*, s. 34.
78 *Ibid.*, ss. 36 and 37.
79 *Ibid.*, ss. 42, 43, 45.

themselves, thus limiting the potential of distress by re-visiting the relevant events. Coupled with the further options at its disposal, this provides a support structure which goes far beyond criminalisation, while the power to refer the matter to the Victoria Police shows that the Commission is hardly a toothless entity. It is a level of support that is rare in laws on conversion practices, and it sets a standard worth pursuing by other jurisdictions.

At the same time, there are aspects in which the Victorian system can usefully be complemented.

The guidance provided to victims, for instance, can be helpfully accompanied by the offer of legal advice on the available options (including remedies under private law). Such an offer is available in other jurisdictions: the website of the German Centre for Health Education indicates that advice on the legal situation is provided by the relevant hotline on conversion practices.[80]

The fact that conversion practices have caused substantial suffering in the past also indicates the need for the documentation of past conduct of that kind and of the role played by public and private organisations in this context. The Victorian Act refers in that regard only generally to research tasks which the Commission may carry out,[81] but when the German draft law was being discussed, the Federal Council suggested more specific measures directed at the historical appraisal and documentation of attempts to change sexual and gender identity.[82] The German government agreed to examine that proposal,[83] but the final version of the Act did not include any such measures.

4.2 Wider Educational Efforts

The importance of educational measures in the context of conversion practices can hardly be overstated. It is a prevailing lack of knowledge about conversion 'therapy' and its harmful effects but also about matters relating to sexual orientation and gender identity that must be held accountable for preparing the ground on which these practices thrive.

The outreach work done by charities and by prominent members of the LGBT community, such as the former professional rugby player Gareth Thomas, who has spoken to young people facing the difficulties of coming out,[84] and the actor Sir Ian McKellen, who talked to school students in a cam-

---

80 Federal Centre for Health Education, 'IDAHOBIT* 2022: BZgA-Initiative LIEBESLEBEN startet Telefonberatung zum Schutz vor Konversionsbehandlung' <www.bzga.de/presse/pressemitteilungen/2022-05-12-idahobit-2022-bzga-initiative-liebesleben-startet-telefonberatung-zum-schutz-vor-konver/>.
81 s. 19 of the Victorian Act.
82 BT-DS 19/17278 (n 24) 27.
83 *Ibid.*, 30.
84 Matthew Bell et al., 'The Pink List 2010' *Independent*, 1 August 2010.

paign against homophobia,[85] are examples of activities capable of reaching large audiences, including young LGBT persons who have concerns about asserting their sexual orientation or gender identity. It is expected that such outreach work is of particular importance in areas where vibrant and visible LGBT communities do not yet exist.

In the context of the German legislation, the Federal Council referred to the beneficial consequences of further educational measures and measures directed at the promotion of societal acceptance. It also highlighted the importance of an 'open and informed society which knows how to meet diversity with respect' when dealing with conversion practices.[86] In the Victorian Act, such measures are in part among the functions of the Commission, which is under an obligation to 'establish and undertake information and education programs' and to undertake informative and educational programmes with respect to 'any other matters relevant to the provisions' of the Act.[87]

Educational initiatives can be expected to be particularly effective if accompanied by engagement with relevant stakeholders.[88] The Magnus Hirschfeld Foundation, in its Final Report on the (then draft) German law, emphasised the importance of dialogue in this context, especially with churches and faith communities, and suggested the establishment and financing of a five-year project to initiate such dialogue and give it academic guidance.[89]

4.3 Denial of State Support

In his 2020 Report, the Independent Expert called on States, inter alia, to ensure that 'public funds are not used, directly or indirectly, to support' conversion practices.[90]

The problem of State involvement arises not only with regard to direct acts by State organs but also in view of public facilities that may be used for conversion practices and in view of the prioritised tax status that some organisations may enjoy, which allows them to fund such practices. A motion to withdraw preferable tax status to organisations that are involved in these practices had been suggested in the debate on the German law, but during the relevant vote in the Health Committee the suggestion did not find a majority.[91]

---

85 *Belfast Telegraph Online*, 'Sir Ian McKellen: Young People Don't Want Labels, Fluidity Is the Future'. 8 February 2018.
86 BT-DS 19/17278 (n 24) 26.
87 ss. 17(1) and 18 of the Victorian Act.
88 See also Independent Expert (n 3), para 87(e).
89 Bundesstiftung Magnus Hirschfeld (ed), *Abschlussbericht* (Berlin 2019) 265 <https://mh-stiftung.de/wp-content/uploads/Abschlussbericht_BMH_neu.pdf>.
90 Independent Expert (n 3), para 87(a).
91 BT-DS 19/18768 (n 43) 17, Änderungsantrag 6 (Left Party).

It was a missed opportunity. The withdrawal of tax benefits – and indeed, of any form of State funding – takes into account the character of larger organisations, some of whose officials may engage in the relevant conduct even where a central policy about such practices is absent. The potential loss of preferential financial status can create a meaningful incentive for organisations to keep a closer watch on the activities of their officials, to check whether their internal structures facilitate the performance of the relevant practices and to institute counteracting measures where that is indicated.

At the same time, States that allow organisations under whose umbrella conversion practices are carried out to keep their preferential tax status contribute to the maintenance of a system that makes such conduct possible, and thus appear to collude in the practices. A legislative ban on State support in any form for conversion practices is thus not an only important aspect of a comprehensive solution but is in the interest of the State itself: it minimises the risk of attracting State responsibility for the performance of the relevant practices.

4.4 A Supervisory Offence

The organisational structure of several providers, which may include an internal hierarchy of authority between its officials, puts another problem in focus. It concerns the fact that responsibility for these cases lies not only with the principal perpetrators but also with those to whose charge the supervision of officials is entrusted. These concerns indicate the need for a solution that, in the field of criminalisation, provides measures that target the responsibility for their supervisory failures. A bishop might thus attract responsibility for allowing the carrying out of conversion practices by a priest, where the supervision of the latter's action falls within his remit.

This is not a step that appears to have been taken by jurisdictions criminalising conversion practices that far. Yet it is clear that the establishment of such an offence corresponds to a need and would make a helpful contribution to efforts to address the relevant practices, especially where the underlying acts are carried out within larger organisations.

At the same time, as the relevant offence targets an aspect that differs from direct perpetration, it seems appropriate to reflect this distinction at the level of the subjective element of the crime. It is suggested that the standard established in Article 28(a) of the Statute of the International Criminal Court (ICCSt) for command responsibility constitutes a useful basis for supervisory offences in the field of conversion practices as well. Under that provision, liability requires that the superior 'knew or, owing to the circumstances at the time, should have known' that subordinates 'were committing or about to commit' the relevant crimes. This standard is lower than that which would arguably be required of principal perpetrators (a circumstance which can be taken into account at sentencing level). But it corresponds to the particular blameworthiness of the offence, which focuses on the negligence of the superior.[92]

5. Concluding Thoughts

The need for criminalisation has been highlighted by various parties who are concerned by the phenomenon of conversion practices, but arguments advanced by opponents to the ban and difficulties that arose in other jurisdictions also point to challenges that await legislation in this field. Contentious points are likely to include the role of victim consent, the concern that criminalisation may have an impact on freedom of religion, the inclusion of gender identity in the relevant law as well as its extension to '*de minimis*' infractions.

Often enough, a reflection on the rationale underlying criminalisation can help in the evaluation of these issues. It helps, in particular, to reposition claims both on the role that individual consent should carry and allegations regarding the lack of significance of certain conversion practices. The validity of both points is restricted from the outset, as the purpose of the relevant criminalisation goes beyond the protection of the immediate victims, but also addresses the discriminatory message these practices disseminate to society as a whole.

In other instances, a consideration of applicable human rights mechanisms provides an understanding that helps to address the challenges. From that perspective, for instance, it is clear that gender identity enjoys the same protection as sexual orientation, while freedom of religion is subjected to restrictions that apply when certain conditions are fulfilled.

At the same time, the design of legislative responses to conversion practices also allows a reflection on solutions that have been found in the past, with some of the most advanced laws going some way in providing a comprehensive support system for victims of conversion practices. The 'Civil Response Scheme' enacted in Victoria has been mentioned as an example that sets standards which other legislatures may endeavour to attain. Wider educational efforts are of similar use: outreach initiatives in particular can provide valuable information about LGBT matters and forestall the conditions that allow conversion practices to thrive.

At the same time, there is room for efforts that go further in addressing the problem. The prohibition of State support for these practices, for instance, renders particularly effective help – especially, where such a ban includes indirect

---

92 It is not suggested that the higher standard for civilian commanders (Art. 28(b)(i) ICCSt) is taken as a basis. That standard is fulfilled only if the superior 'knew, or consciously disregarded information which clearly indicated, that the subordinates were committing or about to commit such crimes'. That, however, would raise the standard of proof for the prosecution to a worrying degree and run counter to the conception of the crime as providing an incentive to establish and follow a system of effective supervision.

help as well, such as financial support to organisations that allow conversion practices to be carried out by their officials. Instruments of criminal law, too, can take the organisational structure of the providers into account – for instance, by establishing an offence which targets the responsibility of superiors for acts of subordinates.

In the evaluation of conversion practices and their harmful consequences, it is the medical profession that has taken the lead – critical statements by organisations in the healthcare sector on the relevant practices can be traced back at least to the beginning of this century.[93] By comparison, the task of evaluating the relevant practices from a legal perspective may seem overwhelming, especially when public controversy can be expected to arise. Yet it is one which no jurisdiction seeking to comply with the Independent Expert's Recommendations can avoid.[94] And there is reason to draw courage from the fact that lawmakers do not have to start at nil: existing laws and their *travaux préparatoires* provide valuable insights not only into the challenges that they encountered but also into solutions they devised. At the same time, a reflection on the rationale for legislation can be of help again and may even inspire legislation that transcends existing efforts to address the problem. The initiative to enact a comprehensive law thus not only gives its creators the chance to formulate a strong reaction to the harm and injustice endured by the victims. It also hands the lawmakers the opportunity to declare that discrimination of LGBT persons will not be tolerated and that the State is willing to work with education where possible, with criminalisation where necessary, to make sure that it does not provide the soil on which such practices can grow.

---

93 See e.g. American Psychiatric Association, 'Therapies Focused on Attempts to Change Sexual Orientation (Reparative or Conversion Therapies)' (March 2000) <https://web.archive.org/web/20110407082738/www.psych.org/Departments/EDU/Library/APAOfficialDocumentsandRelated/PositionStatements/200001.aspx>.
94 Independent Expert (n 3), para 87.

Part 5

Faith and Justice
Religion and the LGBT Community

Chapter 20

Between Understanding and Inclusion

Religious Perspectives

Paul Behrens and Sean Becker

Religions tend to mirror the human condition of the societies in which they take root. That they thus incorporate aspects that intersect with areas of LGBT life should not be a surprise.

And yet, the relationship between religion and LGBT concerns can hardly be described as one which had been untroubled throughout its history. The fact that opposition to LGBT rights was often led by religious groups or utilised religious arguments – be it on the decriminalisation of same-sex activities,[1] LGBT-inclusive education[2] or same-sex marriage[3] – has contributed to that.

At the same time, the portrayal of the LGBT community and religious groups as opposing 'others' would amount to the simplification of a matter that is considerably more complex.

For one, if it is correct to recall objections by certain faith groups to LGBT rights, it is equally legitimate to note that others stood with the LGBT community at a time when this attracted animosity. Even before Stonewall, the Metropolitan Community Church gave space to LGBT members to worship,[4] and as early as 1971 did the Australian Quakers advocate a change in the law 'to eliminate discrimination against homosexuals'.[5] In the following year, Beth Chayim Chadashim was founded – 'the world's first synagogue by and for gay and lesbian Jews'.[6]

---

1 See references in *Dudgeon v United Kingdom* (Application no. 7525/76) Judgment, 22 October 1981, para 25.
2 *BBC News*, 'LGBT Teaching Row: Birmingham Primary School Protests Permanently Banned'. 26 November 2019 <www.bbc.co.uk/news/uk-england-birmingham-50557227>.
3 Rose French and Rachel E Strassen-Berger, 'Bishops Begin Fight for Marriage Vote' *Star Tribune* (Minneapolis), 15 October 2011.
4 Lindsay McIntosh, 'Clergyman Who Is Putting the Case for Gay Marriage', *The Times*, 1 October 2011.
5 Canberra and Region Quakers, 'Quakers and Same-Sex Attracted People' <https://actquakers.org.au/same-sex-marriages/>.
6 Beth Chayim Chadashim, 'Shalom!' <www.bcc-la.org/>.

DOI: 10.4324/9781003286295-26

It is true, too, that in many religious communities, the debate on LGBT issues is far from concluded. After the Catholic Congregation for the Doctrine of the Faith, for instance, had taken position against the blessing of same-sex couples, two priests launched an initiative in Germany, which, in May 2021, led to blessings of same-sex couples in more than a hundred German Catholic congregations.[7] The Church of Scotland, in 2018, voted for the drafting of new laws to allow the performance of same-sex marriage by its ministers;[8] the Church of England opposes it.[9] In 2018, the participation of an Islamic cleric in an exorcism to try to 'cure' a person of their homosexuality was reported;[10] yet in 2019, the Central Council of Muslims in Germany issued a statement on the proposed ban on conversion practices, in which it expressly supported protection of homosexual citizens against discrimination.[11]

Nor are these divides limited to questions of doctrine. A religious group without LGBT members would be a rarity, and a development that can be expected to gain increasing force is their increased visibility – including that of persons who hold official positions within their faith group. For those who come out in their communities, intersectionality is not a theoretical concept but a lived reality, and their path is not always an easy one.

The chapters in this part are dedicated to questions that have arisen on particular matters of LGBT concern in Judaism, Christianity and Islam.

Chapter 21 (Solomon and Holtschneider) engages with Jewish approaches to gender and sexuality. It explores the way in which principles underpinning various Jewish religious movements have affected their treatment of these matters and analyses texts from the Jewish marriage ceremony to demonstrate how such understandings have changed as our perception of humanity evolved.

Chapter 22 (Burbach) analyses several key approaches to tradition in the literature around transgender issues in Catholic theology. It argues that some approaches raise profound methodological difficulties, which challenge the ability of the norms of inquiry embodied in the figure of 'orthodoxy' to guide research in this area. It responds by looking to Pope Francis's apostolic exhortation, *Evangelii Gaudium*, for theological resources to cope with the problems arising from these difficulties.

---

7 *Deutsche Welle*, 'Katholische Gemeinden feiern die Segnung homosexueller Paare'. 10 May 2021 <www.dw.com/de/katholische-gemeinden-feiern-die-segnung-homosexueller-paare/a-57485621>.
8 Press Association, 'Church of Scotland to Draft New Same-Sex Marriage Laws' *The Guardian*, 19 May 2018.
9 *BBC News*, 'Same-Sex Marriage: Church of England "Should Not Change Stance"'. 27 January 2017 <www.bbc.co.uk/news/uk-38768217>.
10 Tasha Wibawa and Erwin Renaldi, 'Islamic Exorcisms Used as Conversion Therapy as Indonesian City Moves Against LGBT Population' *ABC (Australia)*, 5 December 2018. <www.abc.net.au/news/2018-12-06/indonesia-lgbtqi-conversion-therapy/10576900>.
11 Zentralrat der Muslime, 'Stellungnahme zum Entwurf eines Gesetzes zum Schutz vor Konversionsbehandlungen', 18 December 2019.

Chapter 23 (Dalton) explores the danger of marginalisation that LGBT Muslims in the UK face, who, in spite of anti-discrimination laws, may experience alienation from the mainstream Muslim and the predominantly white LGBT community alike. It deals with the difficulty of LGBT Muslims to find a space in which their 'authentic' self can develop and in which Islam and their sexuality can be reconciled.

Chapter 21

Jewish Approaches to LGBT+ in Texts, Culture and Ritual

Rabbi Mark L. Solomon and Hannah Holtschneider

A couple approach their rabbi to discuss their wedding plans. They are both very excited about arranging their wedding. It is the rabbi's job to guide the couple through the Jewish ceremony, and, acting as registrar, the rabbi is there to satisfy the requirements of civil law in Scotland.[1] The rabbi ushers the spouses-to-be into their study and invites them to share their thoughts about their forthcoming nuptials. Aside from settling a date, time and venue, the rabbi has a number of questions to ask, which relate to the distinctly Jewish aspects of this union.

Depending on the Jewish religious movement in question, the rabbi and the couple sitting in the rabbi's study can be very different as will be the requirements for marriage. We present you with two scenarios from two different Jewish religious movements: a heterosexual cis-gender couple who are getting married under the auspices of the Orthodox United Synagogue and a same-sex couple who are members of a Liberal Synagogue.

In the first scenario, a key concern of the rabbi will be to establish the legal Jewish credentials of the couple. This will require them to present him[2] with documentary proof that their mothers were Jewish, usually by producing the ketubot (marriage contracts; singular ketubah) of their mothers from a recognised Orthodox synagogue,[3] or proof that they themselves converted through an Orthodox Beit Din (rabbinic court). If the mothers' ketubot are not available, they could bring their grandmothers', along with birth certificates to prove the relationship. Failing that, the rabbi will make other, exhaustive enquiries to ensure that they are eligible for a Jewish marriage.[4] The rabbi will also insist

---

1 In Scotland, the officiating rabbi acts as registrar and legalises the marriage by signing the Marriage Schedule. In England and Wales, this function is normally performed by the synagogue's Marriage Secretary. Occasionally, the rabbi acts as Marriage Secretary.
2 As of 2019, there are not yet any female Orthodox rabbis in Britain, although women are just beginning to be ordained in the USA and Israel by some on the extreme liberal fringe of Orthodoxy.
3 Proof of the parents' Jewish marriage in a non-Orthodox synagogue would not in itself be sufficient to establish their Jewish status for Orthodox purposes since Progressive (Reform or Liberal) movements use different criteria to determine a person's Jewish status. Progressive conversions are not accepted by Orthodox authorities; therefore, if someone's mother had had such a conversion, the child would not be regarded as Jewish. Some Progressive movements accept patrilineal Jewish status, which is also rejected by the Orthodox.
4 In addition, a *kohen* (descendant of the ancient priestly clan) may not marry a divorcee or a convert, while a person born of an adulterous or incestuous relationship (known as a *mamzer*) may *only* marry another such person or a convert. These restrictions are rejected in Progressive Judaism.

DOI: 10.4324/9781003286295-27

that the bride-to-be immerses in a ritual bath prior to the wedding to cleanse herself of menstrual impurity. He will probably ask the couple to attend a short course of preparation for marriage, which will focus largely on the laws of 'family purity', that is, the monthly abstinence from sex during and for a week after the wife's period.

The Liberal rabbi, too, can only solemnise a legal marriage for two Jews but will usually accept the couple's verbal assurance that they are Jewish. If one of them is not, the rabbi might nevertheless conduct a Jewish blessing for them (after their civil marriage), including some of the Jewish wedding customs. He or she[5] will explain that Progressive Judaism now welcomes LGBT+ couples and offers a wedding ceremony identical in all essentials to a traditional heterosexual marriage. They will be offered the chance to tailor their ceremony to their own taste, with a choice of terminology – 'bride and bride' or 'groom and groom', or perhaps 'loving companions' or 'partners' if they want to be less gender-specific or wish to avoid the traditional patriarchal vocabulary of marriage.

We have deliberately chosen to present examples, which expose stark contrasts between the religious ideologies. We have done so to enable us to delineate clear differences in approaches to questions of sexuality and gender. Between these extremes, there is shared ground in negotiating sexual and gender identities in relation to religious tradition and wider social norms. While Orthodox Jewish movements are slower to change, the guidance on homosexuality in Jewish schools issued by the current Chief Rabbi of the United Hebrew Congregations of the Commonwealth, Ephraim Mirvis, in 2018 offers a welcome opportunity to reflect on the potential for change within mainstream and conservative traditionalist Orthodoxy.[6] Liberal Jewish movements are quicker to adopt changes to Jewish tradition in tandem with, or in response to, wider social change, but it would be short-sighted to underestimate the persistence of negative attitudes to LGBT+ identities.[7] It is important to bear in mind that there is variation within all Jewish religious movements and that arguments for

---

5 Women rabbis have been ordained in the Progressive movements in Britain since 1975. As of 2019, there are approximately equal numbers of male and female rabbis in the Reform and Liberal movements, as well as around 15 lesbian and gay rabbis and one transgender rabbi.
6 Ephraim Mirvis, *The Wellbeing of LGBT+ Pupils: A Guide for Orthodox Jewish Schools* (KeshetUK 2018) <https://chiefrabbi.org/wp-content/uploads/2018/09/The-Wellbeing-of-LGBT-Pupils-A-Guide-for-Orthodox-Jewish-Schools.pdf> (accessed 17 July 2019).
7 In 1996, the announcement by a leading lesbian Reform rabbi that she was to conduct a 'covenant of love' ceremony for two women led to an unexpected and heated controversy, nearly splitting the Reform movement. Up to that point, Reform Judaism had taken a lead in the acceptance and inclusion of LGBT+ people, so the outpouring of homophobic discourse was shocking. This led, after much painful discussion, to a decision that the Reform movement would give no sanction to such ceremonies but would not expel those who participated in them. Since 2012, the movement has revised its view and now supports equal marriage. See Elli Tikvah Sarah, *Trouble-Making Judaism* (David Paul Books 2012) 25–27, 282–289; and a concise account of the events in Jonathan Romain and David Mitchell, *Inclusive Judaism: The Changing Face of an Ancient Faith* (Jessica Kingsley 2020) 176–180.

a better understanding of human sexuality and the embrace of LGBT+ identities can be found in Orthodox Judaism as well.[8]

Where do these different understandings of marriage originate? And how do they relate to the foundational texts constituting the Jewish people and which remain fundamental to Jewish religious self-understanding today? To answer these questions, we will firstly establish the textual tradition on sexuality and its expression, which forms the basis of Jewish religious thought. Secondly, we will outline how the intellectual and religious principles underpinning different Jewish religious movements (Orthodox, Conservative, Reform, Liberal) affect the interpretation of foundational texts and the engagement with gender and sexuality beyond heteronormativity. And finally, we will outline how non-Orthodox Jewish movements have taken new approaches to the social institution of marriage and its expression in wedding rituals.

1. Sexuality and the Jewish Textual Tradition

The Hebrew Bible presupposes that there are two genders that map onto two biologically different human bodies: male and female.[9] These are understood to be complementary in their social roles, which are derived from their biological sex. Elaborated in biblical and post-biblical interpretation, man and woman form a union for the bearing and raising of children (Genesis 1:28; 9:2), and marriage is the only socially accepted context for sexual activity. While it was biblically acceptable for a marriage to be constituted by the sexual act, and for a man to divorce his wife at will, post-biblical rabbinic Judaism instituted a social safeguard for the welfare of women and children: the *ketubah* (marriage contract/divorce settlement).[10] The *ketubah* ensured that even though divorce

---

[8] For one important example, see the 'Statement of Principles' of 2010 <http://statementofprinciplesnya.blogspot.com/> (accessed 29 August 2019), signed by leading Modern Orthodox rabbis. See also Chaim Rapoport, *Judaism and Homosexuality: An Authentic Orthodox View* (Vallentine Mitchell 2004). This book argues for a compassionate and nuanced pastoral approach to gay people, recognising that the traditional advice for gay men to marry a woman is potentially very harmful; that a demand for celibacy is rarely realistic; that being in a stable relationship is the safest and healthiest option for men who cannot remain celibate; and that masturbation is, after all, not the most terrible of sins. The book was endorsed with a foreword by then Chief Rabbi Jonathan Sacks.

[9] Rabbinic legal literature contains extensive discussion of biological gender variance, under the categories of *androginos* (intersex; both male and female genitalia), *tumtum* (no external genitalia), *saris* (literally eunuch, but including men with marked 'feminine' characteristics, presumed to be sterile from birth) and *aylonit* (women sterile from birth, with marked 'masculine' characteristics). The key texts are *Tosefta Bikkurim* 2 (*Mishnah Bikkurim* 4) and *Bavli Yevamot* 81a–84a. See Charlotte Elisheva Fonrobert, 'Regulating the Human Body: Rabbinic Legal Discourse and the Making of Jewish Gender' in Charlotte Elisheva Fonrobert and Martin S. Jaffee (eds), *The Cambridge Companion to the Talmud and Rabbinic Literature* (Cambridge University Press 2007) 270–294. Fonrobert argues that the rabbis' concern is to map these physical variants onto a predetermined binary legal gender template.

[10] Rabbinic tradition attributes this reform to the Pharisaic sage Simeon ben Shetach, 1st century BCE; see *Yerushalmi Ketubot* 8:11, 32c.

could only be instigated by the husband, his wife was due a material settlement for herself and her children, which ensured their economic and social survival.[11]

Jewish tradition generally has positive attitudes towards sex within marriage, recognising mutual pleasure and avoidance of sin as reasons for sex beyond the goal of procreation.[12] The rabbis of the Talmud, the major compendium of post-biblical rabbinic discussion that seeks to make sense of biblical tradition in a changing world, frankly discuss sexual relations within marriage, prohibiting marital rape, prescribing frequent intercourse as a woman's marital right and advising husbands to ensure that their wives experience orgasm.[13] Written from a patriarchal, heteronormative perspective, Talmudic discussion places firm boundaries around what is permitted and seeks to contain both male and female sexual urges within the tightly prescribed context of marriage.

The Hebrew Bible primarily knows of male homosexuality, and the following two biblical verses form the basis of subsequent rabbinic discussion: 'And you shall not lie with a male as one lies with a woman – it is an abomination (to'evah)' (Leviticus 18:22)[14] and 'And a man who lies with a male as one lies with a woman – they have both done an abomination. They shall surely be put to death; their blood is upon them (Leviticus 20:13)'.[15]

Traditional Jewish interpretation since rabbinical times focuses on sexual acts between two men and defines the prohibition in Leviticus 18:22 as restricted to anal intercourse, both active and passive.[16] Other homosexual acts are rabbinically forbidden but not on pain of death.[17] Reasons for these prohibitions are

---

11 For the legal history, see Ze'ev Falk, *Introduction to Jewish Law of the Second Commonwealth, Part 2* (Brill 1978) 295–304. For the ethical intent of the law, see Eliezer Berkovits, *Not in Heaven: The Nature and Function of the Halakhah* (Ktav 1983) 33–37.
12 Michael L. Satlow, *Jewish Marriage in Antiquity* (Princeton University Press 2001) 3–41.
13 See Rabbi Mark L. Solomon, 'Sexuality' in Nicholas de Lange and Miri Freud-Kandel (ed), *Modern Judaism: An Oxford Guide* (Oxford University Press 2005) 401f., for source references.
14 The leading Leviticus scholar Jacob Milgrom, in *Leviticus 17–22* (Doubleday 2000) 1569, makes the radical suggestion that the law in 18:22, which occurs in the context of a list of heterosexual incest prohibitions, only applied to corresponding homosexual acts of incest – that is, with male members of one's own family.
15 The Talmud considers male anal intercourse to be forbidden to non-Jews also, as part of the 'Seven Laws of the Sons of Noah', based on Genesis 2:24, 'Therefore shall a man [. . .] cleave to his wife', where the word 'cleave' is construed to imply 'and not to a male' (*Bavli Sanhedrin* 58a). Rashi *ad loc.* comments that, since the passive partner derives no pleasure, there can be no true 'cleaving' – an assertion with which many, who have more experience of this than Rashi presumably did, might beg to differ.
16 See *Bavli Sanhedrin* 54a-b. The death penalty, while biblically mandated, was frowned upon by some of the leading rabbis of antiquity (*Mishnah Makkot* 1:10) and has not been practised in Judaism for nearly 2,000 years. It is nevertheless treated as a marker of the severity of the sins concerned.
17 This is the dominant legal view; the codifier Moses Maimonides sees other homosexual acts other than anal intercourse as biblically prohibited, although not capital offences; see Rapoport (n 8) 2 and his detailed footnotes analysing the sources 140–142.

advanced in the Talmud, but homosexuality is not frequently discussed because it was understood as a largely non-Jewish vice.[18] When the Talmud does offer discussion, we find the argument that *to'evah* (abomination; abhorrence) means *to'eh attah bah*, 'you go astray by it.'[19] Later commentators offer several interpretations of this: (1) because it is 'against nature', that is, against the way the body is built, and the passive male partner is assumed to derive no pleasure from penetration;[20] (2) because it causes men to desert their wives in favour of other men;[21] (3) or because it does not lead to procreation.[22] Rabbinic discussion has no knowledge of a relatively fixed sexual orientation, which manifests at least from puberty onwards and is consistent throughout a person's adult life. Rather, biblical and talmudic discussion is only concerned with prohibited actions and behaviours.

Lesbianism is never mentioned in the Bible, but when the rabbis commented on Leviticus 18:3, in an early work of *halakhic midrash* (close reading of the biblical text to extrapolate detailed legal rulings), they not only brought the notion of sex between women into the picture, but they explained that the people of Israel were prohibited from following the 'laws' of Egypt and Canaan because in those societies 'a man would marry a man and a woman would marry a woman'.[23] Two talmudic passages discuss whether 'women who rub [against one another]', understood as lesbian activity, have acquired the status of 'harlots' and might be barred from marrying into the priestly caste, and concludes that this is not the case.[24] Since neither penile penetration nor ejaculation is involved, lesbianism is discussed far less than male homosexuality, to the point that it is largely invisible.[25] The legal consensus is that women who engage in lesbian acts have not transgressed a biblical commandment but have nevertheless acted lewdly and should be disciplined.[26]

---

18 *Bavli Qiddushin* 82a, where the majority ruling that two bachelors may sleep under one blanket is explained by the claim that 'Israelites are not suspected of homosexual intercourse'. The rabbis seem to have regarded the Graeco-Roman world, on the other hand, as a 'hotbed of homosexuality' that presented a constant danger to Jewish men and boys, especially those captured as slaves (see e.g. *Mishnah Horayot* 3:7 on redeeming male slaves who are in danger of violation, *Tosefta Avodah Zarah* 3:2 on leaving Jewish children in the care of gentiles, and narratives of slaves violated in *Bavli Gittin* 58a).
19 *Bavli Nedarim* 51a. This uses a rabbinic hermeneutical technique called *notarikon*, which treats a biblical word as shorthand for a longer phrase.
20 Rashi to *Bavli Sanhedrin* 58a, see (n 15) above; *Torah Temimah* to Leviticus 18:22.
21 *Tosafot* to *Nedarim* 51a, *Rosh* (R. Asher b. Yechiel) *ad loc*.
22 *Pesiqta Zutarta* to Leviticus 18:22, *Sefer ha-Ḥinukh*, commandment 209. This is the rationale most commonly invoked today and eloquently advanced by former Chief Rabbi Jonathan Sacks, *Tradition in an Untraditional Age: Essays on Modern Jewish Thought* (Vallentine Mitchell 1990) 169–170.
23 *Sifra, Acharey Mot* 9:8.
24 *Bavli Yevamot 76a* and *Shabbat* 65a; Rashi *ad loc*.
25 For the effect of this invisibility, see the sources in the next footnote.
26 See Maimonides, *Mishneh Torah*, Laws of Forbidden Intercourse 21:8. For full discussion, see Rebecca Alpert, *Like Bread on a Seder Plate: Jewish Lesbians and the Transformation of Tradition* (Columbia

The preceding interpretations of human sexuality are bound to a context in which homosexuality was socially taboo and its prohibition did not require justification. However, the 20th century brought about a more complex discourse about human sexuality and sexual orientation, particularly since the social and sexual revolution of the 1960s and 1970s.

2. Modern Understandings of Sexuality and Their Impact on Jewish Religious Life

Contemporary understandings of sexuality rely on a complex interplay of emotions, physical reactions and social teachings, which enable us to make sense of our feelings and express our sexuality. Interpretations of gender roles and reproduction play into the social context in which sexuality is discussed and performed. The majority of adults are attracted to the opposite sex, and heterosexuality continues to be promoted as socially normative; other sexual orientations and self-understandings remaining the exception.[27] While LGBT+ identities now enjoy partial legal equality in most liberal democracies – an equality based on scientific evidence of the givenness of sexual orientation – full social acceptance is a much slower process in a continued heteronormative cultural environment.

2.1 Jewish Reinterpretations of Homosexuality

Following the legalisation of male homosexual intercourse between consenting adults in 1967 and the Stonewall Riots of 1969 bringing the movement for gay liberation into the centre of society, Jewish movements also moved discussion of homosexuality into the mainstream. The leading American Modern Orthodox Rabbi Norman Lamm critically evaluates the traditional reasons for the prohibition, listed earlier, and finds them unpersuasive.[28] He resorts to what he considers the original meaning of *to'evah* (abhorrence) and concludes that anal intercourse is forbidden simply because it is viscerally disgusting. He then advances the notion, well known in medical and psychological literature since the 19th century, that homosexuality is a 'sickness', seeing the sexual act as an outcome of this 'affliction'. Hence, the 'sinner' is to be understood to have diminished responsibility and needs to be treated with compassion, while

---

University Press 1997) 17–35. See also Sarah (n 7), and 'Judaism and Lesbianism: A Tale of Life on the Margins of the Text' in Jonathan Magonet (ed), *Jewish Explorations of Sexuality* (Berghahn Books 1995) 158–166.

27 J. Michael Bailey, Paul Vasey, Lisa Diamond, Stephen Breedlove, Eric Vilain, and Marc Epprecht, 'Sexual Orientation, Controversy, and Science' (2016) 17:2 *Psychological Science in the Public Interest* 45–101.

28 Norman Lamm, 'Judaism and the Modern Attitude to Homosexuality' in *Encyclopaedia Judaica Yearbook 1974* (Keter 1974) 194–205.

the 'sin' (gay sex) is to be strongly condemned. Lamm, then president of the Orthodox Yeshiva University in New York, inadvertently perhaps, moved the discussion along by making it obvious that his own, subjective, 'visceral' reaction becomes the arbiter of textual interpretation, rather than any objective criteria that can be applied to traditional texts. Since then, the notion that non-heterosexual orientations are 'sickness' has largely been abandoned within Orthodoxy, owing again to better understanding of the unalterable nature of sexual orientation.

Instead, we find a return to the behaviour-based approach of Jewish tradition, which regards homosexual acts as sinful. Many contemporary Orthodox rabbis have embraced the notion that sexual desire cannot be controlled, but that behaviour can be, so that forbidden sexual acts must be avoided.[29] Yet, while homosexual acts are understood as sinful, they are seen as no more so than many other transgressions, such as driving on the Sabbath (which is also, theoretically, punishable by death), and that gay people should be welcomed in synagogues just like everyone else. Some gay Orthodox Jews adhere to the biblical prohibition of anal intercourse but allow themselves to transgress the rabbinical prohibition of other acts of gay sexual intimacy.[30] Most Orthodox Jewish movements hold fast to traditional heteronormativity, but some parts of the community are able to embrace LGBT+ Jews more easily than others.[31]

Outwith Orthodoxy, some Jewish religious movements argue that *halakhah* (Jewish law) needs to change to accommodate new scientific insights into human sexual orientation, just as it has changed in response to other scientific and technological developments.[32] Conservative, Reform, Liberal and Reconstructionist Jewish movements offer different ways of relating *halakhah* to wider social and intellectual influences, and embrace the opportunities and freedoms offered by modern societies. For Conservative Jews, *halakhah* continues to be a primary factor in the interpretation of new scientific and social developments. Therefore, the Conservative movement is concerned to find ways of recognising within *halakhah* the scientifically established fact that sexual orientation is unalterable.[33] Reform, Liberal and Reconstructionist[34] move-

---

29 See, for example, Jonathan Sacks (then Chief Rabbi of the United Hebrew Congregations of the Commonwealth) in his foreword to Rapoport (n 8) ix.
30 For discussion of this, see Steven Greenberg, *Wrestling with God and Men: Homosexuality in the Jewish Tradition* (University of Wisconsin Press 2004) 227, 238–250.
31 See (n 8).
32 For a pioneering example, see Herschel J. Matt, 'Sin, Crime, Sickness or Alternative Life-Style? A Jewish Approach to Homosexuality' (1978) 27:1 *Judaism* 27, 13–24.
33 For the range of views in Conservative Judaism, see Kassel Abelson and David J. Fine (ed), *Responsa 1991–2000, the Committee on Jewish Law and Standards of the Conservative Movement* (The Rabbinical Assembly 2002) 612–729.
34 For British Reform, see Romain and Mitchell (n 7) 163–188. For British Liberal Judaism, see Pete Tobias, *Liberal Judaism: A Judaism for the Twenty-First Century* (Liberal Judaism 2007) 197. For American Reform, see the Union of Reform Judaism, Gay and Lesbian Jews, 2020 <https://

ments place greater weight on the evolution of Jewish tradition in response to social and scientific insights, and evaluate these in relation to what they see as core Jewish concepts and values, rather than the rules of *halakhah*. These core principles include the belief that all people are created in the divine image (Genesis 1:27, 5:1, 9:6), the command to love one's neighbour as oneself (Leviticus 19:18) and to love the stranger as oneself (Leviticus 19:34) and the insight that 'it is not good for a human to be alone' (Genesis 2:18).

The following ways to contextualise the biblical prohibition of *to'evah* (Leviticus 18:22) have made an impact on non-Orthodox Jewish movements and led to the now widespread acceptance of LGBT+ Jews in Conservative, Reform, Liberal and Reconstructionist congregations. Firstly, it is often claimed that the motivation of the taboo was the need for a small, embattled semi-nomadic people to increase their numbers both for production and defence, so that non-procreative acts were seen as wasteful.[35] In a world where overpopulation is a growing concern, this idea carries little moral force for most people. Secondly, there is the notion that the biblical prohibition relates to the Torah's opposition to idolatry and is therefore obsolete today.[36] A third argument suggests that the biblical portrayal of homosexual acts is a reflection of the unequal, violent and exploitative nature of male same-sex relations in the ancient world. Because modern understandings of homosexual partnerships are based on equality and loving respect, they are completely different from the scenarios imagined in the Torah, and thus not prohibited.[37] The fourth, and for us most powerfully explanatory argument, focuses on the biblical wording that a man should not lie with another man *as he would with a woman*, namely that a man should not submit (to) another man as he would submit a woman. Here, the penetrative sexual act between two men is understood as a transgression of the patriarchal heteronormativity on which biblical and post-biblical society is based.

---

urj.org/what-we-believe/resolutions/gay-and-lesbian-jew> (accessed 31 May 2020). For Reconstructionism, see Reconstucting Judaism, Inclusion, 2020. <www.reconstructingjudaism.org/act/inclusion> and Reconstructing Judaism, LGBTQ Inclusion, 2020 <www.reconstructingjudaism.org/topic/lgbtq-inclusion> (accessed 31 May 2020). For a first-hand account of the debates within American Reform, see Denise L. Eger, 'Embracing Lesbians and Gay Men: A Reform Jewish Innovation' in Dana Evan Kaplan (ed), *Contemporary Debates in American Reform Judaism: Conflicting Visions* (Routledge 2001) 180–192.

35 See Greenberg (n 30) 149.
36 See Alpert (n 26) 42. The word *to'evah* is most often used, in the Hebrew Bible, with reference to idolatrous cults. One Talmudic opinion bases the prohibition of passive anal intercourse on Deuteronomy 23:18, 'There is to be no *qedeshah* among the daughters of Israel, nor a *qadesh* among the sons of Israel.' The terms *qadesh* and *qedeshah* are traditionally identified as cult prostitutes, with the males being associated with homosexual cultic activity (*Bavli Sanhedrin* 54b). These interpretations have been called into question by recent scholarship.
37 This is the argument that carries most weight for Steven Greenberg (n 30), especially 192–214. On this view, however, it is hard to account for the fact that Leviticus 20:13 prescribes death for the passive, and presumably abused, partner as well.

Contemporary progressive Jewish movements have rejected such patriarchal power structures and embraced gender equality (with varying degrees of thoroughness) as a fundamental aspect of their self-understanding. The 'transgression' represented by gay sex here becomes subversive as a practice that breaks down patriarchal society and, as such, can and should be embraced as pathbreaking and liberating.[38]

Alongside these approaches that regard the prohibition as obsolete or objectionable are those which seek to reinterpret Leviticus 18:22 in more palatable or relevant fashion, using *midrashic*[39] techniques familiar from rabbinic tradition in creative ways. These focus on details of the wording to yield the idea that only non-consensual, selfish or exploitative sexual acts are prohibited, or that it addresses only situational homosexuality, in which a man is used as a substitute for an unavailable female partner, but says nothing about men whose primary desire is for other men.

2.2 Social Changes in Jewish Religious Life

In addition to *halakhic* discussion, we find social action, which has, since the early 1970s, led to the creation of safe spaces where LGBT+ Jews are able to live their religious identities as LGBT+ Jews. These spaces can take the form of gay and lesbian synagogues as alternatives to attending mainstream congregations, common in the United States,[40] or social groups that act as supportive communities. The oldest such group is the Jewish LGBT+ Group[41] in Britain, founded in 1972. Today, we find LGBT+ Jews accepted and integrated into all non-Orthodox Jewish movements. Liberal, Reform and Reconstructionist

---

38 The conclusion here is Rabbi Mark L. Solomon's (n 13) 407–408, inspired by Judith Plaskow, *Standing Again at Sinai: Judaism from a Feminist Perspective* (Harper Collins 1990) especially 198–210. See the discussion in Greenberg (n 30) 175–191, under the chapter heading 'The Rationale of Category Confusion', and Daniel Boyarin, 'Are There Any Jews in "The History of Sexuality"?' (1995) 5:3 *Journal of the History of Sexuality* 333–335. So also Tikva Frymer Kensky (*The Anchor Bible Dictionary*, s.v. 'Sex and sexuality', 5:1145) who states that the biblical laws on homosexuality are 'best explained as a desire to keep the categories of "male" and "female" intact'. In conversation between Rabbi Mark L. Solomon and Steve Greenberg, the latter acknowledged the force of this view, but explained that, as an Orthodox Jew, he could not accept an interpretation that imputes a limited patriarchal perspective to the, for him, divine Torah. Solomon, as a Liberal rabbi, has no problem seeing the Torah as a human document reflecting the social norms of its time. It is true that in patriarchal societies, such as ancient Athens, homosexuality can support male power structures, so this argument holds best for 20th and 21st century Western society.
39 Rabbinic hermeneutic methods based on a close reading of the biblical text, with special emphasis on supposed redundancies in Hebrew, used to draw out additional legal, ethical and spiritual lessons. For examples of these strategies of reinterpretation, see *Alpert* (n 26) 38–40; *Greenberg* (n 30) 203–209.
40 See Moshe Shokeid, *A Gay Synagogue in New York* (Columbia University Press 1995).
41 Founded as the Jewish Gay Group, it became for many years the Jewish Gay and Lesbian Group, and has recently changed name again to acknowledge the inclusion of bi, trans and other queer people.

movements have accepted LGBT+ students for ordination as rabbis and cantors, and provide marriage and/or partnership ceremonies for all Jews. The Conservative movement continues to be split on the status of LGBT+ Jews in leadership positions and in relation to marriage and partnership ceremonies.[42] While the Conservative movement trains LGBT+ Jews for leadership positions and offers marriage and partnership ceremony options, it is the prerogative of individual communities to decide how to relate to and whether to implement these.[43]

In the State of Israel, since the 1990s, we can observe a huge social and legal liberalisation, even though traditionalist parts of the Orthodox community continue their opposition. Gay soldiers and employees enjoy equal rights.[44] Gay Pride celebrations take place freely and attract huge crowds in Tel Aviv, which has a large and vibrant gay scene, while they continue to encounter violent ultra-Orthodox opposition and little government support in Jerusalem.[45]

3. Changing Views of Jewish Marriage[46]

Heterosexual marriage is a historical institution, which has changed over time. It is uncontroversial to state that the meaning and the content of 'marriage' vary according to its particular religious, cultural, ethnic, geographical, economic and political setting. The evidence from the Hebrew Bible suggests that Jewish marriage began in the form of the acquisition of a young virgin by a man from her father (see Deuteronomy 22:13–28). Polygyny and concubinage were assumed as the legal norm.[47] The rabbis of the Talmud examined the legal texts of the Hebrew Bible and brought these together with the creation narratives (Genesis 1 and 2) and the romantic-love lyricism of the Song of Songs, in their task of creating the rules and rituals of Jewish marriage (see the Babylonian Talmud tractate, *Qiddushin*, redacted 500–600 CE). Although concubinage fell into disuse in later antiquity[48] and polygyny was banned for Ashkenazi Jews by the 12th century CE,[49] these rules and rituals remain largely in force through-

---

42 For a range of Conservative views, with extensive argumentation, see Abelson and Fine (n 33) 612–729.
43 See Abselson and Fine (n 33) above.
44 See Lee Walzer, *Between Sodom and Eden: A Gay Journey Through Today's Changing Israel* (Columbia University Press 2000).
45 The documentary feature film *Jerusalem Is Proud to Present*, dir. Nitzan Gilady, 2007, chronicles the struggle to hold a gay Pride march in Jerusalem in 2006, and the surrounding context.
46 This section includes material adapted from the unpublished *Report of the Working Party on Same-Sex Commitment Ceremonies* of the Union of Liberal and Progressive Synagogues Rabbinic Conference, February 2001, written by Rabbis Elizabeth Tikvah Sarah and Rabbi Mark L. Solomon.
47 Rachel Adler, *Engendering Judaism: An Inclusive Theology and Ethics* (Jewish Publication Society 1998) 129.
48 See Satlow (n 12) 192–195.
49 Ze'ev W. Falk, *Jewish Matrimonial Law in the Middle Ages* (Oxford University Press 1966) 1–34.

out the Jewish world to this day – with some 'progressive' adjustments – in the face of massive social transformations. Thus, Jewish heterosexual marriage retains an element of acquisition of the bride by the groom, known as *qinyan*, an element of reciprocal covenantal love, and an underlying theology of God's dual purpose in creating humanity in two forms, male and female: the imperative of *reproduction* on the one hand (Genesis 1:27–28) and the need for *companionship* on the other (Genesis 2:18–25).

Originally, two ceremonies separated in time – one involving betrothal (*erusin*; also known as *qiddushin*) and one, the marriage itself (*nissu'in*) – the wedding ritual since the Middle Ages incorporates both within one ceremony. In the first part, the dimension of acquisition is emphasised by the groom placing a ring on the bride's index finger and saying the words of a legal formula of betrothal: 'Behold, you are consecrated to me by this ring according to the law of Moses and Israel.'[50] Then the idea of marriage as an economic arrangement is underlined by the reading out of the traditional contract document (*ketubah*), signed by two witnesses before the ceremony, which sets out the husband's marital obligations towards his wife, but especially his financial obligations in the event of his death or of divorce. In the second part of the marriage ceremony, the theme of covenant is expressed, together with the divine purpose underlying heterosexual union, in the recitation of Seven Blessings (*Sheva B'rakhot*), which celebrate 'the groom and the bride' as both a new Adam and Eve and as presaging the joy of the Messianic Age.

As the understanding of marriage as a loving and increasingly equal partnership has become predominant in Western societies during the 20th century, Progressive Jewish movements have altered the traditional ritual and procedures of marriage ceremonies to reflect this, requiring the bride to reciprocate the betrothal formula, supporting couples in their wish to exchange rings, and rewriting the *ketubah* so that it has become a document that expresses the couple's promises to love and support one another.[51] In making these changes, liberal religious Jews have succeeded in completely undercutting the original aspect of *qinyan*, acquisition of the bride by the groom, while preserving the outward forms.[52]

The best-known symbol of a Jewish wedding, the canopy (*chuppah*) under which the bride and groom stand, provides the most dramatic expression of the change in the meaning of Jewish marriage from biblical times to the present day. Originally, there seems to have been little ceremony attached to the

---

50 In traditional ceremonies, the bride does not speak at all, and many authorities argue that, if she gives the groom a ring, this could invalidate the 'acquisition' and thus void the marriage.
51 See Tobias (n 34) 193–197.
52 This assertion contrasts with the argument of Adler (n 47) 169–207 that ceremonies based on the traditional wedding liturgy are irredeemably tainted with patriarchal symbolism and meaning. She proposes instead a novel ceremony based on the laws of business partnerships, called *b'rit ahuvim* (covenant of lovers), and this has enjoyed some popularity in feminist religious circles.

acquisition of a bride by a groom – he would simply take her into his home and have sex with her. The 'memory' of this form of marriage is present in the *chuppah*, originally the marital chamber, possibly decorated for the occasion. The canopy has accumulated further meanings so that today it also represents the *quality* of the home that the couple hopes to create together – the covering cloth symbolising the divine presence, the open sides, the virtue of hospitality.[53]

As homosexual loving relationships were acknowledged in the last quarter of the 20th century, there has been a shift in attitudes to homosexuality in general and the treatment of LGBT+ persons, in particular, so that Western societies have largely established full legal equality, enabling LGBT+ people to marry as heterosexual couples do.

In the Jewish world, the debates were conducted in the context of a need to rethink Jewish attitudes towards same-sex relationships and their celebration through ritual. As early as 1982, the British Reform movement produced a pamphlet, *Jewish and Homosexual*,[54] and the late 1980s and the 1990s saw a wide-ranging debate in the Reconstructionist and Reform movements in the United States.[55] Although the Liberal Jewish movement considered itself welcoming to, and affirming of, all persons, it was not until 1991 that the Rabbinic Conference issued its *Where We Stand on Homosexuality*.[56] It was primarily motivated by the intolerant backlash that followed the AIDS epidemic. It opens with an analysis of the traditional Jewish stance on homosexuality. Rejecting this position and its assumptions and motives, the pamphlet offers ten conclusions. These include a call to reject prejudice and discrimination, and a demand to understand and respect homosexual relationships while at the same time attaching value to 'traditional Jewish family life'. Its central thrust is an affirmation that, whilst deploring both promiscuity and adultery and encouraging chastity for the unmarried, 'the appropriate context for the expression of human sexuality is a lasting relationship of mutual love and faithfulness between two persons'.[57]

In the wake of a bitter controversy within the British Reform movement over same-sex commitment ceremonies,[58] Rabbi Mark L. Solomon raised this issue within the Liberal movement in 1999, where the response was far more

---

53 See, for example, Anita Diamant, *The Jewish Wedding Now* (Scribner 2017) 61.
54 Wendy Greengross, *Jewish and Homosexual* (Reform Synagogues of Great Britain 1982).
55 See (n 34).
56 Pamphlet published by The Union of Liberal and Progressive Synagogues, part of the 'Where We Stand' series. This was largely the work of Rabbi John D. Rayner (1924–2005), the leading rabbinic scholar of Liberal Judaism.
57 The foregoing paragraph is adapted from Rabbi Mark L. Solomon, 'Preamble to Resolutions on Same-Sex Commitment Ceremonies', Union of Liberal and Progressive Synagogues Rabbinic Conference 2001.
58 See (n 7).

positive. A working party was swiftly established, and its recommendation to allow such ceremonies, and create a liturgy for them, was accepted in 2001.[59]

4. Inclusive Marriage Ceremonies

In 2005, Liberal Judaism published *B'rit Ahavah – Covenant of Love: Service of Commitment for Same-Sex Couples*. It was the first such liturgy published by any Jewish movement and fortuitously coincided with the introduction of civil partnerships in English law. While for pragmatic reasons it avoided the word 'marriage', the Hebrew title includes *qiddushin*, the Hebrew word for 'legal marriage'. The introduction states:

> In theory it might be possible to create a commitment ceremony that bears no resemblance whatever to a traditional Jewish marriage service, but in practice Judaism possesses no other set of symbols that conveys the same meaning: the formal and public celebration of an exclusive physical and emotional bond between two people, and the invocation upon this union of God's blessing. Many Jewish gay men and lesbians have grown up with the hope and expectation that they would, one day, stand under the *chuppah* and get married. When they come to seek a Jewish blessing for the central relationship in their lives, the forms and symbols that speak to them most powerfully are those of the wedding service. Thus the broad outline and some of the wording of this liturgy bear strong resemblance to the traditional marriage service. However, much of the text is significantly different, with original concepts, symbols and formulations that mark it out as a new and distinctive ritual for a new social and communal reality.[60]

As well as setting out a full wedding ritual for Jewish same-sex couples, the booklet also indicates appropriate elements of the ceremony for couples where only one partner is Jewish, which is the reality for most LGBT+ Jews.[61] In the years following publication, Liberal Judaism continued to advance in its

---

59 Unpublished working papers of the Rabbinic Conference of Liberal Judaism, copies in the possession of Rabbi Mark L. Solomon. The resolutions were incorporated in the *Madrich*, the guide for rabbinic practice kept, and periodically updated, by the Rabbinic Conference (now the Conference of Liberal Rabbis and Cantors). It should be noted that several rabbis, in Britain as in the United States, had been conducting private LGBT+ 'marriage' or blessing ceremonies outside any official framework, and usually without their congregations' knowledge, for many years.
60 Rabbi Mark L. Solomon (ed), *Covenant of Love: Service of Commitment for Same-Sex Couples* (Liberal Judaism 2005) iii. The more conservative members of the Rabbinic Conference, while supportive of the desire for commitment ceremonies, were still anxious that this should not be identical to marriage. The argument of this paragraph tries to address that anxiety, while defending the use of marriage ritual.
61 See Romain and Mitchell (n 7) 180.

thinking, and together with the Quakers and Unitarians, was among the first religious denominations to embrace, and campaign for, full marriage equality.[62]

A couple of examples will be given here of the creative thinking behind the ceremony. One of the most liturgically significant passages is the Betrothal Blessing (*birkat erusin*). In the Orthodox version, this reads:

> Blessed are You, Lord our God, King of the Universe, who has made us holy through his commandments, and has commanded us concerning forbidden unions, forbidding us those who are betrothed, permitting us those who are wedded to us through the rite of the canopy and sacred covenant of marriage. Blessed are You, Lord, who sanctifies his people Israel by the rite of the canopy and the sacred covenant of marriage.[63]

The Liberal version for heterosexual marriage is considerably shorter and omits any mention of sexual prohibitions: 'We praise You, Eternal God, Sovereign of the universe; You teach us the way of holiness, and by Your laws Jewish marriage is sanctified.'[64]

The *Covenant of Love* version expands this as follows:

> We praise You, Eternal One our God, Sovereign of the Universe: You remember the covenant and have made your creatures wonderfully varied. These loving companions stand here before You today, prepared and ready to enter into a sacred covenant of love. Blessed are You, Eternal One: You sanctify our lives with love.[65]

This draws on two other blessings from Jewish tradition: the blessing upon seeing a rainbow, which includes the words 'who remembers the covenant', and a blessing said upon seeing people of unusual appearance, 'who makes people varied'.[66] While the latter usually refers to unusual bodily appearance, here it is reclaimed to affirm the varied nature of our innate sexuality. The former embraces both the modern LGBT+ use of the rainbow flag as a symbol

---

62 Jessica Elgot, 'Liberal Judaism to Lobby Lords Over Same-Sex Marriage' *Jewish Chronicle*, 23 March 2010 <www.thejc.com/news/uk-news/liberal-judaism-to-lobby-lords-over-gay-marriage-1.14156> (accessed 2 June 2020). See also Lynne Featherstone, *Equal Ever After: The Fight for Same-Sex Marriage – and How I Made It Happen* (Biteback Publishing 2016) chapter 5.
63 Jonathan Sacks (trans.), *The Authorised Daily Prayer Book of the United Hebrew Congregations of the Commonwealth* (Collins 2006) 789.
64 *Siddur Lev Chadash* (Union of Progressive and Liberal Synagogues 2005) 597.
65 See Solomon (n 60) 4. On page 12 there is an alternative version (as with all the blessings in the booklet), which names the divine not in the traditional masculine gender as 'Eternal One our God, Sovereign of the Universe' but using feminine forms (Hebrew has only masculine and feminine, no neuter, and almost every word has a gendered inflection) as 'Divine Presence [*shekhinah*] and Source of life'. Such usages are now being introduced more widely in Liberal liturgy.
66 See Solomon (n 60) 25n4. The source of the blessings is *Bavli Berakhot* 59a and 58b.

of diversity and peaceful coexistence, and the idea of marriage as a mutual covenant, not a hierarchical relationship.

One other example must suffice. The fourth of the Seven Blessings, which constitute the culminating section of the wedding ceremony, reads in the traditional version as follows: 'Bring great happiness and joy to one who was barren [Zion], as her children return to her in joy. Blessed are You, Lord, who gladdens Zion through her children.'[67]

The Covenant of Love supplements the prophetic imagery of barren Zion rejoicing in the return of her exiled children[68] with imagery taken from Genesis 2:18, which deals with the problem of human loneliness, so often experienced by LGBT+ people who feel unable to reach out for love, which is considered sinful, immoral or inferior: 'May the Divine Presence rejoice greatly, for we were not created to be solitary, and these our brothers/sisters have found in each other a partner for mutual support. We praise You, O God, that You unite individuals through love.'[69]

The Jewish wedding ceremony traditionally concludes with the bridegroom stamping on a glass and breaking it, as the congregation shout out *mazal tov*! (Congratulations!) This medieval custom is traditionally explained as a reminder, even in our moment of rejoicing, of the destruction of the Temple and Jerusalem, although many other meanings have been suggested.[70]

This raises the question for a same-sex couple – who will break the glass?[71] Some might break a glass each; others might find a glass big enough that they can stamp on it simultaneously. The text provided in the Covenant of Love includes the words:

> . . . this practice reminds us of the Jewish concept of *Tikkun Olam*, our duty to heal and repair the world in partnership with God. Wherever there is oppression and pain, we are asked to respond. Because so many lesbian, gay, bisexual and transgender people sadly still know the oppression and pain of hiding, because so many LGBT people still lack equality of civil rights in our world, we break a glass/glasses on this day of celebration to remind us that even in this hour of great joy, our world is still incomplete and in need of healing. May the time come soon, speedily and in our day,

---

67 See *Authorised Daily Prayer Book* (n 63) 791. The text of the Seven Blessings comes originally from *Bavli Ketubot* 8a.
68 See Isaiah 54:1, etc.
69 See Solomon (n 60) 7.
70 Ana Prashizky, 'Breaking the Glass: New Tendencies in the Ritual Practice of Modern Jewish Orthodox and Alternative Weddings' (2008) 13 *Sociological Papers: Between Tradition and Modernity: The Plurality of Jewish Customs and Rituals* (Sociological Institute for Community Studies, Bar Ilan University) 2–7.
71 Some feminist-conscious mixed-sex couples also experience this as an important choice to be made; most go along with tradition.

when all who are in hiding shall be free and all who are in exile shall come home. May the shattering of this glass/these glasses by__and__remind them and all of us to work towards this time of wholeness, this *tikkun*, for ourselves and our world. *Amen*.[72]

5. Conclusion

We have sought to demonstrate the textual basis of Jewish understandings of sexuality and their expression in marriage and wedding rituals. A living tradition continues to flow out of an ancient textual corpus. As we have shown, this tradition has developed different understandings of human sexuality and its place in Jewish religious life. At its most conservative, we continue to observe the rejection of LGBT+ sexual identities. Yet, in many Orthodox and Conservative Jewish contexts, a person's sexual orientation is accepted as a given, while homosexual behaviour may still be understood to be a choice and seen as sinful. At its most liberal, not only is sexual orientation understood as innate, but LGBT+ identities are embraced and celebrated. Liberal Jewish movements have devised rituals to celebrate two people entering a lasting commitment of mutual love and support, which are open to couples of all genders. These rituals derive from Jewish tradition and take into account both the changing nature of the social institution of marriage and of the gender identities of the couple. In Liberal Jewish traditions, children are welcomed as much into same-sex partnerships as they are into heterosexual unions.

---

72 See Solomon (n 60) 8, slightly adapted for more recent use.

Chapter 22

Tradition and Transition
Methodological Approaches to LGBT Issues in Roman Catholic Theology After Pope Francis

Nicolete Burbach

1. Introduction

'Mainstream' Roman Catholic theologians have only recently started to think seriously about trans issues.[1] This presents a number of challenges. For example, the pre-existing literature, which might inform them, is very diverse and dispersed and often in ways that inhibit engagement by individuals trained in traditional Roman Catholic theological methodologies. Most trans theology speaks from a Protestant perspective, and explicitly Roman Catholic resources are often disciplinary outliers operating with unusual methodologies that are perhaps, at least on the face of it, incompatible with 'mainstream' approaches. Engaging with these sources thus requires the 'mainstream' Roman Catholic theologian to step outside of their comfort zone and to learn to think beyond the boundaries of their familiar epistemic practices. This brings an additional complication when we start to think about how these practices are part of a communal life or tradition in which they have normative weight: what does it mean for the Roman Catholic theologian to 'think with the Church' while also thinking with writers who, at least as those theologians might intuitively see it, very much do not? And how should this activity shape our reception of these sources?

This chapter attempts to answer this question. It begins by drawing from MacIntyre's understanding of tradition as embodied rationality in order to frame the issue in more detail. It then looks to how the methodological diversity within the existing field of trans theology, along with the requirements of the current situation, undermine simple appeals to tradition as a heuristic for assessing that theology. The chapter concludes by looking to Pope Francis's *Evangelii Gaudium* in order to cope with the problems this context raises.

2. Tradition and Enquiry

The problems this chapter seeks to identify all revolve around tradition and its relation to enquiry. But what is tradition in this context, and what is this relation?

---

1 Thank you to David Albert Jones, who commented on an earlier draft of this chapter.

DOI: 10.4324/9781003286295-28

One way in which tradition is commonly invoked as an epistemic principle is in terms of setting parameters for what enquiry is acceptable within a Roman Catholic ecclesial context. Tradition sets the boundaries for what we can think while still intelligibly being 'Roman Catholic' thinkers or thinking in a 'Roman Catholic way'.

For example, John Paul II's encyclical, *Veritatis Splendor*, seeks to respond to methodological developments in Roman Catholic moral theology, which it claims are 'not consistent with "sound teaching"'.[2] We do not need to go into detail here about the nature of these developments, which it labels 'teleologism' and 'proportionalism'.[3] What is significant is that these methodologies, according to the encyclical, implicitly grant the moral agent the capacity to make decisions about moral situations in ways that go contrary to the stipulations of the moral precepts taught by the Church, restricting the power of the Magisterium to only 'exhort consciences' and 'propose values'.[4] In this context, as Nicholas Lash puts it, the encyclical's 'central and overriding aim' is to reaffirm the specific moral principles challenged by these methodological developments, specifically (albeit implicitly) around sexual norms.[5]

In doing so, *Veritatis Splendor* invokes the authority of the Pope within the Roman Catholic Church in order to canonize (or re-canonize) the modes of enquiry in moral theology supposedly rejected by 'teleologist' and 'proportionalist' theologians. We might understand this in terms of shaping what the philosopher Alasdair MacIntyre would call the 'tradition' of Roman Catholic theology: a 'form of enquiry' that takes place within the life of a community and is governed by the institutionalized methods of that community.[6] Such traditions embody a model of 'rational enquiry', setting the parameters for meaningful conversation about truth within the life of that community.[7]

In this context, the 'Roman Catholic tradition' can be understood as functioning as a tradition in the MacIntyrean sense. Whatever the other theological significances attached to the activity, epistemically speaking, to think 'with the tradition' is to operate according to its canons of rationality, working within the parameters for enquiry that it sets down.

---

2 John Paul II, *Veritatis Splendor* (1993) <http://w2.vatican.va/content/john-paul-ii/en/encyclicals/documents/hf_jp-ii_enc_06081993_veritatis-splendor.html> (accessed 28 August 2019) (§29); see 2 Tim. 4:3.
3 For a detailed discussion of proportionalism, see Bernard Hoose, *Proportionalism: The American Debate and Its European Roots* (Georgetown University Press 1987).
4 *Veritatis Splendor* (n 2), §4.
5 Nicholas Lash, 'Crisis and Tradition in *Veritatis Splendor*' (1994) 7:2 *Studies in Christian Ethics* 22–28, 23.
6 Alasdair MacIntyre, *Whose Justice? Which Rationality?* (Gerald Duckworth & Co. Ltd. 1988) 358.
7 Ibid., 7.

3. Troubling Tradition

3.1 'Orthodoxy' as Heuristic

Granting this, we can move to formulate an intuitive distinction. In a theological context, the parameters that define Roman Catholic 'rationality' are delineated by the terms 'orthodoxy' and 'heterodoxy'. A simplistic reading of these concepts aligns the former with a recognition of the tradition and the latter with a rejection of the tradition.

These concepts have an epistemic and a normative dimension. Epistemically speaking, in this context, 'orthodoxy' and 'heterodoxy' delineate parameters for constructive ('rational') contributions to Roman Catholic theological discussion. The normative component enjoins us as Roman Catholics to only affirm arguments and truth claims made within these parameters of Roman Catholic rationality. As a result, 'orthodoxy' functions as a heuristic, which nominally enables us to disregard certain sources as unable to contribute to our specifically *Roman Catholic* program of enquiry.

The *epistemic* contrast between the two approaches is clearly evidenced in the literature. For an avowedly 'orthodox' example, we might look to the work of David Albert Jones. Jones is a bioethicist who conducts his research according to the norms of traditional Roman Catholic moral theology. For example, his 2018 paper on gender reassignment surgery (GRS) seeks to 'clarify whether GRS is compatible with the ethical and philosophical principles that have developed within the Catholic tradition'. More specifically, he focuses on the 'principles of bodily integrity and totality, as expounded by Pope Pius XII'. In the process, he notes that he does not seek to 'defend' these principles, but rather to work from a position of their acceptance.[8] In doing so, he self-consciously works from 'within the tradition'; a methodological approach that is also born out in his preliminary review of magisterial teachings on or related to GRS, which serves to orient his enquiry.[9]

In contrast, the 'heterodox' label encompasses a diverse range of methodologies. The single uniting factor upon which we are pinning this designation is a rejection of the canonical parameters of enquiry associated with the Roman Catholic tradition. As mentioned earlier, the 'orthodox–heterodox' distinction is a simplistic one, and we will shortly see why it is troubled by the more complex realities of the theological field. However, for now, we will take as a general heuristic what might be described as the 'common sense' criteria for canonical enquiry in the Roman Catholic Church: fidelity to the Magisterium.

---

8 David Albert Jones, 'Gender Reassignment Surgery: A Catholic Bioethical Analysis' (2018) 79:2 *Theological Studies* 314–338, 315.
9 *Ibid.*, 315–318.

Following from this, the most obvious form of heterodox enquiry is (from a Roman Catholic perspective) theology done from the perspective of a different denomination. For example, the Anglican theologian Susannah Cornwall uses the apophatic or negative theology of Pseudo-Dionysius the Areopagite in order to critique 'homonormativity', whereby the rejection of straight identity by queerness leads to the conflation of queerness with homosexuality. Cornwall objects that this obscures the authentic queerness of trans people, who may otherwise be heterosexual.[10] Against this, she sees Dionysius' negative theology, which rejects positive talk about God in all forms, as enabling talk about gender that does not ultimately reduce it to a binary choice of worldly heterosexual or homosexual identity, but instead directs it toward a mysterious divine reality that qualifies all worldly totalizations – binaristic or otherwise. In doing so, she seeks to construct an authentically queer theology, which destabilizes 'constricting, limiting ideologies' about what it means to be human.[11]

The apophatic tradition is well established in the canon of Roman Catholic theology.[12] To this end, Cornwall's argument has some purchase on discussions within the Roman Catholic theological tradition. Likewise, she invokes a Eucharistic theology that will be meaningful to the Roman Catholic reader. However, she also opposes her use of negative theology to positive, or 'kataphatic' theology, which seeks to make determinate claims about the divine nature and thus the human nature that resembles it. This approach, she writes, 'became the one so overemphasized in later Western Christianity . . . which has not exactly thrown open its arms to embrace transgendered (and intersex) bodies and their implications for its doctrines about sex, gender, sexuality, and complementarity'.[13] Against this, Cornwall offers a theology in which a genderless God leads to an anthropology according to which 'gender is not an absolute or ultimate aspect of human identity'.[14] She argues that this destabilizes supposedly total binaristic schemas of gender, opening up a conceptual space in which we can appreciate how 'straight' trans people (and indeed, straight people in general) can nevertheless make 'choices and statements' that are 'subversive' of those binaries.[15] In this context, transgender bodies play a prophetic role, making legible the 'non-ultimacy of traditional sex–gender–sexuality configurations'.[16]

---

10 Susannah Cornwall, 'Apophasis and Ambiguity: The "Unknowingness" of Transgender' in Marcella Althaus-Reid and Lisa Isherwood (eds), *Trans/Formations* (SCM Press 2009) 13–40, 16.
11 *Ibid.*, 17.
12 Which is not to say that these theologians were all 'Roman Catholics', with all the post-Reformation connotations this has today. Merely that they are read and afforded a measure of authority in their insights by Roman Catholic theologians.
13 Cornwall (n 10) 23.
14 *Ibid.*, 28.
15 *Ibid.*, 33.
16 *Ibid.*, 37.

This line of argument puts her at odds with the 'orthodox' methodology, which we found in Jones: as we saw earlier, the 'orthodox' approach seeks to stake out a position that is firmly committed to the positions which Cornwall attacks. In doing so, it takes her beyond the Roman Catholic tradition, and it is not hard to see how a committed 'orthodox' reader might struggle to accept her argument. This difficulty is compounded by the fact that she (quite understandably, being an Anglican) omits from consideration the very factors that would prevent this acceptance, namely the authority (to Roman Catholics) of the teachings that she attacks.

Less obviously, but no less importantly, much trans theology does not cite the conventions that accompany what we would recognize as 'academic theology'. This is often a product of necessity: trans people rarely occupy positions within academic theology departments. Consequently, a lot of trans theology has been produced in ways that diverge from academic methodologies and speak to different audiences.

For example, Virginia Ramey Mollenkott and Vanessa Sheridan's autobiographical approach to the theology of trans identity in their *Transgender Journeys* is predicated upon an assumption that, as Sheridan puts it, 'there is remarkable power in the validity of narrative and in the authenticity of one's personal experience'.[17] This power can motivate 'the active, dynamic development of a new and enriched spiritual environment within our faith communities'.[18] In this vein, informed by their own personal histories as trans Christians, Mollenkott and Sheridan set out an analysis of the situation of trans people in (Protestant) Christian communities, and a manifesto for cultural and spiritual reform in both personal and ecclesial contexts.

This body of work does not meet the requirements for compelling argumentation in the academic context in which most Roman Catholic theological enquiry occurs. For example, Mollenkott and Sheridan use the genre of trans autobiography as the foundation for what might be described as a 'witness' or 'prophetic' mode of enquiry, rather than what might be considered a 'rigorous' academic approach. Hence, they note that the purpose of *Transgender Journeys* is not to be a 'comprehensive, in-depth explanation or summation' of trans issues in theology, and therein distinguish it from the 'scholarly works' that cite academic norms.[19] The divergent methodology of these texts places them in different conversations to 'traditional' Roman Catholic theology: they address what David Tracy would describe as distinct 'publics', or communities with distinct norms for rational enquiry (which Tracy calls 'plausibility structures'),

---

17 Vanessa Sheridan, 'Vanessa Sheridan's Gender-Variant Journey' in Virginia Ramey Mollenkott and Vanessa Sheridan (eds), *Transgender Journeys* (Resource Publications 2003) 53–67, 53.
18 Virginia Ramey Mollenkott and Vanessa Sheridan, 'Introduction: Equipping Ourselves for the Journey' *Ibid.*, 5–15: 13.
19 *Ibid.*, 13.

which intersect with more obvious communities, like the Roman Catholic Church.[20] As a result, they are structured by different canons of enquiry.

These kinds of text might thus also be conceived as at least analogously 'heterodox' on the basis that they admit distinct sources of insight and forms of reflection that Roman Catholic theologians (who predominantly work in an academic context) might reject. They are, we might say, 'unorthodox' scholarship. In both cases, Catholic theologians may see the arguments and insights offered out of these methodologies as failing to speak to their concerns and commitments, a stumbling block for 'rational' enquiry by the standards of their tradition.

3.2 Troubling the Epistemic Distinction

The problem with the intuitive 'orthodox–heterodox' distinction, epistemically speaking, is that it implies an overly simple relationship between different traditions. It is true that conversations between Roman Catholics and non-Roman Catholics often begin to founder when (for example) the former invokes the Magisterium as a measure for theology. However, this is not necessarily where such conversations have to end.

This becomes particularly visible across the confessional boundaries that we have used to frame this contrast. In doing what we have called both 'orthodox' and 'heterodox' theology, we are articulating something about the nature of the tradition, which serves as the basis for our enquiry. A 'heterodox' approach does more than just reject normative Roman Catholic parameters for enquiry: it also makes a claim about what those parameters ought to be. For example, Cornwall might argue not only that apophatic theology enables us to think outside the parameters of the kataphatic approach associated with 'orthodox' Roman Catholic theology, but that this possibility is a challenge to the parameters that restrict enquiry to within those terms. Conversely, Jones may argue that the teachings of the Magisterium pose a corrective to Cornwall's thesis, the argument for which may be sound on its own terms.

With regard to genre, this challenge is expressed in the idea that these excluded voices may have valid insights for academia despite their failure to cite academic norms. Autobiography is a particularly significant example here: famously, Sandy Stone argues that conventional narratives around trans identity are in part the product of writing that reconstitutes trans lives around prevailing social norms, including cissexist and homophobic ones. Most strikingly, she notes that the first academic gender dysphoria clinics helped construct a number of these narratives through enforcing normative performances of

---

20 David Tracy, *The Analogical Imagination: Christian Theology and the Culture of Pluralism* (Herder & Herder 1981) 26.

femininity by only providing services to those who were deemed 'appropriate' to their desired gender. This was enforced in part through the adoption of diagnostic criteria from Harry Benjamin's *The Transsexual Phenomenon*, which prohibited various forms of self-presentation, including certain sexual activities; something which was then anticipated by prospective service users, who read Benjamin's book and adapted their presentation to meet its standards. This in turn leads to a paucity of data on trans lives which transgressed these norms, these being self-selectively occluded and therefore never recorded. Moreover, although this in turn led to a revision of these criteria in the search for a better diagnostic category, this search merely wound up stripping them back to Benjamin's core narrative of being 'born in the wrong body', which remains prominent today.[21]

Arising from these origins, academic discussion of trans issues is always already concerned with autobiography. Moreover, Stone argues that the transgressive nature of actual trans lives renders them texts that disrupt the normative narratives established through these conforming biographies.[22] In this context, autobiography constitutes a challenging continuation of a genre that is not only inseparable from more conventional 'academic' discourse but also a necessary corrective to its historical inadequacies.

In short, the real thrust of 'heterodox' arguments is that we might be wrong precisely in all the ways that lead us to acknowledge one 'orthodoxy' over the other. Their presence in the field of trans theology not only raises questions about trans issues, but problematizes the nature of our tradition itself as that which demands our allegiance.[23]

3.3 Troubling the Normative Dimension: Against Loss Cutting

This more radical conflict tends to be relatively intractable. This is where the normative dimension of the distinction comes into play, enjoining us to remember our commitments to a specifically Roman Catholic project of enquiry and to move on to another source that is more helpful in this context; to 'cut our losses'.

We can see an example of this loss cutting at work in the Congregation for Catholic Education's recent document on 'gender ideology', *Male and Female He Created Them*.[24] One of the striking features of this document is the

---

21 Sandy Stone, 'The *Empire* Strikes Back: A Posttranssexual Manifesto' in Susan Stryker and Stephen Whittle (eds), *The Transgender Studies Reader* (Routledge 2006) 221–235, 227–229.
22 *Ibid.*, 231.
23 Naturally, this includes positions within the tradition around its own infallibility etc.
24 Congregation for Catholic Education, *Male and Female He Created Them* (2019) <www.educatio.va/content/dam/cec/Documenti/19_0997_INGLESE.pdf> (Accessed 22 August 2019).

tension that emerges between its professed call for dialogue with trans people and contemporary gender theory, and its subtle refusal to engage in this dialogue itself.[25] For example, *Male and Female* distinguishes between 'the ideology of gender on the one hand, and the whole field of research on gender that the human sciences have undertaken, on the other'. The document qualifies its call for dialogue based on this distinction, rejecting the former but approving dialogue with the latter. However, it specifies this latter category of work as that which seeks 'a deeper understanding of the ways in which sexual difference between men and women is lived out in a variety of cultures'.[26] In doing so, it disregards any research that does not work in terms of a 'sexual difference between men and women' that exists across cultural contexts. This sets the ground for further enquiry within the parameters of Roman Catholic anthropology, in which this 'sexual difference' is assumed.

Loss cutting is undoubtedly necessary in particular contexts. The range of theological challenges posed by 'heterodox' sources is broad, and it is not possible to engage with the whole of our theology on a systemic basis at any given time; sometimes, we need to assume our premises in order to say something about the world at all. Similarly, it is often more prudent to work within the bounds of our established expertise, rather than seeking to broaden our enquiry beyond them.

However, once we start to look at Roman Catholic theology in general, as a broader project conducted in the community as a whole by a variety of people with diverse expertise, problems begin to arise. Two of them are as follows:

Firstly, loss cutting requires us to have a sense of what we are rejecting. MacIntyre notes that the 'precondition of the adherents of two different traditions understanding those traditions as rival and competing is . . . that in some significant measure they understand each other'.[27] This requires a process of inter-translation whereby members of one tradition at least provisionally adopt the language of the other tradition, enabling them to recognize the relationships of commensurability and incommensurability between the two. As a result, any engagement between our tradition and another requires us to acquaint ourselves with the ways of thinking involved in that other tradition, and this extends to the act of rejecting a tradition as incommensurable with our own. In short, all loss cutting necessarily involves engagement with other traditions; the question is merely one of how informed we are when we come to make

---

25 For a more detailed analysis of this, see Nicolete Burbach, 'The Vatican's New Document on Transgender Issues Is Not Interested in Dialogue, but Dialogue Is What We Need' *ABC Religion and Ethics*, 24 June 2019 <www.abc.net.au/religion/the-vatican-on-transgender-issues-and-the-absence-of-dialogue/11241116> (accessed 22 August 2019).
26 Congregation for Catholic Education (n 24), §6.
27 MacIntyre (n 6) 370.

the cut. To 'cut our losses' is to abandon any further attempts to identify the commensurabilities and incommensurabilities between another tradition and our own, thereby rejecting the information that would come from further exploration. This is not a decision that should be taken lightly, especially as we are more like to reject the other tradition under false pretences the earlier we make the cut.

Secondly, this intertranslatability challenges relativist or perspectivist accounts of logically incommensurable traditions, which could operate according to their own relative and exclusive 'truths'. This is evidenced, according to MacIntyre, in how distinct traditions can enrich and even provide a necessary corrective to one another. MacIntyre describes what he calls an 'epistemological crisis', in which a tradition ceases to make progress according to its own standards, causing disagreements to arise within the tradition over those standards. As a result, its rationality ceases to be able to mediate disagreements, as those disagreements concern the nature of that rationality itself.[28]

These crises are resolved, according to MacIntyre, through the formulation of new theories that fulfill three conditions. The first condition is that they must 'furnish a solution to the problems which had previously proved intractable in a systematic and coherent way'. The second is that they must also be able to explain precisely what rendered the tradition inadequate in its previous formulation. The third is that these previous two tasks must be accomplished in a way that 'exhibits some fundamental continuity of the new conceptual and theoretical structures with the shared beliefs in terms of which the tradition of enquiry had been defined up to this point'.[29]

Crucially, however, because these solutions also address issues with the limitations of the tradition itself, they will not come from the resources already available within the tradition. Rather, '[i]maginative conceptual development will have to occur', which will be justified precisely in the success of the innovations in achieving what was previously impossible.[30] MacIntyre invokes the development of the doctrine of the Trinity, which was predicated on philosophical concepts derived from the live philosophical debates of the time, as well as Aquinas' synthesis of Augustinian and Aristotelean traditions as examples of these developments.[31] This entails an openness to influence from outside of one's tradition, either in the form of translating the resources of other traditions into the language of one's own in order to overcome its limitations, or even in recognising the superiority of another tradition to one's own *despite*

---

28 *Ibid.*, 361–362.
29 *Ibid.*, 362.
30 *Ibid.*
31 *Ibid.*, 362–363.

its discontinuity, leading to the abandonment of the third criterion and a consequent change in tradition.[32]

The point here is not to say that Roman Catholic theology faces an epistemological crisis around trans issues (although approaching those issues theologically may result in such a crisis). Rather, as MacIntyre notes, what this means is that traditions themselves can serve as objects of their own enquiry;[33] in a process, moreover, that is governed in part by their interactions with other traditions. This in turn means that the course of their development cannot be entirely determined from any present perspective.[34]

This in turn means that we cannot take it as a premise that thought from other traditions has no value to our own. At any point, that thought may be the factor that either improves our own tradition or necessitates a shift away from it in order to sustain our project of enquiry. Consequently, any approach to loss cutting that seeks to avoid the possibility of a challenge to or supplementation of our own tradition by another only serves to restrict our access to potential resources, which may prove beneficial, or even crucial, in the future.

3.4 Troubling Identity

There is also at least one reason why loss cutting *cannot* be a solution for the difficulties posed by this variation. Loss cutting involves identifying a given tradition as 'other', in opposition to our own. We have seen how this identification as 'other' does not preclude engagement. However, there is a further difficulty involved in identifying just what constitutes 'our own' tradition in opposition to that other. This difficulty is foregrounded when we look to the ways theologians, in approaching trans issues, contest the very identity of the tradition out of which these approaches purport to speak.

Two ways in which they do this are as follows. Firstly, there is what might be described as the 'deconstructive' approach, which rereads the tradition so as to allow new meanings to emerge and thereby to disrupt its boundaries. In doing so, they purport to reveal that the identity of the tradition itself can be understood in ways that undermine our preconceptions.

For example, Anna Magdalena Patti finds a theological gender fluidity in St. John of the Cross's spiritual canticle, *Dark Night of the Soul*. In St. John's concept of the Dark Night of the soul, self-oriented, 'masculine' desire is transformed into a love that is 'oriented toward God and others'. In this state, St. John gives himself utterly and selflessly over to divine love, which, through the

---

32 *Ibid.*, 365.
33 *Ibid.*, 358.
34 *Ibid.*, 361.

refusal of his own consolation, appears as spiritual 'dryness' and 'alienation'. In doing so, he comes to abide in the 'femininity' of being desired by God.[35]

In short, Patti rereads St. John as articulating a more fluid, feminising understanding of our own gendered nature *vis-à-vis* the divine. In doing so, she finds resources within the Roman Catholic tradition for an understanding of gender that subverts the tradition's conventional understanding. These kinds of approaches thus raise the question of whether we can truly 'know' the tradition that we profess, or at least raises the specter of a fluidity that holds new possibilities for what can be engaged with constructively from within it. They challenge rigid canons of enquiry according to which the distinctions over which our loss cutting operates can be made, in turn posing a more general problem for asserting these canons: it could just be that we do not know our own tradition well enough to make the discriminations necessary for loss cutting. Moreover, we cannot merely dispense with these challenges by rejecting the deconstructive method itself, at least not on the basis of a preconceived idea of what is permissible within the tradition: it is precisely these kinds of preconceptions that deconstructive approaches challenge, and to do this would be to merely beg the question against them.

Significantly, in certain cases, it is difficult to distinguish between deconstructive and 'heterodox' approaches, and not merely in the sense that some deconstructive theologies might be only dubiously 'orthodox'. For example, Cornwall's essay, which we looked at earlier, makes its argument by reference to Pseudo-Dionysius, a figure who enjoys a position of relative canonicity within the Roman Catholic theological tradition. In doing so, despite being an Anglican theologian, she also potentially shows the possibility for an expanded Roman Catholic theological imagination. This is because there is significant overlap between Roman Catholic and certain other theological traditions.

This fact further problematises loss cutting across confessional boundaries: because of the overlap between Roman Catholic and other traditions, developments within those other traditions around shared aspects may impinge directly upon our own. This in turn problematizes easy distinctions between what is internal and what is external to our tradition: some enquiry which is formally 'external' to our own project may function at least analogously to enquiry 'internal' to it in terms of its capacity to speak meaningfully about our own projects.

Secondly, there are approaches that do not so much challenge the boundaries of our traditions as challenge the idea of boundaries *themselves* in the context of our traditions. These approaches question well-established norms, such

---

35 Anna Magdalena Patti, 'The Poetic Feminine: Questions of Spiritual Gender in Percy Shelley's Alastor & John of the Cross's Dark Night of the Soul' *CatholicTrans*, 13 February 2014 <https://catholictrans.wordpress.com/2014/02/13/the-poetic-feminine/> (accessed 30 August 2019).

as continuity and faithful reproduction of prior canons, articulating instead an account of the tradition as finding its fulfillment in the rejection of these canons.

One example of this would be what Marcella Althaus-Reid terms 'indecent theology'. Althaus-Reid responds to the failure of traditional South American Liberation Theology, which allies Roman Catholicism to the pursuit of economic justice, often via Marxist social analysis, to interrogate traditional Roman Catholic sexual and gender norms. She argues that these norms themselves are artifacts of South America's colonial past and constitute distinct occasions of oppression. This, combined with the axiom that 'every theology implies a conscious or unconscious political praxis',[36] leads 'indecent theology' to seek a postcolonial corrective to traditional Liberation Theology by taking the transgressive sexual lives of the urban poor as an authentic locus for social and theological critique. It also seeks to correct in feminist Liberation Theology what Althaus-Reid identifies as a failure to think with 'honesty' about sexuality and gender, specifically in its adoption of idealized and ideological understandings of sexual practices.[37]

In this context, Althaus-Reid proposes an '[o]ut-of-the-closet' theology that refuses to 'compartmentalize' the transgressive sexual aspects of life, which otherwise become objects of reaction against which idealist theologies are formed.[38] In contrast, embracing the 'obscenity' of nominally 'indecent' material sexual practices disrupts the idealized sexuality of traditional theologies, thereby forming the basis for a postcolonial theological critique.[39]

Siân Taylder applies this approach to trans identity in the Catholic Church. Her deliberately 'belligerent – if not aggressive' response to both transphobic Catholicism and anti-Catholic secular 'allies' seeks to account for her life and theology in a way that concedes nothing to those who would attack her.[40] In doing so, she inverts the traditional maxim of 'love the sinner, hate the sin', criticizing it both as a mask for prejudice against those for whom the sin is not so much 'of "doing", but simply of "being"', and unworkably conciliatory for those who have been severely hurt.[41] Instead, she takes an unapologetic approach that deliberately plays with a 'subversive' and 'gloriously inappropriate clash of decent and indecent',[42] foregrounding and revelling in the conflicts that define her life.

---

36 Marcella Althaus-Reid, *Indecent Theology: Theological Perversions in Sex, Gender and Politics* (Routledge 2000) 4.
37 *Ibid.*, 6–7.
38 *Ibid.*, 88.
39 *Ibid.*, 110–111.
40 Siân Taylder, 'Shot from Both Sides: Theology and the Woman Who Isn't Quite What She Seems' in Lisa Isherwood and Marcella Althaus-Reid (eds), *Trans/formations* (SCM Press 2009) 70–91, 88.
41 *Ibid.*, 71.
42 *Ibid.*, 73.

For 'indecent' theology, obscenity is 'a way to transcendence', something that is allied to the pursuit of truth or 'reality', and a 'suppressed aesthetics', which is nevertheless 'of Christianity'.[43] This is, however, tied to a strong critique framed in terms of an imagination that inverts the traditional terms in which the Roman Catholic tradition conveys itself. For example, Taylder embraces trans lives not merely as another form of life within the Church, but as inextricable from a so-called 'sin' that people are encouraged to hate.[44] Whereas deconstructive approaches seek to integrate difference within an expanded theological imagination, 'indecent' theology thus attempts to rupture that imagination by starting from a position of transgression. That is, rather than pursuing unity and continuity through a vision of a more expansive tradition, 'indecent' theology represents the tradition's inconsistency and self-overturning.[45]

The theological situation after 'indecent' theology is one in which accounts of the Roman Catholic theological tradition as fulfilled in continuity are only one kind of account of that fulfillment among others within the tradition. In this context, to simply reject them without discussion on the basis of their rejection of continuity would be to beg the question in favor of one account over these others. In other words, to merely 'cut our losses' with regard to theologians such as Taylder would be to abandon rational deliberation about the nature of our tradition on this point.

3.5 Centralization

One objection to the arguments of the preceding section might be found in MacIntyre's later work, *Three Rival Versions of Moral Enquiry*. In this, he develops his account of the importance of authority to tradition: the figure of the 'master' who has perfected the tradition as a 'craft' and can exercise the skill required not just to work within the tradition but to 'go further' in perfecting it.[46] Porter argues that this model of authority presupposes an additional form of authority, which is that which adjudicates what constitutes the proper exercise of practical reason so as to guide the development of a tradition as a whole.[47] She finds this intimated in MacIntyre's assertion that genuine progress in moral enquiry requires participation in a moral community that enforces canons for enquiry, and in doing so precludes '*fundamental dissent*'.[48] She also reads

---

43 Althaus-Reid (n 36), 111.
44 Taylder (n 40) 71.
45 For a critical discussion of this distinction, see Marika Rose, *A Theology of Failure: Žižek Against Christian Innocence* (Fordham University Press 2019) 29–53.
46 Alasdair MacIntyre, *Three Rival Versions of Moral Enquiry* (Gerald Duckworth & Co. 1990) 65–66.
47 Janet Porter, 'Tradition in the Recent Work of Alasdair MacIntyre' in Mark C Murphy (ed), *Alasdair MacIntyre* (Cambridge University Press 2003) 38–69, 63.
48 MacIntyre (n 46) 60; quoted in Porter (n 47) 62 (emphasis in original).

MacIntyre as giving an example of this in his discussion of Abelard's submission to papal condemnation, which afforded the Pope an authority to adjudicate dialectic.[49]

Prima facie an appeal to this authority seems like it could resolve this issue: an unquestioned authority with the power to adjudicate enquiry could designate the kind of deconstructive or 'indecent' approaches above as unsuccessful developments in the tradition. In turn, this means that we could avoid engaging with these sources as *a priori* lacking epistemic value for Roman Catholic theology.

For example, MacIntyre associates this epistemic authority in the Roman Catholic tradition with that of the Pope. And we see exercises of papal authority which seem to reflect this, such as in John Paul II's *Ordinatio Sacerdotalis*, which teaches that 'the Church has no authority whatsoever to confer priestly ordination on women and that this judgment is to be definitively held by all the Church's faithful',[50] thereby ruling out not only women's ordination on a doctrinal level, but also the possibility of affirming it within the bounds of canonical 'Roman Catholic' theology. We might also think of other authoritative bodies in the Church, such as synods and Ecumenical Councils, which, while potentially admitting plurality within themselves, speak to the Church with a unified voice.

There are two responses to this. Firstly, if this is the case, then at minimum this becomes just another instance of contested 'orthodoxy', and our practical objections to loss cutting come into play. However, this first response itself involves a presupposition about identity that begs the question against Taylder and the challenge she raises. This becomes apparent when we look to two of Porter's objections to MacIntyre's argument.

Porter notes that historical communities have more complex structures of power than that assumed by MacIntyre, and this leads to more complex mediations of discussion within their traditions. Indeed, the case of Abelard found a resolution of sorts not through the unilateral exercise of a centralized power (e.g. that of the Pope to censure), but through a complex process of negotiation by various authorities, including Bernard of Clairvaux, the Pope and the Abbot of Cluny. This in turn means that norms of enquiry are not necessarily enforced unilaterally within historical traditions.[51]

The question then is whether this holds for Roman Catholic theology today. In one sense, it does: as a tradition of enquiry, Roman Catholic theology takes place in various contexts, from independent research to papal institutes to secular universities, and invokes different authorities therein;

---

49 Porter (n 47) 63–64; see MacIntyre (n 46) 89–91.
50 John Paul II, *Ordinatio Sacerdotalis* (1994) § 4 <www.vatican.va/content/john-paul-ii/en/apost_letters/1994/documents/hf_jp-ii_apl_19940522_ordinatio-sacerdotalis.html>.
51 Porter (n 47) 64–66.

authorities that can and do come into conflict. Moreover, these diverse authorities can lead the Church down paths of enquiry that were previously unforeseen by its theology.

For example, in 1879, Leo XIII's *Aeterni Patris* called for a model of Catholic theology that operated within the parameters of a certain tradition of reading Thomas Aquinas, known as neo-Scholasticism. This served as the dominant paradigm in Catholic theology for the next hundred years up until the Second Vatican Council in the 1960s.[52] However, at the Council, a new, more expansive theological program was laid out, led in part by theologians who had previously been censured for their rejection of neo-Scholasticism.[53] This is not to say that the Council was in discontinuity with the prior tradition in theologically problematic ways; only that this seems to be an instance of non-centralized development of the tradition, as evidenced by the eventual recognition of thought from authorities who at one point fell outside the bounds of what was validated by the centralized authority of the day.[54]

The presence of plural, conflicting authority in the tradition would mean that, in turn, appeals to a unilateral authority do more than merely establish boundaries for enquiry. Parallel to how loss cutting asserts a particular account of the tradition's identity against others, they would assert a normative claim about the status of other authorities, to be implicitly or explicitly challenged by the functioning of those authorities themselves. In short, such appeals would invoke a distinctive vision of the program of enquiry itself, over and against other accounts. Rather than setting parameters for enquiry, they would thus enter into a discussion about what those parameters ought to be (i.e. precisely the discussion that is opened by thinkers such as Taylder). As a result, appeals to a centralized authority could no more rationally resolve these discussions than 'loss cutting' can rationally resolve the contested issues of identity that those sources also raise.

Here, we might object that, despite this historical diversity of authorities, the tradition nevertheless affords a unique authority to (for example) the Pope and his Magisterium to operate in this centralized way. However, it is not at all clear how these assertions of unilateral authority actually avoid the issues above: as elements of the tradition's reading of itself, they also fall within the scope of the challenge presented by deconstructive and indecent approaches. To this end, merely asserting this authority does not actually address that challenge.

---

52 For a history of neo-Scholasticism, see John Haldane, 'Thomism and the Future of Catholic Philosophy' (1999) 80:938 *New Blackfriars* 158–169.
53 An excellent introduction to these theologians and their influence within the Church can be found in Hans Boersma, *Nouvelle Théologie and Sacramental Ontology: A Return to Mystery* (Oxford University Press 2009).
54 Albeit a development that was ultimately canonized by a centralized authority ('the Council') into which these plural authorities were integrated.

Note here that this does not amount to reducing the Church to a 'sociological reality', constituted by its *de facto* historical features. We are not arguing from the fact that certain theologians nominally belonging to the tradition invoke decentralized models of authority to the conclusion that these decentralized models of authority are the case. Rather, we are arguing that, in invoking these decentralized models of authority, they problematize centralized models such that these models cannot merely be asserted in response to them. As a result, we cannot simply assume a centralized model of authority as a sufficient condition for rejecting texts that invoke a different model: those texts problematize the very criteria by which they would be rejected.

This, then, creates a situation where we must act *as if* there were competing authorities within the tradition, each making distinct claims about the nature of their authority relative to that of others. The upshot is that, regardless of our own convictions on the matter, we must adjudicate between each side, in the process engaging with them fully, rather than merely negating one in favor of the other from the start.

Furthermore, paralleling our argument around 'loss cutting', Porter argues that the unilateral delineation of norms for enquiry by one authority in a plural context could have a fragmenting rather than unifying effect, limiting the tradition to a project of enquiry that its members come to find inadequate, leading to epistemological crisis.[55] Appealing to an absolute authority to determine the identity of Catholic theology would merely forefront the conflict around the nature of that identity. Drawing hard lines about how to resolve this conflict would then limit our capacity to actually find a resolution, especially if only one side could accept those conditions. Consequently, at least until we find a clear common ground that can serve to underpin a shared approach toward resolution, we cannot yet draw those lines. And this common ground can only be found through engaging seriously and receptively with those others, rather than attempting to negate them from the start.

4. The Problem of Trans Theology

In summary, when Roman Catholic theologians approach trans issues, they are confronted with a literature that is not only methodologically diverse but is so in ways that require us to engage substantively with sources across this diversity, rather than merely ignoring them based on the heuristic of 'orthodox' versus 'heterodox'. The upshot is that we cannot take 'orthodoxy' as a heuristic for determining those with whom we should engage theologically around trans issues. Approaches that fail to meet our criteria for what is proper to the tradition merely invite us to think more broadly about the conditions underpinning

---

55 Porter (n 47), 66.

our conception of, and perhaps relationship to, the Roman Catholic theological tradition. Consequently, they cannot be 'cut as a loss'; rather, we must read and engage with them, in the process allowing them to challenge us not just around trans issues but our broader theological commitments in light of which we approach those issues.

This leaves us in a situation approximating epistemological crisis. The challenge of trans theology is that it requires us to reflect carefully on the nature of the Roman Catholic theological tradition itself, putting into question the longstanding historical certainties and established norms of enquiry in light of which we would otherwise navigate first order questions about trans issues. The situation is not quite one of epistemological crisis, insofar as the tradition has not ceased to make progress by its own standards. Rather, the novelty of the field means that it has yet to begin doing so, and it is unclear *how* it is to make progress when it does.

This throws up two related problems: firstly, a pastoral problem related to uncertainty, and secondly, a practical problem about beginning to make progress. The remainder of this essay will outline these two problems and look to Pope Francis for resources to cope with them.

4.1 The Pastoral Problem

The pastoral problem relates to anxieties about how this situation will be resolved. It arises in the context of the fact that we are forced to recognize the possibility for our sources to challenge not only (as in the case of 'heterodox' approaches) the Roman Catholic tradition's positions on related issues but also (as in the case of deconstructive approaches) our accounts of the nature of the tradition itself *and* (as in the case of 'indecent' approaches) our corresponding commitments to the tradition as it exists today. To engage with trans issues as a Catholic theologian is thus to become involved in a holistic theological project that goes in many different directions and exceeds the capacities of any one person (and perhaps any group of people) to synthesize, anticipate or otherwise determine its course.

However, this project must be accomplished in a context where we must nevertheless formulate specific policies and take concrete courses of action. Consequently, there is almost inevitably going to be a deficit in the development of the field relative to our response to it. As a result, some other principle will have to fill this gap, moving us from indeterminate knowledge to determinate action. The fear is that this additional principle will be arbitrary or coercive, such as the violently enforced exclusion of certain groups from spaces of power and influence.

Pope Francis provides resources for the Roman Catholic Church to move in a direction that enables it to cope with this contemporary fragmented situation. In his 2013 encyclical, *Evangelii Gaudium*, he offers 'four principles related to constant tensions present in every social reality', which seek to guide us in negotiating the difficulties of a pluralistic world.[56] These principles, summarized briefly, are as follows:

Firstly, 'Time is greater than space': this enjoins us to recognize a 'constant tension between fullness and limitation', where fullness corresponds to the fulfillment of our lives and projects in 'the final cause which draws us to itself', and limitation corresponds to our present situation, which falls short of fullness. Time, here, is the movement of the 'horizon' of limitation into fullness.[57] In this context, Francis encourages us to give 'priority' to time over space, not to seek to achieve or obtain everything in the present, but instead to work patiently and to endure difficulty, with a concern for 'initiating processes'.[58]

In short, this principle counsels patience, resilience and long-term planning in the face of conflict. Significantly, it does this through invoking an eschatological temporality, in which our lives are drawn toward fulfilment. This in turn forestalls our anxieties about failure, as well as fears that the tensions in which we find ourselves are unresolvable.

This is illustrated further in his second and fourth principles. His second principle, 'Unity prevails over conflict',[59] invokes an image of the 'profound unity of all reality'; a cosmic reconciliation achieved in Christ, who 'has made all things one in himself: heaven and earth, God and man, time and eternity, flesh and spirit, person and society'. In doing so, it rereads the eschatological vision of the first principle in light of a narrative of salvation in redemption from alienation and conflict. The 'fullness' toward which we are oriented is ultimately that of 'peace' in communion.[60] Hence, the principle provides a hermeneutic of the conflicts that characterize present limitation: the Holy Spirit, which drives history, 'overcomes every conflict by creating a new and promising synthesis'.[61] Consequently, we should work with the Spirit to achieve a resolution in which social differences 'can achieve a diversified and life-giving unity'. Specifically, this means seeking 'a resolution which takes place on a higher plane and preserves what is valid and useful on both sides'.[62]

This image of resolution on a 'higher plane' resists the conflation of fulfillment with the triumph of any one element within conflict: this higher plane opens up a diachronic dimension that transcends the synchronic conflicts

---

56 Pope Francis, *Evangelii Gaudium* (2013) <http://w2.vatican.va/content/francesco/en/apost_exhort ations/documents/papa-francesco_esortazione-ap_20131124_evangelii-gaudium.html> (accessed 28 August 2019) §221.
57 *Ibid* §222.
58 *Ibid* §223.
59 *Ibid* §226.
60 *Ibid* §229.
61 *Ibid* §230.
62 *Ibid* §228.

of the present. We find this reflected in Francis's fourth principle: 'The whole is greater than the part.' This principle navigates the tension 'between globalization and localization', and the universal and the particular.[63] It offers a model of universality conceived by way of the image of a 'polyhedron': a shape that 'reflects the convergence of all its parts, each of which preserves its distinctiveness', in contrast to the 'sphere', which is composed of a single, homogenous surface of erased difference. As Francis notes, the polyhedron 'is greater than its parts'[64] – its universality incorporates the two-dimensional particularity of each face through its transcendence of them into three-dimensional space.

Finally, an important feature of each of these principles lies in how the transcendence of fullness, including its realization in unity and universality, resists reduction before our ideas of fullness. His third principle, 'Realities are more important than ideas', identifies 'a constant tension between ideas and realities'. This tension warns against the detachment of either from the other, resisting a '[f]ormal nominalism' in which the ideal takes precedent over the material and practical realities of life, thereby undermining the impetus for concrete action.[65]

Francis reads this principle as an exhortation toward 'incarnation of the word', analogous to the concrete realization of grace in history in Christ. The 'principle of reality' is that 'of a word already made flesh and constantly striving to take flesh anew'.[66] This enables us to reread this principle in terms of the historical eschatological vision of the other three principles: it means participating in the process whereby we achieve fullness, which also requires the recognition of the transcendence of that fullness over our present limitation and its conflicts, including the parties and positions involved in them. Thus, this principle's warning against idealist reductions of concrete 'realities' to 'ideas' is also a warning against reducing this process to our ideas of this process. The upshot is that recognizing the priority of time over space, as outlined in his first principle, involves recognizing that this process lies outside of our anticipations of that process.

Consequently, *Evangelii Gaudium's* four principles outline an understanding of faith in God's action in history, in which the resolution of conflict is shown to lie beyond the horizon of our present knowledge. This restates the situation presented by trans theology: we are faced with a wide-ranging field of competing claims, with no clear systematic way to resolve them. However, it does so in a fundamentally hopeful way: the process by which this resolution occurs is a redemptive one, and therefore is not arbitrary.

---

63 *Ibid* §234.
64 *Ibid* §236.
65 *Ibid* §232.
66 *Ibid* §233.

In turn, this enables us to accept the limitations of our situation with courage and confidence: they are only human limitations, rather than the limitations of the process itself. Moreover, as Francis's second principle shows us, we can co-operate with the historical work of grace. God works through human actors, even though we cannot always understand or anticipate our roles. This means that this confidence can also apply to our actions: we can play an authentic role in this process, working toward fulfillment even if our limitations mean that we cannot guarantee its success through our actions. This guarantee lies beyond us, in God.

4.2 The Practical Problem

The second problem is practical: we know that we can co-operate with grace in resolving these issues, but *how* can we do so? Where do we, as Roman Catholic theologians, go next?

This problem is predicated upon an impetus to resolve these issues, which is laudable but also ought to be moderated. Francis's four principles exhort us to recognize that fullness lies beyond the capacities and conceptions of the present. This is not to say that we should be satisfied with allowing these issues to go unresolved, especially when they are a source of suffering for so many people. However, equally, Francis's principles encourage us to set more modest goals for our actions in the present: to be realistic about our current limitations, to take a long-term perspective that emphasizes beginning processes rather than trying (and inevitably failing) to secure our ends prematurely, and to refuse to falsely totalize our ideas of what those resolutions would look like.

This prompts us, first and foremost, toward caution in offering supposedly universal solutions and responses to these issues. Consequently, the Church should be hesitant about making any determinate statements on trans issues: with the embryonic status of Roman Catholic theology in this area, it is far too early to do anything other than seek to enable later theologians by providing initial reflections for them to work from.

Secondly, because this field presents something of a systemic challenge to the Roman Catholic tradition and opens up so many avenues of discussion, we ought not to proceed as if there were a neat systematic basis for our work, which could be deployed universally as a kind of reductive framework for difficult problems.

Thirdly, and related to this, Francis's third and fourth principles remind us that grace works toward a unity that embraces difference, refuses to reduce it away and subverts our expectations in doing so. Consequently, our work should likewise tend toward seeking recognition and inclusion of the Other where possible, rather than defensively reacting against them. Theology cannot become another weapon in the culture war: such violence is antithetical to the grace that it seeks to incarnate.

5. Conclusion

There is perhaps a tension between our response to the pastoral and practical problems, and it is with regard to this tension that I would like to conclude. On the one hand, the pastoral response counsels courage and the confidence to act despite lacking all the information. On the other hand, the practical response counsels patience, and, where we cannot see an immediate solution, the willingness to allow God's plan to work itself out in ways that lie beyond our control. Both counsel trust in God, but with a different sense of what this requires: do we trust in God by acting, or do we trust in God by waiting?

Here, we should distinguish between long-term, large-scale resolutions of problems and short-term, small-scale resolutions. Francis's eschatological vision is concerned with long-term, large-scale resolution, in which the Holy Spirit brings creation to its fulfillment. However, all our actions, which must be performed decisively, at a given moment in time, take place in the short-term, even when they set in motion long-term processes.

Even though the Spirit guarantees long-term, eschatological resolution, our actions can go very wrong in the short term. Moreover, as Francis teaches, eschatological resolution lies beyond our anticipations. Rather, our capacity lies in anticipating the short term. Likewise, when things go wrong, we are more capable of anticipating this in the short term than in the long term, especially when this long term takes on cosmic timescales.

We are thus more able to anticipate and avoid short-term harms than long-term harms. Moreover, I would suspect that more short-term harms can be incurred than goods achieved by rash or hasty action. Consequently, although we should have the courage to act, this should be the courage to act only after sufficient reflection on the issues and discernment with regard to our actions, so as to avoid as many short-term harms as possible. As this inevitably slows down our ability to respond to issues, I would suggest that we lean more on trust in patience rather than trust in action. As for precisely how much reflection and discernment are needed before we ought to act, that is a perennial human question for which I do not have an answer.

Chapter 23

Is There a Space to Fight Back? Exclusionary Queer and Islamic Spaces and Resistance from Queer Muslims

Drew Dalton

1. Introduction

In 2019, many queer organisations and individuals in the West celebrated 50 years since the Stonewall Riots of New York and the invention of the pride flag, which is now entering its third decade of existence. Change has been significant in the United Kingdom, with positive changes in law and policy towards queer people, as well as the growing acknowledgement of the acceptability of social attitudes towards 'homosexuality'.[1] Several scholars of sexuality have observed this sea change and have suggested that we now live in a 'post-closet era' where the identity options for queer people have grown significantly and queer people are no longer confined to their 'gaybourhoods' in major cities.[2] Other positive movements have seen the rise of Pride celebrations, a growing acceptance of openness towards sexuality and gender identity within places of employment and even a change in Relationship and Sex Education in schools proposed for 2020 to include queer relationships and families. However, in contrast to this, and within the same year marking this 50th anniversary, the United Kingdom saw parents of predominantly Muslim children protesting outside of Parkfield Primary School in Birmingham against the school's 'No Outsiders' programme, which discussed same-sex family structures, under the notion that this was not suitable for children of ethnoreligious backgrounds (in this case, Islamic and South Asian). These protests raised and brought to light media questions about the intolerance of the predominantly South Asian Muslim community toward queer people and whether Muslims 'fit in' to wider British values and changing social attitudes.[3]

---

1 British Social Attitudes Survey, 'Homosexuality' (2013) <www.bsa.natcen.ac.uk/latest-report/british-social-attitudes-30/personal-relationships/homosexuality.aspx> (accessed 20 August 2019).
2 S Seidman, *Beyond the Closet: The Transformation of Gay and Lesbian Life* (Routledge 2002) 5; A Ghaziani, *There Goes the Gaybourhood?* (Princeton University Press 2014) 29.
3 *The Spectator*, 'Should Muslim Parents Be Allowed to Challenge LGBT Lessons?' (2019) (Online) <www.spectator.co.uk/article/should-muslim-parents-be-allowed-to-challenge-lgbt-lessons-> (accessed 17 March 2020).

DOI: 10.4324/9781003286295-29

In contrast to this event, once Manchester Pride and several other Pride organisations in the United Kingdom announced that they were using a new and updated version of the pride flag, with an additional brown and black stripe to represent people of colour, this caused friction within the queer community. Many argued passionately that it should not be changed from the original colours and that these colours represented all peoples in a 'colour blind' approach to the community.[4] However, this was met with opposition by many others, arguing that stopping this change is a form of racism and stating that the addition of the brown and black stipes is a fitting representation of people of colour within the queer community who have historically been, and continue to be, ignored and who are widely held up as the group, alongside trans people, who started the Stonewall Riots in the first place.[5]

Nonetheless, this wider social acceptance of queer people has not necessarily percolated to all levels of society and neither has racism and islamophobia abated within the United Kingdom at large. With these events and challenges in mind, this chapter will discuss the experiences of queer Muslims within the United Kingdom. It will posit the notion that queer Muslims still face unique barriers on a number of levels, including representations of Muslims and queer citizenship, the heteronormativity of Islamic spaces and finally the nature of racism and islamophobia within queer communities. This intersectionality of issues creates the unique lived conditions of queer Muslims today. So, it is vital to examine where queer Muslims form sites of resistance and seek support whilst they traverse the bridge between their ethnoreligious communities and the larger, predominantly white, queer communities. This chapter will explore the position faced by queer Muslims in the 'cash of cultures' debate in which Muslims are increasingly represented as the ideological 'Other' in post-9/11 politics. It will further examine in light of this how some queer Muslims have fashioned their own sense of belonging in queer spaces of their own making as sites of resistance to political ideology, racism and Islamophobia felt within queer communities and the pressures of heteronormativity within Islamic spaces. As a point of reference, the author uses the term 'queer' to broadly refer and encompass many of the identities included in the sexuality and gender identity spectrum (the LGBTQI+ acronym).

2. Representations of Muslims and Queer Citizenship: A Clash of Cultures?

The representations of Muslims (and of Islam) have altered significantly throughout socio-historical time periods, and this still has effects on how people

---

4 A Kotak, 'Combat Racism by Adding Black and Brown Stripes to the LGBT+ Rainbow Flag' (2019) <www.openlynews.com/i/?id=f81e044d-ae93-44dd-bf89-b7fb9bee68e7> (accessed 20 August 2019).
5 See Kotak (n 4).

in the West perceive Muslim communities to be. This has shaped modern-day discourses of Islam and has fed into Islamophobic tropes of how Muslims act, behave and treat others. Within postcolonial theory, the classic work of Said argues that early 'expert' knowledge of geographical spaces of the Middle and Far East, and their peoples, was developed in the academies of the West, and through the scientific expeditions of academics, they formed the 'exotic object', the 'Orient'.[6] These exotic objects were viewed as different to that of the people of the West and with the 'Orient' full of people ('Orientals'), who were seen as traditional rather than modern, suspicious and corrupt rather than industrious and enlightened and fanatical rather than scientifically interested in the truth. Through discourses of Western enlightenment, Western scholars have created this imaginary place and of the people who inhabit it. Narratives not only from academia but from early film and media emerged of romanticised yet highly sexualised, dominant Middle Eastern men who covet Western, white women and who stand in contrast to Middle Eastern women, who are portrayed as mysterious, submissive and exotic. Said argues that due to this knowledge coming from Western scholars and academics, this formed wider policy decisions of how the West would interact with other people. Despite its inaccuracies and stereotypes, this has become the dominant norm when discussing Muslims, which has garnered modern popular imagination in the media as the 'Other' especially in post 9/11 times.[7] Whilst this argument presented by Said has come under critique via 'Occidentalism',[8] which argues that the 'Orient' has a similar reductive view of the West and so there are misrepresentations on both sides, the power relations are not the same. Whilst some Muslims in Arab states can use anti-Western arguments and some economic influences, this pales into comparison with American and Western economic geopolitical power and dominance over other cultures.[9] Nonetheless, Said's arguments still hold relevance in how Muslims are represented as the 'Other' and conversely, complicated by queer Muslims whereby to exist is to be framed within a wider discourse of queer sexuality and gender identity as a 'Western' invention and not part of a wider Muslim culture. This distancing technique was highlighted in the 2019 Birmingham school protests in the United Kingdom, whereby some Muslim parents campaigned against the teaching of same-sex family structures by using the narrative that they were 'not part of Muslim culture'.[10] Queer sexualities and identities should

---

6 E Said, *Orientalism* (Vintage Books 1978) 160.
7 S Garner, *Racisms: An Introduction* (2nd edn, Sage Publications 2017) 238.
8 I Buruma and A Margalit, *Occidentalism: The West in the Eyes of Its Enemies* (Penguin 2004) 10.
9 Garner (n 7) 239.
10 Donna Ferguson, '"We Can't Give in": The Birmingham School on the Frontline of Anti-LGBT Protests' *The Observer*, 26 May 2019 <www.theguardian.com/uk-news/2019/may/26/birmingham-anderton-park-primary-muslim-protests-lgbt-teaching-rights> (accessed 20 August 2019).

always be analysed in light of ideological, geo-political and nation state framing, which will be discussed next.

In terms of the historical shift from European colonialism to present day neo-colonialism, Bracke argues that homosexuality has 'shifted columns' – whereby once it was used as a descriptor for markers of uncivility and deviance, it is increasingly being framed as a tool of 'civilisation' of cultures.[11] Islam is imagined as an alternative to European modernity, or yet to achieve modernity,[12] and those of Islamic origin as childlike and of another time, who are yet to develop into modern adults.[13] In several EU countries in recent years, conflicts over homophobic violence and racism have increasingly pitted mainstream queer and, in particular, Muslim ethnic communities against each other at the national level as well as the local geographical level. The infamous 'clash of civilisations' argument by Samuel Huntington has received widespread support in the wake of the 'war on terror', which appears to have translated into a 'clash of subcultures',[14] whereby inherently homophobic Muslim men lambast, attack and murder non-Muslim queer people. As a result of this, a narrative has emerged of a Muslim and gay binary with distinct and polarised positions into an 'Islam versus homosexuality tug of populations war'.[15] Within popular discourse, this posits a progressive, secular West versus a conservative, undemocratic and theocratic Islam. This has largely been informed by mainstream and queer media outlets representing examples of images of ISIS attacks toward gay men in Syria or of nation state leaders and some Muslim preachers' condemnation of homosexuality in the Arab world and Sub-Saharan Africa.[16] It has also been further fuelled by feminist and queer condemnations of Islam as deeply patriarchal, homophobic and hostile towards women and minorities as a new formation of racism.[17] The 'Other' as Muslim has become threatening and highlighted to queer people via media outlets, and this fuels the fear of the 'Other' to those who live in a largely secular queer community in Europe.

---

11 S Bracke, 'From "Saving Women" to "Saving Gays"; Rescue Narratives and Their Dis/continuities' (2012) 19:1 *European Journal of Women's Studies* 237–252.
12 J Butler, *Frames of War: When Is Life Grievable?* (Verso 2010) 10.
13 D DasGupta and RK DasGupta, 'Being Out of Place: Non-Belonging and Queer Racialisation in the U.K.' (2018) 27 *Emotion, Space and Society* 31–38.
14 N Heidenreich, 'The Struggle Between the Subcultures – Homophobia vs. Racism?' In EH Yekane and B Michaelis (eds), *Queer Across the Humanities: Perspectives on Queer Theory* (Querverlag 2005) 30.
15 J Puar, *Terrorist Assemblages: Homonationalism in Queer Times* (Duke University Press 2007) 2.
16 Michelle Nichols, 'Islamic State Throw Gay People Off High Buildings UN to Hear' *The Sydney Morning Herald*, 14 August 2015 <www.smh.com.au/world/islamic-state-throws-gay-people-off-high-buildings-un-to-hear-20150814-giyu0t.html> (accessed 17 March 2020).
17 K Kosnick, 'A Clash of Subcultures? Questioning Queer-Muslim Antagonisms in the Neoliberal City' (2015) *International Journal of Urban and Regional Research* 687–703.

Due to these wider ideological positionings, the lines of civility and barbarism have been redrawn in a discourse, which informs who is included and excluded from nation state citizenship as the apparent threat to white female and queer people looms from the differentially 'perverse others' from the Muslim world.[18] This has altered the way in which queer 'subjects' relate to their nation-states as Western queer people are increasingly taken into the 'national fold' as a process, which is deeply racialised.[19] Puar refers to the term 'homonationalism' to refer to the specific use of (homo)sexuality in the discourse of nationalism in the USA and as a post-9/11 strategy of homonormativity within nationalistic and patriotic discourse.[20] Homonationalism becomes a tool in which to position a nation state's 'national gays' higher than that of 'racial and sexual others'[21] who are positioned as from the 'outside'. Similar to this, Puar's concept of 'femonationalism' sees the rights of white Western women as threatened by Muslim outsiders who would seek to cover, veil and limit the freedoms of them. In fact, many mainstream queer movements of the global North have unwittingly, and sometimes not so, become an agent of this racialisation and islamophobia in post-9/11 times, as both femonationalism and homonationalism have redrawn concepts of 'good' and 'bad' nations and the views of their subjects within them. Kosnick presents the notion that the policing of Muslim communities in terms of gender equality is now a global phenomenon in post-9/11 times, due to three key tropes used in the war on terror and its underpinning of the 'clash of cultures' polarisation.[22] These three key figures have evolved from this and have been constructed as the *dangerous* Muslim man, the *imperilled and fragile* Muslim woman and the *civilised* European, creating a threatening 'Other' as outlined by Said. This redefining of 'who belongs' in terms of national citizenship places White Western women and White queer people as 'proper' citizens who are accorded protection by the liberal nation state and who stand in sharp contrast to racialised 'others' who exist to subvert and curtail the rights of both groups, or who exist outside of the fold.[23]

Okin argued that the debate about incompatibility of religious minorities in the West was already forming pre-9/11, and whilst most have focused on gender, some emerged around the incompatibility with sexual diversity and Muslim culture.[24] Anti-immigrant right wing politics has become emboldened

---

18 Puar (n 15) 45.
19 Kosnick (n 17) 690.
20 L Duggan, *The Twilight of Equality? Neoliberalism, Cultural Politics, and the Attack on Democracy* (Beacon Press 2003) 32.
21 A Yildiz, '"Turkish, Dutch, Gay and Proud": Mapping Out the Contours of Agency in Homonationalist Times' (2017) 20:5–6 *Sexualities* 699–714.
22 Kosnick (n 17) 687–703.
23 *Ibid*.
24 SM Okin, 'Feminism and Multiculturalism: Some Tensions' (1998) 108:4 *Ethics* 661–684.

by this, and this has affected the larger White feminist and gay activist movements, as Fekete argues:

> Most alarmingly, even some feminists and gay activists are now part of an overtly right-wing consensus that calls for immigration controls specifically targeted at immigrants from the Muslim world. Central to this process is a generalised suspicion of Muslims, who are characterised as holding on to an alien culture that, in its opposition to homosexuality and gender equality, threatens core European values.[25]

This illustrates the dichotomy of identities amongst queer Muslims, whereby 'queer' and 'Muslim' are viewed as mutually exclusive identity categories, with queer as Western and Muslim as unable to accept public equality of queer people. This assumption becomes highlighted by the press and media as something evident within the attitudes of Muslims and so feeds into their 'Otherness' and continues to position Muslims as an 'Other' to Western ideals of democracy and tolerance of sexual minorities as a result.

Massad argues that there have been policy changes at the national and global level by Western world leaders, who have strategically used sexual minority groups and gender equality to their own ends and to continuously represent Muslim-majority countries as the 'Other.' In reaction to this, Massad contends that LGBT identity politics has been imposed upon Arab and Middle Eastern Societies as part of a 'gay international agenda' of American neo-imperialism in the region.[26] Queer Arabs, he contends in his polemic, are succumbing to a false consciousness levered upon them by Western interests, which exploit them in the false belief that they are protecting their rights. It is easy to see currency within the argument that the West has this agenda, especially notable when former UK Prime Minister David Cameron stated that countries (many of which were Muslim majority) who practice homophobic and transphobia policy making should be denied UK international aid.[27] However, intellectuals, such as Massad, appear more concerned with ethnic solidarity rather than ensuring the safety of the most vulnerable members of a society whom he purports to defend.[28] Furthermore, Massad's arguments have often simplistically dismissed global (and Western) queer rights movements as the 'gay international' lobby, and his argument that Western LGBT identity politics causes harm has been disputed via the protestation of LGBT activist movements across

---

25 L Fekete, 'Enlightened Fundamentalism? Immigration, Feminism and the Right' (2006) 48:2 *Race and Class* 1–22.
26 J Massad, *Desiring Arabs* (University of Chicago Press 2008) 160.
27 H Seckinelgin, 'Same-Sex Lives Between the Language of International LGBT Rights, International Aid and Anti-Homosexuality' (2018) 2 *Global Social Policy* 1–26.
28 S Kugle Siraj al-Haqq, *Living Out Islam: Voices of Gay, Lesbian and Transgender Muslims* (New York University Press 2014) 4.

Sub-Saharan Africa and the Arab world, as well as the lack of evidence of his theory on the lived experiences of queer people in those nation states.[29] As discussed, the 'Other' has emerged through ideological, geo-political and social influences and has seemingly solidified Islam as an apparent monolith, positioned as a threatening and heterosexual (Brown and Black) Muslim culture, which has become framed against that of enlightened Western and White queer sexualities. This polarisation works to reinforce many non-Muslim queer viewpoints toward how they perceive Muslims, as well as how queer Muslims living and born in the United Kingdom are seen and treated in queer communities. In fact, queer space needs to be understood as not just structured through sexuality as 'these everyday spaces intersect with various other scales of spatiality, including national, international and transnational spaces.'[30] Added into this mix are problematic ideas of 'race', racialisation and the enactment of racism and Islamophobia within queer communities, which add problems for queer Muslims as they seek to access queer spaces, which will be examined in the next section.

3. Queer Muslims in Queer Spaces

Before attitudes to queer Muslims are discussed, it is vital to examine what is meant by the concept 'Islamophobia', as it has been debated by several leading academics, and confusion still reigns as to whether it is a form of racism or religious intolerance. Islamophobia as a concept emerged in recent years and was first discussed in the social sciences; yet, it covers a phenomenon that is not new and is largely a process of homogenising all Muslims into a negative, backward and exotic idea of the 'Other' as a group.[31] Islamophobia is a complex phenomenon and has been argued to be more about 'race' than religious prejudice by some authors,[32] although this has been hotly contested by others who have argued that it is more about being about an aversion to Islam as a religion.[33] In critique of the idea that Islamophobia is strictly an aversion to religion, Islamophobia has developed within the public imagery and has developed a 'Muslim-ness' that allows Muslims to become inserted into one category based on physical, religious, cultural and national genealogies rather than only the values and behaviour of religious people themselves.[34] As such, Moodod and Werbner argue that Islamophobia is about *both* 'race' and religion, and it has

---

29 M Rahman, 'Queer as Intersectionality: Theorising Gay Muslim Identities' (2010) 44:5 *Sociology* 944–961.
30 K Browne, J Lim, and G Brown (eds), *Geographies of Sexualities: Theory, Practices and Politics* (Ashgate Press 2007) 12.
31 Garner (n 7) 239.
32 *Ibid.*
33 F Halliday, 'Islamophobia Reconsidered' (1999) 22:5 *Ethnic and Racial Studies* 892–902.
34 Garner (n 7) 240.

become a 'new' form of cultural racism and exclusion which is pernicious as other traditional forms of racism, and in doing so, it has become something that is both biological and cultural.[35] In agreement with this, Garner argues that it is unimportant whether 'Muslims' are a priori a 'race' because the patterns and behaviours of non-Muslims group people under the heading 'Muslim' and deal with them as if they share particular characteristics, beyond that of being identified to a global religion.[36] As such, Islamophobia functions like many forms of traditional racisms by maintaining binary ideals (such as civilised versus barbaric), but it is more complex in that it collapses a complex set of positions into one negative view. This negative view is then projected onto Muslims as a cultural stigma and then works further by jettisoning any non-Muslim communities of any similar practices or norms (for example, domestic abuse, control of women and sexual minorities). This form of Islamophobia as a form of cultural racism involving both 'race' and religion as set out by Moodod and Werbner and Gardner will be the one which is utilised in this chapter moving forward. The following section will look at attitudes toward queer Muslims in queer spaces and the intersectionalities of queer people of colour and Islamic identity, paying specific attention to how racism and islamophobia find outlets within queer communities.

Secularism and notions of 'coming out' form a key backbone of many queer communities and often as a rite of passage to gain access to queer spaces in their entirety; however, this can be problematic for many queer Muslims when this is set as a standard of modern queer politics and identity. As set out by Massad earlier, some mainstream national and global 'gay rights' organisations or groups have also framed queer Muslims in such a way so that they should consider rejecting their religion upon 'coming out', and so they reinforce the negative stereotype of Islam as a threat to modernity whilst pushing queer Muslims to see themselves as 'victims' with no sense of agency.[37] In this light, traditional cultures and perspectives, and especially religion, are often posited as incompatible with a modern queer identity and of an ideal coming out process, which will label them with an identity. The 'freedom of norms' is seen as the 'queer ideal'; however, the atheism of the queer idealised subject often overlooks religion and faith as being a place of identity and difference.[38] In fact, 'queer Muslim subjects are framed as subjects outside the White gay spaces ... and are required to disavow their ethnic-religious identities in order to be read as appropriately queer' and if this is not jettisoned, queer Muslims

---

35 T Moodod and P Werbner (eds), *The Politics of Multiculturalism in the New Europe: Racism, Identity and Community* (Zed Books 1997) 30.
36 Garner (n 7) 242.
37 Kugle (n 28) 4.
38 SD Shannahan, 'Some Queer Questions from a Muslim Faith Perspective' (2010) 13:6 *Sexualities* 671–684.

may face Islamophobia as a result. In the United Kingdom, there is a 'stubborn thread of islamophobia' within queer secular spaces, whereby queer Muslims face Islamophobia within the queer community and beyond as a result of increased stigmatisation of Muslims by the press and by some politicians.[39] This pervasive idea that individuals cannot be queer and religious is still common and is exacerbated by the influence of the media, which also inherently paints religious groups and queer communities in opposition to each other.[40]

Added to this mix, many queer young people of colour perceive a White discourse around the 'coming out' process, whereby this is represented as an individualistic action by queer White people. However, this is often different for many queer people of colour, as coming out is about a larger social change that may involve a greater consciousness about challenging social practices and defying tradition.[41] Furthermore, many British South Asian men may feel hypervisible in queer spaces due to their ethnicity and religious or Islamic identity, and so feel unable to derive feelings of acceptance and inclusion within these spaces[42] and so as a result, anticipate rejection on the basis of their identity as a minority. This is often compounded by the issue that many fear that they will be recognised and identified by ethnoreligious members and their sexual identity may be disclosed by somebody on the gay scene or even by family members who could see them. However, it has been observed in some research that young British South Asian gay men go to queer spaces to seek solace from their estrangement of their ethnic and religious identities.[43] However, this is often to a point, as interpersonal contact in 'gay spaces' can pose additional social and psychological spaces for queer Muslims as they can perceive a risk of sexual disclosure as a result of associating with White British queer people who are perceived as being 'too open' about their sexual identities, as well as the fear of religious discrimination from non-Muslim men. One possible method of managing a stigmatised status is through concealing or 'passing' one's stigma. However, in order to do this with success, the stigmatised individual must be able to hide their stigma in such a way in which to make it invisible to others – however, this can be fraught with inner pressures.[44] To

---

39 DasGupta and DasGupta (n 13) 31–38; M Waites, 'Analysing Sexualities in the Shadow of War: Islam in Iran, the West and the Work of Reimagining Human Rights' (2008) 11:1 *Sexualities* 64–73.
40 SR Smallwood, '"Queerituality": Reforming What It Means to Be a Religious Queer' (2015) 36 *The Vermont Connection* 73–81.
41 OC Fox and TE Ore, '(Un) Covering Normalised Gender and Race Subjectivities in LGBT "Safe Spaces"' (2010) 3 *Feminist Studies* 629–649. See also Shannanhan (n 38).
42 R Jaspal, 'Coping with Perceived Ethnic Prejudice on the Gay Scene' (2017) 14:2 *Journal of LGBT Youth* 172–190.
43 R Jaspal and M Cinnirella, 'Identity Processes, Threat, and Interpersonal Relations: Accounts from British Muslim Gay Men' (2012) 59:2 *Journal of Homosexuality* 215–240.
44 C-S Han, K Proctor, and K-H Choi, 'I Know a Lot of Gay Asian Men Who Are Actually Tops: Managing and Negotiating Gay Racial Stigma' (2014) 18 *Sexuality and Culture* 219–234.

those who could not hide their Islamic identity and due to ethnicity being a visible characteristic, several respondents in Jaspal's research believed that White gay men held erroneous assumptions about South Asian culture and about the Islamic faith due to a growing Islamophobia in the United Kingdom and felt that White gay men fixated their attention on their ethnic identity, which inhibited discussions around 'normal issues'.[45] This made them feel different on the gay scene and exacerbated their feelings of being in the sexual outgroup.

Voices that have dominated Western queer activism, both past and present, have largely been White, and as such the 'community' has become homogenised based on a false sense of cohesion being fostered, which ignored the oppression of people of colour within these 'safe spaces'.[46] The discourse of 'safe spaces' within many queer communities fails to account for intersectionality of experiences, as it relies on a binary logic that focuses on the elimination of homophobia and heterosexism, creating a singular and marginalised identity in how the spaces are organised. This becomes problematic, as the construction of this singular identity means that other privileges and oppressions are unaccounted for or represented in an additive manner (for example, 'double oppression').[47] This additive approach can mean that individuals are perceived to pile up oppressions without any real understanding of the complexity of interaction between them, and therefore, the only safe space is that of a 'colour blind' space on the queer scene. The implication notion that all queer people experience heterosexism and homophobia in the same way leads to a normalised and universalised gendered and racialised experience in these spaces alongside a common practice whereby 'many White people attempt to group all LGBT people of colour together . . . [but] there is no universal experience for LGBT people of colour'.[48] Various grassroot club nights and Black Pride have evolved for queer people of colour in parts of the United Kingdom, and whilst they admirably represent a space for people of colour to have a voice and to be represented, these can also be problematic. These spaces may well appear to be 'safe spaces' free of racism and Islamophobia for queer people of colour; however, this has a secondary effect of transferring responsibility to identify, protect against and address racism onto queer people of colour, rather than it being a collective effort by the whole community. In transferring this responsibility, this absolves many queer White people of this responsibility themselves,[49] and so issues and concerns that should be addressed openly begin to manifest into racism in the queer community since issues are not tackled head on and instead

---

45 See Jaspal (n 42).
46 S Giwa and C Greensmith, 'Race Relations and Racism in the LBGTQ Community of Toronto: Perceptions of Gay and Queer Social Service Providers of Colour' (2012) 59 *Journal of Homosexuality* 149–185.
47 Fox and Ore (n 41) 629–649.
48 *Ibid*.
49 Giwa and Greensmith (n 46) 149–185.

are kept apart. Therefore, there is a need to focus away from creating a 'safe space' into a 'safer space', as this removes us away from the belief that safe spaces can be entirely secured in a way in which they are free of struggle or challenges.

Social geographers have noted how sexuality is made in everyday interactions in certain places and how interaction sexualises spaces. Everyday spaces, such as the home, workplace and the street, are constituted as heterosexual due to repeated heterosexual performances.[50] Within 'gaybourhoods', exclusions are produced on the grounds of identifiers other than sexuality, and so particular identities (White, gay and male) may exclude differences on grounds of social class, 'race', disability and gender. Whilst appearing as 'open to all' and 'colour blind' to all queer people, 'gay bars often act as gated communities keeping out certain classed, gendered and coloured bodies',[51] and so reinforce wider racism and Islamophobic attitudes. This can produce a certain type of homonormativity whereby gay villages focus on able-bodied, male, White, middle-class younger people with expendable incomes.[52] Caluya's research into Asian men on Sydney's gay scene documented how they see this space as a space of segregation filled with racially based sexual rejections and exotification of the Asian body.[53] Brennan-Ing et al argue that ethnoracialised queer people experience racism in other forms, such as physical and verbal assault, as well as fetishised and eroticised due to their 'race' as 'trophies'.[54] Amongst South Asian lesbian and bisexual women, research has examined how they view gay spaces in London as White, not only because of the presence of White women but also because their bodies were 'read' and treated as 'the Other'.[55] There is a clear relationship between 'race' and 'space' in that space is something that is racialised and 'race' is spatialised.[56] Whilst not always apparent, this becomes recognisable when a particular racialisation of space is disrupted or altered when racialised bodies are 'out of place' within these spaces.[57] Groups formed around 'shared Whiteness' are not seen by White people as a racial category, and therefore serve to work as an unmarked and silent 'racial norm'.[58]

---

50 N Held, 'Comfortable and Safe Spaces? Gender, Sexuality and "Race" in Night-Time Leisure Spaces' (2015) 14 *Emotion, Space and Society* 33–42.
51 DasGupta and DasGupta (n 13) 31–38.
52 Held (n 50) 33–42.
53 G Caluya, '"The Rice Steamer": Race, Desire and Affect in Sydney's Gay Scene' (2008) 39:3 *Australian Geography* 283–292.
54 M Brennan-Ing et al., '"I'm Created in God's Image, and God Don't Create Junk": Religious Participation and Support Among Older GLBT Adults' (2013) 25:2 *Journal of Religion, Spirituality & Aging* 70–92.
55 R Kawale, 'A Kiss Is Just a Kiss . . . or Is It? South Asian Lesbian and Bisexual Women and the Construction of Space' in P Puwar and P Raghuram (eds), *South Asian Women in the Diaspora* (Berg 2003) 120.
56 Held (n 50) 33–42.
57 N Puwar, *Space Invaders: Race, Gender and Bodies Out of Place* (Berg 2004) 8.
58 Held (n 50) 33–42.

A group of Black or South Asian queer people coming together becomes much more 'visible as they threateningly fill the space [to White people] in much larger numbers than they literally do'.[59] It is not just a case of seeing the 'race' but of triggering emotions by the perceived practices that produce racialised bodies and so as such, spaces are always racialised even if only White bodies are present. Therefore, brown and Muslim identities threaten to dislocate the heterogeneity supposedly safe spaces.[60]

Manchester's Gay Village was not a source of 'racial neutrality' in the work of Held, who found that exclusions were inbuilt and the space itself was a 'sea of whiteness'.[61] If Black and South Asian people are assumed that they cannot be queer due to their religion or culture, then once they access the Gay Village they are very likely to be perceived as heterosexual and potentially homophobic. Therefore, the 'racial other' becomes seen as sexually oppressed and so 'Muslim' and 'gay' become seen as incompatible within queer spaces. It is of little surprise that many queer Muslims feel alienated in White queer spaces and feel that they are visually marked out as holding an Islamic identity (through beard, hijab or other factor that could lead to suspicion), and once this identification happens, they face Islamophobia within these spaces or exclusionary door practices.[62] Whilst many queer spaces may advertise themselves as tolerant, accepting of all and safe, they are often juxtaposed against other areas that are 'black' or 'South Asian' and which are perceived to be unfriendly and threatening for queer people. This narrative is a powerful one to cultivate the notion that queer spaces are safe spaces; however, this ignores the racialising discourses within queer spaces and sets the queer subject as inherently White.

Comparative studies of gay media print have shown that White gay men are depicted more often on covers and inside pages of commercial LGBT magazines than their racialised counterparts.[63] Online, the Internet represents a frontier whereby racism is propagated and contested and the movement of bodies online has ensured that perpetrators of racism are protected by a shield

---

59 Puwar (n 57) 8.
60 DasGupta and DasGupta (n 13) 31–38.
61 N Held, '"They Look at You Like an Insect That Wants to Be Squashed": An Ethnographic Account of the Racialised Sexual Spaces of Manchester's Gay Village' (2017) 20:5–6 *Sexualities* 535–557. See also S Giwa, *Surviving Racist Culture: Strategies of Managing Racism Among Gay Men of Colour – An Interpretative Phenomenological Analysis* (PhD Thesis, York University 2016) 14; Puwar (n 57) 8.
62 Kawale (n 55) 121; C Bassi, 'Riding the Dialectical Waves of Gay Political Economy: A Story from Birmingham's Commercial Gay Scene' (2006) 38:2 *Antipode: A Radical Journal of Geography* 213–235; J Haritaworn, T Tauqir and E Erdem, 'Gay Imperialism: Gender and Sexuality Discourse in the "War on Terror"' in A Kuntsman and ME Esperanza (eds), *Out of Place: Interrogating Silences in Queerness Raciality* (Raw Nerve Books 2008) 159.
63 T Sonnekus and J Van Eeden, 'Visual Representation, Editorial Power, and the Dual "Othering" of Black Men in the South African Gay Press: The Case of Gay Pages' (2009) 35:1 *Communicatio* 81–100; O Roy, 'The Colour of Gayness: Representations of Queers of Colour in Quebec's Gay Media' (2012) 15:2 *Sexualities* 175–190.

of anonymity against their targets.[64] Within queer communities, queer people of colour may experience racism in dating relationships and social networks, which is sustained by reports from people of colour finding exclusion in queer community events and spaces. Racism in dating and intimate relationships has been reported amongst gay and bisexual men, with 'race' having a greater likelihood of being mentioned in Internet ads for men who have sex with men than in heterosexual online ads. Indirect and direct racism as 'sexual racism'[65] is especially prevalent in personal ad sites used for partner and sexual selection, where sex role stereotypes and racial stereotypes are meshed together to devalue sexual currency or to assume stereotypical sex roles and penis sizes based on racialised fantasies of White men.[66] In terms of Eastern and South Asian men, research has found dominant and stereotypical ideas of feminisation and emasculating bodies to form a submissive sexual position in intercourse.[67] In opposition to this, spaces such as Grindr can become spaces where immigrants and people of colour experience racism and xenophobia.[68] Shield recounts interviews with Arab interviewees who faced online racism and Islamophobia on Grindr, and in particular one account whereby an Arab man received a message from a White gay man who stated 'F*ck [your Arab country]. f*ck Islam, and f*ck you.'[69] Whilst interviewees tended to play downplay these exchanges and placing people as 'bad apples', Shield argues that in light of Europe's turbulent political discourses around immigration and Islam, statements like these become 'entitlement racism' whereby aggressors justify hate speech as simply 'speaking their mind'.[70] Online gay men's dating profiles with 'no Asians' perpetuate common Orientalist stereotypes of Eastern and South Asian people while disavowing them altogether. This brings the classic work of Said to relevance as to why the Orientalist narrative still prevails. The West, Said argues, defines itself by producing an Other, which exists outside of the West's defined boundaries. Therefore, representations produce powerful border-making

---

64 D Callander, CE Newman, and M Holt, 'Is Sexual Racism Really Racism? Distinguishing Attitudes Toward Sexual Racism and Generic Racism Among Gay and Bisexual Men' (2015) 44:7 *Archives of Sexual Behaviour* 1991–2000.
65 VC Phua and G Kauffman, 'The Crossroads of Race and Sexuality' (2003) 24 *Journal of Family Issues* 981–994; LD Icard, 'Black Gay Men and Conflicting Social Identities: Sexual Orientation Versus Racial Identity' (1986) 4:1/2 *Journal of Social Work & Human Sexuality* 83–93.
66 Brennan-Ing et al (n 54) 70–92; C Grov et al., 'Challenging Race-Based Stereotypes About Gay and Bisexual Men's Sexual Behaviour and Perceived Penis Size and Size Satisfaction' (2015) 12:3 *Sexuality Research and Social Policy* 224–235.
67 See Brennan-Ing (n 54).
68 ADJ Shield, 'Grindr Culture: Intersectional and Socio-Sexual. Ephemera: Theory and Politics in Organisation' (2018) <www.ephemerajournal.org/contribution/grindr-culture-intersectional-and-socio-sexual> (accessed 10 August 2019).
69 *Ibid.*
70 P Essed, 'Entitlement Racism: License to Humiliate' in S Pfohman and L Feke (eds), *Recycling Hatred: Racism(s) in Europe Today* (ENAR 2013) 62.

practices, which separate the West and its practices and its Other (the orient, or indeed, the 'Muslim').

For many queer people of colour, racism in whichever form it is expressed, has effects on the quality of life, and racism-related stress has health implications,[71] and some research has suggested that a fragmentation of identities among queer people of colour means that they are often compelled to identify with either their sexual or racial identities.[72] The preferred discourses of a multiracial queer community form around 'Whiteness' as a priority in terms of desire, advertising and basis of many organisations.[73] As such, these 'controlling' images,[74] especially of Black or South Asian men in largely White scenes, form imagery, which is built to satisfy White gay male desire. This representation reinforces the one-dimensional view that ethnicity and sexual orientation are not compatible, and these seemingly incompatible categories feed the narrative that to be 'gay' means to be White. Due to this, the Black gay man or other men of colour become anomalies or inauthentic, and as such, White people can only lay claim to same-sex orientation.[75] Microaggressions become normalised within this context and are characterised as brief, daily assaults on minority individuals, which take a variety of social and environmental forms, which are verbal or non-verbal as well as intentional and unintentional.[76] Three types of microaggressions have been identified – microaggressions, microinsults and microinvalidation, which impact on poor mental and physical health in both queer and racial and minority ethnic communities. Microinsults and microinvalidations (for example, 'you cannot be gay and a Muslim') lead to distress amongst those targeted, and as such, perpetrators may discredit an individual because of wider societal beliefs about their minority group (microinsults). Balsam *et al* noted that these microaggressions were prevalent in three distinct ways: 1) being told that 'race isn't important' by White people (microinvalidation); 2) being framed as a 'sex object' by other queer people due to ethnicity (microinsults); and 3) reading personal ads stating, 'White people only' (microassaults).[77] The queer scene and community can be fraught with difficulties by queer Muslims who often become the 'Other' within these spaces, whereby racism

---

71 A Ro et al., 'Dimensions of Racism and Their Impact on Partner Selection Among Men of Colour Who Have Sex with Men: Understanding Pathways to Sexual Risk' (2013) 15:7 *Culture, Health & Sexuality* 836–850.
72 JM Gibbs and BE Jones, 'The Black Community and Its LGBT Members: The Role of the Behavioural Scientist' (2013) 17:2 *Journal of Gay and Lesbian Mental Health* 196–207.
73 CI Nero, 'Why Are the Gay Ghettoes White?' in EP Johnson and MG Henderson (eds), *Black Queer Studies: A Critical Anthology* (Duke University Press 2005) 241.
74 PH Collins, *Black Sexual Politics: African Americans, Gender, and the New Racism* (Routledge 2004) 149.
75 See Nero (n 73).
76 KF Balsam et al., 'Measuring Multiple Minority Stress: The LGBT People of Colour Microaggressions Scale' (2011) 17:2 *Cultural Diversity and Ethnic Minority Psychology* 163–174.
77 *Ibid.*, 165.

and Islamophobia can go unchallenged and are reinforced structurally. In contract to this, solace within Islamic communities can also be a challenge, which will be discussed next.

4. Queer Muslims in Islamic Spaces

The cultural process of heteronormativity and compulsory heterosexuality is acutely active in Islamic religious communities, and this identity configuration can have detrimental effects on queer Muslims. Heterosexism implies overt and covert manifestations of sexual prejudice against queer people as well as the elevation of heterosexuality as 'the norm', and therefore preferential treatment of heterosexual people at the individual, institutional and cultural levels. By design, heterosexism promotes and assumes that opposite-sex sexuality is the cultural norm within human relationships, which can make it problematic towards queer people. Some studies of South Asian gay men have found higher levels of homophobia within South Asian communities, where there may be a prevalent belief that homosexuality is a Western phenomenon,[78] which echoes that of occidentalism as mentioned earlier within this chapter.[79] This has a secondary effect of socialisation into an environment whereby same-sex sexuality is considered foreign and abhorrent (or 'haram' – forbidden). The voices of queer Muslims are rarely heard and have been both silenced and edited in the past, and when speaking up, they are expected to express contrition. They are voices of an oppressed minority group, 'a minority within a minority', within their religious community.[80] Added to this, contemporary 'gay' culture can also leave much to be desired in the larger Muslim community, with the flamboyancy, perceived indecency and licentiousness that are associated with it can conflict with Muslim ideas of modesty and notions of no sex outside of marriage.[81]

The nature of the family can also cause difficulty in that not only do parents form part of a control method against norm-breaking behaviour, but the extended family offers a host of adult authorities who can act as surveillance and critique.[82] In this sense, the immediate family bleeds into the wider Muslim community and can make stepping outside of regulated and heteronormative boundaries difficult. The family and extended family also act as a role in which to preserve family honour, reputation and their

---

78 R Ratti, R Bakeman and JL Peterson, 'Correlates of High-Risk Sexual Behaviour Among Canadian Men of South Asian and European Origin Who Have Sex with Men' (2000) 12:2 *AIDS Care* 193–202, and see Balsam (n 76).
79 Buruma and Margalit (n 8) 3.
80 Kugle (n 28) 2.
81 A Jama, *Queer Jihad: LGBT Muslims on Coming Out, Activism, and the Faith* (Oracle Publishing 2013) 10.
82 Kugle (n 28) 11.

standing within the Muslim community, which very often can be valued higher than that of the individual's welfare.[83] Given that South Asian ethnic cultures attach great importance to arranged marriage, many young queer South Asian people may feel uncertain and fearful about their future, and as such cope with their threatened identity by denying it and so present their worldview as heterosexual and sexual behaviour as a phase. As such, queer Muslim South Asian men manifest high levels of internalised homophobia and may eschew friendships with other queer people deepening their levels of social isolation.[84]

Familial honour or 'izzat' is an important concept that affects self-disclosure of many queer people of South Asian origin, and linked to this are heteronormative concepts of marriage, family building and pro-creation.[85] For those who hinder or deviate from set heteronormative sexual scripts, they may be at risk of being ostracised, face threats to their identities or forms of violence, and so may attempt to 'pass' as heterosexual in order to deflect attention from the stigma attached to their sexual orientation.[86] Religious heterosexism becomes a system of oppression that contributes to larger hegemonic notions of heteronormativity within ethnoracial communities,[87] and often sources of queer identity in literature are not present and so by examining Islamic books, 'if you check the index in the back of the book, it's rarely mentioned. There's almost a complete silence on the matter.'[88] Not only is silence about queer lives and identities propagated through religious heterosexism, queer Muslims may also face regular denunciation of same-sex romantic relationships in religious communities, and 'out' individuals may face scriptural injunctions hurled at them. As a result, many queer Muslims may feel pressured to choose between their two apparent conflicting identities, their sexual orientation and their religious identity, in the mistaken belief that the two cannot coexist.

As such, ethnoreligious queer people may experience a double-sided homophobia – from both the general population and their ethnoreligious communities.[89] This means that casual homophobic language, concepts of shame and family honour and internalised pain as a result have consistently been found to lead to higher levels of internalised homophobia in South Asian communities amongst queer people.[90] Due to this polarisation of the two identities, an indi-

---

83 *Ibid.*, 55.
84 See Jaspal (n 42).
85 Jaspal and Cinirella (n 43) 215–240.
86 R Jaspal and A Siraj, 'Perceptions of "Coming Out" Among British Muslim Gay Men' (2011) 2:3 *Psychology and Sexuality* 183–197.
87 Giwa (n 61) 13.
88 Jama (n 81) 6.
89 See Jaspal (n 42).
90 Jaspal and Siraj (n 86) 183–197; Jaspal and Cinirella (n 43) 215–240; Giwa (n 61) 16.

vidual may face social and psychological problems due to an identity conflict.[91] This may lead to a perceived obligation to conceal their sexual orientation from their ethnoreligious ingroup members and to conceal their religious identity from sexual ingroup members[92] causing problems of identity authenticity. Due to this identity conflict, religiosity may be much less positive for some queer Muslims who may find that a more personal spiritual relationship with Allah is more preferable[93] in order to reduce the sting and prejudice-induced messages of religious organisations. However, other authors have pointed out the damaging effects of this identity disconnect, as 'there is the type who hates himself and would like to be White or straight or both. Or there is the type who cut off all religious and spiritual aspects, going to the hardcore denial of any form of spirituality.'[94]

Islamic spaces and communities offer sites of safety for many queer Muslims of colour in terms of buffering against structural racisms and Islamophobia. However, they offer only a partial protection in that they often offer silence or condemnation of queer Muslim sexual minorities and gender identity, which is not cisgender. This causes added complications to the lived experiences of queer Muslims and means that many are left in a complex position of intersectional threads, which Orne refers to as the 'intersectional knot', in which one side loosens and offers freedom to an individual, whilst another part tightens offering restrictions.[95]

5. Queer Identity, Resistance and Queer Spaces for Queer Muslims

Within the wider ideological geopolitical framing of Muslims as antithetical to Western and British values, of racism and Islamophobia within queer spaces and heteronormativity in Islamic spaces, how do queer Muslims find resistance to this? It is important to state that there has been very little scholarship on the Queer South Asian diaspora in the United Kingdom.[96] Traditionally, communities have been understood as groups of people who are connected through

---

91 CL Anderton, DA Pender and KK Asner-Self, 'A Review of the Religious Identity/Sexual Orientation Identity Conflict Literature: Revisiting Festinger's Cognitive Dissonance Theory' (2011) 5:3/4 *Journal of LGBT Issues in Counseling* 259–281.
92 See Jaspal (n 42).
93 AL Dahl and RV Galliher, 'LGBTQ Young Adult Experiences of Religious and Sexual Identity Integration' (2009) 3:2 *Journal of LGBT Issues in Counselling* 92–112.
94 Jama (n 81) 8.
95 J Orne, *Boystown: Sex and Community in Chicago* (University of Chicago Press 2017) 77.
96 RK DasGupta, *Digital Queer Cultures in India: Politics, Intimacies and Belonging* (Routledge 2017) 10; A Yip, 'Embracing Allah and Sexuality? South Asian Non-Heterosexual Muslims in Britain' in K Jacobsen and P Kumar (eds), *South Asians in the Diaspora: Histories and Religious Traditions* (Brill Academic Publishing 2004) 294.

faith, ethnicity, social class, nationality and geography. In order for many communities to develop a rally cry as a single point of unity to tackle oppression, this often means supressing difference. However, this is not to state the idea that all South Asian and Islamic spaces (and therefore Muslims) are homophobic by default and that queer Muslims are always caught perpetually between religious–ethnic enclaves and queer spaces. No culture or religion is a monolithic or homogenous entity, and marginal identities of many South Asian and Black Muslims in the United Kingdom do find a way to coexist and resist powerful social norms, despite this being difficult and straining upon the individual.

In fact, the existence of queer Muslims has received much attention in the Global North and in part, due to the international activism of queer Muslim groups, traditional media through television programming and social media, pride marches and distinct communities within predominantly secular queer spaces. Alongside this, there has also been a flourishing of academic and semi-academic interest in the testimonies of queer Muslims.[97] Due to many Muslims living in Western democratic nations, which grant LGBT protections by law, many queer Muslims have been able to organise and to critically engage with their religious identity, family norms, religious authorities and community traditions in ways not possible in Muslim-majority countries.[98] Since the early 2000s, new technology has allowed networks of queer Muslims to become increasingly cohesive and to set up support groups, internet chat rooms, discussion threads and websites. This has developed a community of queer Muslims who can represent and take their concerns to the larger Muslim community and the wider secular world.[99] Online communities are 'part and parcel of the modern queer Muslim experience',[100] whilst the proliferation of queer Muslim organisations in the United Kingdom, such as Hidayah, Imaan and London Queer Muslims, means that they can create their own communities and spaces in which to congregate, worship and meet for Islamic celebrations. This is often within the wider context of much more cisnormative, heteronormative Islamic spaces.[101] For many queer Muslims, being a member of a mosque with people from the same ethnic background is fraught with ambivalence, and many feel that mosques are sites of control.[102] Due to this and in finding their own routes of practice of Islam, many queer Muslims in Peuman's research invited other queer Muslims to their homes during Ramadan for dinner parties. During these celebrations, participants re-appropriated a religious holiday as an embodied practice to give a positive content to their

---

97 DasGupta and DasGupta (n 13) 31–38; Shannahan (n 38) 671–684.
98 Kugle (n 28) 10.
99 *Ibid.*, 221.
100 H Kesvani, *Follow Me, Akhi: The Online World of British Muslims* (Hurst and Company 2019) 221.
101 *Ibid.*, 222.
102 SW Peuman, 'Queer Muslim Migrants in Belgium: A Research Note on Same-Sex Sexualities and Lived Religion' (2014) 17:5/6 *Sexualities* 618–631.

stigmatised identity as a queer Muslim. Queer Muslim organisations, such as Hidayah and Imaan, have nurtured this further with Eid celebrations and queer prayer spaces.[103]

Many queer Muslims in the United Kingdom have implemented key strategies used to buffer against religious homophobia and to destabilise homogenous ideas of queer identity. One such strategy used by many queer Muslims is the queering of religious texts.[104] The interpretation of homosexuality as an offense and therefore sanctioned by stoning to death (rajm) is often interpreted by juristic measures in some nation states that link this to the struggles of the Prophet Lut with his people.[105] However, this punishment is seen as deeply problematic and inaccurate by many queer Muslims, as they argue that the Qur'an does not use any terms corresponding to 'homosexuals' or 'homosexuality' within the entirety of its text, and there are no terms used within the Qur'an that specifically refer to same-sex relations. Nor does the Qur'an prescribe death or any form of punishment for consensual same-sex behaviour. As such, many queer Muslims contest this and refer to the story of the Prophet Lut and how the people of Lut were punished not due to same-sex practices but instead due to rape, incest, stealing and murder. Many queer Muslims point to the notion that the story of Lut 'is male to male rape, involving power and humiliation and so it is not fitrah, it is a choice'.[106] This queer reading of the Qur'an means that these factors led to Allah's destruction of the city and not the occurrence of same-sex loving relationships. In fact, many queer Muslims argue that there is no verse in the Qur'an that unambiguously condemns sexual minorities, and all verses relating to 'sodomites' are referring to ritual rapes of young men and women by the political elites of a vanished people.[107] Furthermore, a commonly cited report in the Hadith in which the Prophet appears to announce the death penalty for homosexual intercourse is highlighted as unreliable, as this does not appear to originate with the Prophet himself but rather a second-generation follower who was prone to exaggeration, fabrication and ideological extremism.[108]

Another strategy used by queer Muslims is to highlight the rich queer Islamic history and to show that 'transgressive' sexual behaviours were tolerated

---

103 Hidayah, 'Homepage' (2019) <www.hidayahlgbt.co.uk/> (accessed 20 August 2019); Imaan, 'Homepage' (2019) <https://imaanlondon.wordpress.com/> (accessed 20 August 2019).
104 AKT Yip, 'Queering Religious Texts: An Exploration of British Non-Heterosexual Christians' and Muslims Strategy of Constructing Sexuality-Affirming Hermeneutics' (2005) 39:1 *Sociology* 47–65.
105 J Rehman and E Polymenopoulou, 'Is Green Part of the Rainbow: Sharia, Homosexuality, and LGBT Rights in the Muslim World' (2013) 37:1 *Fordham International Law Journal* 1–52.
106 Jama (n 81) 16.
107 Kugle (n 28) 49–50.
108 *Ibid.*, 76.

for centuries in the Arab–Muslim world.[109] In terms of gender identity, this rich queer Islamic history has witnessed at least three categories of gender non-conforming persons: the castrated man (khasi, or eunuch); the effeminate man, who may dress, speak or have a feminine gait but is cisgender (mukhannath); and a third gender (hijra), which in Western terms we may recognise as a form of transgender.[110] This strategy argues that the Prophet had formally forbidden attacking effeminate men (mukhannathuns), and in one Hadith, Aisha, the wife of the Prophet, reported that an effeminate man was accustomed to visiting the wives of the Prophet, as they had no sexual desire towards women.[111] Through queering religious texts, queer Muslims do not question the content of religious texts and the Qur'an but instead question the 'accuracy and therefore the hegemony of the traditional interpretation of such texts'.[112] As such, many queer Muslims when queering religious texts argue that they should be placed within a socio-historical and cultural frame in which they have been produced and reproduced by heteronormativity, and through doing this, they are deconstructing the heterocentric history of the faith.[113] Another key strategy used to positively frame queer Muslims' relationship to Islam was to pull upon an essentialist view of sexuality by viewing themselves as fully part of Allah's creation.[114] These strategies combat the role of Islamic homo/bi/transphobia and refashion spaces in which to live as a queer Muslim identity, as well as contesting and destabilising the notion that a person cannot be both 'queer' and a 'Muslim'.

People will also seek out situations where identities that are meaningful to them are verified and supported, and so individuals may possess a variety of identities (Muslim, feminist, friend and so on) in that they may be activated and performed in different social contexts.[115] These identities are also situated within power relations within a society and within social norms and regulatory discourses – for example, identity categories may be given to us by powerful social forces or by our own social ties. As Kugle states, many queer Muslims may have formed their own counter-hegemonic queer theologies that serve to challenge religious spaces that they feel are denied to them.[116] Religious practices may or may not conform to official proclamations by religious authorities

---

109 JW Wright and R Everett (eds), *Homoeroticism in Classical Arabic Literature* (Columbia University Press 1997) 3.
110 Kugle (n 28) 207.
111 *Ibid.*, 241.
112 Yip (n 104) 47–65.
113 Jama (n 81) 115.
114 Kugle (n 28) 14.
115 NT Fuist, '"It Just Always Seemed Like It Wasn't a Big Deal, Yet I Know for Some People They Really Struggle with It"': LGBT Religious Identities in Context' (2016) 55:4 *Journal for the Scientific Study of Religion* 770–786.
116 Kugle (n 28) 21.

but represent the ways in which people enact their faith and construct their own religious identity – a 'doing religion'[117] through agency and interaction. As such, religious identity must take into consideration the agency of the person as well as the sociotemporal context around them. Instead of a strategy of reconciliation, Fuist noted that people engage in selective disclosure, approaching situations with a variety of performances, whilst others adopted a strategy of integration, seeing their religious identities as fully congruent.[118] Neither one is more 'genuine' than the other or are in contradiction to each other. Queer Muslims have used strategies in which to show that queer and Islam are not about being reconciled but are about empowering each other.

Importantly and politically, queer Muslims represent an intersectional location that moves against the clash of cultures' argument and problematises it further, because their very existence challenges the positioning of Western and Eastern cultures as oppositional and mutually exclusive.[119] However, due to being situated within this location, queer Muslims may face oppression, as they remain caught in between cultural/political Islamophobia and homophobia, and so they exist within an 'inside/out' location as they challenge the category of Muslim and the category of queer.[120] Importantly, this positioning and 'impossibility' of queer Muslims mean that they are stood at a site of resistance where they can actively reject dominant narratives of both categories. This is not only a challenge to unchallenged traditions and heteronormativity within Muslim communities, but it is also an equal challenge to the racism, Islamophobia and homogeny within Western queer identities, spaces and organisations.

6. Looking Towards the Future – Is There Space to Fight Back?

When discussing queer Muslims, concepts of nationalism and sexuality are important, as sexuality forms a crucial role in the symbolic enclosure of space in nationalism,[121] and as such, larger geo-political framing of Muslims as the 'Other' in a simplistic binary of 'them' versus 'us' are grounds in which to find space to contest this narrative. Queer Muslims form a distinct part to play in this ideological position, and they face unique intersectionalities, which have the growing potential to destabilise what is meant by both queer and Muslim identities, especially as the movement grows in power and strength in the United Kingdom. Whilst they face distinct pressures, namely the heteronormativity

---

117 See O Avishai, ' "Doing Religion" in a Secular World: Women in Conservative Religions and the Question of Agency' (2008) 22:4 *Gender and Society* 409–433.
118 Fuist (n 115).
119 M Rahman, 'Queer as Intersectionality: Theorising Gay Muslim Identities' (2010) 44:5 *Sociology* 944–961.
120 *Ibid.*
121 J Binnie, *The Globalisation of Sexuality* (Sage Publications 2004) 15.

and religious homo/bi/transphobia from Islamic communities as well as racism and Islamophobia within queer communities, many queer Muslims have found strategies to contest what they have experienced in both. Queer Muslims are marching at gay pride events and even lead pride marches in London Pride, and they are forming online and face-to-face organisations, leading to a flourishing of queer Muslim visibility. Importantly, it must be recognised that not all queer Muslims in the United Kingdom can partake in this growth, and many remain deeply excluded, hidden or discriminated against, facing unique social, cultural, family and identity pressures. In fact, 50 years after the Stonewall Riots, not all queer communities have caught up with the dominant White and secular queer community in terms of progress, and so this chapter aims to act, in its own small way, as a rallying call to the broader queer community to reject concepts of homogenisation and to recognise the problems within the community as a whole regards racism and Islamophobia, as well as the complex intersections faced by queer Muslims and other people of colour. Only by doing this will we ensure that in another 50 years when the riots of Stonewall celebrate their centenary will we see progress made.

Concluding Thoughts

Chapter 24

Stonewall at Fifty

Between Hope and Challenge

Sean Becker and Paul Behrens

This final chapter seeks to draw together the main themes of the book by returning to the question posed in the introduction: is the development of the LGBT community a success story? As so often, the answer to this question is more nuanced than a simple 'yes' or 'no'.

Despite the progress made over the past 50 years, there are still some areas of concern. Especially grim are the threats to life and liberty persons of the LGBT community face in some parts of Africa and Asia, where consensual same-sex acts are still punishable by the death penalty.[1] While some may think that these laws are remnants of a darker past, executions on grounds of homosexuality were carried out in Iran and Saudi Arabia in 2021, with additional executions occurring in six other states,[2] where insurgent groups hold *de facto* control.[3] What is more, some of these laws have been passed only quite recently. In Brunei, the law imposing the death penalty on same-sex sexual acts was adopted in 2019[4] (although capital punishment for these acts was suspended following international backlash).[5] That same year, the Ugandan Parliament generated international outcry for debating a bill, which would have reintroduced the infamous 'Kill the Gays' law of 2014.[6] Utmost worrying, too, are the develop-

---

1 Lucas R Mendos et al., *State-Sponsored Homophobia 2020: Global Legislation Overview Update* (ILGA 2020) 31.
2 Somalia, Libya, Yemen, Iraq, Syria, and Afghanistan.
3 Kellyn Botha, *Our Identities Under Arrest: A Global Overview on the Enforcement of Laws Criminalising Consensual Same-Sex Sexual Acts Between Adults and Diverse Gender Expressions* (ILGA 2021) 19–20.
4 Ben Westcott, 'Brunei to Punish Gay Sex and Adultery with Death by Stoning' *CNN*, 30 March 2019.
5 Bill Chappell, 'Brunei Won't Enforce Death-By-Stoning Law for Gay Sex, Sultan Says' *NPR*, 6 May 2019.
6 Halima Athumani, 'Fear in Uganda's Gay Community After Death Penalty Threat, Arrests' *VOA News*, 30 October 2019. Luckily, the bill was rejected and governmental assent refused for subsequent proposals in 2021, which would have re-criminalized homosexuality with a 10-year prison sentence (see Fox Odoi-Oywelowo, 'No, Uganda Is Not Making It Illegal to Be Gay (Again)' *Aljazeera*, 6 June 2021).

DOI: 10.4324/9781003286295-31

ments in Afghanistan, where members of the LGBT community now face graver danger than ever before amidst the Taliban's seizure of power.[7]

The stakes may not be as high in 'Western' states, in which new legislation tends to expand on LGBT rights rather than restrict them, and the LGBT community generally finds much broader acceptance within society. Nonetheless, this book has introduced a number of challenges that require considerable work yet. From the issue of LGBT youth homelessness[8] to protests against LGBT-inclusive education,[9] there are many aspects of LGBT life in the UK that call for continued improvement and greater societal acceptance. Also, within the LGBT community itself, progress is far from complete. LGBT Muslims in the UK, for instance, struggle to be accepted – both by their faith community as well as within the LGBT community itself, illustrating the added difficulties that result from intersectionality in this context.[10] Some members of the LGBT community additionally struggle with internalized difficulties. Older LGBT couples, whose experiences are informed by the heteronormativity they witnessed during adolescence, are especially affected by these internalized struggles.[11] In sum, societal and internalized pressures still pose considerable obstacles to the successful development of the LGBT community.

To only emphasize areas of concern, however, would negate the host of positive developments the LGBT community has experienced over the past 50 years. While the situation in some African and Asian countries places considerable obstacles in the way of LGBT recognition – this book has referred in particular to the development in Uganda in the context of the introduction of the Anti-Homosexuality Bill – such problems have also met with considerable commitment by LGBT activists in their fight for liberation and with support for the relevant rights by the international community.[12] And there have been victories along the way: in October 2021, the Ugandan government issued its first-ever ID card that identifies a trans person by their correct gender,[13] Sudan abolished corporal punishment and the death penalty for homosexual intercourse in 2020;[14] and in 2021, Botswana's highest appeals court upheld a 2019 high court ruling decriminalizing same-sex relations.[15] In South America, the 2021 Chilean presidential election saw Gabriel Boric, an outspoken supporter of LGBT rights, triumph over the far-right candidate, António Kast, who had

---

7 Kirsty Grant, 'LGBT in Afghanistan: "I could be killed on the spot"' *BBC News*, 20 August 2021.
8 Carin Tunåker, Chapter 4 above.
9 Carolynn Gray, Chapter 8 above.
10 Drew Dalton, Chapter 23 above.
11 Dora Jandrić, Chapter 6 above.
12 Clare Byarugaba, Chapter 5 above.
13 *Mail & Guardian*, 'Meet Uganda's First Transgender Citizen', 9 October 2021.
14 Zoe Tidman, 'Sudan Lifts Death Penalty and Flogging for Gay Sex', *The Independent*, 19 July 2020.
15 Anyana Upadhya, 'Botswana Appeals Court Upholds Decriminalization of Same-Sex Sexual Relations' *JURIST*, 30 November 2021.

been strongly opposed to the same-sex marriage law, which Chile had enacted.[16] And in Asia, the Constitutional Court of Taiwan in 2017 found that the ban on same-sex marriage violated the freedom of people to marry as well as the right to equality as guaranteed under the Taiwanese Constitution.[17]

This book has also discussed a number of positive developments within the 'Western' context. The Catholic church, traditionally a staunch opponent of homosexuality,[18] has entered a new phase of conversation in recent years in which Pope Francis I's apostolic exhortation *Evangelii Gaudium* can be expected to play an important role.[19] Such debate is not limited to one religion: within Judaism, various approaches taken by Orthodox, Conservative, Reform and Liberal movements affect the interpretation of foundational texts and the engagement of the religion with gender and sexuality in general.[20] A developing dialogue between religion and the LGBT community has manifested itself in Islam as well: since 2017, the Ibn Rushd-Goethe Mosque in Berlin, founded by lawyer and feminist activist Seyran Ateş, offers an LGBT-friendly faith community open to all Muslims, regardless of sexual orientation or gender identity.[21] But this initiative also demonstrates the challenges that still lie on the way: Ateş had to be put under police protection after receiving more than 100 death threats within the first few weeks of the mosque's opening.[22]

Law has certainly also played a part in the development of the LGBT community over the past 50 years. The ECtHR's long history of defending the interests of sexual minorities under the ECHR,[23] or the impact of the Equality Act 2010 in the UK,[24] are examples of such development discussed in this book. In 1966, shortly before the passing of the Sexual Offenses Act 1967, only 39% of UK society supported the decriminalization of homosexuality.[25] As such, the 1967 Act preceded society's acceptance of the LGBT community. In some respects, society lags behind the law even today. Instances of

---

16 Tom Phillips and John Bartlett, '"Very Worrying": Is a Far-Right Radical About to Take Over in Chile?' *Guardian*, 16 December 2021; *AFP General Forecasts* (Alberto Peña), 'Leftist Boric Wins Chilean Presidency', 20 December 2021; Michael Chessum, 'If Kast Wins It Would Be Like Pinochet Winning' *i News*, 11 December 2021.
17 Paul Behrens, Chapter 9 above.
18 Gerard Loughlin, 'Catholic Homophobia' (2018) 121:3 *Theology* 188.
19 Nicolete Burbach, Chapter 22 above.
20 Rabbi Mark L. Solomon and Hannah Holtschneider, Chapter 21 above.
21 Sabine Kinkratz and Frank Bachner, 'Everyone Is Welcome at Berlin's Ibn Rushd-Goethe Mosque' *Deutsche Welle*, 16 June 2017; Frank Bachner, 'Berliner Moschee von Seyran Ateş bietet queeren Muslimen Schutz und Beratung' *Der Tagesspiegel*, 25 October 2020.
22 Sabine Beikler, 'Moschee-Gründerin Seyran Ateş Unter Polizeischutz' *Der Tagesspiegel*, 2 July 2017.
23 Helen Fenwick and Andrew Hayward, Chapter 10 above.
24 Lynne Regan, Chapter 15 above.
25 Ben Clements and Clive D Field, 'Public Opinion Toward Homosexuality and Gay Rights in Great Britain' (2014) 78:2 *Public Opinion Quarterly* 523, 524.

disenfranchisement of lesbian mothers within the British healthcare system,[26] the lack of equality and inclusion in the classroom and curriculum[27] and the experiences of transgender students in higher education are examples for that.[28]

However, there is also the danger of oversimplifying the law's role as a 'motor for change'. While this book has pointed out some of the successful developments law has brought about, one must not forget that for the vast part of its history, the law had been a stumbling block for the advancement of the LGBT community.[29] Yet the examination of the law in this regard can also serve to provide insights into the relationship between society and LGBT matters. The law thus offers a useful tool to gauge overall societal acceptance of the LGBT community.[30] At the same time, court judgements can be used to uncover the implicit – and at times not so implicit – homophobic attitudes held by those tasked with interpreting the law.[31] Even today, and even in the Western context, the law can be formed along traditionalist lines, as shown by the ECtHR's reluctance to fully recognize same-sex marriage as a human right.[32] With regard to conversion practices, too, the law trails behind societal opinion. Most experts agree that conversion 'therapy' is not based on scientific evidence,[33] and within the UK, 65% of the population supports a ban on the practices.[34] Yet laws criminalizing these methods are only now beginning to be codified.[35] At the same time, the LGBT community has proven time and again its ability to adapt and thrive in even the most hostile legal and/or social environments. The queer migrant workers on the Arabian Peninsula, who – despite the severe challenges posed by law and society – were able to carve out a niche for themselves, provide a powerful example of the LGBT community's prowess.[36]

This book has presented a multifaceted story of the progress of LGBT rights and the LGBT community. While LGBT persons undoubtedly still face a plethora of challenges – some smaller, some of existential importance – the overall development of the LGBT community over the past 50 years appears to point in the right direction, and more recent developments in areas of the

---

26 Lucille Kelsall-Knight and Ceri Sudron, Chapter 18 above.
27 Eleanor Capaldi and Amanda Sykes, Chapter 14 above.
28 Regan (n 24).
29 Sir Stephen Wall, Chapter 3 above.
30 Kenneth McK. Norrie, Chapter 11 above.
31 Sean Becker, Chapter 12 above.
32 Fenwick and Hayward (n 23).
33 Independent Expert on Protection Against Violence and Discrimination Based on Sexual Orientation and Gender Identity, Practices of So-Called "Conversion Therapy", Report to the Human Rights Council, A/HRC/44/53 (1 May 2020), para 20.
34 Isabelle Kirk, 'Most Britons Want Conversion Therapy Banned, Including That Aimed at Transgender People' *YouGov*, 12 April 2022.
35 Paul Behrens, Chapter 19 above.
36 Gaar Adams, Chapter 16 above.

world which have traditionally been seen as the most challenging for LGBT people – Africa and Asia – give rise to hope for a better future. Nonetheless, the question remains of how to overcome the divide between legislation and societal opinion. Where the relationship between the two is more favourable on the side of societal opinion, such a gap may well be bridged by enhanced involvement of civil society in the law-making process.[37] Where the law is ahead of society in regard to LGBT issues, 'messages from above', including those by leaders of faith communities[38] may be instrumental. Whatever the correct approach within a particular context may be, the past 50 years of progress engender hope that the obstacles that remain will be surmounted over the next 50 years and beyond.

---

37 Behrens (n 17).
38 See Part 2 above.

Index

AB v XY (1917) 149
abortion 15
Abse, Leo 21
acquired gender *see* gender
activism: feminist 23, 312, 333; gay 5, 9, 22, 27, 43, 47, 50–51, 53, 55–56, 61, 63–64, 119, 125, 129, 132–133, 138, 145, 190, 199, 212, 232, 312, 316, 324, 332
Adair, James 3
adoption *see* same-sex couples
Adoption and Children (Scotland) Act 2007 66, 156
adultery 20, 172, 281
Aeterni Patris *see* Leo XIII; Pope
AFAB (Assigned Female at Birth) 92, 94–96, 217
Afghanistan: LGBT Matters in 334
Africa: African Charter on Human and People's Rights (ACHPR) 48; LGBT matters in 8, 55–56, 85, 240, 310, 313, 331–332, 335
age of consent 6, 19, 20, 25, 66, 84, 154, 155, 164, 275
AID (Artificial Insemination by Donor) 95
AIDS (acquired immunodeficiency syndrome) *see* HIV (human immunodeficiency virus)
Albert Kennedy Trust (charity) 29
Alekseyev v. Russia (2010) 141, 143, 144
Althaus-Reid, Marcella 297
Althusser, Louis 165
AMAB (Assigned Male at Birth) 89, 93–94, 96
American Psychiatric Association 239
Andersen v King County (2006) 116
Anderton, James 24
Anderton Park Primary School *see* Birmingham School protests

Anglicanism 37, 289–290, 296
Angola: LGBT matters in 84
Aquinas, Thomas 294, 300
Aristotle 294
Arizona: LGBT Matters in 111, 113
Arran, Lord 21
arranged marriage 322
asexual 12, 198, 203
Asquith, J 151
Ates, Seyran 333
atheism 316
Athena SWAN 28
Augustinus 294
Australia: intersex persons in 83; LGBT matters in 105, 108, 154, 249, 258–259, 267
Austria: same-sex marriage in 131

B v France (1992) 257
Baatour, Mounir 16
Badgett, Lee 51
Baird, John 60
Balsam, Kimberly 320
BAME (Black, Asian and Minority Ethnic) 192–193, 202, 213
Barrett, Mike 28
Bayev and Others v. Russia (2017) 141, 143
Beemyn, Brett 206, 209
Beizaras and Levickas v. Lithuania (2020) 141
beliefs: evaluative 166, 169; factual 166
Bell, David 38
Bell, Megan 90–91
Bellinger v Bellinger 97–98
Benjamin, Harry 93, 292
Bernard of Clairvaux 299
Beth Chayim Chadashim 267
biphobia 99
Birmingham School protests 26, 86

Index

bisexual 5, 7–8, 37, 66, 197–198, 232, 251, 284, 317, 319
Black Lives Matter (BLM) 189
blackmail 17, 24, 48–49, 52
Blood donations 240; and LGBT persons 240
BMA (British Medical Association) 19
Bogarde, Dirk 24
Boric, Gabriel 332
Botswana: LGBT Matters in 84, 118, 332
Bovensiepen, Judith 28
Boyle, Lord 148
Boyson, Rhodes 183
Bracke, Sarah 310
Brazil: LGBT Matters in 16
Brennan-Ing, Mark 317
Briggs, LJ 129
British Medical Association *see* BMA (British Medical Association)
Brown, Rita Mae 190
Brunei: LGBT Matters in 331
buggery 19, 178–179, 183
Burgess, Guy 22
Butler, Judith 42
Butler, Richard Austen 20

California: LGBT Matters in 106, 108–109, 112–113, 117
Caluya, Gilbert 317
Cameron, David 25, 56, 58, 312
Campbell, Stuart 158–160
Campbell v Dugdale (2020) 160, 162
Canada: Bill on conversion practices 252
Carter, David 5
Carter, Jimmy 15
Cashman, Michael 25
'Cassandra' *see* Connor, William
Catholicism 11, 19, 22–23, 117, 268, 286–306, 333; Congregation for the Doctrine of the Faith 268; heterodoxy 288–289, 291–293, 296, 301, 302; orthodoxy 288–292, 296, 299, 301; Pastoral Problem 302–305; rationality 287–288, 290–291, 294, 298, 300
Central Council of Muslims (Germany) 268
Chan, Phil C W 92
chastity 151, 153, 281
Chechnya: 'anti-gay purge' (2017) 8; LGBT matters in 8
Chessington World of Adventures Ltd v Reed (1998) 96
Chicago 4

Chile: LGBT Matters in 332–333
Christianity 31, 60, 107, 268, 289–290, 298; *see also* Anglicanism; Catholicism; Church of England; Church of Scotland; Metropolitan Community Church; Protestantism; Quakers
Christopher Street (New York) 3–4, 8
Christopher Street (publication) 4
Christopher Street Day 5
Church of England 37, 268; *see also* Anglicanism
Church of Scotland 268
Church, Kimberley 201
cisgender 12, 89, 95, 193, 197–198, 201–203, 212, 216, 224, 256, 323, 326
cisheteronormativity *see* cissexism
cissexism 212–213, 291
civil partnership *see* same-sex, partnership
Civil Partnership Act (2004) 66, 127–129
Civil Partnerships (Opposite-Sex Couples) Regulations (2019) 129
Civil Partnerships, Marriages and Deaths (Registration etc) Act (2019) 129
civil solidarity pact *see* same-sex, partnership
civil union *see* same-sex, partnership
Clandinin, D Jean 244
Clerk, LJ 151
Cluny, Abbot of 299
colonialism 27, 48, 297; European 48, 310; postcolonial theory 297, 309
Come Out! (publication) 5
coming out 21, 24–26, 28, 31, 34–36, 40, 72, 74–75, 77, 158, 198, 210, 245, 268
Committee on Homosexual Offences and Prostitution (UK) 151, 163, 177
common nuisance 49
concubinage 279
Congregation for the Doctrine of the Faith *see* Catholicism
Connelly, F Michael 244
Connolly, Mark 191
Connor, William 151
CONODIS (Costa Rican Coalition of Sexual Diversity Organisations and Groups) 119
consensus analysis *see* European Court of Human Rights
consensus doctrine *see* European Court of Human Rights
Conservative Party (UK) 15, 16, 18, 20, 22, 132, 158; conference 16, 158

Constitution 27, 47–48, 53–55, 58–59, 61, 63, 106–109, 111–113, 117, 119–121, 136, 140, 142, 333; ban on same-sex marriage in 107–108, 113, 117, 136, 142; eternity clause 112
consultation 99, 108, 128, 207, 210, 213, 245; on Civil Partnerships (2014) 128, 132; on Equal Civil Marriage (2012) 128; on Reform of the Gender Recognition Act (2018) 99, 207
contraception 22
Convention on the Rights of the Child 251
conversion practices 7, 10, 16, 19, 48, 239–241, 248–264, 268, 334; academic project and 261; children and 48, 250–251, 253–254; consent and 253–255; criminalisation of 7, 16, 249, 252–258, 262–264; de minimis infractions and 257–258; effects of 10, 250–252, 256, 260; electroshock treatment and 4; Equal Opportunity and Human Rights Commission (*see* Equal Opportunity and Human Rights Commission); freedom of religion and 249, 255–256, 263; healthcare providers and 249–250, 252, 256, 260, 264; human rights and (*see* Human Rights); removal of a person for purposes of 253; research and 260; State support to 249, 261–263; supervisory offence 262–263; victims of 249–250, 255, 257–260, 263–264; *see also individual countries*
'conversion therapy' *see* conversion practices
Cooper, Yvette 130
Corbett v Corbett (1971) 89
Cornwall, Susannah 289–291
Cossey v United Kingdom (1991) 94
Costa Rica: LGBT Matters in 106, 119
Costa Rica Advisory Opinion (2017) 121
Council of Europe 7, 126, 137; and East/West divisions 137; and LGBT matters 126
Court of Appeal (England and Wales) 96–97, 170–171, 184
Court of Sessions (Scotland) 147, 148–150, 159; Inner House 148–150, 159
Coutts, J 153
Cowan, Sharon 90–91
Cowan v Bennett (2012) 156–158
criminalisation 6–7, 8, 11–12, 48, 49, 54, 87, 94, 120, 189–190; of 'gay propaganda' 6–7, 189–190; of same-sex relations 8, 11–12, 48, 49, 54, 87, 94, 120; *see also* conversion practices
Criminal Justice (Scotland) Act 1980 74
Crisp, Quentin 18
critical discourse analysis (CDA) 163–186
critical race theory (CRT) 189
Croft, David 24
cross-dressing 227
Cruise, Tom 153
Czech Republic: LGBT Matters in 136

Da Silva Mouta v Portugal (1999) 155
Daughters of Bilitis 4
death penalty 47, 54, 84, 227, 235, 273, 276, 325, 331–332
decriminalisation: of same-sex activities 5–6, 12, 19–22, 65–66, 74, 83–85, 123, 125, 154–155, 163, 171, 176–180, 267, 333
defamation 146–162; in English law 146, 152–153; in Scots law 146–162
Democratic Party (USA) 15
depression 49, 51, 192, 250; among gay men 240
Derrida, Jacques 42
DeSurra, Christopher 201–202
Diagnostic and Statistical Manual (USA) 239
Dilhorne, Lord 21
Diplock, Lord 170, 173, 182
disabled 192–193, 197, 202, 317
discrimination 4, 6, 8, 28, 37, 40, 48, 51–52, 53, 55–56, 63, 68, 71, 91, 96–97, 103, 118, 122, 125, 127, 129, 134–135, 138, 140, 142, 144, 155, 162, 167, 193–194, 197, 205–206, 209, 212–213, 215, 227, 239–242, 251–252, 254, 256, 263–264, 267–269, 281, 315, 328; in housing market 4, 92; institutional 6, 212; in job market 4, 52, 53, 97, 167; and police harassment 3–4, 18, 22, 50–51, 53, 68; in provision of goods and services 92, 155–156; in public sector 4, 6
divorce 60, 95, 272, 280
DNA 243
Donovan, Jason 152
Drumsheugh case *see Pirie and Woods v Cumming Gordon* (1819)
Drumsheugh School 147–148, 157–158
Dudgeon v United Kingdom (1981) 94
Dugdale, Kezia 147, 158–159

Dundas, Lord 150
Dunne, Gillian 33, 45

Eastenders (UK TV series) 25
East/West division (Europe) *see* Council of Europe
Ecumenical Councils 299
EG & 7 others v Attorney General (2019) 120
Elliot, Walter 22
Engels, Friedrich 30
England and Wales: conversion practices and 249, 252, 255–257; decriminalisation of homosexuality 5, 18–21, 65, 71, 163, 169; LGBT Matters in 5–6, 18–21, 28–31, 36, 39, 45, 65–66, 71, 76, 89, 93, 95, 98, 126–133, 150–151, 153, 163–164, 169, 196, 208–209, 219, 242–243, 268, 282
epistemology 166, 286–288, 291, 299; epistemological crisis 294–295, 301–302
Equality Act 2010 100, 161–162, 193, 197, 206, 333; protected characteristic 100, 161–162, 193, 206; public sector equality duty 206
Equality Challenge Unit (UK) 224
Equal Opportunity and Human Rights Commission (Victoria, Australia) 258–260; investigation of conversion practices and 259–260
Estonia: and civil partnership 136
Europe: LGBT matters in 6–8, 86, 126, 133–144, 189–190, 310–312
European Charter of Fundamental Rights 137
European Convention on Human Rights: Article 8 94–95, 98, 100, 115, 127, 129, 137–141, 143, 250–251, 257; Article 9 137, 162, 255; Article 10 161–162; Article 12 94–95, 98, 120–121, 127, 135, 137, 140, 143; Article 14 127, 129, 135, 137–138, 140–141, 144, 155; Article 17 161
European Court of Human Rights 6, 10, 83, 94–98, 100, 115, 120–122, 125–127, 133–145, 155, 161, 250, 255, 257; and consensus analysis 134–135, 143; and consensus doctrine 134; and same-sex marriage 10, 115, 125–127
European Union: Equal Treatment Directive 92, 96
Evangelii Gaudium see Francis; Pope

Facebook 39, 41, 70, 216
fair comment 159–160
family law 97, 130, 155
family values 38, 74, 103
Fedotova and Others v Russia (2021) 140–144
feminism 7, 23, 55, 103, 167, 256, 296–297, 310, 312, 319, 326, 333; gender-critical (*see* gender, critical groups)
FFLAG (Families and Friends of Lesbians and Gays) 124
Fitzpatrick v Stirling Housing Association (1999) 155
Fitzpatrick, Katie 210
Formby, Eleanor 213, 223
Forstater v CGD Europe (2021) 100
Foster v Jessen (2021) 160–161
Foucault, Michel 30–31, 67
France: LGBT matters in 105
Francis I, Pope 11, 268, 286, 302–306, 333; *Evangelii Gaudium* 11, 268, 286, 302–304, 333
Franco-Dutch declaration at the United Nations (2008) 84–85
freedom of belief *see* Human Rights
freedom of expression *see* Human Rights
freedom of religion *see* Human Rights
Fuist, Todd 327

Gardiner, Lord 22
Garner, Steve 314
gay *see* LGBT; same-sex
Gay (publication) 5
Gay Activists Alliance 5
Gay Liberation Front 5, 22
Gay News (UK) 22
Gay Power (publication) 5
gay-related immune deficiency (GRID) *see* GRID (gay-related immune deficiency)
gender 7, 12, 30, 35–36, 38–40, 45–46, 49, 67, 72, 79, 83, 91, 95, 99, 101, 167, 192–193, 199, 203, 204, 206–214, 218–219, 224, 233, 257, 268, 271–272, 278, 285, 289, 292–293, 295–296, 297, 311–312, 316–317, 326, 332; acquired 206–208; assignment 7, 97, 190, 206, 209; cis- (*see* cisgender); critical groups 7, 256–257; diversity 7, 12, 40, 207, 249, 254, 295; dysphoria 207, 291; expression 204, 248; identity 7, 12, 26,

28–29, 33, 36, 41–45, 48–49, 53–54, 56, 84–85, 87, 89, 91, 94–95, 97–100, 102, 122, 192–194, 197–198, 201–202, 204–205, 209–212, 215, 217, 224, 233–234, 248, 250–252, 256–257, 260–261, 263, 271, 285, 288, 307–309, 323, 326, 333; roles 77, 246, 275; theory 167, 214, 293; transition 42, 212, 218, 232, 288; *see also* transgender matters
gender fluid *see* transgender matters
Gender Identity Clinic (UK) 204
Gender Identity Development Service (UK) 217
gender non-conforming *see* transgender matters
genderqueer 40, 204
gender reassignment *see* transgender matters
Gender Recognition Act (2004) 7, 86, 192, 206
Gender Recognition Certificate 89, 207
Germany: Federal Council 260; law on conversion practices in 254, 255, 258–259, 260, 262–263
GLADD (Association of Gay and Lesbian Doctors and Dentists) 241
GLMA; Health Professionals Advancing LGBTQ Equality (USA) 241
Goldberg, Abbie E 208, 210, 212
Goodwin v United Kingdom (2002) 98, 257
Graff, Agnieszka 103
Gramsci, Antonio 165
Greece: LGBT Matters in 16, 138
Greenwich Village (New York) 3–5
Greer, Germaine 26
GRID (gay-related immune deficiency) 183, 239
gross indecency 17, 19, 149, 178, 182

Hailes, Gary 25
Hale, Baroness 130
Hämäläinen v Finland (2014) 140
Harding, Rosie 27
hate crime 37, 134, 158, 192, 197, 209, 319
Hayman, Brenda 246–247
heteronormativity *see* cissexism
heterosexism 201–202, 321–322
heterosexual 20, 29, 31, 34, 38, 48, 51, 66–67, 69, 72–73, 78–79, 122, 131, 152, 184, 193, 197–199, 201–203, 211–213, 230, 256, 270–271, 275, 279–281, 283, 285, 289, 313, 316–319, 321–322

Higher Eduction Academy (UK) 193
Hinds, Damian 26
HIV (human immunodeficiency virus) 23, 51, 55, 60, 74, 183–184, 232, 239–240, 281
Hollande, Francois 105
Holy Spirit 305, 308
homelessness 9, 16, 28–46, 49, 249, 332; among young LGBT persons 9, 16, 28–46, 332
homo/bi/transphobia (HBT) 199; *see also* biphobia; homophobia; transgender matters, transphobia
homonormativity 289, 311, 317
homophobia 25–26, 35, 37, 39, 51–53, 55, 61, 67, 71, 85, 99, 134, 143–145, 147, 152, 156–162, 163–164, 171, 174, 180, 182–186, 201, 242, 255, 261, 291, 310, 312, 316, 318, 321–322, 324, 325, 327, 334; hate crimes 37, 134; institutional 185, 334; internalised 322; State sponsored 56, 227
Homosexual Law Reform Society 21
Hope, Lord Justice Clerk 148
hormone therapy 207
House of Commons (UK) 18, 21, 252
House of Lords (UK) 10, 21, 85, 98, 147, 149, 164, 169–171, 173, 175–186
Hudson, Rock 240
Human Rights: freedom from torture 251; freedom of assembly 53; freedom of association 53; freedom of belief 26, 100, 161–162, 255, 263; freedom of expression 48, 85, 100, 159, 161–162, 212, 255; freedom of religion 26, 100, 249, 255–256, 263; freedom to marry 6, 10, 38, 66, 94–95, 97–98, 105–124, 125–145, 162, 283, 333–334 (*see also* same-sex, marriage); health-related rights 66, 250–251; margin of appreciation 115, 135, 138–139, 141, 143–144; of children (*see* Convention on the Rights of the Child); right to democracy 109; right to family life 51–52, 115, 127, 137, 139, 144; right to identity 89, 92, 94, 97–100, 102, 144, 194, 251, 256–257, 263; right to non-discrimination 48, 63, 91–92, 96–97, 118, 122, 125, 127, 129, 134–135, 138–140, 142, 155–156, 162, 193–194, 206, 251, 256, 264, 267, 269; right to personal autonomy 251; right to personal development 250–257; right to physical integrity 251; right to privacy

19, 22, 61, 83, 94, 115, 127, 139, 144, 154, 163, 177–179, 250, 257; right to self-determination 109
Human Rights Act (1998) 98
Hungary: LGBT Matters in 136, 189–190
Hunt, Stephen 100–101
Huntington, Samuel 310
Huy, Luong The 16

Ibn Rushd-Goethe Mosque (Berlin) 333
Illinois: LGBT Matters in 3, 83
immigration 230, 311–312, 319; *see also* minorities; people of colour
immorality *see* morality
imperialism 312
importuning 22
incest 30, 325
inclusive: curriculum 189, 196, 200–201; education 26, 198, 200–201, 212, 267, 332; LGBT+ 26, 43, 75, 198, 200–201, 203, 208, 210, 212, 219, 241, 245, 282
indecency 17, 19, 22, 49, 148–149, 178, 182, 297, 321; *see also* indecent theology
Independent Expert on Protection against Violence and Discrimination Based on Sexual Orientation and Gender Identity 249, 251, 261, 264
infertility treatment 156
Inman, John 24–25
Inter-American Court of Human Rights: same-sex marriage and 122, 137
International Covenant on Civil, Economic and Cultural Rights 109–110, 251
International Criminal Court 262
intersectionality 12, 35, 42, 67–69, 71, 224, 236, 241, 267–268, 291, 308, 313–314, 316, 323, 327–328, 332
intersexuality 8, 12, 47, 83, 193, 203, 250–251, 289
Iran: LGBT Matters in 331
Ireland: Bill on conversion practices 252, 255; LGBT Matters in 66, 105, 107–108, 111–112
Islam 11, 85, 229, 231, 268–269, 307–328, 332–333; conversion practices and 268; LGBT muslims and 327–328
Islamophobia 308–309, 311, 313–320, 323, 327–328
Italy: LGBT Matters in 136, 138, 139–142
IVF (in virto fertilization) 243

J v St (1996) 95
J. Y. Interpretation 748 (2017) 109

Janus Society 4
Jauncey of Tullichettle, Lord 171, 175, 178, 179, 184, 185
Jenkins, Roy 21
John of the Cross 295
John Paul II, Pope 287, 299; Ordinatio Sacerdotalis 299; Veritatis splendor 287
Johnson, Boris 15–16
Jones, David Albert 288, 290, 291
Judaism: and LGBT matters 10, 268, 333; British Reform movement 276, 281; Conservative 272, 276, 277, 279, 285, 333; Covenant of Love 282–284; Hebrew Bible 272–274, 279; ketubah 270, 272, 280; Liberal 271, 272, 276, 277, 278, 280, 281, 282–283, 285, 333; Orthodox 270, 271, 272, 275–276, 278–279, 283, 285, 333; Progressive 271, 280; Reconstructionist 276, 277–278, 281; Reform 272, 276, 277, 278, 281, 333; Talmud 273–274, 279; Torah 277; and wedding ceremony 10, 270–271, 272, 280, 282, 284
judges: attitudes towards homosexuality 10, 147, 164, 171, 178, 180, 182, 184–185, 334
justice 9, 66, 297

Kadaga, Rebecca 60
Kast, Antonio 332
Kato, David 64
Kennedy, Lady John 150
Kerr, Innes Margaret 150–151
Kerr v Kennedy (1942) 150
Kidman, Nicole 153
Kilbrandon, Lord 170, 181–182
Kingarth, Lord 154
Kirby, J 154
Kitzinger, Celia 130
Knight, David Rolph 154, 156
Knuller Ltd. v Director of Public Prosecutions (1972) 169
Korolczuk, Elzbieta 103
Kosnick, Kira 311
Kozachenko, Kathy 5
Kugle, Scott 326
Kuvalanka, Katherine A 208, 210, 212

Labouchere Amendment 17, 21
Labour Party (UK) 15, 21, 22, 158
Lamm, Norman 275–276
Lane, Lord C J 184

language 10, 11, 26, 61, 68, 75, 103, 118, 149, 190, 202, 219, 242, 293, 294, 322; and LGBT population in Arab peninsula 190, 226, 228, 229, 233, 234, 235
Lash, Nicholas 287
Lawrence, Matson 194
Law Society (England and Wales) 19, 84
Lee v Ashers Bakery Company Ltd (2020) 162
Leo XIII 300
lesbian 5, 8, 12, 23, 25, 26, 35, 77, 131, 147, 149, 150, 151, 152–155, 156, 158, 162, 183, 191, 198, 203, 251, 267, 274, 278, 282, 317; mothers 10, 242, 243, 244, 246, 247, 334
Lesbian, Gay, Bisexual and Transgender Pride Month 5
Lesotho: LGBT matters in 84
Letsweletse Motshidiemang v The Attorney-General (2019) 118
LGBT: anti-LGBT rights movement 15, 49, 86, 92, 99, 100–101, 103; concept 12; inclusive education 26, 196, 200, 201, 267, 332; older LGBT couples 9, 16, 66, 332; queer 29–30, 40, 53, 194, 198, 202, 203, 204, 205, 227–228, 230, 233, 235–236, 289, 307–328, 334; rights 7, 8, 9, 11, 15, 16, 17, 23, 28, 29, 30, 37, 40, 44, 47, 51, 53–57, 58, 59, 63–64, 66, 84–85, 86, 87, 92, 100, 101, 102, 105, 118, 121, 163, 189, 190, 250, 267, 312, 332, 334; *see also* genderqueer; non-binary; same-sex; transgender matters
LGBT Age (NGO) 70
LGBT Health and Wellbeing (NGO) 70
LGBT History Month 212
LGBT Youth Scotland (charity) 195
LGBTI Law Committee of the International Bar Association 84
LGBT+ Lawyers Division (UK) 84
Liberace 151, 152, 154
Liberation Theology 297
Lithuania: LGBT Matters in 138, 141
Lively, Scott 60
Local Government Act (1988) 66, 92, 155, 189, 192; section 28 6, 24, 25, 38, 66, 75, 78, 155, 189, 192
Lokodo, Simon 52
Los Angeles 4
Loughton, Tim (MP) 129, 133
Lowry, Lord 171, 175, 179, 183
Lut (Prophet) 325

McGlashan, Hailey 210
McGoldrick, Dominic 137
McGowan (Sheriff) 157
MacIntyre, Alisdair 286–287, 294–295, 298–299
McKellen, Sir Ian 260
McKendry, Stephanie 194
McKinney, Jeffrey S 221
MacLean, Donald 22
Madison, John 117
Magisterium 287, 288, 291, 300
Magnus Hirschfeld Foundation (Germany) 261
Maine: LGBT Matters in 114
Major, John 25
Malta: law on conversion practices in 249, 252
Marriage (Same Sex Couples) Act 2013 66, 126, 133
Marriage (Same Sex Couples) Bill 38, 130
marriage equality 10, 105, 107, 125–127, 128, 131, 133, 138, 283; *see also* same-sex, marriage
Marx, Karl 165
Marxism 165, 297
Marzetti, Hazel 194, 208, 213
Massad, Joseph 312, 314
Mattachine Societies 4
Maxwell-Fyfe, David 19, 20, 26
May, Theresa 27
Mead, George Herbert 68, 70, 73, 76
Meadowbank, Lord 148, 149
media: British 197; mainstream 63, 310; social 29, 39, 204, 324; Ugandan 60, 61
men who have sex with men *see* MSM (men who have sex with men)
mental health 29, 36, 41–42, 44–45, 240, 251, 320; *see also* depression
Mertova, Patricie 244
Metropolitan Community Church 267
Miceli, Melinda 36
Middle East 232, 309, 312
migrant 10, 226–228, 230, 233, 235–236, 334; *see also* immigration
military: and homosexuals 6, 15, 25
Miller, Daniel 39
minorities 10, 119, 143–145, 186, 310, 311; sexual 92, 122, 126, 134, 143–144, 312, 314, 323, 325, 333; *see also* immigration; people of colour
Mirvis, Ephraim 271
misgendering *see* transgender matters

Mollenkott, Virginia Ramey 290
Montague, Lord 18
Moodod, Tariq 313–314
morality 9, 11, 177–180, 186; laws 227; sexual 173, 179, 186
Morris of Borth-Y-Gest, Lord 170, 173–175, 177, 181–182
Mozambique: LGBT matters in 84
MSM (men who have sex with men) 232, 239, 240, 319
Mudde, Cas 101
Mundell, David 158
Mundell, Oliver 158
Museveni, Yoweri 49, 58
muslim *see* Islam
Mustill, Lord 171, 175, 179–180, 183, 185

National Gay Task Force 5
National Health Service (UK) 43, 94, 203, 242, 245–246
National LGBT Survey (UK) (2017) 217, 249
National LGBT+ Bar Association (United States) 84
National Union of Students (UK) 195, 199, 208, 211, 213–214, 219–220
Netherlands: LGBT matters in 84; same-sex marriage in 131
Neugarten, Bernice 69
New Labour 25
New Zealand: Bill on conversion practices 252; transgender students in 210
NHS *see* National Health Service (UK)
Niestedt, John 117
non-binary 27, 40, 83, 97, 99, 104, 193, 195, 198, 202–203, 204, 207–208, 210, 212, 217
Norrie, Kenneth 85, 131
Northern Ireland: LGBT matters in 66, 94, 160
Nott-Bower, Sir John 18
NUS *see* National Union of Students (UK)

Obama, Barack 5
Obergefell v Hodges (2015) 114, 123
Offences Against the Person Act 1861 (UK) 171, 179
Okely, Judith 28
Okin, Susan 311
Oliari and Others v Italy (2015) 115, 120, 121, 138, 140–143
Orban, Viktor 190

Orlandi v Italy (2017) 138
Ormrod, Roger 89–90
'othering' 66, 210
outing 61–62, 199, 206, 208–209

P v S and Cornwall County Council (1996) 96
pansexual 198, 203
Pappas, Christine 102
Pastörs v Germany (2019) 161
pathologisation: of homosexuality 3, 252; of transgender identity 3–4, 207, 252
patriarchal 144, 271, 273, 278, 310
Patti, Anna Magdalena 295–296
Peluso, Daniela 28
people of colour 308, 314–316, 319–320, 328
Peter Tatchell Foundation 132
Peuman, Wim 324
PG and JH v United Kingdom (2001) 257
Pine, Seymour 3
Pirie and Woods v Cumming Gordon (1819) 147
Pius XII, Pope 288
Polari 234
Pope 287, 299, 300
Porchlight (NGO) 43
Porter, Janet 298–299, 301
postcolonial 297, 309
post-industrial 30
Prain, Sheriff-Substitute 88
Pratt-Boyden, Keira 28
Prendergast, Shirley 34
Pride 4, 50–52, 86, 279, 308, 316, 328; flag 307, 308 (*see also* rainbow flag); marches 99, 324, 328; parades 5, 37, 52
pronouns 42, 44, 199, 201, 208–210, 215, 217, 219, 224
Prophit v BBC (1997) 153, 157, 159
Proposition 8 (California) *see* referendums, plebiscites etc on same-sex marriage
Proposition 22 (California) *see* referendums, plebiscites etc on same-sex marriage
Proposition 102 (Arizona) *see* referendums, plebiscites etc on same-sex marriage
Proposition 107 (Arizona) *see* referendums, plebiscites etc on same-sex marriage
prostitution 19, 93, 173
Protestantism 286, 290
Pseudo-Dionysius the Aeropagite 289, 296
Puar, Jasbir 311
public: decency 19, 170, 184, 186; morals 170, 180–182

Quakers 267, 283
queer *see* LGBT
queer studies 214
Quilty v Windsor (1999) 153, 157
Qur'an 325–326

R (on the Application of Steinfeld and Keidan) (2018) 129
R v Brown (1994) 171
R v Tan (1983) 93
racism 149, 160, 162, 224, 308, 310, 313–314, 316–320, 323, 327–328; cultural 314
rainbow flag 43, 283
Ramsay, Michael 21
rape 20, 39, 49, 172, 228, 250, 325; marital 49, 273
Rawlinson, Peter 18
Reagan, Ronald 23
Redgrave, Gemma 25
Rees v United Kingdom (1987) 94
referendums, plebiscites etc on same-sex marriage 85–124; Arizona (2008) 111, 113; Australia (postal survey) (2017) 105, 108; Bermuda (2016) 107–108, 110; California (2000) 106, 109, 113; Costa Rica (intended 2010) 106, 119; Croatia (2013) 107; Finland (2013) 108; Ireland (2015) 104, 107–108, 111–112; Maine (2009) 114; Minnesota (2012) 117; Proposition 2 (California) 106; Proposition 8 (California) 108, 112–113, 117; Proposition 102 (Arizona) 101, 111, 113; Proposition 107 (Arizona) 113; Slovakia (2015) 107, 110; Slovenia (2015) 107, 110; Taiwan (2019) 84, 107, 109
refugee 55; rights 55
Register of Corrected Entries 88
registered partnership *see* same-sex, partnership
Registration of Births, Deaths and Marriages (Scotland) Act 1854 88
Reid, Lord 170, 173–174, 176–178, 182
religion *see* Christianity; Islam; Judaism; Quakers
Rohleder, Poul 208, 210, 212, 219
Rooke, Allison 35
Ross, Sheriff 159–160, 162
Roughead, William 149
Russell, Catherine 25
Russell, LJ 95
Russia: LGBT Matters in 6, 140–142, 189

sadomasochism 171, 175–176, 178–180, 184–185
Said, Edward 309–310, 319
Salvesen, Lord 150
same-sex: couples, adoption by 66, 156; couples, legal protection of 115, 122, 125–126, 134, 137, 139–140, 143–144; marriage 10, 16, 36–38, 46, 66, 73, 83–85, 105–118, 120–123, 125–132, 134–138, 140, 143–144, 162, 192, 268, 333–334; partnership 10, 83, 125–127, 130–131, 133–136, 138–144, 156, 285; practices 19, 53, 325; registered partnership 83, 125–127, 130, 133–136, 138–142, 144; relationships 66, 71–72, 78, 98–99, 102, 104, 114, 125, 130, 134, 136, 141, 144, 155, 281, 322, 325; *see also* referendums, plebiscites etc on same-sex marriage
Saudi Arabia: LGBT Matters in 227, 331
Schalk and Kopf v Austria (2011) 136–137
Scotland: conversion practices in 240, 252, 268; Higher Education Institutions (HEI) in 194; LGBT Matters in 6, 10, 21, 65–66, 71, 74, 93, 155, 157, 161–162, 192, 240; LGBT students in 26, 208–209; non-binary students in 195, 198, 202, 208, 210, 212, 217
SDA *see* Sex Discrimination Act (1975)
section 28 *see* Local Government Act (1988)
Seelman, Kristie L 207, 209
Seidman, Steven 172
self-harm 41, 45
Sex Discrimination (Gender Reassignment) Regulations (1999) 97
Sex Discrimination Act (1975) 91–92, 96–97
sexual identity 9, 33–34, 43–44, 65–68, 71, 73, 79, 193, 197–198, 202, 232, 260, 315
Sexual Offences Act 1956 (England and Wales) 178
Sexual Offences Act 1967 (England and Wales) 178
Sheffield and Horsham v United Kingdom (1999) 94
Sheridan, Vanessa 290
Sim v Stretch (1936) 147, 152, 154
Simon of Glaisdale, Lord 170, 177, 186
Simpson, Alfred 186
sin 157, 162, 276, 284–285, 297–298

Slovenia: LGBT Matters in 105, 107, 136
Slynn of Hadley, Lord 171, 175, 179
Smith, Chris 6
society: and perception of LGBT matters 7, 9–11, 20, 24, 30, 35–38, 40, 47, 53, 55, 61–63, 92, 112, 117–118, 123–124, 150–152, 154–159, 163, 180, 186, 190, 212, 253, 261, 277–278, 308, 332, 333; societal norms 11
sodomy 17, 149, 169
SOGI (Sexual Orientation and Gender Identity) 87–89, 94, 98, 100–101, 103–104; see also LGBT
Southern Poverty Law Center 248
STEM (Science, technology, engineering and mathematics) 214
stigmatisation 44, 65, 74, 232, 252, 315, 325
Stone, Sandy 291–292
Stonewall (New York): Inn 3–5, 68, 87; riots 5, 8, 28, 46, 54, 65, 78, 83, 86–88, 158, 194, 236, 248, 275, 307–308, 328; uprising 5–6, 47, 64
Stonewall (Nongovernmental Organisation, UK) 44, 128, 132–133, 192–193, 209, 211, 213, 220
Stonewall Inn Editions 4–5
Stonewall National Monument 5
Storrie, Rhiannon 208, 210, 212, 219
'Straight pride' 86, 99
Sudan: LGBT Matters in 332
suicidal 24, 45, 51; see also self-harm
Sumner, Edward 23
surrogacy 156, 243
Syria: LGBT matters in 310

Taiwan: LGBT Matters in 84, 107, 109, 333; same-sex marriage and 84, 107, 109, 333
Tatchell, Peter 132
Taylder, Siân 297–300
Tegeder, Mike 117
Templeman, Lord 171, 175, 184
Thatcher, Margaret 23, 66, 190
theology: academic 290; eschatology 303–304, 306; eucharistic 289; indecent 297–298, 300, 302; moral theology 287–288; teleologist 287; trans 286, 290, 292, 301–302, 304
Thomas, Gareth 260
Tom of Finland 23
Tracy, David 290

TransEdu Scotland 195, 209
transgender matters 7, 15–16, 26, 52, 98, 204, 206–207, 234–235, 240, 249, 256–257, 268, 284, 289, 326; anti-trans rhetoric 197; division of sex and gender 91; gender fluid 40, 204, 207, 210, 295; gender identity 7, 12, 26, 28, 33, 41–45, 48–49, 53–56, 84–85, 87, 89, 91, 94–95, 97–100, 102, 122, 192–194, 197–198, 199, 201–202, 204–205, 210–212, 215, 217, 224, 233–234, 248, 251–252, 256–257, 260–261, 263, 307–309, 323, 326, 333; 'gender identity disorder' 94; gender non-conforming 40, 56, 204; gender reassignment (see gender, assignment) 7, 88–89, 96–97, 190, 206, 235, 288; gender transition 40–42, 89, 93, 95–96, 208, 211–212, 219, 234, 240 (see also gender); genderqueer (see genderqueer); misgendering 199, 209, 210–211, 223, 290–291, 297; trans equality 206; trans identity 87, 95, 195, 233; transphobia 44, 52, 61, 186, 190, 199, 201, 205, 207, 209, 211, 214–215, 220, 224, 312, 326, 328; trans rights 8, 26, 37, 83, 85, 86–90, 96–98, 100, 104; trans students 10, 190, 205, 208–210, 214–215, 221, 334; see also gender, expression; gender, identity; LGBT, rights
Trump, Donald 15
Tunisia: LGBT Matters in 16
Turing, Alan 17
Twocock, Paul 132

UAE (United Arab Emirates): Federal Supreme Council 235; LGBT Matters in 229–230, 233–234
UDHR see Universal Declaration of Human Rights
Uganda: Anti Homosexuality Act 2014 50; Anti Homosexuality Bill 2009 47, 53–64, 332; Children's Rules (1997) 51; Children's Statute 1996 51; Civil Society on Human Rights and Constitutional Law (The Coaltion) 47, 55–60, 62–63; High Court 61; LGBT matters in 9, 16, 47–64, 331–332; National Resistance Movement (NRM) 58; Non-Governmental Organizations Act 49–50; Penal Code 48–49; Police Act 49; Public Management Order Act 2016 50; Sexual Offences Bill (2015) 49

Index

Unitarians 283
United Kingdom: conversion practices in 252
United Nations: Committee on Economic, Social and Cultural Rights 250; Committee on the Rights of the Child 251; Human Rights Council 85; Security Council 85; Special Rapporteur on Freedom of Religion or Belief 256; Special Rapporteur on Torture 251
Universal Declaration of Human Rights 48
USA; conversion practices and 248, 256; LGBT matters in 4–5, 21, 23, 29, 47, 60, 74, 83–84, 88, 99, 106, 113–114, 191, 194, 207, 241, 278, 311; non-binary students in 208, 210, 212; Supreme Court 106, 114, 194

Vallianatos v Greece (2014) 138
van Dijk, Teun 165–168
Vatican Council, Second 300
Veritatis splendor *see* John Paul II, Pope
Vickerstaff, Sarah 29, 69
Victoria (Australia): Equal Opportunity and Human Rights Commission (*see* Equal Opportunity and Human Rights Commission); law on conversion practices in 253, 258–261, 263
Vietnam: LGBT Matters in 16

Walker, David (Bishop of Manchester) 257
Webster, Leonard 244
Werbner, Pnina 313–314
Weston, Kath 31, 35
WH Smith (Store) 22–23
White v British Sugar Corporation (1977) 92
WHO *see* World Health Organization
Wilde, Oscar 17
Wildeblood, Peter 18
Wilkinson, Sue 130
Williams, Claire 28
Williams, Robbie 152
Wolfenden, Sir John 20
Wolfenden Inquiry *see* Wolfenden Report
Wolfenden Report 12, 20, 151, 164, 177–178, 180, 184
World Health Organization 66, 69, 239
WPATH (World Professional Association for Transgender Health) 241

X, Petitioner (1957 Case) 88–89
X, Y & Z v United Kingdom (1997) 94

Yatromanolakis, Nicholas 16
Yemen: LGBT Matters in 227, 228–229
Yogyakarta Principles (2006) 84

Zion 284